D-DAY

THE FIRST 72 HOURS.

WILLIAM F BUCKINGHAM completed his PhD on the establishment and initial development of British Airborne Forces in 2001. His other books include *Arnhem 1944* also published by Tempus. He lives near Glasgow.

Praise for *Arnhem 1944*

'Startling... reveals the real reason why the daring attacks failed'

The Daily Express

'The originality of this book lies in its exploration of the long term origins of the battle as well as in its account of the fighting itself... an excellent read'

Professor Hew Strachan

D-DAY

THE FIRST 72 HOURS

WILLIAM F. BUCKINGHAM

TEMPUS

Cover Illustration: British troops go ashore on Sword Beach, D-Day, 6 June 1944. Photograph courtesy of The Imperial War Museum (B5114).

First published 2004

Tempus Publishing Limited
The Mill, Brimscombe Port,
Stroud, Gloucestershire, GL5 2QG
www.tempus-publishing.com

British Library Cataloguing in Publication Data.
A catalogue record for this book is available from the British Library.

ISBN 0 7524 2842 X

Typesetting and origination by Tempus Publishing Limited
Printed in Great Britain by Midway Colour Print, Wiltshire

CONTENTS

PREFACE

In the early hours of 6 June 1944, 20,000 British and American airborne soldiers descended by parachute and glider in the areas of Ranville and St Mère Église in Normandy. Employing 1,200 transport aircraft and 188 gliders, this was the largest airborne landing executed to that date. It was, however, merely the opening phase of a larger operation, the next stage of which commenced six hours or so later. A fleet of 6,000 assorted vessels, ranging from battleships to miniature submarines, delivered getting on for a quarter of a million Allied soldiers onto a sixty-mile stretch of the Normandy coast, extending from the mouth of the River Orne in the east to the coast of the Cotentin Peninsula in the west. Years in the making and codenamed Operation OVERLORD, this was and remains the largest amphibious invasion in history. It began the liberation of German-occupied North-West Europe and led ultimately to Allied victory within the year.

Unsurprisingly, such a momentous event has generated a great deal of interest. Researching this book, for example, involved consulting almost a hundred works and documents dealing wholly or partially with the Normandy invasion, and there are many, many more. Generally speaking, these can be divided into two broad groupings. Leaving aside the official histories, which do a creditable job of covering all the angles in detail, the largest category tends to focus on the strategic 'big picture' and deals with the Normandy campaign as a whole, up to the breakout after Falaise or the liberation of Paris. Within this treatment, the initial assault usually merits a few pages at best or a few lines at worst. Works in the other category take the opposite tack and concentrate almost exclusively on the events of

Tuesday 6 June 1944, through oral histories or by examining the activities of specific units or arms of service within that narrow time frame.
A similar tendency exists in the treatment of the airborne and
amphibious elements of the invasion, which are frequently dealt with
in virtual isolation and along national lines.

These approaches are of course perfectly valid, and in sum provide
thorough coverage of Operation OVERLORD from inception to
completion. However, the problem with minimising or maximising
the initial assault is that it gives a distorted impression of that event
and its relevance in the wider context. The casual observer reading
two randomly selected works, for example, could be forgiven for
forming the view that the Normandy invasion consisted of a twenty-
four hour flurry of activity on the beaches, seamlessly followed by
three months of massed tank attacks near Caen that went on until the
Americans rode to the rescue from the west and closed the Falaise
Gap. They would likely not be aware that in reality the initial assault
went on for three days, or that the course of events in that period
totally shaped the following three-month campaign and arguably
what came after. Neither would they be aware that the initial assault
also highlighted command, doctrinal and organisational shortcomings
that were to dog Allied operations for the rest of the war in North-
West Europe.

The primary aim of this work is thus to provide a coherent and
comprehensive account of the first seventy-two hours of the
Normandy invasion, amalgamating the two approaches cited above
and incorporating both the Allied and German perspectives. The time
frame is not accidental. It took seventy-two hours for the assault force
to achieve most of their D-Day objectives, and the end of the period
marks the point where the burden began to pass from the assault divisions to follow up formations. In addition, the events and imperatives
that led to OVERLORD will be examined, along with the planning,
preparation and forces assigned to both carry out and prevent the
invasion, in order to put the operation into its proper perspective. In
the process, a critical eye will be cast on received wisdom regarding
the D-Day invasion. The American landings on the UTAH beaches, for

example, are almost invariably lauded for their low casualties and efficient disembarkation and logistics build-up. Rather less attention has
been paid to the performance of the US 4th Infantry Division once
ashore, although this was to have serious implications at the time and
later. Similarly, much is made of the alleged failure of the British 3rd
Infantry Division to seize the city of Caen on 6 June as ordered, but
the question of whether or not that objective was realistic or indeed
achievable is rarely addressed, if ever.

On the German side, there has been an unquestioning acceptance
that the British airborne lodgement around Ranville could have been
swiftly eliminated had the senior commanders not reacted in a slug-
gish and hesitant manner. The biggest piece of received wisdom,
however, relates to the American OMAHA landing beaches. Over the
years events these have attained near-legendary status as the unparal-
leled Calvary of D-Day, a perception reinforced recently by the
feature film *Saving Private Ryan*. This has led to a widespread assumption that the beaches assigned to the British and Canadian forces were
a pushover in comparison. The OMAHA defences are thus automatically
assumed to have been formidable, although there is no shortage of
evidence to challenge the assumption, and the possibility is rarely
considered that there might have been deeper problems among the
American assault troops.

This work will therefore assess the accuracy or otherwise of these
assumptions, and hopefully provide a considered and balanced
account of the initial, vital but largely overlooked stage in the Allied
invasion of Normandy. In conclusion, I would like to thank Jonathan
Reeve at Tempus Publishing for his forbearance with my sometimes
elastic approach to deadlines, and once again my son Chris for putting
up with my life being virtually on hold for the past few months, and
for once again acting as unpaid sounding board and proof reader.

William F. Buckingham
Bishopbriggs, Glasgow
January 2004

1

RHETORIC, RAIDERS AND THE EVOLUTION OF THE OVERLORD PLAN

JUNE 1940-JUNE 1944

At 04:30 hours on the morning of 10 May 1940, forty-two *Luftwaffe Junkers 52* transport aircraft lifted off from airfields around Cologne, each towing a DFS 230 troop-carrying glider. Two machines were obliged to abort after take off due to tow-rope failure. An hour later, in the last minutes of pre-dawn darkness, the remaining gliders cast off just short of the Belgian-German border. As first light tinged the sky, they began landing on the meadow atop the Belgian fortress of Eben Emael, protecting three nearby bridges across the Albert Canal. The gliders carried assault pioneers from *7 Flieger Division*, who moved to their objectives with the fluidity and speed generated by intensive practice. A mere ten minutes after touchdown, the fort's observation cupolas and gun turrets had been destroyed or disabled with specially designed shaped charges and flame-throwers. Two of the three bridges were also seized, and a bridgehead established at the third after the defenders triggered their demolition charges.[1]

The attack on Eben Emael was the opening move in Operation *Sichelschnitt* (Cut of the Scythe), which involved three German Army Groups fielding a total of ninety-three divisions. The Eben Emael operation heralded a feint attack into the Low Countries while the main focus of the German attack was an armoured thrust through the Ardennes region, which forced the River Meuse at Dinant and Sedan on 13 and 14 May 1940. Allied counter-attacks failed to stem the German advance, and the *Panzers* reached the Channel coast south of

Boulogne on 21 May, trapping the bulk of the British Expeditionary Force (BEF) in the Pas de Calais. An *ad hoc* evacuation, codenamed DYNAMO, was launched on 27 May. Over the next week 311,586 British, French and other Allied personnel were lifted from Calais, Dunkirk and adjacent beaches.[2] The rest of the BEF was evacuated from ports along the north and western French coast by 20 June 1940.[3] The price of the evacuation was high. The BEF lost 68,111 of its personnel in France killed, missing or as POWs, and mere fractions of its stores and heavy equipment were salvaged. In all, 2,472 guns, 63,877 vehicles, 105,797 tons of ammunition, 415,940 tons of assorted stores and 164,929 tons of fuel were left behind.[4]

This then was the sequence of events that made a cross-Channel invasion necessary almost exactly four years to the day after the end of Operation DYNAMO. In the more immediate term, it also provided the catalyst for a number of practical measures without which the Normandy invasion in June 1944 would have been far more difficult, or even impossible. The main driver behind this was Winston Churchill. Made Prime Minister on the same day the German offensive began, Churchill actually began issuing directives aimed at returning to the offensive before Operation DYNAMO had run its course. On 3 June 1940, in a minute to the Military Secretary to the Cabinet, General Sir Hastings Ismay, warning against the dangers of adopting a defensive mindset, Churchill also mooted raising a 10,000-strong raiding force.[5] He expanded on the latter topic two days later in a further minute that ended with a number of specific proposals. These included a call for suggestions for delivering tanks onto enemy-held beaches, setting up intelligence gathering networks along German held coasts, and the establishment of a 5,000-strong parachute force.[6]

The War Office and Air Ministry response was commendably swift in the circumstances. On 6 June 1940 the War Office authorised raising a raiding force, dubbed Commandos in honour of the Boer guerrillas of the same name,[7] and three days later the Army's Director of Recruiting and Organisation (DRO) called for volunteers for unspecified special service.[8] On 10 June the Air Ministry formulated its response to Churchill's demand for a parachute force, and the Army

Chiefs of Staff included additional parameters for prospective parachute volunteers into Commando recruiting instructions.[9] Two days
later Lieutenant-General Sir Alan Bourne RM was appointed the first
Director of Combined Operations;[10] his higher ranking successor,
Admiral of the Fleet Sir Roger Keyes supplanted him on Churchill's
instructions on 17 July.[11] Bureaucratic measures were accompanied by
the practical. By July 1940 twelve 500-strong Commandos were
forming, and the new joint-service Parachute Training Centre at RAF
Ringway had been established. Combined Operations carried out its
first live operation on the night of 24-25 June 1940; Operation COLLAR
saw five small parties landed at three separate spots south of Boulogne.
A second raid, codenamed AMBASSADOR, was aimed at the airfield and
installations on recently occupied Guernsey on the night of 15-16 July
1940.[12]

This was commendable but by no means flawless progress. The
Commando idea was not universally accepted, and there were difficulties in obtaining volunteers, obliging a second recruiting drive in
October 1940.[13] Even then, the War Office department tasked to
implement the Commando directive had to invoke the CIGS to force
recalcitrant Commandos to comply with its instructions.[14] The pecu-
liar Commando conditions of service were also problematic. Such
postings were temporary,[15] and units were soon agitating for the
return of their volunteers,[16] and morale suffered when the separation
between volunteer and parent unit caused problems with pay and
allowances for dependants. In addition, Commando volunteers were
not provided with billets or rations, but were expected to make their
own arrangements with a monetary allowance, amounting to thirteen
shillings and four pence per day for officers, and six shillings and eight
pence for other ranks.[17] This still brought the War Office into conflict
with the Ministry of Food, particularly when Commando units
moved into rural areas for training.[18]

These teething troubles do not detract from what was highly creditable progress, given the threat of seemingly imminent invasion and
the need to rebuild the British Army. According to received wisdom,
Churchill's rationale in demanding the formation of Commando and

Airborne forces was to carry out pin-prick raids to boost British civil-ian morale, which by happy accident later developed into one capable of spearheading more conventional operations as well. In the process this involved a largely needless and wasteful diversion of high quality manpower and other resources that would have been better employed elsewhere. This explanation is very popular with Churchill's critics and those generally opposed to the creation of so-called 'elite' forces alike.[19]

It is easy to see how this view was formed. Arguably the biggest culprit was Churchill himself, because of the language in which he couched his directives. His initial minutes, for example, advocated developing a 'reign of terror' along German-held coastlines via a 'butcher and bolt' policy. This language was mirrored in internal War Office communications, which invariably referred to the new Commando force as a basis for 'irregular units' and 'special parties' with no fixed organisation and intended for 'tip and run tactics depending on speed, ingenuity [and] dispersion'.[20] Churchill's badger-ing for action without delay reinforced this interpretation, if only because the lack of time and resources made small-scale raiding the only immediate option.

This interpretation also fitted neatly with a pre-existing War Office interest in irregular warfare. This went back at least to the end of the First World War, with British involvement in such operations in Russia and Ireland. A small section entitled General Staff (Research) was set up in the mid-1930s, being expanded and renamed Military Intelligence (Research) in early 1939. As well as publishing pamphlets on guerrilla operations, MI(R) carried out covert intelligence gather-ing in Rumania, Poland and the Baltic States, and was involved in an abortive scheme to assist the Finns in the Winter War.[21] In April 1940 ten 'Independent Companies' were formed for irregular operations in Scandinavia, five of which briefly saw action.[22] Administrative convenience may also have played a part in focusing Churchill's direc-tives into raiding. This appears to be the only reason the War Office folded the parachute requirement into the Commando recruiting effort,[23] for example, and the Air Ministry used the same excuse for its unilateral reduction of the parachute requirement from 5,000 to 500.[24]

However, there is evidence to counter the raiding interpretation of Churchill's directives, starting with what Churchill actually asked for. The first minutes called for the raising of not less than 10,000 raiders, with an additional and separate requirement for 5,000 parachute troops. This clearly shows that Churchill did not consider the two requirements indivisible, and a total force of 15,000 men was a considerable force for small-scale raiding under any conditions. This in turn strongly suggests Churchill had a more substantial purpose in mind, and he was not alone. In July 1940 Major John Rock RE, ranking Army officer at the Parachute Training Centre, requested the War Office reserve the new parachute force for key tasks like the '…capture of a Channel port for an invasion of France'.[25] In fact, planning for an airborne brigade group was already underway, leading to a formal requirement for two all-arms 'Aerodrome Capture Groups'.[26] Such thinking was not restricted to the embryonic airborne force either. Captain Lord Louis Mountbatten, who replaced Keyes as Director of Combined Operations in October 1941, claimed that he was left in no doubt that the primary focus of his new command was to be preparation for a large-scale cross-Channel invasion.[27]

It is possible that Rock was expressing a personal opinion, but it is unlikely that the Director of Combined Operations was doing the same. A closer examination of his directives suggests Churchill was thinking along similar lines from the outset too. The minute of 3 June 1940, for example, referred to the need to play the Germans at their own game. Only the Eben Emael operation and a *coup de main* against bridges in Rotterdam can be construed as raiding operations, and it is therefore logical to assume that Churchill was instead referring to the German employment of 'shock troops'.[28] Yet more pertinently, on 25 August 1940 Churchill briefed Secretary of State for War Anthony Eden on the requirement for 5,000 parachutists and 10,000 raiders, which were to be

> … capable of lightning action. In this way alone will those positions be secured which afterwards will give the opportunity for highly trained regular troops to operate on a larger scale.[29]

This clearly shows that Churchill viewed raiding as a means to an end, rather than an end in itself, and the scale and scope of the operations carried out under the raiding umbrella reinforces the point. These ranged from Operation BITING, the seizure of apparatus from the German radar station at Bruneval on the night of 27-28 February 1942, to the operation to destroy the 'Normandie' dry dock facility at St Nazaire on 28 March 1942. The former employed 119 men from the 2nd Parachute Battalion, supported by a thirty-two strong Army covering party, six assault landing craft, five motor gunboats and two destroyers.[30] The latter involved over 600 Commandos and naval personnel, three destroyers, one of which was converted into a floating time bomb, and eighteen smaller craft.[31] Despite their disparate scale, these operations required exactly the same skills, expertise and detailed planning as a large-scale invasion. The sheer number of such operations also generated a considerable amount of research and development data and operational training and experience; by early 1942 Mountbatten was pushing for an operation every two weeks.

In fact, some operations were launched purely to test operational concepts, as Mountbatten pointed out to personnel training to attack the defended port on the Norwegian island of Vaagsö.[32] Launched on Boxing Day 1941, Operation ARCHERY involved 800 Commandos, supported by the cruiser HMS *Kenya*, two dedicated landing ships (HMS *Prince Leopold* and HMS *Prince Charles*), four destroyers and the submarine HMS *Tuna*. The latter vessel acted as a guide to place the attack force in the correct fjord, and RAF bombers dropped smoke pots to cover the landings and provided daylight air cover for the duration of the operation.[33] The Vaagsö was thus in essence a small-scale invasion, and used a number of techniques employed in the cross-Channel invasion two and a half years later.

It is therefore clear that Churchill intended the new forces to play a larger role than small-scale raids for British public consumption from the outset. The creation of Combined Operations, the Commandos and what was ultimately to become British Airborne Forces was intended to provide the British military with a vital capability totally lacking in its order of battle in mid-1940. This was a properly trained, configured and equipped shock force, capable of operating from the sea or air, and controlled by an independent executive command answerable to the highest British command echelon. The primary purpose of this force was to spearhead a future large-scale invasion of German-occupied Europe, which it did at the beginning of June 1944. It can therefore be argued that, thanks largely to Churchill's foresight and prompting, British preparations for the invasion began as the last British and Allied troops were being lifted from Dunkirk, and exactly four years before British, Canadian and US troops set foot on the Normandy beaches.

Planning for the cross-Channel invasion commenced only slightly later than these practical measures. In October 1941 the British Chiefs of Staff drew up a scheme codenamed ROUNDUP, which envisaged landing just twelve divisions and six tank brigades north and south of Le Havre. ROUNDUP was not intended to fight through serious opposition, but as a pursuit operation to take advantage of a German withdrawal following a decisive defeat in Russia. Given German success in the Soviet Union at the time ROUNDUP was conceived, this was somewhat optimistic, and the scheme was probably intended as a first step for planning purposes.[34] Nonetheless, the Chiefs of Staff ordered Combined Operations HQ and Home Forces Command to prepare a collective outline in April 1942, based on a detailed survey of coastal topography, intelligence on German defences and research and development work on assault landing techniques and equipment.[35]

At this time it was an article of faith that the logistics of a large-scale landing required the seizure of a port at the outset or immediately thereafter, and the larger the better. The ROUNDUP landing area included several ports beside Le Havre, and Dieppe to the north was selected as the venue for a scaled-down dry run for ROUNDUP in August 1942. The operation, initially codenamed RUTTER, was first mooted in April 1942, presumably in response to the Chiefs of Staff directive cited above. The primary stated aim of the operation was to test the feasibility of seizing a defended port, with the secondary aims of investigating possible problems inherent in controlling a large and disparate invasion fleet, and to test assault techniques and equipment.

Dieppe stands at the mouth of the River Arques, overlooked by flanking headlands. The harbour lay to the east of the town, which was fronted by almost a mile of steep shingle beach backed by a concrete sea wall, a 150-yard wide esplanade and a row of seafront hotels ending with a large casino built into the western end of the seawall. *Infanterie Regiment 571* was stationed in the town, the beach was laced with mines and barbed wire, concrete obstacles were placed in the narrow streets leading inland from the esplanade, the casino was fortified and the eastern headland was reinforced with concrete artillery positions and machine-gun emplacements. This allowed the defenders to enfilade the beach from both ends, and the esplanade formed a secondary killing zone. Defences were also constructed covering two outlying beaches to the east and west, and four batteries of coastal defence guns provided long-range support.

The initial plan was scheduled for July 1942, and envisaged landing troops east and west of Dieppe, with a parachute attack on the out lying coastal artillery batteries. It was postponed at the last minute when an unexpected weather front grounded the parachute force.[36] Thereafter the parachute element was discarded along with the intensive pre-landing bombardment. Ostensibly the latter was to avoid French civilian casualties, and the former to remove weather-dependent factors from the plan.[37] These were undoubtedly valid concerns, but there was also the fact that the RAF was unable to provide sufficient aircraft to lift even a single parachute battalion without borrowing operational aircraft from Bomber Command, and that the 1st Parachute Brigade was significantly under-strength.[38] Whether or not, dealing with the coastal batteries was given to the Commandos, and the scheme then snowballed in size and scope. The major focus became a frontal assault with tanks on Dieppe, with flank landings to seize the headlands overlooking the port. Later additions included seizing the airfield at St Aubin-sur-Scie and an attack on a nearby German divisional headquarters, a rather tall order given that the latter objectives were 3 and 6 miles inland respectively, and that the entire raid was scheduled to last a maximum of seven hours.

Nonetheless the scheme, renamed JUBILEE, went ahead and ultimately involved delivering the 2nd Canadian Infantry Division and Nos 3 and 4 Commandos onto five separate beaches. The Canadian contingent made up 4,693 of the 6,100-strong attack force, which included fifty men from the US 1st Ranger Battalion attached to various units to gain experience. The landing force employed 252 other assorted ships and landing craft, supported by a flotilla of minesweepers, five destroyers and sixty-nine RAF and RCAF fighter and light bomber squadrons.[39] The operation began at 04:50 on Wednesday 19 August 1942, with the neutralisation of the German coastal defence batteries. One attack went like clockwork, and the Commandos involved were back aboard their vessels within three hours. The other went less smoothly. The landing force was scattered after running into a German coastal convoy, and only a handful landed late in the correct place. One group of Commandos was captured by a German counter attack, and the rest were only able to temporarily distract the battery from firing on the attack force. The supporting attacks by the Queen's Own Cameron Highlanders of Canada and The South Saskatchewan Regiment on the headlands overlooking Dieppe did not go as planned either. One landing was unopposed, but the other came under heavy fire and suffered a number of casualties. Stiffening resistance and unrealistic timetabling prevented either objective being achieved; the attackers had to fight their way back to the beach and their evacuation was delayed by a lack of landing craft. Both battalions were virtually destroyed; the Queen's Own Highlanders lost 346 men killed, wounded, missing and captured, and the South Saskatchewans lost just over 500.

The real disaster unfolded on the Dieppe seafront. After a five-minute bombardment from the supporting destroyers and single strafing run by RAF fighters, the Essex Scottish went ashore at 05:20 into a storm of enfilading fire from both headlands and fortified seafront buildings. Between forty and seventy-five per cent of its effective strength was lost within thirty minutes. The Royal Hamilton Light Infantry managed to take the casino at 07:12, but few survived to cross the fire-swept esplanade. The first wave of nine Churchill tanks arrived fifteen minutes late, and only three tanks managed to surmount the sea wall and engage the fortified seafront buildings. They and a further twelve from succeeding waves were trapped on the esplanade by the concrete obstacles blocking the streets into the town, and eventually fell back to the cover of the sea wall. The reserve battalion from the Fusiliers Mont Royal was committed at 07:00 following an erroneous report that the Royal Hamiltons had penetrated into Dieppe. They too were effectively wiped out, losing 512 all ranks from the 583 committed to the landing. At around 08:00, Royal Marine A Commando was also despatched to the main beach, with orders to bypass the town and eliminate the German positions on the east headland. The first wave, accompanied by their commander, Lieutenant-Colonel J.P. Phillips RM in a launch, were again pinned down immediately on landing. Realising the futility of landing more troops, Phillips donned white gauntlets, moved into the open and succeeded in waving off some craft from the succeeding waves before being killed.

The 2nd Canadian Infantry Division took 4,693 men to Dieppe. 2,892 remained there, 1,895 as prisoners or missing; the remaining 907 were dead. The supporting units also suffered relatively heavily. Sixty-six men from the Royal Marine A Commando were killed or captured on the beach, No. 3 Commando lost 120 killed, wounded and/or captured, while No. 4 Commando lost twelve dead, twenty-one wounded and thirteen missing.[40] In addition, the fifty-strong contingent from the US 1st Ranger Battalion lost six dead, seven wounded and four captured.[41] Lieutenant Loustalot, who accompanied No. 3, earned the dubious honour of being the first US serviceman killed in ground combat in the European theatre.[42]

Unsurprisingly, the Dieppe débâcle has spawned a great deal of controversy. Churchill, for example, has been charged with deliberately setting up the operation to fail, to provide a credible counter to vociferous Soviet demands for a Second Front in 1942. In Canada, Dieppe is widely viewed as an example of British carelessness with the lives of their colonial subjects, although this conveniently overlooks the Canadian enthusiasm for the operation. One recent author has argued, not altogether convincingly, that Mountbatten overstepped

his authority and launched JUBILEE without the knowledge or sanc-
tion of his superiors.[43] Be that as it may, with hindsight the Dieppe
operation contained a number of flaws. The close naval escort proved
insufficient, and the near total reliance on surprise was a mistake. A
five-minute bombardment from heavy naval units would have been
insufficient, and that from a mere four destroyers did little more than
provide a morale boost for the first assault wave and alert the German
garrison of the impending landing. While undoubtedly courageous, the
landing craft crews required more marshalling and forming up training,
and some of their craft were poorly configured and constructed for
large-scale landings. The British Landing Craft Personnel (Large), for
example, lacked a ramp and obliged passengers to jump down from a
high prow, and the craft's wooden construction was not sufficiently
robust; several were holed on rocks during the landings.[44]

These flaws were undoubtedly costly, but that has to be set against the
fact that the Dieppe operation was explicitly intended to combat test
command and control arrangements and assault equipment and techniques, hardly a recipe for playing safe. Mountbatten may thus have
been wise after the event in claiming that the success of the Normandy
landings was won on the beaches of Dieppe,[45] but he was essentially
speaking the truth. JUBILEE did not fail in every respect, and those that
did yielded valuable experience and lessons that were later incorporated
into the Normandy plan. The majority of the Dieppe attack force was
delivered accurately and on time, which suggests that amphibious planning and procedures were largely sound. The destruction of one coastal
battery proved that eliminating such installations in this way was feasible, and the performance of the Commandos showed their selection
and training was turning out troops with the necessary high levels of
initiative and flexibility. The flank landings also proved the feasibility of
inserting flank guards for the main landings, and it should be noted that
things only began to seriously unravel for the South Saskatchewans and
the Queen's Own Cameron Highlanders of Canada during the extrac-
tion phase. This would not have been a factor in a permanent invasion.

However, arguably the most significant outcome was the impact on
German and Allied perceptions. Their apparent success reinforced

German conviction that any Allied invasion would involve seizure of a major port, and they continued to invest a great deal of time and resources fortifying ports and constructing supporting coastal defences along the entire coastline of occupied Europe. For their part, the British took the opposite tack, and drew the conclusion that seizing a major port would be extremely costly and probably imposs ible, at least before the garrison had demolished the port facilities. The alternative was therefore to think the previously unthinkable – plan for a cross-beach assault, and work out a way to get around the logisti- cal handicap this would entail.

In the event, the cross-Channel invasion was to be an Anglo- American affair, and liaison between the two militaries predated US entry into the war. The US Navy Department stationed a semi-official observer in London in the summer of 1940, the US War Department regularly despatched officers on 'special missions', and there was a mutual exchange of military missions in the spring of 1941. These agreed the Germany-first principle for Allied strategy, which was formalised after the Japanese attack on Pearl Harbor on 7 December 1941 and Hitler's declaration of war on the US four days later. The ARCADIA conference held in Washington on 31 December 1941, however, accepted that circumstances precluded a direct attack upon Germany, and agreed to a strategy of peripheral attacks and an aerial bombing offensive against the German homeland. The long-term aim was thus a full-scale invasion of Western Europe by 1943.[46]

However, both parties held fundamentally different views of the arrangement. The British viewed it as but one option in a step-by-step approach, partly due to a long-standing principle of attempting to avoid Continental entanglements, and partly in acknowledgement of post-Dunkirk military weakness and more recent maulings in Greece and the Western Desert. The aim was to wear down German opera- tional capabilities via peripheral operations and only then use the cross-Channel invasion to deliver the *coup de grace*. This line of think- ing was clear in the British ROUNDUP plan of October 1941, which was intended to take advantage of a sudden German collapse on the Eastern Front.[47] The Americans took the opposite tack, favouring the concentration of overwhelming force against a single point to bring matters to a speedy and favourable conclusion. Had they possessed the means, the Americans would have insisted on a cross-Channel invasion in 1942.

Perhaps fortunately, the blunt fact was that the US Army was incapable of properly protecting the continental United States, let alone prosecuting a global war. These differences reinforced less than helpful mutual preconceptions. Many of the British viewed American self-confidence as unwarranted cockiness at best and outright arrogance at worst, allied to profligacy with materiel and personnel. For their part, not a few American officers viewed their new British allies as erstwhile colonial oppressors, and considered the British preference for the indirect approach as an excuse to cover an unwillingness to come to grips with the Germans. On a more practical level, there was also a lack of administrative arrangements necessary to undertake operational planning. Thus in May 1942 the Americans imitated the British Combined Chiefs of Staff Committee and its associated machinery by creating a whole new command and planning organisation headed by the US Joint Chiefs of Staff and a dedicated Joint Planning Staff. There was also an Anglo-US Combined Chiefs of Staff office, consisting of the British and US Chiefs of Staff or their representatives, with a subordinate group of Combined Staff Planners and a direct line to Churchill and Roosevelt.[48]

Unsurprisingly given all this, American planning for the cross-Channel invasion predated these arrangements. In February 1942 US planners drew up a scheme for an invasion of the Pas de Calais, similar to the British ROUNDUP plan of the previous October, although their efforts were handicapped by a lack of suitable landing craft and troops. According to the US Army Chief of Staff, the Americans would only be able to deploy a maximum of three and a half divisions to the UK in 1942.[49] Any invasion would thus have to rely on British support that was unlikely to be forthcoming given their more realistic appraisal of German capabilities, the accuracy of which was graphically illustrated at Dieppe. In addition, the invasion area was dictated by the operational range of the available fighter aircraft, which restricted the projected area of operations to the region between Abbeville and Dunkirk, an unsuitable location for a number of reasons. The beaches there were shallow and thus unsuitable for British landing craft, they lacked suitable exits, the handful of ports in that area were too small to host a large-scale logistical effort, and the German defences were at their strongest. The US Army thus accepted, albeit reluctantly, that a cross-Channel invasion was not feasible in mid-1942. The plan was thus codenamed SLEDGEHAMMER, modified and filed as a contingency measure.

The Americans were not discouraged, however. In March 1942 the US planners began working on a much larger scheme, provisionally scheduled for the spring of 1943. The result was the 'Marshall Memorandum' passed to President Roosevelt on 2 April 1942. This envisaged a raiding phase to wear down the German defenders and camouflage the location of the invasion before landing forty-eight astride the mouth of the River Somme. The similarity of the US design to the British ROUNDUP scheme of the previous year led to it being dubbed '1943 ROUNDUP'. The plan was presented to the British Chiefs of Staff in April 1942, who received it more favourably than SLEDGEHAMMER. However, they were unwilling to give a firm commitment, even when Marshall promised a million US troops and a top priority build-up called BOLERO in return for an undertaking to launch the invasion in 1943. Marshall was trying to placate Roosevelt's impatience for action, maintain the President's commitment to the Germany First principle, and to forestall his US Navy counterpart from diverting resources to the Pacific theatre. The result was a compromise, and at the Washington Conference in June 1942 Marshall thus signed up to the invasion of Algeria in November 1942 and reluctantly put Sledgehammer on the back burner.

BOLERO nonetheless went ahead and logistical planning bodies called BOLERO Combined Committees were established. One of their main functions was to prepare bases for US troops slated for the invasion, 32,000 of which had arrived in the UK by June 1942.[50] However, BOLERO was hamstrung by the demands of Operation TORCH.

Three of the first four US divisions assembled in the UK, totalling 150,000 men, were redirected to North Africa and their replacements did not start to arrive in the UK until March 1943. The supply effort was similarly retarded, dropping from 240,000 tons in September 1942 to 20,000 tons in February 1943. It took a further five months to re-attain the former level.[51] The situation changed for the better after the Casablanca Conference in January 1943 when, with badgering from Churchill, the British Chiefs of Staff finally made a firm commitment to a cross-Channel invasion in 1944. This was the first of a number of developments that shifted the invasion from a disputed abstract to a concrete undertaking. BOLERO was given precedence over the requirements of subsequent operations in the Mediterranean, and the groundwork was laid for a single, dedicated command to oversee the preparation and execution of the operation. No Supreme Allied Commander was appointed, but the necessary staff and planning organisation was set up in anticipation.

Thus in March 1943 British Lieutenant-General Frederick E. Morgan was summoned to the War Office, presented with all mate-rial relating to the cross-Channel invasion, and informally requested to draw up a proposal for the next step.[52] By April 1943 he had produced a number of propositions and a suggested structure for a new, Anglo-American planning staff. Morgan was then officially appointed Chief of Staff to the Supreme Allied Commander (Designate). After some wrangling over structures, delineation of authority and the precise wording of the Casablanca agreement had been resolved,[53] Morgan's new office opened on 17 April 1943. It was named COSSAC, the initials of Morgan's title, and initially concen-trated on three specific plans. COCKADE was a scheme aimed at supporting the Soviets by keeping as many German units in the west as possible. RANKIN was an updated SLEDGEHAMMER, intended to take advantage of a sudden German collapse. OVERLORD was the opera-tional plan for full-scale, cross-Channel invasion. With mid-1944 pinpointed as the time for the latter, the next step was to establish the location.

In November 1942, after the Dieppe débâcle, British planners re-examined the requirements for invasion. Multiple and widely separated landings were abandoned in favour of a single, large but defensible landing area capable of accommodating a rapid build up, and a list of factors was compiled to aid selection. An invasion site had to be within range of UK-based fighters, not too strongly defended, protected from the weather, suitable for over-the-beach supply, contain suitable and sufficient beach exits, be linked to a developed road net, and be near a major port. Unfortunately, the planners were unable to locate a site meeting all these criteria, and only two came close. Both were in Normandy, on the Cotentin Peninsula and in the area of Caen, and the latter was judged the more suitable, although it lacked a port; the nearest was Le Havre, 30 miles east on the other side of the River Seine.

This appreciation was accepted by the Combined Chiefs of Staff on 1 March 1943, and formed the basis for the last American invasion plan before responsibility passed to COSSAC. SKYSCRAPER envisaged landings near Caen and the east coast of the Cotentin Peninsula. Two airborne divisions were to be delivered behind each landing area, and Commandos were to carry out simultaneous attacks along the entire coast. Two divisions were to land initially at each area, followed by a second wave of three divisions. After securing the port of Cherbourg at the tip of the Cotentin Peninsula, the force would break out to the east. Ironically given its similarity to the final OVERLORD plan, SKYSCRAPER was rejected by the British Chiefs of Staff, who claimed it minimised likely German opposition, and that insufficient resources were available.[54]

Morgan made his own study of past work before setting his staff to preparing appreciations and outline plans for landings at Caen and the Pas de Calais. Their conclusions, which appeared in mid-June 1943, rejected the Pas de Calais and recommended a three-division assault on a thirty-mile front west of the River Orne. The scheme was deliberately broad-brush, and made no effort to address details like the composition of the assault force or timings, although the need to frame future planning around predicted weather and tidal conditions and the conflicting needs of the various forces involved were noted. The likelihood of speedy and powerful German counter-attacks was also acknowledged, with the recommendation that the assault wave and initial follow-up forces should contain a high proportion of armoured and anti-aircraft units.

The COSSAC scheme also broke with previous thinking by making no provision for seizure of a port, advocating using prefabricated artificial ports that could be towed across the Channel and assembled in place instead. This was a bold step, given that the idea was untested and that many of the components were still on the drawing board. The scheme also omitted any landing on the Cotentin Peninsula because the British Chiefs of Staff were unwilling to guarantee sufficient landing craft, and similar concerns over aircraft provision restricted the airborne contribution to a single rather than two such divisions. The latter highlights the most pressing handicaps faced by the COSSAC planners at this stage. Morgan lacked executive authority, he had no superior with sufficient clout to obtain additional resources or force compliance, and his position was complicated yet further by the lack of a clear chain of command. This left COSSAC open to all kinds of interference, well meaning or otherwise. Churchill, predictably, was a particular offender in this respect.

The ongoing strategic disagreement compounded these difficulties. Success in Sicily and seemingly imminent Italian collapse led to a further 66,000 US troops being diverted from the BOLERO build-up, and the British Chiefs of Staff, still keen to pursue the indirect approach, suggested redirecting a further 50,000. This was a step too far for the US Chiefs of Staff, however, and the result was yet another strategic debate at the QUADRANT Conference in Quebec, beginning on 12 August 1943. This both reaffirmed the primacy of BOLERO and significantly advanced the OVERLORD cause. Morgan's outline plan was endorsed, with the proviso that it be expanded to include the Cotentin landing. In addition, several battle-tested divisions were to be transferred from the Mediterranean for the invasion, and COSSAC was directed to continue with preparations and planning.

Ironically, this exacerbated Morgan's problems. The outline OVERLORD plan presented at Quebec fulfilled his brief in full, and COSSAC was not configured to deal with the myriad details required to turn the outline into an operational reality. Those required direct participation and input from corps, army and army groups, many of which were not fully established, and COSSAC lacked the authority and chain of command necessary to work with them in any case. The Combined Chiefs of Staff invested Morgan with limited executive powers after he complained in September 1943, but this could only be a stopgap.[55] Further progress thus depended on finalising the command structure for OVERLORD by designating a Supreme Allied Commander.

This, however, raised the potentially vexed questions of finding a candidate and deciding nationality. The Chief of Imperial General Staff, General Sir Alan Brooke, was considered briefly and Churchill suggested the US Chief of Staff, General George C. Marshall, at the Quebec conference.[56] Roosevelt also favoured Marshall, but hesitated after being warned of the potentially serious consequences of removing him from the highest levels of Allied decision making. The matter came to a head at Tehran in November 1943, when Stalin asked point-blank who was to lead the much-promised cross-Channel invasion. Forced into a corner, Roosevelt finally recommended General Dwight D. Eisenhower. The choice was both popular and wise. Churchill considered Eisenhower the only US officer beside Marshall qualified for the job and the selection of a long-standing protégé doubtless eased Marshall's disappointment. Eisenhower had been involved in the initial planning for the invasion in February 1942, and as Commander Allied Forces in the Mediterranean had gained experience with amphibious operations, and demonstrated the skills vital for effective command of a multi-national force. He was therefore appointed Supreme Commander, Allied Expeditionary Force on 6 December 1943, and he arrived in London six days later, presumably amid rejoicing from Morgan and the COSSAC staff.

With a Supreme Commander in place, the detailed planning for OVERLORD moved ahead rapidly. COSSAC was superseded by Supreme Headquarters Allied Expeditionary Force (SHAEF), and General Sir Bernard L. Montgomery was appointed to command 21st Army Group, the top British command slot. Eisenhower designated

Montgomery temporary Supreme Commander while he returned to the US for a brief leave. Montgomery was tasked to explore ways of expanding the outline OVERLORD plan, which both considered too small. This Montgomery duly did, whilst ruthlessly remodelling 21st Army Group HQ to his liking.[57]

The re-evaluation was presented to Eisenhower on 21 January 1944, and advocated widening the landing area to include the entire length of coast between the River Orne and the eastern side of the Cotentin Peninsula, with airborne landings to secure the flanks. The British were to land in the east and Americans west of Bayeux, which was selected as the demarcation line. The initial landing had three major objectives. These were to seize Caen and the surrounding area suitable for airfield construction; to block and destroy German reserves moving to oppose the invasion; and to facilitate the rapid seizure of Cherbourg, all of which were to be carried out concurrently. Eisenhower accepted the plan, and directed SHAEF to pass it to the Combined Chiefs of Staff for authorisation. This was granted on 1 February 1944, after the first stage of the invasion was delineated into a distinct sub-operation with its plan. This was codenamed the NEPTUNE Initial Joint Plan, leaving the OVERLORD codename for the overall strategic scheme. NEPTUNE envisaged delivering six British, Canadian and US divisions onto five landing areas, codenamed UTAH, OMAHA, GOLD, JUNO and SWORD.

This still left the matter of resolving the precise timing and date, which involved balancing a number of sometimes mutually exclusive factors. A daylight assault would have greatly aided navigation and gunnery observation, but at the cost of conferring the same advantage on the defence. A night landing, on the other hand, would initially conceal the scale and direction of the assault. The choice was thus between an aggressive daylight fight through and a more stealthy approach to get the leading waves ashore under cover of darkness. A detailed study recommended that the attack should go in approximately an hour after first light, permitting the preliminary approach to be carried out in darkness but allowing sufficient daylight to direct an intense pre-landing barrage. The date of launch was dependent on moon and tide. Airborne landings were impossible without some natural illumination, and the seaborne landings had to be made on a rising tide to avoid stranding landing craft after delivering their loads. This narrowed the choice down to one or two three-day periods in any given month. As 1 June had been selected as the approximate date for the invasion, the nearest favourable period fell on 5, 6 and 7 June 1944. Monday, 5 June was therefore designated D-Day, with H-Hour three hours before high tide.

With the location, date and time fixed, preparatory activities and operations could go ahead. Planning for NEPTUNE required a huge amount of information, ranging from beach gradients, composition and obstacles to the location, equipment and morale of German units. Monitoring communications yielded an abundance of such data, thanks largely to total German confidence in their ENIGMA encipherment machine. This used interchangeable lettered wheels to encrypt signals prior to despatch, and offered up to 150 billion possible permutations of any given message. Thus the Germans, unsurprisingly, considered ENIGMA to be unbreakable. However, a team of mathematicians and cryptographers based at Bletchley Park in Buckinghamshire, building on Polish and French intelligence work, succeeded in doing just that.[58] Codenamed ULTRA, the resulting decryptions allowed the Allies to read virtually any German military communication they could monitor. This, in conjunction with data gathered by the Resistance, permitted SHAEF to assemble an extremely accurate picture of German dispositions and activities in France and Belgium.

The planners also required visual information. Allied reconnaissance aircraft took tens of thousands of photographs of the landing area, and specially configured aircraft with oblique or side mounted cameras obtained low-level close-ups of specific objectives and pictures of the landing beaches, some while flying parallel at very low level up to 1,500 yards offshore. The latter photographs were assembled into panoramas issued as navigation aids to landing craft crews and junior commanders in the initial assault waves. To avoid alerting the Germans to the target of the invasion, this activity was extended along the entire coast of occupied Europe, with three sorties being flown elsewhere for every one over Normandy. For more detailed information on the beaches the planners could also call on the combat swimmers of the Combined Operations Pilotage Parties (COPPs). Originally formed to reconnoitre and mark landing sites for Commando raids using dinghies or canoes, by January 1944 they were using modified nine-ton landing craft dubbed Landing Craft Navigation (LCN) equipped with echo sounders, radar and radio navigation equipment, and X-Type miniature submarines. Both craft were used to carry combat swimmers close inshore to carry out surveys, and later to mark the route for the invaders.

The first COPP survey of the landing beaches was carried out on the night of 31 December-1 January 1944 off la Rivière, primarily to investigate the make up of old peat workings behind the beach. Another party was despatched to the area off Laurent-sur-Mer on the night of 17-18 January 1944, when tidal conditions permitted an X-Craft to cross the Calvados Reef. It remained on station for three days, carrying out periscope surveys during daylight and sending in combat swimmers for close-reconnaissance at night; on one occasion a German sentry unwittingly stepped across a marker line while the swimmers gathered samples of beach material for analysis. They returned with details of beach exits, and the location of German fortifications, minefields and the number and type of beach obstacles. Sand samples proved the beach could support tanks and heavy vehicles, confirming the site as suitable for an artificial harbour.[59]

Not all preliminary activity was passive. Aerial bombing of German coastal defences began in mid-April 1944, again with three raids elsewhere for every one in Normandy. Thus only approximately ten per cent of the total tonnage delivered was directed against the coastal batteries there; more concentrated attacks against targets in the invasion area were planned for the night of D Minus 1, and attacks by medium bombers were incorporated into the assault fire plan.[60] Targets were also struck well inland. The US 9th Air Force, for example, destroyed or badly damaged twenty-one of the twenty-four bridges over the Seine north of Paris, and hit thirty-six airfields as far afield as Belgium. The RAF's 2nd Tactical Air Force carried out 2,000 raids against ninety-two radar stations along the German occupied coast; seventy-six were put out of action, including almost all those covering the landing area.

The Continental railway system received equally intensive treatment. The TRANSPORTATION Plan pinpointed key marshalling yards, track junctions and repair facilities in France, Belgium and western Germany, and struck them in a way that appeared to focus on the Pas de Calais while actually cutting rail links with Normandy. Allied heavy bomber squadrons delivered 75,000 tons of bombs via 21,949 sorties between February and June 1944, while fighter-bombers caught elements that avoided bombing of the marshalling yards; by June 1944 three-quarters of the locomotives in Northern France and Belgium had been destroyed or rendered unserviceable.[61] The air effort was paralleled by Plan VERT, a covert sabotage campaign co-ordinated by the British Special Operations Executive (SOE). Beginning in July 1942, SOE had cultivated resistance activity among French railway workers. Among the most successful SOE initiatives was the introduction of abrasive paste into the wheel bearings of flat cars capable of carrying German tanks and armoured vehicles. This rapidly seized the wheel bearings and rendered the cars useless.[62] In the year beginning June 1943, saboteurs destroyed 2,500 freight cars, and damaged a further 8,000 along with 1,822 locomotives and 1,500 passenger carriages. The result was a slow but steady reduction in the flow of rail traffic into the invasion area that increased as the invasion neared. Between March and June 1944, the total volume of rail traffic across France and Belgium was reduced by sixty per cent, and in northern France generally the proportion was as high as seventy-five percent.[63]

The Allies also put an immense amount of effort into disinformation and deception operations. Operation FORTITUDE created the fictitious 1st US Army Group or FUSAG in south-east England, poised to attack the Pas de Calais. The illusion was maintained with an elaborate radio network that generated spurious traffic, and huge dummy camps complete with inflatable trucks and tanks for the benefit of German reconnaissance aircraft. Large numbers of timber and canvas aircraft and landing craft were also shuttled between locations by specially trained detachments. This supported the German conviction that the Pas de Calais was the most likely area for invasion, which was subtly reinforced by feeding the German high command corroborating disinformation via the totally compromised German spy network in the UK. The Spanish reporter Luis Calvo, codenamed GARBO and turned by British intelligence in February 1942, was particularly noteworthy. The British built an elaborate and totally fictitious spy ring around GARBO, which the Germans came to view as one of their most reliable intelligence assets. Another deception plan created a complete British 4th Army with a headquarters in Edinburgh, and a phantom US 14th Army based around Stirling and Dundee. Around sixty signallers succeeded in persuading the Germans that one armoured, four infantry and one airborne division were poised to invade Norway,[64] a deceit that kept twenty-seven German divisions tied up in Scandinavia for over a month after the launch of OVERLORD.[65]

As preparations advanced and the invasion drew nearer, maintaining security became increasingly complex, necessitating a new category of top secret. Codenamed BIGOT, this was created to cover information connected to NEPTUNE, and officers so cleared were thus dubbed BIGOTS. In one grisly incident, divers had to be employed to account for the bodies of two BIGOTS killed when German E-Boats sank two LSTs engaged in a landing exercise on the Devon coast on the night of 26-27 April 1944.[66] On a lighter note, physics teacher Leonard Sidney Dawe was arrested while walking his dog one Sunday morning, and interrogated by MI5. Dawe was senior crossword puzzle compiler on *The Daily Telegraph*, and was singled out after the words Utah, Omaha, Mulberry, Neptune and Overlord appeared in his puzzles during May 1944.[67] A Czech military writer caused a similar stir when it was noticed that map-diagrams relating to the employment of airborne troops in one of his works virtually replicated the actual OVERLORD airborne plan; he too was investigated and exonerated.[68] Some were not so fortunate. The Quartermaster General of the US 9th Air Force was relieved of his command, reduced in rank and sent back to the US in disgrace following unguarded remarks at a dinner party in April 1944. A British officer who left a copy of the OVERLORD communications plan in a London taxi was presumably treated equally harshly; the offending briefcase was actually handed in to Scotland Yard's lost property office by the cab driver.[69] Despite these and other scares, security remained unbreached and as we shall see, the cross-Channel invasion achieved total surprise.

This then was the two-and-a-half-year process of discussion, argument and outright disagreement that shaped the Allied cross-Channel invasion. Before examining the operational detail of the invasion plan, we shall first take a look at the other side of the hill, to see what the Germans had in the area slated for the invasion, and how they planned to meet such an eventuality.

2

WIEDERSTANDNESTE, BODENSTÄNDIGE DIVISIONS AND PANZERS

THE GERMAN DEFENCE IN NORMANDY

Wherever the Allies had elected to invade in 1944, they would have faced fixed defences of some description. These ranged from Fort Austrått in Norway, which incorporated a triple 128mm gun turret lifted from the German battlecruiser *Gneisenau*, to the *Ringstand*, a roughly 4 x 3-metre concrete shelter capable of housing a machine-gun team and ammunition.[1] These and a host of other fortifications formed part of the Atlantic Wall, stretching from the Arctic Circle to the Spanish border, and were presented by Nazi propaganda as the impregnable result of a seamlessly implemented masterplan. The reality was somewhat different in all respects, however, for the evolution of the Atlantic Wall was at least as convoluted as that of the OVER-LORD invasion that overran the stretch covering the Normandy coast.

It is generally accepted that the concept and term Atlantic Wall came out of two directives. *Generalfeldmarschall* Wilhelm Keitel, *Oberkommando der Wehrmacht* (OKW) chief of staff,[2] issued the first on 14 December 1941. It contained detailed instructions for the construction of a new *Westwall*, the fixed defensive line erected on the western German border, popularly known as the Siegfried Line.[3] Like the inland defences, the new coastal line was to consist of reinforced concrete field defences sited to cover similarly protected coastal artillery batteries.[4] Keitel's directive was followed on 23 March 1942 by *Führer* Directive No. 40. This complemented the earlier Directive by section laying out the logic for building the fortifications, contained operational instructions for coastal defence, and delegated responsibility for the different sectors of the German occupied coast-line to the various regional high commands.[5] Actual construction predated these directives, however, at least in France and Belgium. The *Heer* had begun erecting defensive fortifications as part of its normal routine after the fall of France, while the *Kriegsmarine* commenced construction of a number of heavy coastal batteries and associated fire-control radar installations near Calais, Boulogne, Le Havre and Cherbourg in July 1940.[6] The latter installations formed part of the preparations for Operation *Seelöwe* (Sealion), the aborted invasion of Britain.[7]

On the surface, the directives from Keitel and Hitler seem to constitute a pretty straightforward order to implement the construction of defences along the western coast of the occupied territories. However, they did not establish priorities, responsibilities or a clear chain of command for the *Heer*, *Kriegsmarine* and the third agency involved, the Organisation Todt. The latter was a civilian organisation created by Dr Fritz Todt in 1938 to complete the *Westwall* defences, and subsequently undertook military construction projects throughout the German occupied territories. Todt went on to head the German Armament Ministry until his death in an air crash in February 1942. All three organisations shared a strong disinclination to co-operate, and the unfettered competition this engendered turned the Atlantic Wall project into a microcosm of the Nazi state. Indeed, the turf war between the *Heer* and *Kriegsmarine* reached such a pitch that Hitler intervened in late 1942, and while this toned things down somewhat, it did little to rationalise channels of communication or normalise relations between the services. This led to the ludicrous situation where *Generalfeldmarschall* von Runstedt, the senior military commander in the West, was unable to issue direct orders to *Heer* artillery personnel seconded to man *Kriegsmarine* coastal batteries. Instead he had to route 'requests for assistance' to the naval high command via OKW.[8] Neither was this kind of behaviour restricted purely to the military. Albert Speer, Todt's successor as Minister for Armaments, was obliged to institute tightly controlled monthly cement quotas to curtail the common practice of one organisation seizing entire shipments to the detriment of its competitors.[9]

In the event, the Organisation Todt came out on top and was given sole responsibility for Atlantic Wall construction early in 1942. This, however, proved to be very much a two-edged sword. Speer encountered further problems in trying to rationalise the Organisation Todt's highly compartmentalised internal structure, not least from the head of the organisation, Franz Dorsch, formerly a deputy of Todt's.[10] The German military enjoyed less success than Speer, who eventually succeeded in driving his reforms through. Even the office of *Oberbefehlshaber West* (Commander-in-Chief West) had no authority over the Organisation Todt and could only request co-operation that was frequently not forthcoming. When this failed the only recourse was an appeal to OKW or Hitler, which was usually futile because of the Führer's preference for parallel and competing agencies in all government business. According to one senior *Heer* officer, the Organisation Todt did much of its work with little or no reference to tactical necessity or military advice, and frequently undertook construction work for no discernible reason.[11] This was a matter of no small importance given the amount of resources involved. A six-man bunker with ammunition storage required 500 cubic metres of concrete, twenty-three tons of steel reinforcing rods and six tons of sheet steel, while a two-storey command bunker required almost three times these amounts; these were among the smaller fortification elements.[12] Between the middle of 1942 and 1944, Atlantic Wall construction consumed 1,200,000 tonnes of steel, five per cent of the entire German production total, and 13,234,500 cubic metres of concrete, at a cost of 3.7 billion *Reichsmarks*.[13]

The only centralised direction came, such as it was, directly from Hitler. This, however, exacerbated the situation because Hitler changed construction priorities to match his shifting strategic perceptions, and because *Führerprinzip* brooked no opposition. Thus in October 1941 he made turning the Channel Islands into an impregnable fortress top priority on the assumption that the British would assign similar importance to retaking the only piece of British sovereign territory under German occupation.[14] The following year, unsettled by the British attacks on St Nazaire and Dieppe in March and

August, priority was shifted to fortifying ports, in line with received wisdom that large-scale invasion was impossible without access to port facilities. In November 1943 Führer Directive No. 51 shifted priority yet again to the Pas de Calais and Denmark. The former was selected as the most probable objective for the Allied invasion, and because the region was slated as a launch area for the V-weapon offensive against Britain; the latter merely because Hitler thought it a likely target for Allied diversionary attacks.[15]

However, while it may have been achieved in a somewhat haphazard manner, a good deal of progress was made nonetheless. By mid 1944 12,247 of the 15,000 fortifications originally envisaged had been completed, mostly in the Pas de Calais including the area astride the mouth of the River Seine.[16] Most of the remaining defensive development was centred on the U-boat bases at Brest and Lorient, and Cherbourg at the head of the Cotentin Peninsula. By the time construction ceased in 1944, over 250 distinct building designs had been drawn up for use in the Atlantic Wall.[17] However, this seemingly excessive total reflects the fact that designs were drawn up to meet all conceivable eventualities. Thus some designs existed only on paper and in other cases only single or handfuls of examples were built. The variety of designs was also offset by the inclusion of common design features. This modular approach rationalised and thus speeded up the construction process.

At the lower end of the scale were the so-called Tobruks, small concrete shelters based on a design used in North Africa. The basic design, which was also known as a *Ringstand* or Type 58c, housed a machine-gun team and ammunition. Other versions included one configured to take a 50mm mortar (the Type 61c), and the *Panzerstellung* which mounted a small tank turret, frequently taken from ex-French Renault R 35s mounting a short 37mm gun and a co-axial machine gun. Leaving aside giant constructions such as the Lindemann Battery housing 406mm guns at Sangatte near Calais, at the other end of the scale was the Type 636 Observation Post, a structure almost 20 metres square with a heavily protected observation room connected to a large plotting room. It also contained separate quarters for an officer and nine men, a radio and communications room, and some were configured to mount a Giant *Wurzburg* radar array. A mock-up of a Type 636 appears cast as a rather unlikely machine-gun emplacement in the opening segment of the feature film *Saving Private Ryan*. Other structures included casemates to accommodate artillery pieces of varying calibres and types, such as the Type M272 for 150mm artillery pieces, or the Type 677 capable of mounting 210mm artillery pieces or an 88mm PAK designed for enfilading fire and equipped with protective wing walls.[18] There were also a variety of personnel shelters, the most common of which was the Type 621 housing ten men and incorporating a *Ringstand* Tobruk.[19]

Hitler may have been happy to promote competition among the agencies and individuals tasked to build the Atlantic Wall, but he also expected the project to be finished on schedule. At a conference in September 1942, Hitler insisted on a completion date of 1 May 1943. When this failed to materialise he ordered von Runstedt's *Oberbefehlshaber West* to carry out a survey of progress. This duly appeared in October 1943, although Hitler was less than impressed with von Runstedt's critical assessment of both the state of the defences and the troops manning them. Neither did he appreciate von Runstedt's recommendation that it was essential to back up the defences with a strong mobile reserve. The Führer then did what he usually did when faced with unpalatable news. He issued yet another order to the agencies involved to give the task of improving defences top priority, and turned to a reliable favourite to rectify matters. Thus *Generalfeldmarschall* Erwin Rommel was appointed Inspector General of Coastal Defences and commander of *Heeresgruppe* B in November 1943, with a direct line to Hitler. Rommel then conducted his own survey, the first part of which was presented to Hitler in mid-December.

Rommel's overall conclusion was even more critical than von Runstedt's. In Rommel's view only thirty per cent of the completed fortifications were of use. That was as far as agreement between the two went, however. As von Runstedt's October 1943 report implied, he and other senior *Heer* officers viewed the Atlantic Wall defences as essentially a tripwire that would trigger deployment of mobile reserves for a counter-attack, and would at best impose some delay on the invaders. This defensive philosophy was based on that employed by the *Kaiserheer* during the First World War; thus the coastal defences merely formed the leading edge of a thinly manned outpost zone that extended up to 1.5km inland. The main defence zone, made up of an interlinked series of strongpoints and artillery positions several kilometres in depth, came next and beyond that lay a third line from which the mobile reserves could launch counter-attacks. A scaled-down version of this defensive system was employed with deadly effect against the succession of British and Canadian offensives east and south of Caen in June and July 1944.[20]

Rommel, however, was less confident of the ability of German mobile reserves to deploy to meet an Allied invasion unhindered. This was based on his experiences in North Africa, where he had witnessed first hand the Allied materiel superiority and, more importantly, the burgeoning capabilities of Allied tactical airpower. Rommel therefore took the view that any assault had to be stopped immediately at the water's edge, and set about turning the Atlantic Wall into an enlarged version of the defensive lines he had employed in North Africa. To this end he ordered the existing outpost zone to be transformed into the main defence line, and halted all construction work outwith that zone. When the Organisation Todt displayed its usual obduracy, Rommel simply directed *Heer* engineers to do the work instead. The main focus of effort were the areas in between already fortified locations, and especially those Rommel identified as being suitable for an invading force; this included the stretch of Normandy coast between the Rivers Orne and Vire.

By the time Rommel was appointed Inspector General of Coastal Defences, even Hitler recognised the Allied cross-Channel invasion was a matter of when rather than if. Speed was therefore of the essence, and the key to this was improvisation. Rommel therefore set his engineers and local garrison units to preparing field defences at key locations, even though Hitler had specifically forbidden such construction in 1943. He was also adamant that the manual labour required to construct the defences was a task for all, and not just the enlisted men. *Leutnant* Arthur Jahnke, a Knight's Cross holder assigned to *709 Infanterie* Division after being wounded on the Eastern Front, forestalled a tirade during one of Rommel's frequent inspections by removing his gloves to reveal calluses and cuts amassed from stringing barbed wire.[21] Rommel also pushed the forward edge of the defensive line out into the sea, using thousands of beach obstacles, again fabricated and emplaced by *Heer* engineers and local garrisons; by June 1944 half a million had been produced and emplaced.[22]

The obstacles were generally laid out in belts beginning at an offshore depth of around 2 metres, and thereafter corresponding to the low, half and high tide marks. The most basic obstacles, which were often set the furthest out to catch incoming landing craft, were simply stout logs driven into the sand tilted seaward at a slight angle, and topped with a waterproofed Teller mine.[23] These were sometimes supplemented with moored rafts also carrying mines. The next obstacles, dubbed *Hemmelbalker* or 'Ram Logs', pointed inland at about thirty degrees with two shorter supports at the raised end, which was surmounted with either a metal cutting edge or a mine. These were intended to snag landing craft backing away from the beach after delivering their loads.

Interspersed among the Ram Logs were Element C obstacles, large moveable steel or wooden frames carrying mines or other types of explosive charge; these were sometimes called Belgian Gates. Finally, at the high-tide level were the tetrahedra, fashioned from three or four lengths of metal girder welded together and intended to foul and otherwise damage landing craft ramps and hulls. These too often mounted mines or booby-traps, and were called hedgehogs by Allied troops.[24] As well as these common obstacle types there were specialised items for specific applications. In at least one location with a sea wall, for example, 6-metre lengths of curved rail were mounted at 1.5-metre intervals at right angles to the wall. The object was to deny attackers cover and prevent them surmounting the wall, and the rails were thus interlaced with mines and barbed wire.[25] Rommel also instigated the widespread erection of anti-airborne obstacles, consisting of wire-braced poles projecting up to 2 metres above the ground, sometimes laced with mines or booby-traps. Popularly known as *Rommelspargel* (Rommel Asparagus), these were capable of severely damaging gliders and injuring or even killing paratroopers unlucky enough to come down on them.

The first line of defence above the water line was mines, which Rommel had used extensively in North Africa. His stated aim was to achieve a density of one mine per square metre in the selected areas of the main defensive zone, and to this end 6.5 million assorted mines had been laid by June 1944.[26] Apart from those mounted on beach obstacles, many of these were placed in fields blocking beach exits. Large proportions of the remainder were laid to protect the various concrete Atlantic Wall fortifications and the field works erected in their stead. The smallest of these, referred to as *Wiederstandneste* or resistance nests, were self-contained positions housing up to two infantry squads, anti-tank guns and mortars. Heavy weapons were housed in bunkers, linked by communication and fire trenches, and surrounded by barbed wire and mines. Some were independent and sited to protect beach exits or other key terrain, and others were placed as outlying elements of the larger *Stützpunkte*, or strongpoints. These were multi-purpose fortifications, generally 400 metres or so in diameter, sited to protect installations like gun batteries or radar stations as well as tactically valuable terrain, and were frequently placed to provide mutual support for neighbouring strong points. Infantry *Stützpunkte* held a company or so of troops with machine-gun bunkers and fire trenches, reinforced with mortars, anti-tank guns of various calibres and light flak.[27] Others were built around field or medium anti-aircraft artillery batteries and their observation and fire control installations, protected by the same defence works as the infantry strongpoints.[28]

This leaves the question of the number and type of fortifications erected along the stretch of coast the Allies selected for their invasion. In fact, the Norman coast was long considered a low priority, largely because it lacked any sizeable ports and thus did not fit the German template for a suitable invasion site. The nearest fully fortified areas were Le Havre to the east and Cherbourg at the tip of the Cotentin Peninsula to the west. The situation changed after Rommel inspected the area in January 1944, and he noted the suitability of the wide sandy beaches running east from the mouth of the Seine for large-scale invasion. Despite this relatively late start, by June 1944 approximately seventy-five assorted field defence works and nineteen battery positions had been prepared between Cabourg in the east and Quinéville, mid-way up the Cotentin Peninsula to the west. The works were spread pretty evenly along the water line, but were only developed in depth in the eastern end of the frontage, between Ouistreham and Port-en-Bessin.

Many of the artillery positions consisted of open concrete emplacements, but some within range of the Allied invasion beaches mounted their guns in concrete casemates, sometimes with a full complement of fire control posts, personnel and defensive bunkers. Among the most easterly was the Merville Battery, located a mile east of the mouth of the River Orne and the same distance inland. It was covered from the sea by two strongpoints, which contained a total of thirty bunkers, including an observation post linked to the battery by field telephone. The battery proper consisted of a command post bunker, two blockhouses, a light flak emplacement and four casemates capable of mounting 150mm guns. All this was distributed over an area roughly 400 metres in diameter, enclosed by an inner barbed wire fence, a minefield and an outer ring of barbed wire that included an anti-tank ditch covering the north-west quadrant of the perimeter.[29]

A cluster of strongpoints and battery positions were located 2 miles or so to the west, on the other side of the River Orne south and west of Ouistreham. The town itself housed a 17 metre-high artillery command post and a strongpoint with six 155mm guns in open concrete emplacements; the latter incorporated the town's heavily fortified casino. Two out of three strongpoints to the south-west of Ouistreham contained four-gun batteries of 100mm and 155mm guns, all but one of which were enclosed in Type 699 casemates; the three strongpoints were codenamed Daimler, Morris and Hillman by the British.

More strongpoints were grouped around Douvres-la-Delivérande, on the edge of a ridge 3 miles inland from Langrune-sur-Mer, and in and around Courseulles-sur-Mer and la Rivière. Another fortified battery, equipped with four 100mm howitzers in Type 669 casemates was located near the village of la Mare-Fontaine, 2 miles or so inland from la Rivière. Moving west from la Rivière, both Arromanches and Port-en-Bessin also housed strongpoints. Midway between them lay the Longue Battery, positioned on the coast just north of the village of Longue-sur-Mer. Four Type M272 casemates mounting ex-*Kriegsmarine* 150mm destroyer guns were lined out parallel to the cliff line 350 metres away, and a Type M262 Fire Control Post, protected by machine gun and mortar Tobruks, was set into the top of the cliff.

The most formidable artillery position lay a further 14 miles to the west of Port-en-Bessin, on a triangular promontory called the Pointe du Hoc. A wide sand beach ran for most of the distance in between, backed by high sand bluffs that turned into rocky cliffs 2 or 3 miles short of the Pointe. A number of resistance nests were scattered along this stretch, with strongpoints defending four gullies or draws leading through the bluffs near Colleville-sur-Mer, St Laurent-sur-Mer and Vierville-sur-Mer. Only around fifteen per cent of the bunkers in these strongpoints were sufficiently hardened to withstand artillery fire, however.[30] The Pointe du Hoc position, which is sometimes mistakenly rendered Pointe du Hoe, was protected on its two seaward sides by 100-ft cliffs. It housed a battery of six 155mm guns, numerous large personnel shelters, flak and defensive bunkers, protected inland by minefields. A Type 636 Fire Control Post constructed at the very tip of the promontory controlled the guns, which were originally mounted in open concrete emplacements. In June 1944 the battery was in the process of being upgraded; two of the open emplacements had been replaced with Type 671, and two more were under construction.

The stretch of coast between Port-en Bessin and the Pointe du Hoc contained fewer defences than to the east, and the lower Cotentin contained fewer still. This was partly because the fortification work was carried out from east to west, and partly because there was only a limited area of dry ground available in the Cotentin; the land immediately behind the beach was partly inundated marsh. The only way inland from the beach was along number of raised causeways, and the field defences thus consisted almost exclusively of resistance nests placed to dominate the seaward end of these causeways. *Wiederstandnest 5*, sited at the end of the causeway linking la Grande Dune to St Marie-du-Mont, was typical of these installations. The position, which measured 400 metres long by 300 metres deep, was fronted by a concrete anti-tank wall running along the top of the beach, and encircled to the flanks and rear by a double apron of barbed wire with mines in between. Within this boundary were three machine-gun bunkers, six Tobruks (four *Ringstande*, one *Panzerstellung* and one mortar), a single 47mm and three 50mm anti-tank guns (one enclosed in a Type 667 casemate), an ammunition bunker and five assorted personnel shelters, most of which were linked by trenches.[31]

The beach defences were backed by ten prepared artillery positions for 105mm, 122mm, 155mm and 210mm batteries. Most of these consisted of open concrete or earth emplacements but at least two were fully protected. The St Marcouf Battery was a *Kriegsmarine* installation, armed with four 210mm guns and a single 150mm piece, protected by a number of light and medium flak emplacemnts, machine-gun bunkers, barbed wire and mines. Like the battery at the Pointe du Hoc, the St Marcouf Battery was being upgraded in June 1944. Two of the 210mm pieces had been enclosed within Type 683 casemates with another under construction, and a Type M272 casemate was being erected over the 150mm. The St Marcouf site also contained a fire control bunker for the other hardened battery at Azeville, located a mile or so farther inland. The Azeville battery consisted of four 105mm guns, protected by two Type 650 casemates, surmounted by 37mm flak emplacement, and two Type 671 casemates, all camouflaged to look like buildings from the nearby village from which the battery took its name. They were protected by the usual array of personnel shelters, defensive bunkers and Tobruks, linked together and to the casemates by concrete-lined tunnels.[32]

Thus by June 1944, a mere five months after Rommel's first inspection of the area, the Normandy coast boasted a defensive line that was at least adequate, and in places significantly more than that. However, static defence requires men as well as fortifications. Responsibility for defending the north French coast was divided in two, between *Generaloberst* Han von Salmuth's *15 Armee* and *Generaloberst* Friedrich Dollmann's *7 Armee*. The former's frontage ran from just east of Cabourg in Normandy to the River Scheldt in Holland, covered by fifteen *Heer* infantry and three *Luftwaffe* Field divisions.[33] Eleven of these were positioned to defend the Pas de Calais, reflecting Hitler's and the German High Command's view that the region was the most likely target for an Allied invasion. By contrast, *7 Armee* had only thirteen divisions to cover almost twice the length of coastline, extending west to the mouth of the River Loire on the Atlantic coast. Five of these divisions, along with a mobile infantry brigade and three independent regiments made up *84 Korps*, commanded by *General der Artillerie* Erich Marcks from a headquarters in St Lô. *84 Korps* was responsible for the Normandy coast from the Cotentin Peninsula to the boundary with *15 Armee* near Cabourg.

Three of *84 Korps'* divisions were located in the Cotentin Peninsula. *243 Infanterie Division* was tasked to defend the western side of the Peninsula, while *709 Infanterie Division* was responsible for Cherbourg and the eastern side down to the mouth of the River Douve. The resistance nests running north from the mouth of the River Douve to Quinéville were manned by elements of the *Grenadier Regiment 919*. Both Divisions were so-called *bodenständige* or static defence formations, made up of overage conscripts, the physically unfit and recovering casualties from other fronts. They thus lacked a third of the infantry strength, the reconnaissance battalion and much of the organic artillery fielded by normal infantry divisions.[34] The third division was also *7 Armee's* reserve formation, *91 Luftlande Division*. This was a *Heer* unit trained and equipped for air landing operations, which only arrived in the Cotentin from Germany in mid-May 1944 with *Fallschirmjäger Regiment 6*. The latter was based in Carentan on the River Douve at the base of the Peninsula.[35]

The unit assigned the sector between the River Vire and Arromanches was, on paper at least, a rather different animal. *352 Infanterie Division* was raised from scratch in the Hanover area in early November 1943, using a cadre of experienced, pre-war regular personnel from *321 Infanterie Division*, a formation destroyed on the Eastern Front the previous summer. *352 Division* moved to St Lô in December 1943, where it commenced training whilst being brought up to full strength. Despite the relatively poor physical standard of some of the recruits and shortages of materiel and equipment, by the spring of 1944 the formation was officially classified an attack division, the highest category of combat readiness. Rommel inspected the formation in February 1944, and on 15 March it was ordered up to the coastal defences. Seven of the Division's ten infantry battalions were distributed among the coast defences, backed by the five divisional artillery battalions. The remaining three infantry battalions were stationed around Bayeux as the division reserve.[36] The last sector of *84 Korps'* frontage, running from Arromanches to Cabourg on the east side of the River Orne was the responsibility of *716 Infanterie Division*. This was also a *bodenständige* formation, and its nine infantry battalions were spread across the sea-front resistance nests and the larger inland strongpoints south-west of Ouistreham.

In addition there were several units which, though not assigned to *84 Korps*, were capable of rapidly meeting any landings on the Corps' front. The nearest was *15 Armee's* most westerly formation, *711 Infanterie Division*, which was deployed on the right flank of 716 Infanterie Division. Stationed further back from the coast were three *Panzer* divisions, all of which had been designated reserves of one kind or another.[37] *Generalleutnant* Edgar Feuchtinger's *21 Panzer Division* was *Heeresgruppe B's* reserve formation, and was quartered around Caen, hub of the local road net 10 miles or so inland from Ouistreham. The Division had played a key role in Rommel's *Afrika Korps*, but was destroyed when the Germans were ejected from North Africa in 1943. It was then reformed in France around a cadre of experienced survivors, equipped with a mixture of obsolete German and captured French vehicles. The effectiveness of the latter was hugely improved by modifying them to carry German 75mm Pak guns or howitzers for direct support. According to one source, much of the conversion work was arranged outside official channels by one of the Division's artillery officers, whose family ran an armaments business in Krefeld. By June 1944 these improvised vehicles had been augmented with ninety brand-new *Panzer IVs*, giving the Division's combat power a significant boost.[38] In June 1944 *21 Panzer Division* included *Panzer Aufklärungs Abteilung 21, Panzer Regiment 22, Sturmgeschütze Bataillon 200, Panzergrenadier Regiments 125* and *192*, and *Panzer Artillerie Regiment 155*.[39]

The remaining two *Panzer* divisions belonged to the OKW reserve, and were an even more formidable proposition. The first formed half of *I SS Panzer Korps*, alongside the *1 SS Panzer Division 'Leibstandarte Adolf Hitler'*, which in June 1944 was quartered around Beverloo in Belgium. *12 SS Panzer Division 'Hitlerjugend'* was raised in response to a Führer Order in June 1943, originally as a P*anzergrenadier* formation; this status was upgraded at the end of October 1944. There was a strong ideological underpinning for the creation of the Division, over and above the fact it was a *Waffen SS* formation.[40] *12 SS Panzer* was intended to be a symbolic statement of the commitment of German youth to the Final Victory and National Socialism. Apart from a cadre of experienced officers and NCOs drawn from the *Leibstandarte* and a smaller contingent transferred in from the *Heer*, the Division's person-nel were seventeen and eighteen year-old volunteers from the *Hitler Jugend*, the Nazi youth organisation. Given the enduring myth that *12 SS Panzer* was made up of schoolboys, it is important to note that this means that the volunteers were over eighteen by the time the Division was committed to combat in June 1944. A nominal roll captured the following month, for example, showed that thirty-five per cent of the Division's *SS Panzer Grenadier Bataillon 1* were nine-teen or over, and none were under eighteen.[41]

The volunteers were put through an atypical training regime that dispensed with drill and spit and polish in favour of matters connected more directly to the realities of the battlefield. To this end, virtually all training was conducted in the countryside, and focussed on fitness training, character development, weapon handling and fieldcraft. Much importance was placed on night training and unarmed combat, while working on tank production lines in Nürnberg introduced personnel from the Division's *Panzer* unit to the innermost workings of their vehicles.[42] At the beginning of April 1944 the Division moved from its concentration and training area around Beverloo in Belgium to a forward assembly area near Falaise in Normandy, 40 to 50 miles from the Normandy coast. By June 1944 *12 SS Panzer Division* was 20,000 strong, and fielded almost 500 tanks and other armoured vehicles.[43]

The last unit was the *Panzer Lehr Division*, a *Heer* formation located almost 100 miles inland, in the area of Chartres and Le Mans. The Division was commanded by *Generalleutnant* Fritz Bayerlein, and had returned to France in May 1944 from Hungary, where it had been deployed as part of measures to prevent Hungary from making peace with the Soviets.[44] *Panzer Lehr* was the only totally armoured and mechanised formation in the *Heer* order of battle, and thus fielded almost 200 tanks, forty self-propelled guns and over 600 armoured half-track troop carriers and other vehicles. As its personnel were drawn from demonstration units at a variety of specialised training establishments, the Division also enjoyed a very high level of expert-ise. As a veteran of the fighting in North Africa, Bayerlein shared Rommel's respect for Allied airpower, and he tailored the Division's activities to suit. Training stressed the need for effective dispersal and camouflage, daylight vehicular movement was forbidden, and the Division was dispersed across the farms, woods and villages in its concentration area with full stocks of fuel and ammunition. On 1 June 1944 *Panzer Lehr* was, like 352 *Infanterie Division*, officially declared fully capable of offensive action.[45] It consisted of *Panzer Aufklärungs Lehr Abteilung 130, Panzer Lehr Regiment 130, Panzergrenadier Lehr Regiments 901* and *902*, and *Panzer Artillerie Lehr Regiment 130.*[46]

These then were the defences and defenders that would face the Allied cross-Channel assault. Before investigating how well they fared, however, it will be necessary to move back across the English Channel to examine the detail of precisely how and by whom the invasion was to be carried out.

3

THE MEANS

LANDING CRAFT, FIREPLANS
AND FUNNIES

Interestingly, despite the long and convoluted development of the Allied invasion plan and the Atlantic Wall defences, both the attackers and defenders on the spot in Normandy ended up with roughly the same and relatively short period for training and preparation. The final version of the NEPTUNE Initial Joint Plan did not emerge until 21 January 1944, roughly simultaneously with Rommel's drive to fortify the Normandy coast. Once the decision had been taken, the Allied units had just under five months to make their preparations, and in particular, to locate and concentrate the necessary landing and naval escort, transport aircraft and gliders, and to finalise the fire support plan.

The provision of landing vessels had been a recurring problem throughout the gestation of the OVERLORD and NEPTUNE plans. The root of the problem lay in the competing priorities generated by the relative paucity of resources, for there was simply not enough steel, marine power plants or shipyards to meet all demands. An emergency building programme was instigated in the spring of 1942 to provide landing vessels for 1943 ROUNDUP, which caused a good deal of disruption to the overall naval construction effort. This farmed out construction to numerous small American shipyards and engineering contractors, many located on waterways many miles from the coast. Such dispersion created a not inconsiderable additional burden for the US Navy, which had to provide transit crews and co-ordinate their movements over considerable distances before they even reached the sea. The emergency programme ended in February 1943, when most of the production capacity was switched to building escort vessels. In the event, many of the vessels produced were diverted for the TORCH landings in November 1942.

The US Joint Chiefs were thus understandably less than impressed when the British requested another increase in landing craft production in March 1943 and the COSSAC planners reiterated it at the Washington Conference in May 1943 with a requirement for 8,500 assorted landing vessels. This figure was so in excess of projected production that some, notably Admiral Ernest J. King, suspected a deliberate British ploy to stymie the cross-Channel invasion by asking for the impossible and then withdrawing from the enterprise when it was not forthcoming. In fact, the figure was based on a ten-division invasion, and after a re-examination by the Joint Chiefs' own planners, COSSAC was instructed to base its planning around 4,054 assorted landing vessels. Of these, 3,257 were to be British built, while the remainder were to be produced in the US.[1] In the event, a total of 2,955 craft were employed in the first wave on 6 June 1944.[2]

The problem was exacerbated by the fact that initially, there simply were no landing craft, and there was a limited pool of experience around which to frame specifications and designs. What little experience there was came from the British, who carried out a limited amount of research in the inter-war period. In 1920 they produced a landing craft capable of delivering the current model of medium tank directly onto the beach. Later dubbed the Landing Craft, Mechanised (LCM), it was used alongside more conventional landing boats in annual amphibious exercises from 1924. Larger landing exercises were held in 1930 on the Isle of Wight, and in 1934 the British 5th Division carried out landings on the Yorkshire coast.[3] In 1938, following investigations by the newly formed Inter-Service Training and Development Centre (ISTDC), the LCM was joined by the Landing Craft Assault (LCA), a wooden-hulled vessel capable of carrying twenty-five troops. These vessels were used in the attack on Dieppe in August 1942.

Landing vessels were divided into two basic categories: ocean-going ships capable of moving troops and equipment from friendly ports to the selected stretch of coast, and smaller craft for shuttling them from ship to shore. Prompted by a directive from Churchill on 5 June 1940, the British developed tank landing vessels in both categories.[4] The Landing Craft Tank (LCT) was originally capable of delivering three forty-ton tanks directly onto the beach via a bow ramp, and appeared in November 1940. The design was stretched a year later to accommodate six tanks and to allow operation on shallow beaches. The ocean-going design was based on shallow draft oil tankers used on Lake Maracaibo in Venezuela. Three examples were modified by removing their bows and oil tanks to create an open well deck, and then refitting them with a new bow with integral doors to become Landing Ship Tanks (LST). The final version of the LST was 328-feet long and displaced 1,780 tons. Unloading was carried out via the bow doors directly onto the beach or, for unloading personnel and light cargo offshore, up to six small landing craft carried on davits. All LSTs were built in the United States. Several smaller designs were also configured to carry tanks or other vehicles. These included several versions of the Landing Craft Mechanised (LCM) capable of carrying a single tank, and the nine-ton Landing Craft Vehicle Personnel (LCVP) capable of carrying a three-ton truck or thirty-six troops; both these vessels were unloaded via a bow ramp.

The personnel equivalent to the LST was the Landing Ship Infantry (Large) or LSI(L). The standard design for these vessels was capable of carrying almost 700 troops, and twelve LCAs or equivalent. There were also at least three British non-standard LSI(L)s, based on converted fast cargo liners. Christened *Glengyle*, *Glenearn* and *Glenroy*, these 500-ft vessels had approximately the same troop capacity as a standard vessel, but carried twenty-four LCAs and three LCMs, the former deployable by davit and the latter by thirty and fifty-ton derricks. Of similar size were the Landing Ship Dock (LSD), 450-ft vessels displacing 8,700 tons, with floodable well decks capable of accommodating fourteen LCAs or five LCTs. Other smaller craft included the steel Landing Craft Infantry (Large) or LCI(L), and wooden Landing Craft Infantry (Small) or LCI(S). The former displaced 386 tons and carried around 200 troops, while the latter displaced 110 tons and could accommodate half that complement; troop egress on both these craft was via gangways located on either side of the bow. The smallest and probably most numerous infantry landing craft was the 41-ft Landing Craft Assault (LCA), displacing thirteen tons and carrying thirty-five troops who exited the vessel via a bow ramp.

There were also a wide variety of specialised craft adapted for specific functions such as the Landing Ship Headquarters, HMS *Bulolo*. Converted from an armed merchant cruiser, *Bulolo* was modified with command and communication facilities capable of processing over 2,000 radio messages per day, and carried 258 personnel and six landing craft. The Landing Craft Flak was a LCT modified with protected mountings for automatic anti-aircraft guns; a typical outfit consisted of four 40mm Bofors and eight 20mm guns. At the other end of the scale was the nine-ton Landing Craft Navigation, equipped with echo sounders, radar and radio navigation equipment. These were used to guide the first wave of the landing force into the correct approach lanes to the landing beaches. Even more unusual was the Landing Barge Kitchen, a floating cookhouse capable of feeding 900 men for a week.

As we have seen, the invasion plan made extensive use of deception to conceal the location of the assault. Targeted bombardment of the beach defences was thus delayed until literally the last moment, in order to maintain operational secrecy for as long as possible. The aerial side of the NEPTUNE support plan involved RAF heavy bombers striking the Pointe du Hoc battery on the night of D Minus One, followed by daylight attacks by medium and heavy bombers on selected targets on or just behind all the beaches. The Naval Bombardment Plan was to commence just after first light, and was divided into three phases. The first was to silence the German gun batteries capable of engaging the landing beaches, according to a prioritised list. The second phase shifted fire to the German beach defences, in order to saturate them with fire as the first wave of landing craft delivered their passengers onto the beach. Thereafter the naval guns were to switch to phase three, the provision of close support fire controlled by forward observer teams attached to the ground forces.[5]

The gunfire was to be provided by a number of landing vessels and more conventional warships. Some of the former were merely standard self-propelled artillery pieces and tanks firing from their landing craft during the run in to the beach.[6] Specially configured vessels included the Landing Craft Gun (Large), mounting two five-inch guns, and the Landing Craft Tank (Rocket). The latter was a standard LCT with the tank deck filled with launch rails for five-inch rockets, capable of carrying between 762 and 1,062 rockets, depending on the mark of craft involved. The rockets could be fired in salvoes of varying size, and the vessels were equipped with radar as a firing aid because the rigid mountings required the rockets to be launched at a precise, predetermined distance from the target.[7]

More conventional fire was provided by 137 warships drawn from the Royal Navy, the US Navy and a number of Allied navies. These were organised into a Western Task Force responsible for delivering the American assault force onto the OMAHA and UTAH landing areas, and an Eastern Task Force for SWORD, JUNO and GOLD landing areas. A Landing Ship Headquarters was allocated to each landing area, along with a dedicated bombardment group. The latter included the battleships HMS *Ramillies*, *Rodney* and *Warspite*, and USS *Arkansas*, *Nevada* and *Texas*, twenty-three cruisers, 101 destroyers and two bombardment monitors, HMS *Erebus* and *Roberts*. These were specially built hulls carrying a single big gun turret and a fire control tower. Most of the cruisers and destroyers were British, augmented with US, French, Polish and Norwegian vessels. The larger ships were tasked to carry out the initial counter-battery phase of the Naval Bombardment Plan, while the destroyers and some of the cruisers moved inshore to suppress the beach defences.[8]

The Normandy plan differed from those employed in the Mediterranean and the Pacific. The former relied on darkness to achieve tactical surprise, while the latter went in during daylight after increasingly protracted air and sea bombardment to neutralise the defence. The Normandy scheme was a combination of both, and according to a recent work on the OMAHA landings by Adrian R. Lewis, compounded the drawbacks of each while discarding their advantages. According to this analysis, the Normandy pre-landing bombardment was too short to neutralise, let alone destroy the German coastal batteries and defence works, and flew in the face of experience gained against Japanese defences in the Pacific. The OMAHA landing thus amounted to a direct assault against a 'deliberate defence years in the making'[9], that only avoided complete disaster thanks to the training and initiative of the landing force at OMAHA, and more by luck than judgement at the other landing areas.

There are number of problems with this analysis, beginning with the fact that the OMAHA sector was among the least developed parts of the German coastal defence scheme, and the artillery and defence works there had been months or even weeks in the making rather than years. More importantly, there were significant differences between circumstances in the Pacific and North-West Europe that render comparison between them questionable at best. Neither was the Pacific doctrine especially effective, being merely a technologically updated version of the tactic that repeatedly failed to overcome prepared defences during the First World War, despite some of the longest and most concentrated artillery bombardments in history. In extolling the virtues of the firepower approach championed by the US Marine Corps in the Pacific, Lewis points out that an estimated fifty to sixty per cent of the Japanese defenders on the Roi–Namur Atoll in the Marshall Islands were killed by the pre-landing bombardment. The point is reinforced with a quote from the Japanese commander on Iwo Jima warning his superiors in Tokyo that US naval bombardment was capable of destroying beach defences with impunity.[10]

However, this overlooks the fact that forty to fifty per cent of the Roi–Namur defenders survived to contest the landings, as did a great many of those on Iwo Jima despite enduring the longest bombardment in the Pacific War at seventy-two days. Sufficient Japanese guns survived to extract a heavy toll of the Iwo landing force on the beach, and over the next thirty-six days the Iwo defenders inflicted the highest proportional casualty rate in Marine Corps history on the 4th and 5th Marine Divisions, including 6,000 dead.[11] As the island was only 5 miles long by half that wide, this would seem to provide a pretty solid argument for the limitations rather than the efficacy of protracted bombardment. Of course, the German defences at OMAHA, or indeed elsewhere in Normandy did not approach the density or sophistication achieved by the Japanese on Iwo Jima, but the point is that protracted and unrestrained bombardment was not the automatic panacea Lewis appears to suggest.

In any event, protracted bombardment was not an option for the Normandy invasion for a number of reasons. Firstly, there was the matter of resources. The fact that preparatory bombing for the invasion severely disrupted the strategic bombing programme suggests that there was little additional bombing capacity, and the same applied to the provision of warships. Most of the US Navy contribution of three battleships, two cruisers and thirty-four destroyers were only assigned to the invasion force in April and May 1944 after it became apparent that the Admiralty were unable to supply sufficient vessels. The Royal Navy was itself stretched by the need to maintain a capital force in the North Sea, in case the remnants of the *Kriegsmarine*'s surface fleet sought to interfere with the invasion.[12] In addition, had more ships been available, there may not have been the sea room to deploy them. The invasion was to put over 6,000 Allied vessels into the sixty-mile wide Bay of the Seine on D-Day; the complexity of the NEPTUNE landing plan can be deduced from the fact it ran to 700 pages of typed foolscap.[13] Warships engaged on counter-gunnery work also need room to move, and with 137 warships so engaged at the margins of the landing fleet, manoeuvre space was clearly at a premium.

Neither was lengthening the bombardment an option, because that would have alerted the German defenders to the location of the invasion, the consequences of which should not be underestimated. Aside from the German divisions garrisoning the coastal defences, there was a parachute brigade, an infantry division and a *Panzer* division within 10 miles of the landing area. A further two *Panzer* divisions were billeted between 25 and 80 miles from the Normandy coast, and two more *Panzer* and a *Panzergrenadier* division were located within 150 miles of it. Even a proportion of this combat power was capable of inflicting serious if not mortal harm to the Allied landings. Little wonder then that the Allies were willing to expend an enormous amount of effort and material on deception measures. Beginning the bombardment earlier still would merely have compounded the problem by gifting the Germans even more reaction time. This point is the crux of the differences between landing operations in the Pacific and the Normandy invasion.

With the arguable exception of those conducted against Papua New Guinea and the Philippines, Pacific landings were against islands that could be isolated and totally dominated from sea and air, which made tactical movement by the defenders costly if not suicidal. Even on the occasions where the Japanese succeeded in shaping a meaningful counter-blow, such as the armoured counter attack on Saipan on the night of 15-16 June 1944, US materiel superiority proved decisive. An invasion against a continental landmass, and especially against one with a sophisticated transport net like that in North-West Europe, was a completely different prospect. The operational area could not be isolated or dominated to anywhere the same degree, and the disparity between the Allied and German forces was nowhere near as marked as in the Pacific. Indeed, German operational abilities and materiel were in many instances superior to those of their opponents.

It can therefore be argued that the Normandy invasion had little in common with the amphibious model practised over comparatively vast sea distances by the US forces in the Pacific. Rather, it was more akin to an opposed river crossing, albeit one on a grand scale, an analogy that also explains why the night landing tactic practised with success in the Mediterranean was not an option. First, the landings were to be preceded by a series of vital airborne operations. Launching these in daylight would have negated the deception plan at a stroke and, more importantly, likely have been suicidal for the airborne troops. Second, because of its sheer size, a night sea landing would have required the NEPTUNE landing force to set sail long before dusk on D Minus One. This again would have negated the Allied deception measures, warned the Germans that invasion was imminent and allowed them ample time to monitor progress, deduce the destination and set counter-measures in motion.

Be that as it may, the surest way to neutralise coastal batteries and defences was not with aerial bombing or artillery, but by direct assault prior to the main amphibious landings. As we have seen, this method was to be employed against the Merville and Pointe du Hoc batteries, a discarded US airborne plan tasked the 101st Airborne Division to eliminate the German defences covering OMAHA, and the 82nd Airborne had significantly assisted the US Sicily landings despite an appalling drop.[14] Given this, it is curious that Lewis dismisses the concept out of hand, finding it '…almost inconceivable that a professional military organisation would plan to neutralize a beach defence with airborne soldiers'.[15] British and US airborne development and practice differed somewhat, but missions of this type were well within their remit and capabilities.

Be that as it may, there was further source of support available to the D-Day assault force. As we have seen, the Germans put a great deal of effort into blocking beaches suitable for invasion with mines and a wide variety of obstacles. Swift and efficient removal of these obstacles was therefore essential if the invading force was not to be pinned down on the beach, as happened to the luckless Canadians at Dieppe. This would normally have been a task for engineer troops, but they would have been terribly vulnerable to artillery and small-arms fire, and many of the obstacles were too large to be cleared easily by hand. To get around this problem, the British developed a whole series of specialised armoured vehicles, created by or under the supervision of Major-General Sir Percy Hobart.

Hobart was a First World War tank pioneer and something of an armoured visionary. Command of the British 1st Tank Brigade from 1934 to 1937 gave him the opportunity to develop his ideas. He was a rather difficult personality however, which led to him being retired and banished to Egypt, where he applied his ideas to the embryo Mobile Division formed there in 1938. Renamed the 7th Armoured Division in 1940, the unit proved the efficacy of Hobart's ideas and his skill as a trainer against the Italians that year, but he was sacked from the command and returned to the UK as a civilian. Hobart was thus serving as lance-corporal in his local Home Guard unit when

Churchill, ever the champion of innovation and unorthodoxy, brought him back into the Army to develop special armoured vehicles for the forthcoming invasion. To this end he was given command of the 79th Armoured Division in 1943; the unit was an umbrella organisation rather than an armoured division in the accepted sense, and its vehicles and personnel were parcelled out and fought as attachments to more conventional formations.

The results of Hobart's work were dubbed 'Funnies' and mainly utilised the British Churchill and US M4 Sherman tanks although other models, particularly the British Valentine, were used for research and development and training. Some vehicles were adapted to purely engineering tasks, while others were configured with a more aggressive role in mind. Most of the former were Churchill derivatives. Perhaps the most versatile was the Churchill Armoured Vehicle Royal Engineers (AVRE). Armed with a 290mm-petard spigot mortar capable of throwing a 40-pound charge nicknamed 'the flying dustbin' 80 yards, the AVRE had a crew of six including an assault engineer. It could also be fitted with a dozer blade and a cradle to deploy a fascine, a bundle of thin logs several feet in diameter used for filling ditches or bomb craters. Two other Churchill obstacle-crossing Funnies were the Churchill Bridgelayer, equipped with a 30-foot scissor bridge, and the Churchill Ark, a turretless vehicle with foldable ramps at the front and rear. The body of the vehicle proper acted as a bridge by driving into a ditch or gulley, and it could also be used as a means for other vehicles to surmount sea walls. A training vehicle developed from the US M4 was dubbed the Sherman Twaby Ark. There was also the Bobbin, which unrolled a carpet of logs or canvas strip from a reel to provide a firm path for other vehicles over mud or soft sand that would otherwise have bogged them down.

The Churchill could also be fitted with a number of devices for clearing minefields, such as the Farmer Deck, the Canadian Indestructible Roller Device, and the Bullshorn Plough. The first two were basically rollers mounted in line with the vehicle tracks, which then detonated any mines prematurely; the Farmer Deck incorporated armoured scoops to deflect blast. The latter consisted, as the name suggests, of two large ploughs mounted ahead of the tank's tracks, which would shovel mines to one side. A more common mine clearing solution was the Crab, based on the Sherman. The Crab mounted a roller fitted with numerous lengths of heavy-duty chain between two hydraulic jibs projecting from the front of the vehicle. When engaged to the tank's engine, the roller rotated rapidly, causing the chains to beat the ground and detonate any mines buried therein, an action that led to the vehicle's other nickname of 'Flail'. The most fearsome Funny was the Churchill Crocodile, which replaced the hull machine gun with a flame-thrower capable of projecting a burning jet of fuel over 80 yards. Four hundred gallons of top-secret fuel for the flame gun were carried in a special armoured container, which could be jettisoned via a remote release, after which the Crocodile could operate as a standard gun tank.[16]

The British factored the Funnies and their various capabilities into their assault plan, and demonstrated the vehicles to the commander of the US 1st Army, Lieutenant-General Omar Bradley. Bradley rejected them all except one, ostensibly because the Churchill was not used by US units and thus had special maintenance requirements and a separate supply line for spares. There may also have been an element of 'not invented here' syndrome; if so, the OMAHA landing force were to pay a terrible price for their leaderships' prejudices. Whether or not, Bradley did accept one of Hobart's Funnies: the Duplex Drive (DD) Sherman. Invented by Hungarian military engineer Nicholas Staussler in 1941, DD equipment could be used to convert any standard tank into an amphibian with the aid of propellers linked to the vehicle's gearbox and a collapsible canvas screen. The screen was sealed to the tank via a metal flange welded all the way round the hull, and was erected via rubber tubes inflated with compressed air. Once ashore the screen could be jettisoned from within the tank by firing a charge of explosive detonator cord waterproofed into the bottom of the flange.

The idea was to launch the DD tanks from LCTs or similar vessels and allow them to accompany the leading wave of LCAs under their own power. This would put fully combat-ready tanks onto the beach simultaneously or slightly ahead of the first wave of infantry, in order to provide the latter with immediate fire support. The shock value of the DD is frequently extolled as justification for their deployment, although it is difficult to see much practical advantage over merely delivering tanks by LCM; perhaps the attraction lay more in the fact that there were insufficient of the latter craft available. Whatever the reason, the DD Sherman was nonetheless the most widely employed of the Funnies, but it was also arguably the most hazardous to operate. Once in the water the tank was actually suspended beneath surface level within the canvas screen, and the latter's low freeboard made them very vulnerable to swamping. DD crews were therefore trained and equipped with the same Davis Escape Apparatus issued to British submariners, and each vehicle was equipped with a large inflatable rubber dinghy. The system was largely developed on the British Valentine Infantry Tank, numbers of which were used by the British for training, but by D–Day all British crews had converted to the DD Sherman, which employed tracks and two propellers for propulsion and steering. The British and Canadians deployed the equivalent of a full brigade of DD Shermans for the invasion, and the Americans used two battalions.[17] According to one source, around 900 were employed in the first wave of the invasion.[18]

There was one further element deployed in support of the seaborne landing. Although the sea and airborne elements of the D-Day landing are often studied in isolation, the overall landing plan saw them as a mutually supportive whole. The airborne plan envisaged delivering the better part of three airborne divisions, totalling in excess of 20,000 men, to areas on the flanks of the sea landing areas six to eight hours before the sea landings commenced. The vast majority of these were paratroopers, and most of them were carried to battle in Douglas C-47 transport aircraft, the military version of the Douglas DC-3 airliner. Christened the Dakota by the British, the C-47 was an all-metal, twin–engine monoplane with a cruising speed of 185 miles per hour, and was capable of lifting twenty fully equipped paratroops who exited via a large door set in the rear port side of the aircraft. It could also tow Horsa or Waco CG4 gliders and carry over 8,000 pounds of cargo; special tracks were fitted into the floor of the aircraft to allow the rapid dropping of large crates or containers by parachute. The US 9th Troop Carrier Command's three Transport Groups deployed 882 C-47s for the initial airborne landing, and the RAF's No. 46 Group contributed a further 150.[19]

In addition to the C-47 the RAF's other dedicated troop carrier unit, No. 38 Group, used several types of converted bomber. Four of No. 38 Group's ten squadrons were equipped with 104 twin-engine Armstrong-Whitworth Albemarles. Originally designed as a medium bomber, the RAF declared the wooden Albemarle surplus to requirements due to poor payload and short range before deploying it operationally, and bequeathed the hundred or so produced for airborne use. The aircraft was configured to carry ten paratroopers, who exited from a large aperture in the rear floor of the fuselage, and could also be used as a glider tug. Cruising speed was 130 miles per hour, with a combat radius of 230 miles.

A further four squadrons from No. 38 Group were equipped with the Short Stirling, an obsolete four-engine bomber also farmed out for airborne use. The Stirling had a maximum speed of 270 miles per hour and a combat radius of 800 miles, or 525 miles towing a glider. It was capable of carrying twenty-two paratroopers, who used a large aperture in the rear fuselage floor. The type does not appear to have been popular, however, and a relatively high number of experienced paratroopers refused to jump from it when it became available in April 1944, preferring a court-martial.[20] Nonetheless, it remained in service in the parachute transport role and as a glider tug, and one hundred and four took part in the D-Day airborne landing.[21] The final aircraft deployed by RAF transport squadrons was the Handley Page Halifax, another four-engine machine. Because it could only carry ten paratroopers the Halifax was employed mainly as a glider tug, and forty Halifaxes from No. 38 Group's remaining two squadrons served in this capacity on the initial airlift into Normandy.[22]

Finally, the D-Day airborne force also employed three unpowered aircraft. The smallest was the US built Waco CG4 glider, used exclusively by US Airborne Forces in Normandy. The CG4 had a wingspan of just over 83ft and was of tubular metal and canvas construction with an upward hinging nose to assist loading and unloading. It could carry thirteen troops, or a quarter-ton Jeep and four men, or just over 4,000 pounds of cargo in addition to a crew of two; 107 of these machines were included in the initial US lift. The British-built Airspeed Horsa was a much larger machine of laminated plywood construction; at least one US writer claims this was significantly weaker than the tubular metalwork of the CG4, and that this caused many unnecessary US casualties.[23] This is rather unlikely, given that far more widespread British usage indicated no such problem, quite the opposite in fact. The US perception may therefore have had more to do with poor US piloting than flaws in the machine's construction.

The Horsa could carry up to twenty-nine troops depending on the mark of machine, or a variety of loads including Jeeps, with and without trailers, a single six-pounder anti-tank gun or a small bull-dozer. Loading was through a large door on the front port side, an awkward arrangement that led to the machine being modified with a removable tail to speed unloading after landing. This system included a rather alarming back up, a permanently attached length of explosive detonator cord encircling the rear fuselage of the machine. Called a 'surcingle', this permitted the crew to blow the tail off the machine if it proved resistant to removal with tools, as was frequently the case. The Mark II Horsa was equipped with a sideways hinging nose to assist loading and unloading, but most of those despatched to Normandy used the former system. All varieties were equipped with very large flaps powered by compressed air, which allowed the Horsa to make very steep landing approaches to very short landing runs. In conjunction with two drogue parachutes it was possible to bring a fully laden Horsa to a dead stop within 100 yards of touchdown.[24]

The General Aircraft Hamilcar was also a British-produced lami-nate wood machine, as well as being the largest and heaviest combat glider used by the Allies during the Second World War. With a wingspan of 110 feet, the Hamilcar could lift a seven-ton light tank. More common loads included Bren gun carriers, and seventeen-pounder anti-tank guns complete with prime mover, ammunition and an eight to ten man crew.[25] The initial British Normandy lift included four Hamilcars, all of which carried the latter load. The remaining ninety-four gliders were all Horsas, carrying troops, motor cycles, Jeeps, trailers, six-pounder anti-tank guns, bulldozers and assorted engineering equipment including two motor boats.[26]

These then were the methods and tools with which the Allies intended to pierce the Atlantic Wall and commence the liberation of German-occupied Europe. All that remains before moving on to examine how effective they were in practice is to look at the troops tasked to use them, and how they fitted into the overall landing plan.

4

RED DEVILS, ALL AMERICANS, SCREAMING EAGLES AND RUDDER'S RANGERS

THE FIRST PHASE OF THE NORMANDY PLAN

The NEPTUNE Initial Joint Plan envisaged delivering the sea landing force along a sixty-mile stretch of the Normandy coast, running from the River Orne to Quinéville on the eastern side of the Cotentin Peninsula. The flanks of the landing area were to be secured by two airborne landings that, in total, comprised the largest Allied airborne operation to date. Of these, the one at the eastern end of the beach-head was the most vital. This was partly because the bulk of the German forces gathered to face the invasion lay to the east, and more immediately because *21 Panzer Division* was quartered around Caen, around 12 miles inland from Ouistreham at the mouth of the Orne. The unit selected to secure and hold the eastern flank was the British 6th Airborne Division.

The 6th Airborne Division was born from a War Office order issued on 23 April 1943. The order originated in October 1942, when the War Office decided to double the number of airborne divisions in its Home Establishment. As with virtually everything connected to the British airborne force, the Air Ministry vehemently opposed this expansion and put forward a counter-proposal that envisaged limiting the size of the airborne force to two parachute brigades, augmented by a small force of gliders to carry heavy weapons and equipment. Unsurprisingly, CIGS General Sir Alan Brooke rejected this, and Churchill was called on to arbitrate. The Prime Minister reluctantly backed the Air Ministry proposal, and also ordered a halt to glider production, prompted by alleged problems with storage. Brooke, however, flatly refused to disband any of the existing airborne units and vociferously objected to halting glider production because he feared the specialist workforce would be lost to other areas of the war economy. His courageous stand paid off, for the British airborne force was retained at its existing level, and Horsa glider production was slowed rather than stopped.[1]

Brooke resurrected the requirement for a second airborne division on 24 February 1943, following the firm British commitment to the cross-Channel invasion at Casablanca the previous month. When the Air Ministry reprised its objections, Churchill ordered the General and Air Staffs to carry out a complete review. The root of the RAF objection was the additional training burden the expansion would place on the glider pilot training programme. This was an ongoing bone of contention, for although it initially insisted only qualified bomber pilots were capable of flying gliders,[2] the Air Ministry was unwilling to come up with the goods when requested in mid-1941.[3] The RAF then suddenly discovered that Army personnel were able to fly gliders after all, recommended that Army officers and NCOs of aircrew medical standard be merely seconded for flying training, and that they also be fully trained for ground combat.[4]

This was accepted by the War Office, and led to the formation of the Army Air Corps on 21 December 1941, and the establishment of the Glider Pilot Regiment within that Corps in February 1942. By August 1942 the Glider Pilot Regiment had grown to two battalions, commanded by Lieutenant-Colonel John Rock RE and then Lieutenant-Colonel George Chatterton after Rock was killed in a gliding accident in October 1942.[5] The Army trained its glider pilots to be 'total soldiers', and put them through an exhaustive selection and ground combat training to platoon command level before letting them near a glider. RAF involvement was reduced to providing flying training in the same way it provided parachute training for the Army's parachute troops. As we shall see, members of the Glider Pilot Regiment were to play an absolutely crucial role in the Normandy airborne landings.

The Air Staff was placated by the Army's agreement to restrict its airlanding brigades to two infantry battalions on 21 April 1943, and the 6th Airborne Division was born two days later. Technically, it was the second British airborne division, as a 1st Airborne Division had been established in November 1941. This, however, was initially a purely administrative headquarters to oversee British airborne development generally, and did not become an operational formation until January 1942, with a single parachute and airlanding brigade. A second parachute brigade was added in July 1942, but 1st Airborne HQ remained a largely administrative body until the end of May 1943, when it concentrated in North Africa for the Sicily invasion. Even then, 1st Airborne did not function as an operational whole until 1944, in a divisional training exercise codenamed 'RAGS' in May, and at Arnhem in September. It can therefore be argued that the 6th Airborne Division was actually the first British airborne division, insofar as it was intended as a fully functional, operational entity with a properly thought out organisation from the outset. Even the new Division's number was the result of forethought, being chosen as a disinformation measure.

The 6th Airborne's formation was a three-phase process, extending over a period of just under six months beginning in April 1943. Divisional HQ was established at Syrencot House near Netheravon in Wiltshire on 3 May 1943, and the Division's glider formation, logically named the 6th Airlanding Brigade, established a HQ at nearby Amesbury. The first units assigned to the new division had originally been raised for the 1st Airborne Division. They included the Airborne Armoured Reconnaissance Regiment, the 3rd Parachute Squadron RE, 224 Parachute Field Ambulance, and two glider infantry battalions, the 1st Battalion the Royal Ulster Rifles and the 2nd Battalion the Oxfordshire and Buckinghamshire Light Infantry. The latter were assigned to the 6th Airlanding Brigade, commanded by Brigadier the Honourable Hugh Kindersley MC. The first complete formation was the 3rd Parachute Brigade, commanded by Brigadier James Hill, DSO, MC, a pre-war regular officer who had commanded the 1st Parachute Battalion in North Africa. Hill's Brigade was raised on

5 November 1942, and consisted of the 7th, 8th and 9th Parachute Battalions. The Division's second parachute formation, the 5th Parachute Brigade, was established on 1 July 1943 and consisted of the 12th and 13th Parachute Battalions, commanded by Brigadier Nigel Poett. Other newcomers included the 3rd and 4th Airlanding Anti-Tank Batteries, the 2nd Airlanding Light Anti-Aircraft Battery and the 53rd (Worcestershire Yeomanry) Airlanding Light Regiment.

In the event, the 6th Airborne Division was augmented with a further two infantry units. The all volunteer 1st Canadian Parachute Battalion was raised on 1 July 1942. The first volunteers trained at the US Army Parachute Training School at Fort Benning, Georgia until a Canadian facility was completed at Camp Shiloh, Manitoba. The Battalion arrived in the UK on 28 July 1943, and joined the 6th Airborne Division on 11 August after a parachute conversion course at RAF Ringway; this was necessary because British and US parachuting equipment and techniques differed significantly.[6] The second unit was the 12th Battalion, The Devonshire Regiment. Originally a coastal defence unit, the 'Red Devons' were assigned to the 6th Airlanding Brigade on 18 September 1943. The decision to add a third battalion to airlanding brigades was based on combat experience in the Mediterranean, which showed that two-battalion brigades lacked sufficient manpower for intensive combat. The arrival of the 1st Canadian Parachute Battalion prompted an organisational reshuffle. The newcomers were assigned to the 3rd Parachute Brigade, and Hill was obliged to transfer his senior unit to Poett' 5th Parachute Brigade. The final 3rd Parachute Brigade line-up was thus the 1st Canadian, 8th and 9th Parachute Battalions, while the 5th Parachute Brigade ended up with the 7th, 12th and 13th Parachute Battalions.

It is interesting to note that these parachute units contradict the common charge that the Airborne Forces siphoned off high-calibre personnel to the detriment of their earthbound infantry brethren.[7] This appears to be based on an erroneous belief that all British parachute units were made up of volunteers. This was true of the original Commando parachute cadre that became the 1st Parachute Battalion, and it was also true of the 2nd, 3rd and 4th Parachute Battalions. However, the quantitative and qualitative limitations of the voluntary principle became increasingly apparent. The flow of volunteers was not infinite, and line units abused the system by using official calls for volunteers to rid themselves of malcontents and other undesirables. A report in July 1941 noted that up to twenty-five per cent of parachute volunteers were rejected for involvement in crime or refusing to jump,[8] and the same problem was noted among the volunteers at the Airborne Forces Depot at Hardwick Hall.[9]

As a result, the voluntary principle was abandoned in July 1941 and existing infantry battalions were simply converted to the parachute role, with only the medically unfit being permitted to opt out.[10] All the 6th Airborne Division's parachute battalions were raised in this way apart from the 1st Canadian Parachute Battalion. Thus the 7th (Light Infantry) Parachute Battalion was originally the 10th Battalion, Somerset Light Infantry, for example, and the 12th Parachute Battalion the 10th Battalion the Green Howards.[11] Many units maintained the illusion of voluntary service by holding battalion parades and asking personnel to volunteer, although a positive result was largely guaranteed in a properly functioning battalion. Individual volunteers were still recruited to replace the medically unfit, training losses and operational casualties, but they were slotted into existing units rather providing the basis for them.

The man selected to command the 6th Airborne Division was Major-General Richard Gale MC, a regular soldier with over a quarter of a century of service. Commissioned into the Worcestershire Regiment in 1915, he was posted to the Machine Gun Corps, was awarded the Military Cross in March 1918, and subsequently volunteered for service in India where he successfully completed the Staff College Course at Quetta. Gale returned to the UK in January 1936, and after a year of regimental service worked in staff posts at the War Office and the planning section of the General Staff, where he was promoted to major. In January 1941 he took command of a Territorial battalion from the Leicestershire Regiment, which was being rebuilt after suffering at Dunkirk the previous summer.

Gale's connection with airborne matters began in September 1941, when he was given the task of raising the 1st Parachute Brigade. In that capacity and with the notable assistance of Lieutenant-Colonel E.E. Down, he transformed the British airborne force from a handful of poorly disciplined, freebooting raiders to highly trained, conventional shock troops that merely used a novel method to reach the battlefield. In June 1942 he was posted to the Air Directorate of the War Office Staff Duties section, which he subsequently headed; the Directorate oversaw liaison between the Air Ministry and War Office on airborne policy and requirements.[12] Gale's experience and grasp of airborne warfare proved invaluable, but he was not a desk soldier and returned to his preferred operational role on 3 May 1943, when he assumed command of the 6th Airborne Division.

Gale faced a formidable task, for he was allowed only fifteen weeks to turn his new command into a cohesive entity. Most of his commanders were unfamiliar with their new situation, and four of his parachute battalions had to be introduced to their new role from scratch. This meant putting them through the hardening course at the Airborne Forces Depot and the Parachute Training School at RAF Ringway, and the 12th Devons had never seen a glider. Having studied past airborne operations, Gale formulated a carefully thought out training programme. Command exercises familiarised the Divisional HQ staff with their tasks in likely operations. Exercise PEGASUS, held soon after the HQ was set up, dealt with precisely the tasks that 6th Airborne would be given in Normandy; attacking fortified gun positions, holding key terrain and interfering with enemy deployment.[13] The divisional intelligence staff monitored German dispositions and compiled information on their defences and equipment, while administration and support units practised their operational tasks under simulated combat conditions by day and night. The Division's medical units, for example, routinely ran simulated casualties through every aspect of the Divisional casualty care and evacuation process.

Great emphasis was placed on physical fitness. The Divisional standard required all personnel to be capable of covering 50 miles in twenty-four hours in full battle order. This requirement was ruthlessly enforced on all ranks, and the 1st Canadian Parachute Battalion cut the time to eighteen hours on 19 November 1944, which may have been a 3rd Parachute Brigade requirement.[14] Gale himself constantly monitored performance, offering advice and encouragement, and his common exhortation to 'Go to it!' became the Divisional motto. All infantry units underwent intensive musketry training in an effort to minimise ammunition requirements, and they cycled through tactical training from rifle section to full brigade level, including week-long field exercises. The latter frequently began with a parachute or glider insertion, and ended with a route march of 20 miles or more. In August 1943, for example, the 9th Parachute Battalion route marched 30 miles to Bath, and carried out an eight-day tactical exercise that ended near Blandford. The battalion commander then dismissed the pre-arranged transport and led his men on a further thirty-mile route march back to Bulford.[15]

The 6th Airborne Division was declared ready for operations on 1 February 1944. The 3rd Parachute Brigade made a mass drop five days later, and the whole Division deployed by air for Exercise BIZZ II at the end of March. Drops were carried out to ascertain the best method for putting an entire brigade onto single or multiple drop zones, and tests were carried out to ascertain the suitability of every conceivable piece of equipment for delivery by parachute. On 21 April the full Division participated in Exercise MUSH, a five day affair controlled by newly created British 1st Airborne Corps HQ.[16] Although only Gale and a handful of his senior staff appear to have been in the know, MUSH was specially configured to simulate the terrain and conditions in Normandy. Gale's autobiography clearly states that Lieutenant-General Frederick Browning, commanding 1st British Airborne Corps, informed him on 17 February 1944 that the 6th Airborne Division was to secure the eastern flank of the upcoming Normandy invasion.[17]

Browning initially outlined a brigade operation due to a shortage of aircraft, but when the RAF's Nos. 38 and 46 Groups became available the mission was expanded to include the whole of the 6th

Airborne Division. The Division's overall mission was to hold the eastern flank of the invasion front by dominating the area between the Rivers Orne and Dives north of Caen. The mission was to start with three preliminary missions. These were to seize the twin bridges over the Orne Canal and River Orne at Benouville, 7 miles north of Caen. The bridges were to be seized intact and held by a glider *coup de main* party, which was to be rapidly reinforced by parachute troops. The second mission was the destruction of five bridges across the River Dives in or near Troarn, Bures, Robehomme and Varaville, to seal the eastern flank of the beachhead. Third came the elimination of the German gun battery at Merville, 4 miles north-east of Benouville.[18]

The 6th Airlanding Brigade was initially selected to spearhead the landing but a mass night glider landing was ruled out in April 1944 when the Germans began coincidentally erecting obstacles across the landing zones. Dubbed *Rommelspargel* or Rommel asparagus, these consisted of wire-braced poles projecting 2 metres or more above the ground laced with mines and booby-traps to damage landing gliders and injure paratroops. Gale therefore rejigged the plan to put both parachute brigades in the first lift, accompanied by only enough gliders to carry their heavy equipment. The airlanding brigade was to land later in daylight with the divisional units, which would allow the parachute sappers attached to clear the obstacles, or at least give the glider pilots a chance of avoiding them.

The final plan assigned all the primary tasks, with the exception of the Benouville glider *coup de main*, to Hill's 3rd Parachute Brigade. Hill allocated the individual missions according to the character of his battalions.[19] Eliminating the Merville Battery was assigned to Lieutenant-Colonel Terence Otway's 9th Parachute Battalion, due to that unit's reputation for detailed planning. Because of its effervescence and elan, Lieutenant-Colonel George Bradbrooke's 1st Canadian Parachute Battalion was detailed to clear the village of Varaville and to destroy the two northern Dives bridges at la Bac de Varaville and Robehomme. The destruction of the remaining three Dives bridges at Bures and Troarn was handed to Lieutenant-Colonel Alastair Pearson's 8th Parachute Battalion, due to its phlegmatic attitude and the colourful character of its commander.

Pearson had commanded the 1st Parachute Battalion in the Mediterranean, and had forced the reluctant pilot of his American Dakota to fly inland to their assigned Drop Zone (DZ) at pistol point during the Primasole Bridge on Sicily, and acted as lead scout for the armoured counter-attack that secured the bridge.[20] He was transferred to the 8th Parachute Battalion in December 1943, as part of an initiative to provide the new parachute battalions with a leavening of experienced officers. Pearson only took the job after ascertaining he would not be 'buggered about by senior officers', and refused to return to his former because he felt his place was with his newer charges.[21] Other units attached to 3rd Parachute Brigade for Operation TONGA, as the first British lift into Normandy was codenamed,[22] included the 3rd Parachute Squadron RE, a troop from 591 Parachute Squadron RE, 224th Parachute Field Ambulance and a section from the 4th Anti-Tank Battery RA.

Brigadier Poett's 5th Parachute Brigade was made responsible for the *coup de main* attack on the Benouville bridges. The actual seizure was entrusted to Major John Howard's D Company, 2nd Battalion, The Oxfordshire and Buckinghamshire Light Infantry, reinforced with two platoons from B Company, twenty or thirty sappers from 249 Field Company RE, and sixteen specially selected glider pilots.[23] Immediate relief was assigned to the 7th Parachute Battalion, commanded by the somewhat unsettlingly named Lieutenant-Colonel Geoffrey Pine-Coffin. Pine-Coffin was to seize the bridges if Howard failed, and was equipped with inflatable dinghies for this contingency. The whole of Brigadier Poett's 5th Parachute Brigade was to land on a DZ half a mile east of the Orne Bridges thirty minutes after the *coup de main* party landed. The 12th and 13th Parachute Battalions were tasked to secure the DZ and assist in converting it into a glider landing zone (LZ), before establishing a defensive perimeter to the south of Ranville. Elements of the 4th Anti-Tank Battery RA, 591 Parachute Squadron RE, a detachment from the 286th Field Park Company RE and the 225th Parachute Field Ambulance were also attached to the 5th Parachute Brigade.

The commanders of the units selected for special missions were informed of their tasks around a month before D-Day. Otway was recalled from leave in April 1944 to take command of the 9th Battalion from Lieutenant-Colonel Martin Lindsay, and was informed his new command had been selected for a 'grade A stinker of a job'. This was the elimination of the German gun battery at Merville no later than thirty minutes before daybreak on D-Day. Otway spent a week studying intelligence on his target with Captain Robert Gordon-Brown, and then moved his battalion and attachments to West Woodhay, south-west of Newbury, on the night of 8 May 1944. The attachments were a troop from the 4th Anti-Tank Battery RA and sappers from 591 Parachute Squadron RE. They then constructed a scaffolding and canvas mock-up of the target on Walbury Hill, with every bunker, trench, minefield, hedge and track. The mock-up was the same distance from the Battalion's bivouac as the real thing was from the projected DZ.

Otway planned to attack the battery from the south east, where there was no anti-tank ditch. The assault was to commence with a diversionary attack on the main entrance, just as three Horsa gliders carrying sappers from 591 Parachute Squadron RE and men from the Battalion's A Company landed within the battery perimeter. At the same time B Company would force an entry through the perimeter minefield with Bangalore torpedoes,[24] and C Company would attack through the gap and clear the bunkers and casemates so the sappers could destroy the guns with specially configured explosive charges. Otway's men made four daylight and five night attacks on the mock-up before returning to Bulford for three days' leave. Security was extremely tight, and WAAFs in civilian clothes were ordered to try to elicit information from the battalion's personnel. Leave was followed by full divisional exercise, which ended with another night attack on the mock-up using live ammunition.

While the assault force practised on their mock-up, six selected volunteers from B Squadron, The Glider Pilot Regiment, practised landing their laden Horsas within the battery perimeter. The gliders were to be guided in to their hazardous LZ with radar homing equipment.

The latter consisted of a Eureka ground beacon that responded to a fixed frequency signal transmitted by the Rebecca apparatus mounted in the aircraft or glider. On 1 June, three days before the provisional D-Day, it was realised that the glider pilots were not trained to use Eureka/Rebecca. The three co-pilots were thus hurriedly despatched to RAF Netheravon to take a specially compressed version of the standard two week course.

The Benouville *coup de main* force underwent a similar process. Although they were unaware of it D Company, 2nd Ox and Bucks had begun practising for their mission in April 1944. Gale discussed his idea to seize the Benouville bridges with a *coup de main* with Brigadiers Poett and Kindersley, and arranged a three-day exercise that assigned D Company to seize and hold three small bridges. The exercise was a success, and Gale praised the glider soldier's dash and verve in a post-exercise address. According to one account, Howard was informed that his company had been selected to carry out a similar assignment to spearhead for the upcoming invasion, and that another practice run had been built into the next divisional exercise, codenamed MUSH. Howard's men did not fare so well on this occasion as the umpire declared the bridges blown before they could be secured, and when the defending paratroopers from the 1st Polish Independent Parachute Brigade refused to desist, the exercise degenerated into a number of brawls.[25]

Brigadier Poett informed Howard that his company had been selected to seize the Orne bridges on 2 May 1944, and stressed that they were to be seized intact at all costs, even though they were rigged for demolition; the primary task of the sappers from 249 Field Company RE was to neutralise the demolition charges. Howard's briefing also included full details of the upcoming invasion, making him the only BIGOT-cleared officer in the Benouville operation, which was code-named DEADSTICK. He was thus forbidden to remove his written orders, notes or any intelligence material from 6th Airborne's planning HQ. The intelligence was garnered from French resistance sources, RAF aerial photography and probably ULTRA decrypts too. A 12-ft square scale model of the bridges and surrounding area was constructed, complete to the smallest detail and updated on a daily basis. When the German garrison at the bridges demolished some nearby buildings, the model was amended to suit within twenty-four hours.[26]

Howard laid out the outline of the bridges and watercourses with tape and set his men to practising in varying combinations to replicate the effect of casualties or timetable errors. Because arrival of all the force's Horsas could not be guaranteed, each platoon had to be prepared to stand in for any other, or to carry out the mission alone if necessary, and the infantrymen and sappers cross-trained on the basics of each others' specific tasks too. Howard insisted on strict silence until the first shot, after which his men were to make as much noise as possible, by shouting their sub-unit call signs. This would permit the attackers to maintain contact in the darkness and confusion, and enhance the shock effect of the assault and dupe the defenders into thinking the attackers were more numerous than they were. The realism of the training was enhanced by the provision of 'enemy' troops complete with German uniforms and weapons, with which Howard's men were permitted to familiarise themselves.[27]

Nonetheless, after ten days of attacking taped outlines by day and night, the troops were becoming understandably restive. Howard called a company parade and went as far as his BIGOT clearance allowed in stressing the importance of the operation they were train-ing for. Moving to Countess Wear on the outskirts of Exeter, where two bridges crossed the River Exe and a nearby canal, proved a more effective morale booster. Howard's men spent six days storming the bridges with blank ammunition and thunderflashes,[28] and practising with the collapsible canvas assault boats they would employ if the bridges were demolished. The local reaction was mixed. Many turned out to watch the training, but an angry householder buttonholed Howard after a smoke bomb from a carelessly aimed mortar damaged his roof, and the local council took a dim view of fishing with thun-derflashes. D Company cemented the relationship by tearing up the town and brawling with the locals on its last night in Exeter. Howard was obliged to smooth things over with the head of the local constabulary.

Noting from his medal ribbons that the latter was a First World War veteran, Howard strongly hinted that the night's antics would quite possibly be the last for at least some of his men, and the matter was resolved without official complaint.[29]

Trial runs confirmed that inserting the assault force into small LZs on the strip of land between the two bridges offered the best prospect of success. Two sites close to the bridges were selected, but they were very small and required pinpoint accuracy. Gale therefore turned to Colonel Chatterton, commander of the Glider Pilot Regiment, to confirm their feasibility and that of the projected glider landing on the Merville Battery. Chatterton placed Flight-Lieutenant Tom Grant DSO, who had worked with the Glider Pilot Regiment in the Mediterranean, in charge of selecting and training the DEADSTICK glider pilots. He selected sixteen men, sufficient to man six Horsas with four reserves, and moved them to RAF Tarrant Rushton to train alongside the Halifax-equipped RAF Nos. 298 and 644 Squadrons. Shortly thereafter Chatterton laid on a daylight demonstration at RAF Netheravon for Gale and Browning, which successfully placed six Horsas in a LZ the size of a soccer pitch.[30] Training then concentrated on doing the same by moonlight. The landing approach required extremely precise dead reckoning using compasses and stop watches, and the Horsas to be cast off at 6,000 feet and 7 miles from their objective. Grant permanently paired the tug and glider crews to establish a close working relationship, because skills of the tug crews, and especially the navigators, were as crucial to the success of the mission as the glider pilots or Howard's infantrymen.

The glider pilots used a number of innovative training aids. The most basic were tinted goggles worn in daylight training to simulate moonlight conditions. The most sophisticated was a film produced from thousands of aerial photographs that ran through the entire flight into both LZs from cast-off to landing, with a running commentary supplying airspeed, altitude, bearing and so on. It was the brainchild of Squadron-Leader Lawrence Wright, who had been involved in the British glider effort from October 1940.[31] The film allowed the DEADSTICK and TONGA pilots to thoroughly familiarise themselves with the fly-in between actual training flights, and proved both effective and popular.[32] The effectiveness of their training was graphically demonstrated when Chatterton organised another demonstration at Netheravon in the immediate run up to D-Day, again involving six Horsas carrying a 5,000lb Bailey bridge spar apiece. This was a common expedient to avoid injury to human passengers in the all too frequent training crashes. Five gliders landed precisely within the small LZ marked out in hazy moonlight. The last machine, slightly misjudging its approach, landed spectacularly atop those that had gone before. Thankfully, the most serious injury was a sprained ankle.[33] In all, the DEADSTICK pilots made forty-three training landings, mostly by night.[34] At the end of May they were finally introduced to their passengers, when Howard's men moved into accommodation at RAF Tarrant Rushton.

The remainder of the TONGA force was not idle while the pilots and troops assigned to the DEADSTICK and Merville missions practised and repractised their tasks. The sappers attached to the 5th Parachute Brigade used large amounts of explosives demolishing specially erected replica *Rommelspargel*. The 7th Parachute Battalion followed in the footsteps of the DEADSTICK force by parachuting in to secure the Countess Wear bridges. The 8th Parachute Battalion spent fourteen days and much blank and live ammunition practising battle drills in a specially acquired wood. This last-minute skills update came after it occurred to Pearson that his men had no experience of operating in wooded areas, even though they were assigned to hold the Bois de Bavent ridge.

Opportunities for live training ceased on 22 May 1944, when the 6th Airborne Division moved into sealed camps, located on or near the airfields housing the aircraft and gliders that would carry them to Normandy. Emphasis then shifted to detailed briefings that provided the actual location and purpose of individual missions and their place in the wider scheme, updated with additional intelligence as it came in. One of the 12th Parachute Battalion's officers noticed two circular patches near his units DZ that looked suspiciously like anti-aircraft emplacements shortly before D-Day. Within twenty-four hours the emplacements were revealed to be the grazing pattern produced by two tethered cows. There was also time for relaxation; the 12th Parachute Battalion's officer's mess tent was comprehensively demolished in the course of a lively party with the RAF officers who were to carry them into battle.[35]

The western airborne landings were to be carried out by two US airborne divisions, which carried the traditions of older units. The 82nd 'All American' Infantry Division deployed to France as part of the American Expeditionary Force during the First World War, the divisional nickname reflecting the fact that the division drew its volunteers from all forty-eight states of the Union. They established a formidable combat reputation; the 82nd Division spent more consecutive days in the front line than any other US formation, and earned battle streamers for actions in Lorraine, at St Mihiel and in the Meuse-Argonne. By contrast the 101st Airborne Division's immediate forebear saw no action during the First World War, as it was still forming when the war ended in November 1918. The formation's nickname 'Screaming Eagles' came from its shoulder patch, which depicted a bald eagle's head on a black shield and was based on that of the Union 'Iron Brigade' in the American Civil War.[36] Both formations were deactivated after the First World War and remained so until 1942.[37]

Like that of their British allies, the US airborne effort was prompted by the German parachute and glider operation in the Low Countries in May 1940. On 25 June 1940 the US Army Adjutant General ordered a Test Platoon formed to investigate the concept.[38] The success of the latter led to the formation of the 501st Parachute Infantry Battalion on 26 September 1940; five hundred series numbers were used to avoid confusion with US Marine Corps parachute units.[39] By May 1942 the American airborne force had expanded into four parachute infantry regiments, and the formation of two airborne divisions was authorised in July 1942. An all arms format similar to the British pattern was adopted, which organised 8,000 men into one parachute and two glider infantry regiments, one parachute and one glider artillery battalion, and assorted support units.[40]

The first airborne division was created by simply converting the 82nd Infantry Division, which had been reactivated at Camp Claiborne, Louisiana, on 25 March 1942.[41] The 82nd was redesignated an airborne formation on 15 August 1942, and was immediately ordered to provide a cadre for the 101st Airborne Division, which was activated the next day.[42] The 82nd Airborne relocated to Fort Bragg in mid-September 1942 for parachute training, although this was complicated by the loss of men unsuitable for parachuting and a cadre for the newly activated 98th Infantry Division, and an ongoing short-age of aircraft.[43] Despite this, in February 1943 the 82nd Airborne Division was selected to participate in the invasion of Sicily. This left Major-General Matthew B. Ridgeway less than four months to turn his partly trained formation into a properly functioning operational instrument, and to integrate new units. These included the 505th Parachute Infantry Regiment, commanded by Colonel James M. Gavin. Gavin's Regiment had a rather high opinion of itself; a lieu-tenant from the 505th Parachute Infantry allegedly reported to Ridgeway with the words 'Sir, Colonel Gavin sends his regards and told us he wants us to co-operate to the utmost with the 82nd Division'.[44] A West Point graduate, Gavin had served on the Airborne Command staff, wrote the first American manual on the employment of airborne forces, and took command of the 505th in July 1942. By the Normandy invasion he was deputy commander of the 82nd Airborne Division, and subsequently became the US Army's youngest divisional commander.[45]

The 82nd Airborne disembarked at Casablanca on 10 May 1943 and moved to a tented camp at Oujda two days later.[46] The Division was to be delivered to Sicily in two lifts. HUSKY ONE, scheduled for the night of 9-10 July, envisaged dropping the bulk of the 82nd Airborne near Gela to protect the US 1st Infantry Division's sea landing; HUSKY TWO was a reinforcing drop scheduled for the following night.[47] In the event, the overly complex air plan, transport aircraft crew inexperience and strong cross-winds severely disrupted HUSKY ONE. Twenty-three aircraft dropped their sticks of paratroopers in the British invasion zone, 60 miles east of their intended destination, 127 sticks were scattered in between, and only 400 men were delivered on or near the correct DZ.[48]

Despite this, one party of badly scattered paratroopers overran and secured the main objective, a strongpoint overlooking the landing beaches, and another blocked a main road 5 miles to the north, where they held out for three days until relieved. The single battalion delivered intact came down 21 miles east of its assigned DZ, in the middle of a fortified position on the US 45th Infantry Division's front; this was subdued after an all day fight.[49] HUSKY TWO fared even worse. The first few aircraft dropped unscathed, but the rest were hit by a tremendous volume of 'friendly' anti-aircraft fire, possibly prompted by an accidental discharge from a machine gun ashore.[50] Whatever the reason, the effect was devastating. Of one hundred and forty-five C-47s, twenty-three were shot down, thirty-seven were damaged and eight returned to North Africa with their passengers aboard. Ninety-seven paratroopers and sixty aircrew were killed or missing, and a total of 162 were wounded.[51] The paratroopers who jumped were as badly scattered as their compatriots the previous night. Nonetheless, the 82nd Airborne made a significant contribution to the invasion. The paratroopers secured their primary objective despite the confusion, blunted several counter-attacks toward Gela and assisted the US 45th Infantry Division in getting off the beach. Other elements rallied by Gavin successfully defended the Biazza Ridge against the Tiger tank-equipped *Hermann Göring Panzer Division*,[52] and scattered groups of paratroopers sowed confusion in the enemy rear by attacking any enemy troops or installations they happened upon.

In all, the 82nd Airborne's experience presaged almost exactly the circumstances they were to face in Normandy a year later. However, the débâcle shook non-airborne American confidence in the airborne method, which was only restored after Marshall launched a high level investigation. This included pitting the US 11th and 17th Airborne Divisions against one another in a large-scale exercise to test the operational suitability of the airborne division concept. The exercise proved to be a resounding success, and the US airborne effort was authorised to continue as before on 16 December 1943.[53] There were also differences of opinion with the 82nd Airborne. Ridgeway concluded that parachute landings were not viable and recommended converting the Division into an air landed unit, using only gliders and transport aircraft. Unsurprisingly, Gavin and the commander of the 504th Parachute Infantry Regiment, Colonel Rueben H. Tucker, disagreed and argued that the problem was purely due to insufficient aircrew training and a lack of parachute pathfinder units to mark DZs for the main force. The outcome of the wider investigation settled the matter, and Ridgeway simply requested that his Division be employed in its entirety in future.[54]

The 82nd Airborne's next airborne operation, consisting of two emergency reinforcing jumps into the Salerno lodgement on the nights of 13-14 and 14-15 September, proved the correctness and viability of Gavin and Tucker's view. A newly created, fifty-strong pathfinder force marked the DZ with Eureka beacons and special lights, with highly favourable results. On the second jump, for example, only seven of the one hundred and twenty-seven C-47s employed failed to deliver their sticks on or within a mile of the DZ; Gavin considered it the most successful 505th Regiment jump to date.[55] The Division then fought as part of the US 5th Army until mid-October 1943, when it was withdrawn to the UK apart from the 504th Parachute Infantry Regiment and some of the Divisional artillery assets, which were retained in Italy.

While the 82nd Airborne was trailblazing in the Mediterranean, the 101st Airborne Division was grappling with the problems of hasty activation. Initially the Division contained a high proportion of men over thirty-three, and twice the norm from the lowest Army intelligence category. The situation was remedied by granting Major-General William C. Lee complete discretion in the dismissal or reassignment of personnel. Thus the unfit or otherwise unsuitable were weeded out with a minimum of bureaucratic fuss, and replaced with high-calibre volunteers from an army-wide airborne recruiting campaign.[56] The Division thus filled out its organisation through the autumn and winter of 1942, although such piecemeal formation complicated training even after Airborne Command laid down a standardised divisional training programme on 4 November 1942.[57] Nonetheless, the

101st Airborne had completed its Unit and Combined Training Phases by 18 January 1943.[58]

Initially, the 101st Airborne consisted of the 327th and 401st Glider Infantry Regiments and the 502nd Parachute Infantry Regiment, augmented by the 506th Parachute Infantry Regiment on 10 June 1943. Commanded by Lieutenant-Colonel Robert F. Sink, the 506th was activated on 20 July 1942 using personnel drawn direct from Army reception centres; Sink was a popular commander and his men took to referring to their unit as the 'Five-oh-Sinks'. The entire Division took part in a series of large-scale exercises in Tennessee through June and July 1943, including the first US mass glider landing. On 4 September 1943 the Division sailed for Britain, where it concentrated around Newbury in Hampshire, within easy reach of the US 50th and 53rd Troop Carrier Wings. In January 1944 the Division's parachute component was increased with the arrival of Lieutenant-Colonel Howard Johnson's 501st Parachute Infantry Regiment.

The 82nd Airborne Division arrived at Belfast in December 1943, where it was joined by the green 507th and 508th Parachute Infantry Regiments, commanded by Lieutenant-Colonel's George V. Millett and Roy Lindquist respectively. The Division moved to billets in and around Nottingham and Leicester in the East Midlands in February 1944, adjacent to the US 52nd Troop Carrier Wing. In April the 504th Parachute Infantry Regiment rejoined the Division, fresh from fighting at Anzio in the ground role. Having suffered twenty-five per cent casualties at Anzio, including an officer replacement rate of over 300 per cent, the 504th was excluded from the upcoming Normandy drop, although around fifty of Tucker's men jumped into Normandy as volunteer pathfinders.[59]

By early 1944 the two US airborne divisions were both parachute heavy formations, consisting of three parachute and one glider infantry regiments, and two each parachute and glider field artillery battalions.[60] Unlike the British 6th Airborne Division, their precise role was not fixed at the outset, but evolved over the period February to May 1944, with a series of ideas of variable feasibility coming under consideration. The most ambitious of these was a late 1943 scheme by Marshall and the chief of the USAAF, Major-General Henry 'Hap' Arnold, to establish a multi-division airhead near Evreux, north-west of Paris. This, it was claimed, would severely disrupt German lines of communications and cripple their ability to respond to the landings in Normandy. Unsurprisingly, Lieutenant-General Morgan was horrified, and Air Chief Marshal Sir Trafford Leigh-Mallory, one of the chief SHAEF planners, labelled it suicidal. Marshall, however, continued to advocate his plan, and it was not finally discarded until February 1944, when Eisenhower sought informed opinion from Gavin, Lee, Ridgeway and others. They overwhelmingly endorsed Leigh-Mallory's opinion, after which Eisenhower tactfully sidelined the scheme.[61]

Lee had been working with the SHAEF planners in London since March 1943, and was joined by Gavin in December; the latter assumed the role of Senior Airborne Advisor when Lee suffered a severe heart attack in February 1944.[62] The first American scheme envisaged deploying the 101st Airborne behind the OMAHA landing area. Gavin, probably influenced by his experience in Sicily, opposed the scheme on the grounds that the terrain would leave the lightly armed airborne force especially vulnerable to armoured counterattack, and his opposition led to the operation being discarded.[63] As we shall see, this was perhaps one of the most serious errors committed by the SHAEF planners. Gavin then put together a more ambitious scheme that included both US airborne divisions. He was supported by Lieutenant-General Omar Bradley, commander of the US 1st Army and one of the few senior US commanders impressed by the airborne contribution in Sicily.

Gavin envisaged dropping both US airborne divisions at the base of the Cotentin Peninsula, to safeguard egress from the UTAH landing beaches and prevent German reinforcements moving through Carentan to interfere. The 82nd Airborne Division was to land northwest of St Mère Église, seize the town and two causeways over the River Merderet at la Fière and Chef-du-Pont, and occupy the area around La Haye-du-Puits to the west, to dominate the western route into the Cotentin Peninsula through St Sauveur-le-Vicomte. The 101st Airborne was to land east of St Mère Église, and was tasked to secure four causeway exits from the UTAH beaches, crossings over the River Douve at la Barquette and le Port south-west of the landing beaches, and to eliminate a German gun battery near St Martin-de-Varreville. The parachute regiments were to be augmented with fifty-two gliders per division, carrying anti-tank guns, ammunition and key personnel. A second, much larger glider lift was scheduled for dusk on D-Day.[64]

The plan was rejigged on the very eve of D-Day when *91 Luftlande Division* and *Fallschirmjäger Regiment 6* were located near St Sauveur-le-Vicomte on 25 May 1944. Leigh-Mallory felt this made the US airborne landings untenable, and demanded their cancellation to avoid certain destruction of both US divisions. Bradley disagreed and after consulting Ridgeway and the 101st Division's new commander, Major-General Maxwell D. Taylor, proposed shifting the 82nd Airborne's landing area eastward. Leigh-Mallory rejected this at an emergency conference on 27 May 1944, less than a week before the scheduled invasion, and Bradley flatly refused to land on the UTAH beaches without US airborne support. Eisenhower had to adjudicate, and he approved Bradley's revised scheme on 30 May 1944.[65]

The most striking difference between the British and US airborne plans was the lack of American special operations, even though there was no shortage of suitable targets. The German resistance nests guarding the causeway exits from the UTAH landing beaches were ideal objectives for a glider *coup de main* attack, for example, as were the la Barquette locks and the Merderet causeways. Similarly, the German coastal battery at the Pointe du Hoc was a perfect candidate for a combined glider/parachute attack like that planned for the Merville Battery. Part of the reason appears to have been innate US Army conservatism, which tended and indeed continues to view special operations and irregular warfare with some suspicion. The US airborne force was in itself something of an unconventional departure, but its employment was overwhelmingly conventional. Senior American commanders viewed airborne divisions as miniaturised, lightly equipped versions of regular units that merely used unorthodox transport to reach the battle-field, and frequently employed them as such.

The US airborne force also lacked the raiding heritage of its British counterpart, which had originally been raised as a raiding force. While the practical results of such raiding were mixed, the British airborne plan shows the experience bequeathed a high degree of flexibility. The sole American experience of airborne raiding was less positive. On the night of 24-25 December 1942, thirty men from the US 509th Parachute Infantry Regiment and two French guides set out to destroy a railway bridge near El Djem in Tunisia. Dropped over 20 miles wide, the raiders never reached their target, and only eight men made the one hundred and 10 miles back to friendly lines. A further sixteen were taken prisoner, and eight remain missing, believed killed.[66]

Perhaps most significantly, the Americans did not possess the tools for the job. The key to most British airborne special operations was the glider, flown by members of the Glider Pilot Regiment. These men were trained according to the 'total soldier' concept, which viewed the glider pilot not just as a flyer, but as a highly trained combat soldier whose duties merely included piloting. To this end recruits went through a gruelling course that weeded out the mentally and physically unsuitable, and trained the remainder in infantry tactics and the myriad skills likely to be encountered among their likely passengers. Only then did they undergo twelve weeks at an Elementary Flying Training School, twelve weeks at a Glider Training School, and six weeks at an Operational Training Unit. Survivors were then posted to one of the Glider Pilot Regiment's two battalions for further training.[67] The American approach was officially defined by the USAAF Director of Individual Training on May 12, 1942: 'The role of the glider pilot in combat will be primarily to land his glider safely, expedite the rapid debarkation of his passengers, secure his glider on the ground, assure that transport which may land after his glider-borne troops have secured the airdrome or locality to permit reinforcement by transport-borne troops. The glider pilot will participate in ground combat only in exceptional circumstances or after his glider has been wrecked in landing.'[68]

Disparity was also apparent between British and US glider troops. American paratroopers were volunteers whose hazardous calling was rewarded with jump-pay at $100 per month for officers and $50 per month for enlisted men. Even though glider landings were proven to be more hazardous than parachuting, American glider soldiers received no special pay until late 1944, when they were belatedly awarded flight pay at the same rate. Neither were they volunteers. Nobody bothered to ask the men of the 401st Infantry Regiment if they wanted to be glider soldiers, and they were denied special insignia or uniform items. Only their divisional shoulder patch and later the Airborne hat patch differentiated the American glider soldiers from line infantrymen, whereas paratroopers were issued distinctive footwear, the much vaunted 'jump boots', field uniforms and parachute insignia. These status symbols were jealously guarded, and US paratroopers frequently went out of their way to emphasise their perceived superiority.[69] Similar British rivalry undoubtedly existed, but was far less marked. As a result British paratroopers and glider soldiers considered themselves airborne first and foremost, partly because the glider had been integral to the British airborne force from the outset, and partly because of the common format and distribution of special insignia. Thus with their maroon Airborne berets, Pegasus sleeve flashes, airborne pattern helmets and camouflaged Denison smocks, British glider soldiers were virtually indistinguishable from their parachute brethren, and they shared the same high standard of physical and tactical training.

Be that as it may, one American special operation was included in the opening phase of the cross-Channel invasion, but was assigned to US Army Rangers rather than airborne troops. The Rangers were a direct equivalent to the British Commandos, raised in June 1942 after an investigation into British developments, and were named in honour of irregular units that fought in North America in the mid-1700s. Two thousand volunteers were whittled down by a two-week selection course, and Major William O. Darby's 500-strong 1st Ranger Battalion was activated on 19 June 1942. The new unit was then put through the Commando course at the British Commando Training

Centre at Achnacarry, followed by four weeks of amphibious training in the Western Isles. It was during this period that fifty men were detached to participate in the Dieppe raid with Nos 3 and 4 Commandos.[70]

The two Ranger battalions that participated in the cross-Channel invasion were raised in the US in response to a US Army Ground Forces directive issued on 11 March 1943. The 2nd Ranger Battalion was activated at Camp Forrest, Tennessee on 1 April 1943, and was commanded by Major James E. Rudder from June 1943. After winnowing a mass of volunteers to the required 500, the Battalion underwent small boat training at the Scout and Raider School at Fort Pierce, Florida, and thence to Fort Dix, New Jersey, for advanced tactical training. In November 1943 Rudder's Battalion established a new US Army speed march record, covering 15 miles in two hours. Arriving in the UK in December 1943, the Rangers trained alongside No. 4 Commando, learning cliff assault techniques on the Isle of Wight and at Swanage in Dorset, and attended the British Assault Training Centre in Devon.

Lieutenant-Colonel Max Schneider's 5th Ranger Battalion was also raised at Camp Forrest in September 1943, and arrived in the UK on 18 January 1944. After attending the Commando Training Centre in March 1944 and the British Assault Training Centre the following month, the 5th Rangers carried out amphibious assault training until linking up with the 2nd Rangers at Dorchester in April 1944. On 6 May 1944 both battalions were officially designated the Provisional Ranger Group, headed by the recently promoted Lieutenant-Colonel Rudder, who also retained command of the 2nd Battalion.[71]

The two Ranger battalions had been selected to eliminate a German coastal battery on the western flank of the OMAHA landing area. Located on a triangular promontory flanked by 100ft cliffs, the Pointe du Hoc Battery was a formidable target. The battery consisted of six 155mm guns, controlled from an observation bunker at the tip of the promontory. Two guns were enclosed in concrete casemates, two were in open concrete emplacements, and two were being converted into enclosed casemates. A number of large personnel shelters, flak and defensive bunkers were intermixed with the gun positions, protected inland by minefields. The OVERLORD planners estimated the range of the battery's guns at 25,000 yards, which made it capable of hitting the marshalling areas from whence the landing craft were to be loaded and despatched to the beaches. Elimination of the battery was therefore vital, and RAF heavy bombers were to hit it on the night before D-Day, followed by a heavy naval bombardment. Lieutenant-Colonel Rudder's Provisional Ranger Group was then to finish the job by attacking the Pointe du Hoc from the sea.

Rudder planned to land on the narrow shingle beaches on either side of the promontory, climb the cliffs and assault the German positions. The attackers were divided into two waves because the beaches were too small for a full battalion. The first wave, headed by Rudder, consisted of 225 men from the 2nd Ranger Battalion carried in ten British LCAs, two of which were to carry demolition charges, ammunition and other equipment. The remainder were fitted with six rocket-powered grapnels carrying 200-ft of rope apiece, and carried seven 16-ft sections of lightweight scaling ladder. The first wave was also equipped with four DUKW amphibious trucks, two of which were fitted with 100-ft extendable turntable ladders used by the London Fire Brigade, with machine guns mounted in place of the hose nozzles.

The second wave was commanded by Lieutenant-Colonel Schneider, and was made up of two companies from the 2nd Ranger Battalion and Schneider's Battalion in its entirety. Schneider was briefed to hold his force offshore and await the code-word 'Tilt' as a signal to proceed; as a back up Rudder's men were to fire flares on reaching the cliff top. If no signal was received by H Plus 30, Schneider was to assume that the first wave had failed and land at the western edge of the OMAHA landing beaches and move cross country to attack the Pointe du Hoc from inland.[72]

The initial phase of the Normandy invasion was thus a complex and multifaceted scheme in its own right, with the airborne component comprising the largest single airborne operation to date. Even this, however, paled into relative insignificance in comparison to the amphibious assault that was to follow.

COMMANDOS, REGINAS, DORSETS AND TWENTY-NINERS

THE SEA LANDING PLAN AND TASKS

The NEPTUNE Initial Plan was to deliver its airborne spearhead onto French soil up to seven and a half hours ahead of the sea landings, which were to commence an hour after first light. The precise timings were dictated by tidal conditions in the Bay of the Seine. The landings required a rising tide, to avoid stranding landing craft after discharging their loads, and low tide differed by an hour from the west to eastern end of the landing area. A further complicating factor was the Calvados Reef, off the boundary between the GOLD and JUNO areas, which could not be negotiated until the tide had risen sufficiently. Thus H Hour at UTAH and OMAHA was set for 06:30, 07:25 at GOLD, 07:35 at JUNO, and 07:25 at SWORD. Contrary to popular usage, these codenames did not refer to beaches, but to landing areas. These were originally divided into seventeen sectors, each identified with a letter from the then current phonetic alphabet. These ran from Able on the right of the OMAHA area to Roger on the left of SWORD. A further eight sectors were added when the landing frontage was extended to include the UTAH landing area. The sectors were sub-divided into beaches identified by the colours Green, Red and White, depending on frontage.

The SWORD landings were assigned to the Queen sector, west of Ouistreham at the mouth of the Orne. It included Lion-sur-Mer and the smaller resort of La Brèche, and was sub-divided into Queen Red, White and Green Beaches, with a frontage of just under 2 miles. The sector was allocated to the British 3rd Infantry Division, commanded by Major-General T.G. Rennie DSO, MBE. Returning from Dunkirk in relatively good order, the formation was earmarked for defence against the seemingly imminent German invasion, and was specifically exempted from the Commando recruiting effort.[1] By 1944 the Division was designated an assault formation, and had undergone extensive combined operations training at Loch Fyne and the Western Isles, reinforced by divisional exercises in the Moray Firth and the south coast of England.

For the invasion, the 3rd Infantry Division consisted of the 8th, 9th and 185 Infantry Brigades and the 27th Armoured Brigade; the 1st Special Service Brigade was attached for the landing. It was given the most ambitious D-Day mission, the seizure of Caen, 10 miles inland. One brigade was to breach the German defences, opening the way for a second brigade to advance inland to occupy Caen, while the third brigade formed a reserve. DD Shermans from the 13th/18th Hussars were to be first ashore, to cover Sherman Crabs from the 22nd Dragoon Guards and Westminster Dragoons, and Churchill AVREs from 5 Assault Regiment RE. These were to provide safe lanes through the minefields, breach the seawall and demolish beach obstacles for succeeding waves of landing craft. They were to be followed by elements of the 8th Infantry Brigade from the 1st Battalion the South Lancashire Regiment and the 2nd Battalion the East Yorkshire Regiment. Their immediate task was to overrun a strongpoint at la Brèche codenamed 'Cod'.

The rest of the South Lancs and East Yorks were to come ashore half an hour later and deal with a strongpoint, codenamed 'Sole' and a fortified gun battery codenamed 'Daimler'. Daimler was one of three such installations on the rising ground south and west of Ouistreham, with a panoramic view of the SWORD beaches. Each contained four 100mm or 155mm guns, most of which were enclosed in Type 699 casemates, protected by concrete machine gun and mortar positions, mines and barbed wire. The other two strongpoints were 'Morris' and 'Hillman', almost 2 miles inland; they were assigned to the 1st Battalion the Suffolk Regiment, scheduled to arrive sixty minutes after the DD Shermans.

The Suffolks were to land alongside Lord Lovat's 1st Special Service Brigade, consisting of Nos. 3, 4, and 6 Commandos, 45 (RM) Commando and two French Troops from No. 10 (Inter-Allied) Commando. No 41 (RM) Commando from the 4th Special Service Brigade was attached for the landing phase; its task was to move west and link up with the JUNO landing area. No. 4 Commando and the French Commandos were to eliminate a 155mm battery and a strongpoint in Ouistreham. The rest of the 1st Special Service Brigade were to bypass German opposition and link up with the British 6th Airborne Division holding the bridges at Benouville, 4 miles inland from the beach.

Next came 185 Infantry Brigade, scheduled to land in the late morning and tasked to move directly on Caen. The 1st Battalion the Royal Norfolk Regiment was to eliminate a strongpoint south of St Aubin d'Arquenay, codenamed 'Rover'. The 2nd Battalion the Royal Warwickshire Regiment and 2nd Battalion the King's Shropshire Light Infantry were to secure Blainville-sur-Orne on the main Caen-Ouistreham, on the way. The 3rd Division's final formation was the 9th Infantry Brigade. Consisting of the 1st Battalion the King's Own Scottish Borderers, the 2nd Battalion the Lincolnshire Regiment and the 2nd Battalion the Royal Ulster Rifles, supported by Sherman tanks from the 1st East Riding Yeomanry, the 9th Brigade was scheduled to land in the early afternoon.

The 8th Infantry Brigade's landing plan was a standard British scheme used by the assault brigades on the SWORD, JUNO and GOLD beaches. The first wave was made up of sixteen DD Sherman tanks launched from four LCTs to land at H-Hour Minus 5 Minutes. The second wave, timed to arrive precisely on H-Hour, was made up of four more LCTs carrying the sappers and specialised armour to clear the beach obstacles. At H-Hour Plus 7 Minutes the third wave, consisting of two infantry companies aboard eight LCAs, arrived followed at H-Hour Plus 20 Minutes by another two companies in the same number of LCAs. A fifth wave consisting of two LCAs carrying beach control units arrived five minutes later, followed by more specialised armour including bulldozers, at H-Hour Plus 35 Minutes.

At H Plus 1 Hour came nine LCTs carrying Sexton self-propelled guns, followed at H Plus One Hour 30 Minutes by more LCTs carrying a full squadron of tanks. The final wave consisted of more landing craft carrying additional artillery and twenty-one DUKW amphibious trucks carrying ammunition and other stores. The scheme could be adjusted to suit specific brigade assault plans. At SWORD for example, the 3rd Infantry Division's Forward HQ came ashore at H Plus 30 Minutes, and the 8th Infantry Brigade's third battalion and the 1st Special Service Brigade came in at H Plus One, alongside LCTs carrying self-propelled artillery.

British 1st Corps' second responsibility was the JUNO landing area. This was allocated to the Canadian 3rd Infantry Division. Commanded by Major-General R.F. Keller, this formation had been in the UK since leaving Canada in 1941. Adjacent sectors either side of Courseulles were selected for the assault. Mike sector, divided into Mike Green and Mike Red beaches, extended a mile west of the mouth of the River Seulles and was assigned to the 7th Canadian Infantry Brigade. The assault wave was made up of the Regina Rifles and the Royal Winnipeg Rifles, supported by the DD tanks from the 6th Canadian Armoured Regiment, followed by the 1st Battalion the Canadian Scottish Regiment.

The 8th Canadian Infantry Brigade was assigned the Nan sector, running east from Courseulles for 3 miles, divided into Nan Green, Nan White and Nan Red beaches. It was to be preceded by DD tanks from the 10th Canadian Armoured Regiment (The Fort Garry Horse), with the North Shore (New Brunswick) Regiment and the Queens Own Rifles of Canada making up the assault wave, backed up by the Régiment de la Chaudière. No. 48 (RM) Commando was attached for the landing, and was to move east to link up with No. 41 (RM) Commando from SWORD Queen Green beach. Once ashore, the 7th Canadian Infantry Brigade was to press south, aiming for the main Caen-Bayeux road that ran roughly parallel and 9 miles inland from the coast. The 8th Brigade was to angle south–east toward Caen, supported by the 9th Canadian Infantry Brigade, which was scheduled to land in the early afternoon. The latter formation was made up of the Highland Light Infantry of Canada, the North Nova Scotia Highlanders and the Stormont, Dundas and Glengarry Highlanders, augmented with tanks from the 27th Canadian Armoured Regiment (the Sherbrooke Fusiliers).

The GOLD landings were entrusted to the battle-tested 50th (Northumbrian) Infantry Division, commanded by Major-General D.A.H. Graham. After fighting in Belgium and France in 1940, the Division was despatched to the Mediterranean in the spring of 1941. After operations in Syria and Iraq, it was involved in the Western Desert fighting culminating in the Battle of El Alamein in 1942. Thereafter it fought in Tunisia and the invasion of Sicily, before being withdrawn to the UK, accompanied by the 7th Armoured Division and 51st Highland Division. All three divisions were intended to provide a leavening of experience for the largely untried British Liberation Army gathered for the cross Channel invasion. For the invasion the 50th Division was also larger than the British and Canadian 3rd Infantry Divisions, having a fourth infantry brigade under command.

The GOLD landings were assigned to the Jig and King sectors, each divided into Green and Red beaches. The King sector ran for a mile and a half west from La Rivière, and was assigned to the 69th Infantry Brigade, backed up by the 151st Infantry Brigade. DD tanks from the 4th/7th Royal Dragoon Guards led the way for the specialist armour from the Westminster Dragoons and 6 Assault Regiment RE. The two lead infantry battalions were the 5th Battalion the East Yorkshire Regiment and the 6th Battalion the Green Howards, followed by the 7th Green Howards. The 69th Brigade's task, for which it was allowed two hours, was to overcome the beach defences and expand the beach-head south to Crépon, 2.5 miles inland, and then onto St Léger, 9 miles inland on the main Caen to Bayeux road. The 151st Infantry Brigade, made up of the 6th, 8th and 9th Battalions the Durham Light Infantry was then to pass to the west and consolidate the centre of the GOLD lodgement along the Caen-Bayeux road west of St Léger.

The Jig beaches had a combined frontage of a mile and a half, although the western Jig Green was significantly narrower. They were assigned to 231 Infantry Brigade with No. 47 (RM) Commando attached for the landing. The first wave consisted of the 1st Battalion the Hampshire Regiment and the 1st Battalion the Dorset Regiment, supported by DD tanks from the Nottinghamshire Yeomanry and more specialised armour from the 6 Assault Regiment RE and the Westminster Dragoons. The Brigade's third battalion was the 2nd Battalion the Devonshire Regiment. Because the Jig sector contained a heavy concentration of defences, 231 Brigade was also allocated the 1st Royal Marine Armoured Support Regiment, equipped with Centaur IV tanks mounting 95mm howitzers,[2] along with 90 and 147 Field Regiments RA; the latter were to provide fire support from their landing craft. On landing, No. 47 (RM) Commando was to occupy Port-en-Bessin, 10 miles to the west, while 231 Brigade eliminated German strongpoints at le Hamel, les Roquettes and Asnelles-sur-Mer. It then expanded the lodgement toward Arromanches-les-Bains Bayeux. 56th Infantry Brigade, consisting of the 2nd Battalion the Essex Regiment, 2nd Battalion the South Wales Borderers and the 2nd Battalion the Gloucestershire Regiment was to land at midday and move straight on to Bayeux.

The US landing at the OMAHA were assigned to Dog, Easy and Fox sectors. The eastern half of the landing, on Easy Red and Fox Green beaches, was allocated to Major-General Clarence R. Huebner's 1st Infantry Division. Raised in May 1917 as the 1st Division of General John J. Pershing's American Expeditionary Force (AEF), the formation was initially nicknamed 'Pershing's Own', and earned seven battle streamers for service in Lorraine, Picardy, Montdidier–Noyon, Aisne-Marne, St Mihiel and the Meuse-Argonne. The 'Pershing's Own' tag was dropped following adoption of a shoulder insignia consisting of a red Arabic figure 1 on a green shield toward the end of 1918. Thereafter the division was referred to as 'The Big Red One'.

In 1939 the Division was reorganised into a triangular structure, built around the 16th, 18th and 26th Infantry Regiments, Regular Army formations that could trace their lineage back to 1901 in the latter case, and to the American Civil War in the former two. It took part in the TORCH landings in Algeria in November 1942 and fought throughout the remainder of the North African campaign, including the setback at the Kasserine Pass, and invaded Sicily in July 1943. Service there cost the Division 267 dead, 1,184 wounded and 337 missing.[3] The formation underwent a period of retraining and reorganisation before embarking for the UK, arriving in November 1943.

The 1st Infantry Division's initial landing plan was essentially similar to that employed by the British. DD tanks from the US 741st Tank Battalion were to be first ashore, followed by Colonel George A. Taylor's 2nd Battalion, 16th Infantry Regiment; a US infantry regiment, sometimes referred to as a regimental combat team, was roughly equivalent to a British infantry brigade. Taylor's unit was spread across Easy Red and Fox Green beaches, four companies being assigned to each in two waves.[4] The spearhead companies were temporarily reorganised into special assault platoons, with mortars, extra machine guns and dedicated wire-cutting, flame-thrower and bazooka teams.[5] They were to be followed by 270 assault engineers, tasked to clear lanes through the mines and demolish the beach obstacles before they were submerged by the rising tide.

The 2nd Battalion's primary objectives were the draws running inland toward St Laurent-sur-Mer and Colleville-sur-Mer. After securing these it was to advance to the Beachhead Maintenance Line, which followed a ridge of high ground running parallel to the coast 2 miles inland from the OMAHA beaches. The 1st and 3rd Battalions were to fan out east and south, the former to a firm base around Engranville, 4 miles inland while the latter secured Huppain on the boundary between the OMAHA and GOLD landing areas. The lodgement was to be expanded by the 18th and 26th Infantry Regiments, angling south and south-east respectively to the D-Day Phase Line, 8 miles inland and running west of Bayeux to Isigny, near the junction of the Rivers Aure and Vire.[6]

The western OMAHA landing was assigned to the US 29th Infantry Division, commanded by Major-General Charles Gerhardt. The 29th was a National Guard formation raised in July 1917 for service with the AEF, using National Guard units from Delaware, New Jersey, Maryland and Virginia. This mix of States from both sides of the

American Civil War divide was reflected in the new division's shoulder insignia, a circular half blue, half grey device intended to signify American solidarity; it earned the nickname of the 'Blue and Grey Division'. After fighting in the Meuse-Argonne campaign in 1918, the Division reverted to National Guard status. It was mobilised in February 1941, and concentrated at Fort George G. Meade, Maryland, where it overcame poor accommodation, uniform shortages and absorbed large numbers of conscripts. Like the 1st Infantry, the 29th Division converted to the new triangular divisional structure in March 1942. This entailed some internal reorganisation, but the core of the formation remained the 115th, 116th and 175th Infantry Regiments, which could trace their origins back to the Colonial period.[7] The 29th Division left for the UK on 27 September, and was initially stationed at Tidworth in Wiltshire, before moving to billets in Devon and Cornwall in May 1943. There it remained until the invasion, spending most of its time training and hiking across the bleak landscape of Bodmin Moor and Dartmoor, and the Division's infantry regiments were the first to pass through the US Army Assault Training Centre at Woolacombe in September 1943.[8]

Colonel Charles Canham's 116th Infantry Regiment was selected to lead the 29th Division onto OMAHA, under operational control of the US 1st Division for the initial landing. The 116th deployed all three of its battalions in a single echelon spread, again spread in two waves over four beaches, supported by DD Shermans from the 743rd Tank Battalion. Four companies and an attached company from the 2nd Ranger Battalion were assigned to Dog Green Beach, which was also to host part of the Provisional Ranger Group if the Pointe du Hoc assault did not go to plan. Dog White, Dog Red and Easy Green beaches were assigned two companies apiece. The regiment's primary objectives were two draws through the bluffs, one leading to Vierville-sur-Mer, and the other fronted by the hamlet of les Moulins. Once off the beach, the 1st Battalion, 116th Infantry was to move west to relieve the Pointe du Hoc assault force, while the 2nd Battalion advanced inland 2 miles to the Beachhead Maintenance Line around Louvières. The 3rd Battalion was then to move through Louvières to the D-Day

Phase Line, at the western end of the Longueville plateau. The 15th Infantry Regiment, scheduled to land at 10:00, was tasked to occupy the eastern sector of the D-Day Phase Line, linking up with the 1st Division's 16th Infantry Regiment near Engranville. The 175th Infantry was scheduled to land D Plus One, and was earmarked for an advance west to secure Isigny at the extreme western end of the OMAHA landing area.[9]

The UTAH landings were assigned the Tare and Uncle sectors, between les Dunes-de-Varreville and la Madeleine. The sectors were divided into Red and Green Beaches, and fronted four elevated roads leading inland through marshland to Pouppeville, Houdienville, Audouville-la-Hubert, and St Martin-de-Varreville. The formation chosen to lead the UTAH assault was Major-General Raymond O. Barton's 4th Infantry Division, consisting of the 8th, 12th and 22nd Infantry Regiments. Like its running mates, the US 4th Infantry Division was raised to serve with the AEF, made up of conscripts rather than Regular or National Guard personnel. The Division was nicknamed the 'I-V' or 'Ivy' Division, a play on words reflected by its shoulder insignia, a khaki square bearing four ivy leaves pointing outward to the corners; the Divisional motto was 'Steadfast and Loyal'. The Division participated in the Aisne-Marne, St Mihiel and Meuse-Argonne campaigns, and was deactivated in 1919. It was reactivated as an experimental motorised formation in June 1940, and redesignated the 4th Infantry Division in August 1943. After amphibious training in Florida, the Division sailed for the UK in January 1944, and was based around Tiverton in Devon before embarking for Normandy.

The UTAH landing was to be preceded by two companies of DD Shermans from the US 70th Tank Battalion. The 4th Division's assault was to be led by the 8th Infantry Regiment, commanded by Colonel James A. Van Fleet, with an attached battalion from the 22nd Infantry Regiment. The 1st and 2nd Battalions, 8th Infantry Regiment made up the first wave onto Tare Green and Uncle Red Beaches, followed by the 3rd Battalion, 22nd Infantry and 2nd 8th Infantry respectively. The two waves were to land fifteen minutes apart, and the second was to include LCTs carrying the 70th Tank Battalion's third company, some of which were fitted with bulldozer blades to assist the combat engineer battalions tasked to clear the mines and beach obstacles for the follow-on forces.

After overcoming the beach defences the 8th Infantry Regiment was tasked to move down the causeways to relieve the 101st Airborne Division units holding their landward ends. The 1st Battalion, 8th Infantry was then to establish a blocking position near St Martin-de-Varreville, while the 2nd and 3rd Battalions moved west to occupy high ground between St Marie-du-Mont and les Forges, just south of St Mère Église. They were then to prepare for a further advance west into the 82nd Airborne Division's area around Amfreville, on the other side of the River Merderet.

The 3rd Battalion, 22nd Infantry was to prepare the way for the rest of the regiment, by eliminating German strongpoints guarding the northern causeway and then following the coast road to the D-Day Objective Line, which ran from Quinéville to le Port Brehay on the River Merderet, 8 miles inland. The rest of Colonel Hervey A. Tribolet's 22nd Infantry Regiment was scheduled to land on Tare Green Beach at H Plus 1 Hour 25 Minutes. It was to cross the northern causeway and occupy the high ground at the east end of the Objective Line, north-west of Fontenay-sur-Mer. The remainder of the Objective Line, between Fontenay-sur-Mer and la Port Brehay was to be occupied by the 4th Division's 12th Infantry Regiment, commanded by Colonel Russell P. Reeder. The latter formation was scheduled to land at H Plus 4 Hours, and was also tasked to seize a bridge over the Merderet at la Port Brehay.[10]

This then was the plan for the Normandy amphibious assault. Perhaps the most striking feature of the plan was the variable distances the assault formations were expected to cover in the first few hours after landing. The OMAHA D-Day Phase Line, located between 4 and 5 miles inland, seems the most reasonable although it was largely dictated by the terrain. The ground immediately inland from the beach was broken and lacked roads wide enough for heavy military traffic. It was also constricted by the inundated Aure valley that ran parallel with the sea 7 miles east from Isigny, over half the OMAHA D-Day Phase Line frontage. The UTAH Objective Line appears more ambitious, being located around 10 miles from the landing beaches, but a good portion of this distance was supposed to be made through territory already secured by US airborne troops.

The British planners were more ambitious, and especially with regard to the JUNO and SWORD landings. Their D-Day objectives were the Caen–Bayeux road and Caen itself, 10 miles inland from the landing beaches. This may have been a reasonable distance for a landing exercise, but it seems a rather tall order for an opposed tactical advance carried out mainly on foot, and following hours cramped aboard landing vessels with minimal facilities. Indeed, Caen was much further from the landing beaches than the initial objectives assigned to previous landings in Sicily or the Italian mainland. At Salerno in September 1943, for example, the D-Day objectives included Salerno Harbour, Montecorvino airfield and the small town of Battipaglia, all of which were within 5 miles of the landing beaches. Despite the British 10th Corps having 23,000 men, almost a hundred tanks, 2,000 other vehicles and over 300 guns ashore within twelve hours of the landings, the badly overstretched and outnumbered German defenders were able to prevent any of these D-Day objectives being secured as planned.[11]

The Salerno example illustrates the relatively poor British record in moving rapidly inland after amphibious landings, even when issued with explicit orders to do so. In particular, there appears to have been an over-concentration on the disembarkation process, a tendency which can be traced back at least as far as Gallipoli in 1915 and also occurred at Anzio in January 1944. In assigning Caen as an immediate D-Day objective, therefore, the planners may have been partly motivated by a desire to offset this tendency to tarry on or near the beach. If so, it is doubly ironic that the failure to reach Caen on D-Day has been a recurring criticism of the British performance on D-Day. Not only were the formations assigned to achieve that objective facing the most formidable portion of the Normandy defences, but they were not provided with all the available intelligence on the opposition either.

The area between Caen and the SWORD and JUNO landing areas was the only part of the invasion frontage where the German defences had been developed in depth. In addition to three fortified gun batteries, the two mile zone immediately behind the beaches contained eight *Stützpunkte* and sixteen *Wiederstandneste*.[12] These were self-contained positions manned by up to a platoon of infantry in the latter case, and a company or more in the former, and included machine guns, mortar and anti-tank bunkers, linked by trenches and surrounded by barbed wire and mines. They were sited to provide mutual support, which meant any direct Allied advance toward Caen would be anything but a quick and straightforward matter.

In addition, this line of advance led straight to the nearest and most potent of the German units positioned for a rapid response. *21 Panzer Division*, commanded by *Generalleutnant* Edgar Feuchtinger, was *Heeresgruppe B's* reserve formation and had been quartered around Caen since the end of April 1944, a fact known to the Allied planners well in advance of the invasion. French agents appear to have informed SHAEF intelligence that German armour was arriving at Caen on 10 May 1944,[13] which was confirmed by ULTRA decrypts five days later.[14] Thus SHAEF Weekly Intelligence Summaries reported *21 Panzer's* departure from Rennes on 13 May 1944 and confirmed its presence at Caen a few days later.[15] How rapidly this information was disseminated is clear from a similar document issued by British 2nd Army HQ on 22 May 1944. This explicitly highlighted the danger posed by the *21* and *12 SS Panzer Divisions*, specifically warned of the likelihood of immediate counter-attack by the former, and warned that the latter could expected to weigh in strongly by the evening of D-Day.[16]

However, all this information does not appear to have been passed down to the men at the sharp end. The British 3rd Infantry Division was aware of 'unconfirmed reports' that *21 Panzer Division* was located on its front from at least 14 May 1944, but laboured under the illusion it was quartered around Falaise, 30 miles south of Caen.[17] This misconception may have arisen through confusion between the *21 Panzer* and the *12 SS Panzer Division*, which moved into the Falaise area at around the same time the *21 Panzer Division* arrived at Caen. Be that as it may, both the British and Canadian 3rd Infantry and British 50th Infantry Divisions were passing the same erroneous information down to their subordinate formations over a week later, as they moved into their sealed concentration areas.[18] These final intelligence updates were accompanied by general warnings that large numbers of German tanks located 20 or more miles inland might be encountered at some point after landing. That, however, was a long way short of providing all the verified and relevant information to the assault troops, as they had a right to expect. This was all the more serious because *21 Panzer Division*'s *Panzergrenadier Regiment 192*, reinforced with an anti-tank unit, was deployed on the Périers Ridge, just over 4 miles north-west of Caen. It was thus perfectly positioned to block any advance on Caen from the SWORD landing beaches.[19]

This was clearly a dangerous basis on which to embark on a mission as vital as that of securing the left flank of the invasion area. The omission is all the more puzzling given the efficiency of the OVERLORD intelligence gathering effort generally. As one writer has suggested, the information may simply have became lost in the great mass of intelligence being routinely processed on German activity in France.[20] This is perfectly possible, although one would have assumed that intelligence relating directly to the initial D-Day assault would have accorded a higher priority than say, the activities of German formations in the south of France. There is another, less palatable possibility. This is that someone at British 2nd Army HQ deliberately suppressed the information, possibly to avoid upsetting carefully worked out and rehearsed plans, or perhaps to avoid damping the morale of the troops.

This may sound far fetched, but it is precisely what happened three months later, in the run up to Operation Market Garden. On that occasion British 1st Airborne Corps HQ deliberately withheld intelligence indicating the presence of SS armoured units from the British 1st Airborne Division. The officer who uncovered the intelligence was swiftly diagnosed as suffering from nervous exhaustion, and was given the option of immediate compulsory sick leave or a court martial. The information did not appear in the intelligence summaries on which the 1st Airborne Division based its planning to seize the bridges at Arnhem.[21] The men at the sharp end would likely not have appreciated the distinction, but the stakes on D-Day were higher than for Market Garden, and thus presented even greater temptation to avoid rocking the boat at the last minute.

Be that as it may, these then were the units tasked to carry out what remains the greatest amphibious operation in history. Before examining how the plan translated in practice, however, it may be illuminating to take a look at how the invasion force was gathered and organised, and the precise manner in which the venture was launched.

6

ON THE BRINK
IMMEDIATE PREPARATIONS AND
LAUNCHING THE INVASION

20 MAY-5 JUNE 1944

Having examined the initial Normandy plan and those tasked to carry it out, all that remains is to detail the sequence of events leading up to the launch of the invasion. However, the execution of the best plan can only be as good as the men tasked to carry it out. In order to gain a properly rounded picture of the events in Normandy, therefore, we shall first make a brief examination of the condition and training of the units assigned to the invasion, and especially those committed to the initial landing. This is doubly advisable as there appear to be a number of misconceptions surrounding the issue.

For example, there is a widespread perception that the American conscript selection system resulted in a US Army above the national average in health, education and general intelligence.[1] Overall this may have been true, but it was not the case in the infantry. With the exception of the all-volunteer parachute and Ranger units, US Army infantry formations at the time of the Normandy invasion contained a preponderance of personnel from the lower recruitment categories, while their rear echelon counterparts were manned with a high proportion of men from the top two categories. In practice, the US system boiled down to allowing all the US Army's constituent branch to take their pick of the conscript pool, and then assigning what was left to the Infantry Branch. A large-scale investigation in November 1944 showed that the US infantryman was physically below the US Army average, being almost an inch and a half shorter than men from other branches.[2] The drawbacks of this were recognised and rectified, initially by redirecting higher calibre personnel into the infantry replacement system, but the beneficial effects were not apparent until well after the Normandy invasion.

This casts a rather different light on the equally common claim that the US Army assigned to the Normandy invasion was, while inexperienced, better trained, educated and physically fitter than its British counterpart. According to this view, the British spent the entire time since 1940 sitting in barracks, or being badly beaten and/or surrendering to the Germans or Japanese at various times and locations, and its only victory at El Alamein had been achieved against an 'undersupplied, outgunned and outmanned' enemy. This was, apparently, due to the fact that the British lacked a killer instinct, because their equipment was inferior to its German and American equivalents, and because the War Office was '…afraid to impose discipline too strictly in a democratic army on the odd notion that it might dampen the fighting spirit of the men in the ranks'.[3]

There is undoubtedly an element of truth in this. However, the same facile analysis could be used to criticise the American defeat and surrender to the Japanese in the Philippines, and for the humiliating setback at German hands in North Africa *after* El Alamein. It could also be pointed out that it was the US rather than the allegedly poorly disciplined British Army that was obliged to resort to capital punishment in late 1944 in an effort to stem a wave of indiscipline, and particularly desertion. That aside, the crux of the matter is that this view of the British Liberation Army is quite simply wrong. It is based on flawed and highly selective evidence, including the hoary chestnuts that the British happily and regularly abandoned operations to brew tea, lacked initiative and surrendered readily once fuel and ammunition began to run low.[4] This somewhat sweeping condemnation appears to be based on German testimony from the initial stages of the desert war, and presumably based in no small measure on British rear echelon troops overtaken by Rommel's rapid armoured thrusts.

Be that as it may, this popular perception overlooks the fact that the British Army was still relearning its business at that time. More crucially, the British Army of mid-1944 was a very different animal, not least through strenuous efforts to gather, analyse and disseminate the combat experience accrued by its constituent elements in a number of ways. As we have seen, the battle tested British 7th Armoured and 50th and 51st Infantry Divisions had been brought back to the UK to act as an experienced leavening for the Normandy invasion force. There was also a programme of posting officers with combat experience to untried formations to provide a similar leavening from within. In the 6th Airborne Division, Brigadier James Hill and Lieutenant-Colonel Alastair Pearson were transferred in to command the 3rd Parachute Brigade and 8th Parachute Battalion respectively, for example.[5] Similarly, John Foley's memoir of service as a Troop commander in an armoured regiment includes an amusing account of the impact of a new, combat experienced Squadron Commander on the preparation of his unit for Normandy.[6]

These programmes were paralleled by organisational and administrative measures. Following an initiative by the 47th Division in mid-1941, a Battle School was established under GHQ auspices at Barnard Castle in December 1941 to oversee low-level tactical training, and every division the UK was ordered to create similar training facilities shortly thereafter. A School of Infantry was set up in July 1942, tasked to formulate a common tactical doctrine for employment across the Army.[7] The War Office disseminated tactical experience and innovations through publications such as the monthly Army Tactical Memorandums or ATMs, and the 'Current Reports from Overseas' or CROs. The latter were produced on a monthly and often weekly basis, and contained accounts and analysis of recent actions. CRO No. 4, dated 26 June 1943, contained four sections entitled 'A division in the battle for Tunis', 'Notes on patrols', 'Artillery in North Africa' and 'The German ten commandments for employment of tanks', for example.[8]

This is not to suggest that the British Army of 1944 was perfect, far from it. Senior officers including Montgomery were not above suppressing or censoring the material compiled for publication in the CROs.[9] The measures detailed above did not totally centralise the

Army's tactical training and doctrine,[10] the battle drills created by the Battle Schools were often implemented as rigid *diktats* rather than as flexible guides, and co-operation between infantry and armour was often found wanting. Neither were all the experienced units brought in to provide leavening suitable or indeed inclined for that role. A replacement officer posted to the 4th Armoured Brigade after its return from the Mediterranean found his new unit was virtually burned out. Senior NCOs in the 1st Battalion, The Royal Tank Regiment complained openly to their commanding officer that they had done their bit in North Africa and Sicily, and relayed similar sentiments from their wives. The 3rd RTR went further, painting slogans including 'No Second Front' on their barracks in Aldershot and coming close to actual mutiny in the opinion of a staff officer witness.[11] On some occasions the discontent may have become potentially murderous; one company commander found a number of live hand-grenades rigged as booby-traps in a camp recently vacated by a similarly disgruntled unit.[12] Neither was this war weariness confined to individual battalions. The British 7th Armoured Division, for example, did not perform especially well in Normandy or thereafter, and retained a reputation for stickiness that outlasted several different commanders.[13]

However, this kind of behaviour was the exception rather than the rule, and does not alter the fact that the British Liberation Army was arguably the best trained and equipped British conscript force ever committed to battle. In particular, the units assigned to the initial wave of the cross-Channel assault do not seem to have been affected. The British 50th Infantry Division returned to the UK with good morale, which withstood rumours of expendability in the forthcoming invasion.[14] For their part, the untried British 6th Airborne and 3rd British and Canadian Infantry Divisions were eager to put their training into practice, and the latter to also put an end to long years of inactivity.

The US Army formations assigned to the invasion suffered similar problems. The US 1st Infantry Division had established an exemplary battlefield reputation alongside one for off-duty indiscipline, thanks to the antics of its personnel in Tunisia and Oran. This led to the

Divisional commander being replaced before the formation sailed from Sicily to the UK in November 1943. Major-General Clarence R. Huebner was a strict disciplinarian, but could not prevent his men objecting vociferously to being placed in the forefront of their third amphibious invasion. Similar sentiments were expressed by troops from the US 9th Infantry Division which was shipped to the UK for the Normandy invasion at the same time[15]; the untried US 4th and 29th Divisions do not appear to have suffered from morale problems of this nature. Whichever, the most significant problem faced by the US divisions lay in the sufficiency and nature of their training. Arriving in the UK in January 1944, the US 4th Infantry Division had only around fifteen weeks to get into shape, sharpen its skills and undergo specialist assault training. The 29th Division had been in the UK since October 1942, but did not begin serious training until Major-General Charles Gerhardt assumed command in July 1943. This seems to have consisted mainly of route marching across Dartmoor until September and December 1943, when assault and amphibious training facilities respectively became available.[16]

There were two dedicated facilities, both in the West Country.[17] The US Army Assault Training Centre was located near Woolacombe on the north Devon coast, and consisted of 4 miles of beach and a replica of a German strongpoint, complete with concrete bunkers and other defences.[18] Although activated in April 1943, it did not open until September, when the 29th Division's three infantry regiments cycled individually through the Centre's three week course. This included boat training with LCAs and LCTs, small unit tactics, live firing and practice with engineer equipment including flame-throwers and Bangalore torpedoes.[19] The second facility was an amphibious training area set up at Slapton Sands. This was a five-mile stretch of beach running north from Start Point on the south Devon coast, with a large live-fire training area extending inland behind it.[20] Landing exercises commenced in December 1943, and exercises codenamed DUCK, PARROT, BEAVER, TIGER and FABIUS I through VI were held before the invasion was launched. Amphibious and live fire training is hazardous by nature, but the danger level was increased by the possibility of interference from German E-Boats. On the night of 26-27 April 1944 nine of the latter attacked a convoy en route to Slapton Sands for Exercise TIGER, and sank the fully laden LSTs. Four hundred and thirteen men were lost, two hundred and seventy of which were missing, and the fact that two engineer officers were BIGOT cleared sparked a security alert until their bodies were accounted for.[21]

Slapton Sands and the Assault Training Centre were indisputably useful facilities, but their benefits were more restricted than a cursory examination suggests. As we have seen, the Assault Training Centre was only capable of handling a single infantry regiment or equivalent at a time, and it did not open until September 1943. Given that the invasion force moved into closed camps in the latter half of May 1944, and that the Centre's course ran for three weeks, there was only sufficient time to run a maximum of twelve training cycles. This was not much considering that the three assault divisions contained three infantry regiments apiece, and that the two-battalion Ranger Provisional Group, the 82nd and 101st Airborne Division and various engineer formations also needed to use the Centre's facilities. In the event, the US 4th Infantry Division's three infantry regiments cycled through the Centre once each, as did two of the 29th Division's sub-units; the 116th Infantry Regiment managed a second visit. None of the 1st Division's units attended the Centre, allegedly because the formation's combat experience made such training superfluous.[22] This meant that in effect, most of the D-Day assault units embarked for Normandy with a maximum of three weeks specialised training, plus however many practice landings they carried out at Slapton Sands. Whether this was sufficient would not become apparent until the assault formations went ashore in earnest in Normandy.

Be that as it may, the training clock ran out in the latter half of May 1944. Thereafter all the invasion troops undertook a two stage move that would lead to their embarkation on the vessels that would carry them to Normandy, first to concentration areas and then to marshalling areas near their embarkation points. The concentration areas were codenamed 'Sausages', due to their map outline, and stretched along the south coast of England from Falmouth to

Newhaven, and up to 100 miles or more inland. The 5th Battalion the East Yorkshire Regiment, which was slated for the first wave onto the GOLD landing area, moved into a camp in Canning Town, near London docks, for example.[23] Placement was dictated partly by the location of the formation involved, and partly by their objective. Thus the US 29th Division was concentrated along the Cornish coast between Falmouth and Plymouth, the US 4th Division from Plymouth to Exmouth, and the US 1st Division between Weymouth and Poole. The British 50th Infantry Division and Canadian 3rd Infantry Divisions concentrated in the area of Southampton and Portsmouth, and the British 3rd Infantry between Portsmouth and Newhaven. The airborne divisions were concentrated near the airfields where their transport and tug aircraft were based. The US 101st and British 6th Airborne Divisions thus occupied overlapping areas running east from Exeter to Newbury, and north from Salisbury to Oxford respectively. The US 82nd Airborne Division was concentrated 150 miles to the north, around Nottingham and Leicester.

Merely getting the troops slated for the amphibious operation and all their vehicles and equipment into the assembly areas was a Herculean task, and a masterpiece of staff work in its own right. Traffic Control Posts manned by Royal Military Police regulated road movements across the whole of the south of England. Vast tented camps, surrounded by barbed wire, armed military police and adorned with signs warning the public to stay clear had been erected to accommodate the troops, complete with twenty-four-hour cookhouses and temporary cinemas. A force of 54,000 men, including 4,500 specially trained cooks, was required to man and run these camps, which also employed 3,800 trucks for troop and supply movements. Neither was this a totally risk-free activity; a German air raid on the night of 30 May inadvertently hit one of the 29th Division's marshalling areas near Falmouth.[24]

British units assigned to camps equipped and run by the Americans counted themselves especially fortunate, and not just because the food was of a generally higher standard. Commandos from the 1st Special Service Brigade were impressed to discover that their accommodation

not only included one officially designated urinal bucket per tent for
night use, but also a US Army private to empty them in the morning.
Similarly, a soldier from the Green Howards noted that American
cookhouses provided three separate containers of hot water for the
men to rinse out their mess tins in sequence. British practice was to
provide a single dixie, which rapidly became an unsavoury grey soup
for all except the first few lucky users.[25] Even American troops considered their treatment above average; a member of the 116th Infantry
Regiment reported the food at his concentration area being the best
of his entire military career, and recalled being allowed plenty of
opportunity for sleep, sport and other recreational activities.[26]

The camps in the concentration and marshalling areas were sealed
as each formation completed their final rehearsal exercises, and some
units spent almost a month in confinement as a result. The real destination of the invasion could then be revealed, allowing the troops to
be fully briefed, provided with intelligence updates as appropriate,
and to make final preparations. For vehicle and particularly tank
crews, the latter process had actually begun up to several weeks previously. All vehicles assigned to the landing had to be waterproofed,
even if they were scheduled for delivery onto the beach. For tanks
especially this was a messy and laborious task that involved filing every
rivet on the belly of the vehicle clean before coating them with
waterproof paint, and sealing inspection plates, periscope housings,
hatches and the turret ring with rubber solution and balloon fabric.
Lengths of explosive detonator cord were included in the sealing;
these were wired up to an electrical switch to allow the waterproof-
ing to be blown off from within the vehicle. Finally, extension pipes
were fitted to engine air intakes and exhaust openings. The bulk of
this was supposed to be carried out prior to arrival, but special
Sealing Stores with all the necessary materials were located within
concentration and marshalling areas as a contingency measure. This
proved fortuitous for Lieutenant John Foley, commanding a troop of
Churchills; one of his inexperienced drivers succeeded in setting off
the detonator cord on Foley's vehicle during the road march to the
concentration area.[27]

The troops were issued with French phrase books and currency, field and emergency rations, anti-gas clothing and goggles, life preservers of various designs, seasickness pills and brown greaseproof paper bags, 'Vomit, For the Use Of'.[28] They were also issued with ammunition, grenades, mortar bombs, demolition charges and other munitions. Many of the units assigned to the first wave were provided with special assault vests in lieu or addition to their normal combat equipment. These vests, or 1942 Battle Jerkins to use the official nomenclature, had been designed by Colonel E.R. Rivers-Macpherson as an alternative to the standard British 1937 Pattern Webbing Equipment. Made of waterproofed cotton duck, the jerkin weighed less than three pounds empty, and was essentially a sleeveless jacket with a number of reinforced pockets. These had a greater carrying capacity and flexibility than the issue webbing equipment, and were favourably received by the troops.[29] They were issued to the 1st Special Service Brigade and troops from the British 3rd and 50th Infantry Divisions, and an American copy dubbed the 'Assault Vest' with slightly different pockets was issued to their US counterparts.

Some specialist troops, including Commandos and combat engineers were also issued with large, framed Bergen rucksacks originally intended for mountain and ski troops. Perhaps the most heavily laden of all were the paratroopers from the US airborne divisions. A typical load consisted of a .45 automatic pistol, M1 Garand rifle with over 100 rounds of ammunition, two cans of belted .30 machine gun ammunition, an entrenching tool, bayonet and water canteen, a Hawkins mine, a Gammon bomb, four blocks of explosive, three first aid kits, K rations for three days, two days supply of D ration chocolate, six fragmentation grenades, two smoke grenades, a cerise air identification panel, a blanket, raincoat, socks and underwear and two cartons of cigarettes. When one adds two uniforms, one worn under the other, a Mae West type life preserver, main and reserve parachutes and a steel helmet, it is scarcely surprising that many American paratroopers were unable to climb aboard their C-47s without assistance. Neither was this all. Additional items such as Bangalore torpedoes, bazooka rockets, machine-gun ammunition, medical supplies and extra rations delivered by container would have to be divided up and carried after landing.[30]

With so much lethal ordnance around, fatal accidents were perhaps inevitable. A sergeant from the 101st Airborne Division's HQ was shot in the side by a comrade demonstrating the action of his Thompson sub-machine gun.[31] Reporting the death of at least one British soldier killed by another negligent discharge was deliberately delayed so he would be listed as a combat casualty, and several assault engineers were killed when one of the wire-breaching devices they were servicing exploded.[32] Despite these tragic accidents, however, there were also lighter moments. One young British tank crewman awoke from an illicit nap atop his Sherman to find the metal heel reinforcements on his boots welded to the tank deck; the prank was his crewmates' way of marking the victim's twenty-first birthday.[33] One member of the US 4th Division's 8th Infantry Regiment spent a good deal of time burgling delicacies to order from QM stores, and on one occasion provided his comrades with garrottes made from piano wire. The wire, it transpired, had been purloined from the sole piano in the unit's recreation hall.[34] As ever, gambling proved popular and many men were swiftly relieved of their newly issued French Francs by their luckier or more astute companions, often without properly grasping the value of the unfamiliar notes.

The date of the invasion was provisionally set for Monday, 5 June 1944 via an order from Supreme Commander Eisenhower at the beginning of May 1944. The date was confirmed on 23 May, and those holding sealed copies of the NEPTUNE plan were authorised to open them on 25 May. The date and time of the invasion were then disseminated to subordinate commanders three days later. On 29 May SHAEF's senior meteorologist, Group-Captain J.M. Stagg, informed Eisenhower that there was a high probability of fair weather for the first week in June. In conjunction with the previous decision and revelation, this information set a huge military machine spread across the length of the UK into motion. The assault and initial follow up waves began boarding their assigned vessels on 30 May, a process that took three days. Each of the landing areas was assigned a specific naval force, codenamed with the first letter of the area codename. Thus

Force U, for example, carried the UTAH landing force, and Force S those assigned to SWORD. Each Force was made up of between nine and twelve separate convoys, and their sailing times were staggered according to the distance from their specific beaches.

On 31 May the Royal Navy began covertly marking the boundaries of the German minefields on the invasion route with sonic buoys, and Admiral Sir Bertram H. Ramsey assumed command of the invasion force the following day. Over the next two days the heavy units assigned to support the landings set sail from as far afield as Scotland and Northern Ireland. In the late evening of 3 June two British midget submarines, x20 and x23, left port and headed directly for the Normandy coast. Each was equipped with radio and sonar emitters, and an 18ft-high telescopic mast mounting powerful flashing lights. Their mission was to surface just before H-Hour and act as live markers for the invasion force.[35] Then, in the late evening of 3 June, Group-Captain Stagg reported a downturn in the weather. Rather than being fair, 5 June would in fact be stormy, with high winds and a cloud base no higher than 500 feet. Even worse, the erratic nature of the developing weather patterns made accurate forecasting virtually impossible. Nonetheless, the first elements of the invasion fleet began to get underway as scheduled, at 03:15 on 4 June 1944. At 04:30 on 4 June Eisenhower presided over a meeting of his senior commanders, including Montgomery and Bradley, at Admiral Ramsey's HQ at Southwick House near Portsmouth. The latest weather report indicated the sea state would probably be within acceptable bounds, but the overcast remained unchanged. Eisenhower therefore postponed the invasion for twenty-four hours.[36]

The recall signal was transmitted to the invasion fleet at 05:00 on June 4, but it almost came too late for one of the Force U convoys carrying the US 4th Infantry Division to the UTAH landing area. Because it was to be among the first to land and had the furthest distance to cover, Lieutenant-Commander George D. Hoffman's convoy had sailed from Plymouth several hours ahead of the rest of the invasion force. As a result, his convoy had closed to 38 miles from the French coast, and there was some concern that the Germans might spot them as they turned away. They remained unseen. Hoffman's passengers and those of the rest of the invasion fleet then spent a miserable day aboard their rolling and pitching vessels, battling widespread seasickness and rising tension that forced inactivity could only heighten. The vessels carrying the US 4th Infantry Division and other troops assigned to UTAH, for example, spent almost twenty-four hours circling off the Isle of Wight because it was too far to return to their ports of embarkation. Other vessels, such as those carrying the 29th Division's 115th Infantry, were able to return to port, but their luckless passengers were obliged to remain on board, their billets ashore having been occupied by the follow-on waves.[37]

Although they were at least spared the seasickness, the airborne troops fared little better. Because its airfields were located over 100 miles further north of its running mates, the 82nd Airborne Division was scheduled to begin taking-off first. Thus some of the All Americans were airborne and en route to France before the cancellation came through. The psychological impact of this can be well imagined; a British parachute officer whose unit received the postponement while fitting their parachutes described the twenty-four hour delay as being the most unnerving period in the whole invasion.[38]

The tension was, if anything, even greater at the Southwick House HQ. Eisenhower may have taken the decision to postpone and recall the invasion fleet after consulting with his senior staff, but the responsibility remained his and his alone. It was therefore a courageous judgement given the circumstances. As we have seen, there was only a three-day window when the tidal and moonlight conditions vital for the invasion coincided, on 5, 6 and 7 June. If the invasion were postponed a second time, there would be insufficient time to reorganise the sea convoys to go in on 7 June. There would be no recurrence of the necessary sea conditions until 19 June, and at that time there would be no moon, which would make the airborne landings problematic. In addition, it was not merely a matter of sitting back and waiting for 19 June to come around.

The process of getting the invasion force to their concentration and marshalling areas and onto the ships was akin to a huge conveyor belt.

Thus the camps and loading areas vacated by the units embarked in the three days leading up to 1 June had been automatically filled by the next landing wave, and so on up the chain. Simply leaving the assault wave afloat was impossible, partly because the landing vessels were neither designed nor equipped for anything more than short voyages of hours rather than days, and because of the deleterious effects such a hiatus would have on the mental and physical health of the troops. The other alternative was barely less daunting. Attempting to unload the assault wave in the conditions cited above was a virtual recipe for chaos, and one that might well take longer than two weeks to disentangle. It would also entail a very high risk of compromising the security screen that had been so painstakingly maintained over the invasion preparations. In short, by postponing the invasion Eisenhower was facing the very real prospect of being responsible for the ruination of Allied hopes for opening a second front against the Germans.

As if that were not enough, the decision of whether or not to go ahead with the invasion after the twenty-four-hour postponement had to be taken no later than 22:00 on 4 June. Any later and there would be insufficient time to reorganise the naval convoys to rendezvous for a dawn assault on 6 June. At around midday on 4 June, Group-Captain Stagg's meteorologists detected a developing break between two incoming weather fronts in the Atlantic that might conceivably improve conditions in the Channel. At 21:30 Stagg passed the news on to Eisenhower and the other senior commanders at Southwick House, and predicted a short period of improved weather beginning in the afternoon of Monday 5 June. It was likely to continue into Tuesday 6 June, with not more than 50 per cent cloud cover, a cloud base above 2-3,000 feet, and moderate winds of between 25 and 30 knots. The ensuing discussion did little to assist Eisenhower in choosing which course to follow. Admiral Ramsey merely reiterated the ramifications of failing to reach a decision by 22:00. The two RAF representatives, Air Chief Marshals Leigh-Mallory and Tedder, felt that the predicted weather was still too poor for effective bombing.

Only Montgomery was unconditionally supportive, recommending emphatically that the invasion be launched forthwith. At 21:45 Eisenhower announced his decision: 'I'm quite positive we must give the order... I don't like it, but there it is... I don't see how we can possibly do anything else.'[39]

Eisenhower's decision prompted a flurry of activity. The signal rescheduling the invasion for Tuesday 6 June had been transmitted and acknowledged by the landing fleet by 23:00, and within an hour the invasion convoys had begun to reform for the voyage across the Channel. Eisenhower retired to his caravan located near Southwick House to snatch a few hours sleep, but was up again at 03:30 for the latest weather update and a final staff meeting. The weather remained unpromising, with high winds and heavy rain, but Group-Captain Stagg's briefing contained both good and bad news. Meteorological reports showed the predicted improvement in the weather was more certain, and the current storm was predicted to end by dawn on 5 June. However, the improvement would likely only extend through Tuesday 6 June before deteriorating again on 7 June. This raised the unpalatable prospect of the initial waves being cut off from support if the weather worsened to the point where the follow up units could not be landed. Opinion among the senior commanders remained divided along previously established lines. Once again, the weight of decision lay solely with Eisenhower. He talked over the pros and cons for some minutes while pacing around the conference room. Finally, at 04:15 on Monday 5 June, he stopped, turned to face the assembled officers and said 'OK, let's go.'[40]

Thus was launched the largest combined airborne and amphibious landing in the history of warfare.

7

D-DAY
H MINUS 6 HOURS 30 MINUTES
TO H-HOUR

(00:30 TO 06:30, TUESDAY 6 JUNE 1944)

The twenty-four-hour postponement left the 20,000 strong Allied airborne spearhead in limbo for several hours. In American units this was perhaps softened by the pre-embarkation meal of unlimited steak with all the trimmings, followed by ice cream.[1] It was probably not the case with the 1st Battalion, 508th Parachute Infantry, which returned from its nerve-stretching false start to torrential rain that collapsed troop tents, one of which was also struck by lightning.[2] The 506th Parachute Infantry also spent a soggy night at Upottery after humping all their kit to flight line in the rain, and back again after the cancellation. At RAF Tarrant Rushton, officers from the 2nd Ox and Bucks finished off two bottles of whiskey, while their men repaired to the camp cinema tent.[3]

Confirmation that the invasion was on again was received at midday on Monday 5 June 1944. Thereafter, the day passed in much the same way as Sunday 4 June, except the weather was clear and sunny, if windy in places. Briefings were repeated, weapons and equipment were checked, double-checked and checked again. The 506th Parachute Infantry, at least, were supplied with another special meal, but with fried chicken instead of steak, while British airborne units were served a special fat-free meal as an anti-airsickness measure.[4] At Broadwell, the 9th Parachute Battalion was ordered to bed in the afternoon for a last-minute sleep.[5] At Tarrant Rushton, the TONGA glider pilots spent the early afternoon sunbathing, before being issued with cigarettes, two compo ration packs and morphine for their first aid kits. At 16:00 they had a final showing of the aerial approach film before their preliminary briefing.[6]

The troops moved to their aircraft in the late afternoon or early evening. It took the 101st Airborne's HQ Company an hour to reach RAF Greenham Common, travelling via the centre of Newbury. The local population, inured to convoys of fully armed American para-troopers and unaware of the significance of their journey, paid little attention. Many of the 6th Airborne's paratroopers were also driven to their airfields, often amid ribald banter with rear echelon personnel. A correspondent for *The Times* witnessed the surreal sight of a truckload of British airborne soldiers belting out the Nazi-street fighting anthem, the 'Horst Wessel' song.[7] At Upottery the 506th Parachute Infantry simply marched to the aircraft from their adjacent camp, with sticks of men peeling off as they reached their designated C-47.

The paratroopers then busied themselves fitting parachutes, apply-ing personal camouflage with grease paint, burnt cork or soot, and making last minute adjustments to their kit. They nonetheless found time to avail themselves of free char (tea) and wads (sandwiches), or coffee and doughnuts for the Americans, dispensed from specially provided canteen trucks. At North Witham the 508th Parachute Infantry were presented with free Pall Mall cigarettes by the American Red Cross, and all American paratroopers were issued Dramamine pills as an anti-nausea measure; at least one unit ordered the troops to take the pills under the supervision of an NCO.[8] Air Marshal Leigh-Mallory visited several airfields including RAF Harwell where he talked to the 6th Airborne's commander, Major-General Richard Gale, shortly before the latter's departure. Eisenhower visited the 502nd Parachute Infantry at Greenham Common, and mingled among the troops asking names, enquiring about hometowns and wishing everyone good luck. The visit went down extremely well, although one officer who spoke to Eisenhower rightly suspected the moral boost went both ways.[9] Eisenhower remained while the troops emplaned at dusk and watched from a rooftop until the last C-47 was airborne.

The troops began boarding an hour before dark, and it was not an effortless procedure. As cited above, the American paratroopers were loaded down with immense loads of ammunition, rations and other equipment; one sergeant from the 506th Parachute Infantry estimated his load doubled his body weight to 250 pounds.[10] British parachutists used kit bags, reinforced versions of the standard item, capable of carrying up to eighty pounds, fastened to the paratrooper's leg with a quick release device. The device was operated after the parachute deployed, and left the kit bag suspended on a 20ft rope.[11] The US 506th Parachute Infantry was issued with leg bags, as the Americans called them, just before the Normandy jump.[12] Most, however, simply crammed items into jump suit pockets and strapped knives, field dressings, ammunition and explosive devices like Hawkins grenades to their lower limbs,[13] a hazardous and potentially lethal expedient. At RAF Spanhoe there was an explosion as the 505th Parachute Infantry were boarding; three men were killed, ten wounded and the aircraft caught fire.[14]

British paratroopers were no less heavily laden; one likened his comrades to 'pregnant ducks carrying everything but the kitchen sink'.[15] In addition to a parachute, a typical load included a Sten gun and several magazines, a .45 automatic, a fighting knife, two pints of water, a forty-eight-hour ration pack, groundsheet, two Bren gun magazines, two belts of Vickers machine-gun ammunition, four pounds of plastic explosive, two hand grenades, a GS shovel, wire cutters, three spare radio batteries, spare underwear and socks, washing and shaving kit, mess tins and, most importantly of all, an enamel tea mug.[16] That this load was borne by a company commander from the 13th Parachute Battalion emphasises the point. The British burden was exacerbated by the unsuitability of the converted bombers the RAF used as parachute transports. Boarding the Armstrong-Whitworth Albemarle involved literally crawling under the rear of the aircraft and heaving oneself through a small hatch into a narrow, low and seatless fuselage, for example. The process was invariably accompanied by a good deal of sweat, swearing and bad temper.[17]

First off were twenty C-47s carrying 260 pathfinders from the American airborne divisions, which took off at around 22:00. Their mission was to mark the six DZs behind the UTAH beaches with EUREKA beacons and Holophane lights. The latter were to be set out at twenty-five yard intervals in a T shape, with the stem following the line of flight; the lights were colour coded by DZ, and flashed the DZ code-letters in Morse.[18] One aircraft carrying thirteen pathfinders from the 101st Airborne ditched after a malfunction; paratroopers and crew were rescued. No further problems were encountered until they reached the Cotentin Peninsula, where the remaining nineteen aircraft ran into an unexpected layer of low cloud and associated turbulence. Formation was lost as pilots instinctively sought to avoid collision, and the error was exacerbated by German flak on leaving the cloudbank.

Thus most of the American pathfinders were dropped wide of their designated DZs. Sergeant Elmo Jones' team, which was assigned to mark the 82nd Airborne's DZ O north-west of St Mère Église, were dropped accurately but low; Jones' parachute had barely opened when he hit the ground.[19] At least two of the team tasked to mark DZ N also arrived in the right place, and set up their EUREKA beacon without interference.[20] The remainder made some unwelcome discoveries. The dense embanked hedgerows that divide the small fields in the Normandy region, called *bocage*, were a far more formidable obstacle than aerial photographs suggested, and made cross-country move-ment a nightmare. Aerial photography also failed to detect a far more insidious threat. The Germans had deliberately flooded the area adja-cent to the rivers Merderet and Douve, creating large tracts of inun-dated land indistinguishable from normal grassland from the air. The stray pathfinders discovered this the hard way, and some drowned in water up to 6-feet deep. Those that managed to wade to safety or landed dry shod had all too little time find their assigned location, for the first echelon of the main force was only thirty minutes away.

The British DEADSTICK force began taking off from Tarrant Rushton at 22:56.[21] Six Albemarles carrying pathfinders from the 22nd Independent Parachute Company took off from RAF Harwell between 23:00 and 23:20; each of the 6th Airborne's three DZs were assigned two sticks of pathfinders as a redundancy measure.[22]

They were followed by another sixteen Albemarles carrying elements of the 9th Parachute Battalion, 3rd Parachute Brigade HQ and the 1st Canadian Parachute Battalion. The Canadians were to provide security for DZ V. At around the same time five more Albemarles, carrying the lead elements of the 5th Parachute Brigade, left RAF Brize Norton in Oxfordshire.[23]

The remainder of the 6th Airborne's first lift was divided into three parts, the first and largest of which was to trail the pathfinders by half an hour. It consisted of 239 Dakotas and Stirlings and seventeen Horsa gliders, carrying the bulk of the 3rd and 5th Parachute Brigades and their heavy equipment. They were scheduled to land at DZ N, north of Ranville, and DZ K between the villages of Escoville and Sannerville at 00:50. The second, scheduled to arrive at DZ N at 03:20, was made up of sixty-five Horsas and four Hamilcars carrying 6th Airborne HQ, most of the Divisional units and an anti-tank battery. The third consisted of three Horsas, carrying airborne sappers and men from the 9th Parachute Battalion, and was scheduled to land atop the Merville Battery at 04:30.[24] A further wave of 220 Horsas and thirty Hamilcars carrying the 6th Airlanding Brigade and Divisional units was to land on DZ N at 21:00.

The initial wave was scheduled to land at 00:20, but the DEADSTICK force landed slightly earlier. The three gliders assigned to the Orne Canal Bridge were to approach LZ X, on the narrow strip of land between the River Orne and Orne Canal, from the south. The lead machine was flown by Staff-Sergeants Jim Wallwork and John Ainsworth, and carried Major Howard and Lieutenant Den Brotheridge's 25 Platoon. The second, carrying Lieutenant David Wood's 24 Platoon, was piloted by Staff-Sergeant Oliver Boland and Sergeant Bruce Hobbs, and the third by Staff-Sergeant Geoff Hobbs and Sergeant Peter Boyle. The latter contained 14 Platoon, commanded by Lieutenant R.A.A. 'Sandy' Smith.[25] The lead Horsa was released at 00:07, and began its final run in at 00:15, with the order to passengers to link arms and brace for impact. As the Horsa's under-carriage touched down Wallwork deployed and jettisoned the drogue parachute specially fitted to the DEADSTICK gliders. This brought his speed down from 90 to 60 miles per hour, raised the machine's tail and forced the nose wheel into the ground. The machine then bounced, tearing off its wheels, and skidded before coming to a dead stop.

Howard had asked the pilots to land as close as possible to an earth bank carrying the road, 25 yards from the bridge; Wallwork rammed his glider into it. Both pilots went through the windscreen, unconscious and still strapped to their seats. They were thus arguably the first Allied troops to touch French soil. The second glider came down precisely sixty seconds later, and had to swerve to avoid collision, breaking its back and throwing Lieutenant Wood clear in the process. The third landed intact, but skidded into a pond to the right of the LZ. The two front seat passengers were ejected through the windscreen, another was killed and several were trapped in the partly submerged fuselage. The time was 00:18, three minutes since Wallwork commenced his run in.

The violence of the landing temporarily stunned the occupants of the lead glider. Nonetheless, they were out of the wreckage and moving toward their objective before the second glider touched down. The presumably inexperienced German sentry patrolling on the canal bridge heard the glider crash-land, but assumed it was part of a damaged bomber falling to earth; instead of investigating he continued his route away from that side of the bridge. When he turned to retrace his steps he was confronted by Lieutenant Brotheridge and most of 25 Platoon erupting out of the darkness towards him. Behind them three men were grenading a bunker believed to hold the firing mechanism for the bridge demolition charges. On the LZ, 24 Platoon were gathering around the fortunately uninjured Lieutenant Wood, preparing to launch their assault on the trenches and gun pits along the canal's east bank. A matter of yards away Lieutenant Smith was rallying 14 Platoon before crossing the bridge to assist 25 Platoon in clearing the German defences on the western bank.

The sentry sensibly took to his heels. Another fired the first shot of the engagement, and a third fired a signal flare and was promptly killed. 25 Platoon, shouting 'Able! Able!' fanned out to deal with the defences. One of the attackers, temporarily tongue-tied by a tension-dry mouth, rectified the problem by hurling foul language. The proprietor of the bridge-side Café Gondrée made the mistake of showing himself at a window, which was promptly shattered by a burst of automatic fire. He wisely and rapidly withdrew with his family to the cellar.

The firefight was prolonged briefly by an NCO from *Fallschirmjäger Regiment 6* who had driven west over the bridge only minutes before. Recognising his British counterparts and disgusted by the poor performance of the bridge guard, he exchanged fire with 25 and 14 Platoons until his ammunition was expended, and then retired to raise the alarm. The sole survivor from the bridge guard fled to his commander's billet in Benouville village. Two off-duty men amusing themselves in a nearby brothel did the same, after firing all their ammunition into the air to support a tale of fighting with the attackers.[26] Meanwhile the airborne sappers discovered that the bridge was not rigged for demolition; the charges were stored in a nearby shed. This and word that the bridge was secure was relayed to Major Howard, who had established his command post in a cleared trench, at 00:24, eight minutes after the first glider touched down.

Events did not unfold as planned at the Orne River Bridge. The first Horsa into LZ Y, flown by Staff-Sergeants Roy Howard and Fred Baacke and carrying Lieutenant Dennis Fox and 17 Platoon, landed unscathed within 300 metres of the objective at 00:20. This was no mean feat, as the LZ was bounded with tall trees. They were followed by Staff-Sergeants Pearson and Guthrie, with 23 Platoon commanded by Lieutenant H.J. Sweeney. The third glider was carrying the DEAD-STICK second in command, Captain Brian Priday and Lieutenant Tony Hooper's 22 Platoon, and was flown by Staff-Sergeants Lawrence and Shorter. Their Horsa was released awry, after the Halifax crew mistook the mouth of the River Dives for that of the Orne. They landed near a bridge over the Dives at la Bac de Varaville, 8 miles east of their real target; ironically, it appears this was one of the 1st Canadian Parachute Battalion's objectives for later that night. After reorganising and realising their error, in the process of which Lieutenant Hooper was captured and then rescued by Priday, they set out for Benouville.[27]

Back at the Orne River Bridge, 17 Platoon suppressed a lone machine gun with two-inch mortar fire and found it otherwise undefended. Sweeney's platoon arrived shortly thereafter, and the two platoons rapidly established a defensive perimeter and radioed Howard that their objective was secure. Howard immediately ordered his radio-operator to transmit the success signal 'Ham and Jam' and not to stop until he received an acknowledgement.[28] The DEADSTICK force thus succeeded in securing both their objectives within fifteen minutes of touchdown. In the process all three platoon commanders from the LZ X force became casualties. Lieutenant Brotheridge was killed in the melee at the west end of the bridge, Lieutenant Smith was wounded by grenade shrapnel nearby shortly thereafter, and Lieutenant Wood received three bullets in the leg while moving back to report the west bank cleared.

Things did not run so smoothly for the 22nd Independent Parachute Company's pathfinders. Two sticks were supposed to have been delivered to DZs N, K and V, but thanks to cloud and poor navigation only one pathfinder team was dropped accurately, and some aircraft had to make two, and in at least one case, three runs over their respective DZs. The official history blames this on poor aircraft drills, although the real reason was the unsuitability of the Albemarle, as the following episode clearly demonstrates.[29]

The team commander in one of the DZ N aircraft fell half out of the floor hatch whilst opening the doors over the English Channel. The number two in the stick was either not strong enough or too heavily encumbered to help which obliged the number three, Sergeant Len Drake, to climb around him to help. Because of the cramped fuselage – there were no seats and the lack of height obliged paratroopers to 'bunny hop' along the floor to the hatch – Drake first had to unstrap his kit bag containing a EUREKA beacon. Unable to pull him to safety, Drake hung on until the aircraft was over land when the team commander chose to drop independently. Drake struggled back to his place in the stick, but the number two was then unable to fully open the hatch, obliging Drake to squeeze back again. He opened and secured the hatch just as the red stand-by light went on, followed swiftly by the green jump light. Drake could not simply drop because his static line was entangled with that of the number two, which would have been fatal for both men; he also needed to reach his kit bag. He therefore requested the pilot go round again for another pass, through a hail of flak. Even then Drake was unable to re-attach his kit bag and jumped with it clasped in his arms.[30]

The pathfinders assigned to DZ N were dropped wide and did not reach their assigned location for thirty minutes, by which time the main force were beginning to jump. A team destined for DZ K dropped onto DZ N and, not realising their mistake, set up their EUREKA beacon and Holophane lights. In some instances standing crops obscured markers, and one set was set out correctly but well away from any of the assigned DZs. The advance parties also ran into trouble. Brigadier Poett, the 5th Parachute Brigade's commander, found himself alone. Unable to see any of the recommended visual reference points, he began moving toward the noise of the firefight at the Orne Canal Bridge instead. There was also the enemy to contend with. Private Arthur Platt of the 22nd Independent was captured by a German patrol while laying out flares on DZ K; his captors executed him on the spot.[31]

At DZ V Lieutenant Donald Wells' pathfinder team landed in good order, and rapidly set out two Ts of green Holophane lights and a EUREKA beacon. The 9th Parachute Battalion stick used an unorthodox exit drill of their own invention, and almost all landed accurately and in a compact group. The two exceptions were Major Allen Parry, whose parachute rigging lines were twisted by an awkward exit, and the last man in the stick, Sergeant Sid Knight, whose parachute harness snagged briefly as he exited the aircraft. Both men landed safely, but wide of the DZ. The company of Canadian paratroopers was less fortunate. One stick was dropped 10 miles wide, and another on the wrong side of the Orne Canal within a mile of the SWORD invasion beaches.[32] The thirty men who landed on or near the DZ moved off to secure Varaville, half a mile to the east.[33]

The 9th Parachute contingent was made up of two five-man parties. The RV Party, led by Major Parry, was to mark out the rally points for the Battalion's various elements with white cloth markers and coloured lights. The Troubridge Party, commanded by Major George Smith and named after an admiral who carried out a vital reconnaissance for Nelson before Trafalgar, was to move straight off to reconnoitre the Merville Battery.[34] They were to assess the impact of OBOE, a raid on the battery by a hundred RAF Lancasters carrying 4,000 and 8,000 pound bombs, scheduled for 00:30.[35] OBOE came in dead on time, but overshot the target by 2,400 yards and hit DZV and the surrounding area instead. The ten-minute raid almost wiped out the Troubridge Party and nearly killed Parry, who was making his way back to the DZ with two stray Canadians. More seriously, it destroyed the EUREKA beacon and most of the Holophane lights.

Thus, when the 9th Parachute Battalion began to jump at 00:50, there were only two green lights showing, and the DZ was obscured by smoke and dust from the bombing. An unexpected twenty-five knot cross-wind and flak exacerbated the situation further. Many of the heavily laden paratroopers were thrown off their feet as their pilots took evasive action, and at least two men were prematurely ejected from their aircraft, one of them the 9th Battalion's Commander, Lieutenant-Colonel Otway. In another Dakota parachute dog Glenn's handler had to enlist help from the despatcher to drag the animal from under the seats and throw him bodily out of the door.[36] Another dog broke free as his handler exited and fled to the other end of the aircraft, obliging that despatcher to pursue, catch and eject the canine refusee alone.[37]

Half a stick from B Company almost ended up returning to England. Number fourteen became stuck in the door and by the time he was clear the red light was illuminated, stopping further jumps. The pilot at first refused to make another run despite the entreaties of the sergeant in charge of the stick, but when he relented the sergeant stopped the jump because he could see they were nowhere near the DZ. The pilot then refused point blank to go round again despite the foul language and mutinous threats emanating from the angry para-troopers, who were loath to miss out on the operation for which they had trained so hard. After discussion among the flight crew the pilot again relented, but the stick were still dropped to the east of the DZ on the edge of the inundated area along the Dives. One disgruntled sergeant from A Company was not so lucky. The last man in his stick, he was thrown off his feet and became entangled with the parachute strops clustered by the door. It took the combined efforts of the despatcher and navigator to free him, by which time the aircraft was heading for home; the pilot responded to his demand to be returned to the DZ with a two word expletive.[38]

The results were similar at the other two DZs. The wrongly placed markers at DZ N near Ranville caused fourteen aircraft to drop their sticks from the 3rd Parachute Brigade HQ and the 8th Parachute Battalion accurately but on the wrong DZ. Another stick straddled a command post belonging to *Pionier Bataillon 716* in Hérouvillette. A vicious, close range fight ensued as the paratroopers went to ground in the German billets, where they held out until relieved several hours later.[39] Elements from the 5th Parachute Brigade's formations were dropped on or near DZ K, almost 2 miles south-east of their proper destination, and many were scattered much further afield. Of the seventeen gliders attached to the main landing, six were assigned to LZ K. Only two got there. A combination of tug error and wrongly placed or missing markers put three more on DZ N, and one came down somewhere to the south of Ranville. The pilots of the latter, Staff-Sergeant W. Ridgeway and Sergeant P. Foster, were captured, although Foster escaped and was killed later fighting with the French Resistance.

The remaining eleven gliders assigned to DZ V were also dogged by ill luck. One came down in the sea after the towrope parted. There were no survivors. Staff-Sergeant Maurice Bramah and Sergeant Ron Bartley also lost their tow over the Channel, but reached the coast and came down in a wood near Villers-sur-Mer, 9 miles north east of DZ V. One Horsa landed safely at a properly configured 'T' of Holophane lights, only to discover they were nowhere near any assigned landing area. Four Horsas came down at various locations between 2 and 8 miles from their target, one in 3 feet of water near Briqueville and another in a minefield. Staff-Sergeant Victor Ockwell was killed after striking a *Rommelspargel* pole, as were Staff-Sergeant V. Saunders and Sergeant J.H. Fuell when they came down 7 miles south-east of the LZ. Two more glider pilots were injured, one losing an arm. Only one Horsa, carrying a Jeep, trailer and motor cycle actually put down on DZ V.[40]

All this had obvious implications for the 6th Airborne's plan. The 12th and 13th Parachute Battalions were to secure the area around DZ N and establish a defensive perimeter to cover the approaches to the Benouville bridges from the south and east. The bulk of the 12th Battalion was scattered to the east of the DZ, and did not begin to rally at the Battalion RV for the better part of an hour. Lieutenant-Colonel John Jackson waited as long as he dared before moving off for his objective in the area of le Bas de Ranville with only 60 per cent of his men. They got there at 04:00, and immediately began digging in. The 13th Battalion moved off in a similarly understrength condition to secure Ranville, which was also done by 04:00 after dealing with German troops in and around the town. A Company remained on the DZ, providing security for 591 Parachute Squadron RE as they demolished the *Rommelspargel* ready for the later glider landings.

The 7th Parachute Battalion, which was to move swiftly to the Benouville bridges, dropped two minutes late at 00:52. By 01:10 only between seventy and a hundred men, including Lieutenant-Colonel Pine-Coffin, had rallied to a green lamp operated by Lieutenant Rogers from the battalion's advance party. They included Captain Richard Todd, who was to portray John Howard in the feature film *The Longest Day* eighteen years later. Mindful of the vital nature of his mission, Pine-Coffin decided to move off, leaving Major Eric Steele-Baume at the RV to direct stragglers. Before the 7th Battalion arrived, however, Howard's men had received a small reinforcement and rebuffed two German attempts to penetrate their perimeter.

Brigadier Poett arrived at the Orne Road Bridge as the 7th Parachute Battalion began to jump, accompanied by a stray paratrooper private. After conferring with Sweeney he walked the 600 yards to Howard's command post. Howard was annoyed Sweeney had not warned him of the Brigadier's arrival, and he also presumably told his signaller to stop sending the Ham and Jam signal, which was supposed to be going out to Poett's HQ. Shortly afterward an open Mercedes touring car and motorcycle escort raced into Sweeney's perimeter, moving so swiftly the car was actually on the river bridge before anyone reacted. The troops on the east bank dealt with the motorcycle while those on the west riddled the car and captured its badly wounded occupants, Major Hans Schmidt and his driver. Schmidt was a company commander from *Infanterie Regiment 736*, and had been visiting his mistress in Ranville when he heard the firefight at the bridges. The driver lost both legs and died shortly afterwards while the severely shocked Schmidt alternated between telling his captors in English that the Führer would shortly throw them back into the sea and demanding they shoot him to restore his honour. He calmed down somewhat when Captain John Vaughan RAMC dosed him with morphine. To add insult to injury, Major Howard appropriated Schmidt's binoculars.

The second incident was more serious. The Benouville bridges were the responsibility of *716 Infanterie Division*, a *bodenständige* formation commanded by *Generalleutnant* Wilhelm Richter. Reports of the airborne landings began to reach Richter's HQ from 00:40, and at 01:05 the Divisional readiness level was raised in response. The British airborne *schwerpunkt* was identified in the area bounded by Benouville, Hérouvillette and Bréville. At around 01:40 control of a number of *716 Division's* sub-units west of the Orne was given to *Infanterie Regiment 736*. These included two engineer companies, *Panzerjäger Kompanie 716* and *Ost Bataillon 642*; the latter was made up of former Red Army POWs. *Infanterie Regiment 736* was ordered to concentrate at Salanelles on the east bank of the Orne and then attack into the British airhead.[41] This meant traversing the Benouville bridges, and brought them up against Howard's DEADSTICK force.

Some German units appear to have investigated the bridges on their own initiative, given that the Ox and Bucks engaged an armoured probe at 01:30, ten minutes before *716 Division* issued the attack order.[42] Howard had pushed his defensive perimeter out to the western edge of Benouville, where the route running across the bridges intersected the Caen-Ouistreham road. His sole anti-tank weapon was a PIAT wielded by Sergeant Thornton from 17 Platoon, which was located at the T-junction.[43] The DEADSTICK force were supposed to have brought a supply of Gammon bombs, but they were either left behind to lighten the load or lost after landing; the search for them caused some acrimony between Howard and Staff-Sergeant Wallwork.[44]

At around 01:30, two German armoured vehicles slowly approached the junction from Benouville. In a testament to their training, the airborne soldiers held their fire until the lead vehicle, identified as a *Panzer IV*, was within 30 yards. Sergeant Thornton then put one of his two PIAT bombs into it. The tank promptly exploded with a spectacular firework display that illuminated the surrounding area for the better part of an hour; the other tank withdrew and ascribed the destruction of the lead vehicle to a six-pounder anti-tank gun. The 7th Parachute Battalion arrived shortly afterwards and moved straight over the bridges to reinforce and expand the western perimeter.[45] The reinforcement was welcome and not before time, if depleted; by dawn the 7th Battalion still only numbered in the region of 200 men. Word of the loss of the Orne bridges reached *716 Division* HQ by 02:10, and a warning order was issued to the divisional mobile reserve to force the Orne bridges at 02:35.[46]

While the 6th Airborne Division was grappling with the consequences of poor delivery by the RAF, events were unfolding in a similar manner over the Cotentin Peninsula. The American main force began taking off at 22:30, and formed up into serials of forty-five aircraft divided into nine-strong V formations. The serials were slotted into a corridor of sky 1,000 feet wide and 300 miles long, following a carefully worked out route across southern England marked with EUREKA beacons; the lead C-47 in each serial was equipped with the REBECCA or equivalent receiver. A shortage of trained personnel meant the lead aircraft in many serials was also the only one carrying a fully qualified navigator. After crossing the coast the C-47s dropped to 500 feet to avoid detection by German radar and flew 30 miles south-west to waypoint GALLUP. Thirty miles further on waypoint HOBOKEN was marked by a surfaced Royal Navy submarine. There the aircraft turned south-east and climbed to 1,500 feet to avoid German guns on the Channel Islands.

The first wave consisted of 6,900 paratroopers from the 501st, 502nd and 506th Parachute Infantry Regiments of the 101st Airborne Division, in 433 C-47s from the US 50th and 53rd Troop Carrier Wings. These were arranged in ten serials flying in three groups, and an eleventh serial was made up of fifty-two gliders carrying a further 155 men and Jeeps, anti-tank guns and other equipment. The Division commander, Major-General Maxwell D. Taylor, was among the paratroopers despite a painful leg injury. The Normandy jump was to be only Maxwell's second, and he became the first US Army general to parachute into combat. The plan was for the C-47s, still flying in tight, nine aircraft V formations, to cross the west Cotentin coast at 1,500 feet. They were then to descend and throttle back to the optimum jump height and speed of 600 feet and 90 miles per hour.

However, the lead serials flew into the cloud that had wrong-footed the pathfinders, with identical but even more serious results. The carefully maintained formation disintegrated as the largely inexperienced pilots instinctively sought to avoid collision by banking, climbing or diving. Some aircraft emerged in company of their fellows, others without a friendly aircraft in sight. The situation was exacerbated by German flak, already stirred up by the bombing that had commenced just after midnight, and the pathfinders. The psychological effect was heightened by the fact that most was from light 20mm or 37mm weapons using tracer ammunition.

Many aircraft were hit; one paratrooper from the 502nd Parachute Infantry likened the projectiles piercing the stressed metal skin of his aircraft to the sound of corn popping.[47] A C-47 carrying the 506th Parachute Infantry took a serious hit as the paratroopers were jumping, and the last five men in the stick were thrown violently together as the aircraft pitched over on one wing. One managed to dive through the door head first, two managed to drag themselves over the threshold prone and the last man, who managed to keep his footing, half-heaved out the fourth and operated the release switch for the containers slung on the aircraft's racks before jumping himself.[48] Some were not so lucky. One pilot watched as flak peppered a C–47 flying just ahead, which rolled over on one wing, recovered and then hit the ground and exploded before a single paratrooper emerged.[49]

Perhaps understandably, many pilots took evasive action despite explicit orders to the contrary. Understandable or not, this had predictable results on the heavily laden paratroopers, who were standing, hooked up and waiting for the green jump light. Many aircraft instinctively dived to minimise their exposure to the flak, but this meant they were too low to identify landmarks or the few DZ markers set up by the pathfinders, and put them below the specified 600ft jump height. One paratrooper from the 506th Parachute Infantry estimated his jump height at no more than 300ft and landed so hard he was temporarily stunned. He then clearly saw a stick of eighteen paratroopers deliberately despatched at roof top height; he likened the sound of their impact to that of ripe melons dropped onto a hard surface.[50] Many aircraft were also travelling far above the specified 90 miles-per-hour jump speed. The opening shock of the standard US T-series parachute was relatively severe under normal conditions, especially with loads like those carried by the D-Day paratroopers. At speeds higher than the recommended maximum of 120 miles per hour the experience was at best painful and could result in items of equipment being shaken adrift and lost; many of the leg bags enthusiastically packed by the 506th Parachute Infantry were lost in this way. At worst, the magnified shock could render the paratrooper unconscious, or rupture panels in the parachute canopy, both with potentially fatal results.[51]

The upshot of all this was to scatter the 101st Airborne Division far and wide across the Cotentin Peninsula and beyond. The Division was supposed to land on three DZs. Not a single stick landed on the 502nd Parachute Infantry's DZ A, just west of St Martin-de-Varreville. Instead most were scattered along a line running parallel but north of the DZ, extending from St Mère Église to the sea, 6 miles away. A relatively tight grouping of the 502nd Regiment's sticks landed just south of DZ C, a few hundred yards west of St Marie-du-

Mont, presumably attracted by the markers. DZ C was actually assigned to the 501st Parachute Infantry. Ten sticks of the latter landed there, and the bulk of the remainder around St Marie-du-Mont itself. DZ D, a mile north of the la Barquette locks on the River Douve, enjoyed the best accuracy. Forty-three sticks of the 506th Parachute Infantry landed on or adjacent to the DZ, and most of the remainder nearby to the south.[52]

Last in was the 101st Airborne's glider serial, which was assigned to LZ E, adjacent to DZ C. One glider, loaded with radio equipment for Division HQ, aborted over the UK with a broken towrope. Another was released far to the south after the tug lost its bearings, and one combination was shot down by flak over the Cotentin. Of the remaining forty-nine gliders, six landed on the LZ, fifteen within half a mile and a further ten came down in a compact group near les Forges, just under 2 miles west. The other eighteen were widely scattered, and almost all were badly damaged by *Rommelspargel*, which the Americans appear to have made no effort to clear. In all, five men were killed, among them the 101st Airborne's deputy commander, Brigadier-General Donald Pratt. He was crushed when the Jeep aboard his glider broke loose, and thus gained the dubious distinction of being the first US Army general to die in a combat glider landing.[53]

Of the rest, clusters and individual sticks were distributed randomly in all directions. A stick from the 501st landed 11 miles to the south, and a stick each from the 501st and 502nd were delivered 15 and 20 miles north respectively, near Cherbourg. Two sticks from the 506th came down behind the OMAHA landing area, 12 and 14 miles east of DZ D respectively. These widely scattered elements appear to have given the Germans the first inkling that something was afoot. At 01:00, *Oberstleutnant* Hoffman, commanding a battalion of *Infanterie Regiment 919*, saw six C-47s flying low directly over his HQ bunker near Montebourg. As he watched, parachutes blossomed from the machines. At first Hoffman thought they were in trouble, but he swiftly realised there were too many parachutes and called the alarm; within minutes his HQ guard was involved in a firefight with American paratroopers.[54]

Hoffman commanded the units defending the UTAH landing

beaches, and among those alerted was *Leutnant* Jahnke, the officer
with the labour-scarred hands. Jahnke commanded *Wiederstandnest* 5
at la Grande Dune, and he immediately called an alert and despatched
a patrol. It returned within half an hour with nineteen sodden
American paratroopers, two of whom had been wounded in a firefight with their captors. Jahnke ascertained they were from the 506th
Parachute Infantry Regiment and was relaying this information to his
superiors when the telephone line went dead. At 02:45 the medic
attending to the wounded Americans reported to Jahnke that the prisoners were agitated, repeatedly asking the time and demanding to be
evacuated inland. Eight miles to the north, a security patrol from the
German artillery battery near Crisbeq also captured a number of US
prisoners from the 502nd Parachute Infantry. Their captors were
fascinated by the paratrooper's equipment, especially the silk scarf
escape maps and miniature compasses. They were also alarmed at the
highly detailed and accurate information about their positions marked
on the American's conventional maps.[55]

The American second wave came in thirty minutes behind the
101st Airborne. It consisted of 429 C-47s and fifty-two Waco CG4
gliders and tugs from the US 52nd and 53rd Troop Carrier Wings,
carrying 6,400 men from the 82nd Airborne Division. The lead serials
carried Colonel William E. Ekman's 505th Parachute Infantry,
followed by the 508th Parachute Infantry commanded by Colonel
Roy Lindquist, and finally Colonel George V. Millet's 507th Parachute
Infantry Regiment. Once again the cloudbank and flak disrupted the
formation. Lieutenant-Colonel Benjamin Vandervoort, commanding
the 2nd Battalion, 505th Parachute Infantry countermanded the green
light when his pilot mistook the River Douve for the Merderet, and
warned him the aircraft was travelling too fast. When they reached the
correct spot and jumped, his aircraft was still flying at an estimated 400
feet and far above the safe jump speed.[56] A private from the 505th
assessed his jump height to have been above 2,000 feet, and noted the
alarming sight of C-47s passing below him after his canopy
deployed.[57]

The succeeding serials suffered similar tribulations.

One C-47 carrying men from the 507th Parachute Infantry was struck in the upper fuselage by a large calibre shell as the stick were beginning to jump; the number six man barely made it out of the door as the aircraft heeled over, raising the door to chest height.[58] Another aircraft took three hits from what were identified as 88mm shells, but were more likely 37mm; an 88mm round would likely have totally destroyed the aircraft. The third round came through the bottom of the fuselage killing three men, blowing a large hole in the floor and filling the fuselage with smoke. At the frantic urging of Sergeant Dan Furlong, the stick jumped without waiting for the green light. Furlong slipped and put a leg through the hole before reaching and diving headlong out of the door. He only just made it; his parachute had barely deployed when he crashed into the upper branches of a tree, having exited at an estimated height of 200 feet.[59]

The 82nd Airborne was also assigned three DZs, located west of St Mère Église. The 505th Parachute Infantry had the most accurate and compact drop pattern of the whole operation, with thirty-six sticks landing on or immediately adjacent to DZ O, and most of the remainder within a two mile radius. At least two sticks overshot the DZ and landed in St Mère Église proper, where the preparatory bombing had set a building in the town square ablaze. The fire illuminated the area, allowing the Germans to shoot at the airborne soldiers as they descended. At least one unfortunate paratrooper fell directly into the conflagration, which swiftly and mercifully detonated his load of ammunition and explosives. German troops shot up another paratrooper who landed in a tree in the square before he could free his weapon. The parachute of Private John Steele, of the 2nd Battalion, 505th Parachute Infantry, became snagged on the church spire, leaving him dangling helplessly. Already wounded in foot, Steele feigned death and avoided attracting unwelcome attention; he was captured later when German troops stationed in the bell tower decided to haul in and loot his 'corpse'. By that time he was also deaf due to the constant ringing of the church bell. A series of desperate close-range fights erupted in the town square and surrounding streets as other paratroopers managed to divest themselves of parachute harnesses and reach their weapons. The town's volunteer fire brigade and many of the townspeople who had turned out to watch them fight the fire were caught up in the confused fighting.[60]

The 508th Parachute Infantry fared worst of all, with only a handful of sticks landing on DZ N. The rest were widely dispersed to the south and west, many landing near Picauville where they ended up fighting the German garrison. The 82nd Airborne's deputy commander, Brigadier-General Gavin, jumped with the 508th Regiment. Both he and the Regiment's commander Colonel Lindquist landed over 2 miles to the north of DZ N. On establishing their location both officers began moving independently toward the bridge over the River Merderet at la Fière, collecting stray paratroopers as they went. Only two sticks of the 507th Parachute Infantry landed on DZ T, although over thirty more overshot by a quarter of a mile and landed in a relatively compact group. Unfortunately this straddled the flooded River Merderet. Many men were drowned and the flooded terrain prevented the Regiment from concentrating effectively. Once again, some sticks were delivered miles from their intended DZs. Ten sticks of the 507th were dropped 20 miles south of their DZ, and a total of eight sticks from all three Regiments were delivered in the area of Cherbourg, up to 15 miles astray.[61]

The 82nd Airborne's fifty-two gliders, which came in at around 04:15, underwent an even worse experience than their forebears from the Screaming Eagles. One aborted after losing its tow over England, and seven either cast off or were released in the cloudbank over the Cotentin, of which five were never seen again. Seven more were cut loose prematurely and came down west of the River Merderet. Of the remaining thirty-seven, twenty-three landed on or near DZ O as assigned, and the rest were scattered further afield. All were severely damaged by *Rommelspargel* or collision with trees, walls, buildings and, in one case, a herd of cows. Three men were killed, twenty-three injured, and only eight of the sixteen 57mm anti-tank guns and eleven of the Jeeps were salvageable.[62]

To an extent, the badly botched delivery was due to unforeseen circumstances, specifically the unexpected cloudbank over the western Cotentin and the absence of markers on the DZs. The situation was not helped by the shortage of trained navigators and electronic navigation aids. As cited above, in many instances only the aircraft leading serials carried navigators and EUREKA/REBECCA apparatus, and there was a similar shortage of GEE receivers. This was a British device developed for RAF Bomber Command that allowed aircraft to establish their location by triangulating radio signals from ground transmitters. Like the weather, responsibility for these shortages can hardly be placed on the pilots, and the same can be said of the air plan under which they flew to Normandy. The latter was seriously flawed by the rigid imposition of radio silence, which prevented the pathfinder aircraft issuing a warning about the cloud over the Cotentin coast. As one writer has suggested, the problem could have been alleviated by sending an aircraft ahead of the formation to relay back weather reports, a sensible and basic precaution given the unsettled state of the weather.[63]

Leaving aside material and planning shortcomings, the poor performance of the US troop carriers is frequently blamed on insufficient and inadequate training, allied to a lack of combat experience. Even though night insertions were the airborne norm at that time, night flying training does not appear to have been a priority, and many of the transport units had little or no night flying experience. The Normandy lift was the first combat experience for the vast majority of aircrew in the eight Troop Carrier Groups deployed by the 50th and 53rd Troops' Carrier Wings. Only the 52nd Wing had any combat experience, gained in the Mediterranean. This would appear to explain why the 82nd Airborne's drop pattern was more compact than that of the 101st Airborne, if only marginally more accurate.

On the other hand, there is evidence that combat experience did not significantly enhance performance. The 52nd Troop Carrier Wing provided the air transport for the British 1st Parachute Brigade's Exercise TONY, carried out on 11 May 1944. Despite near perfect conditions, the drop was widely scattered and several aircraft landed with their sticks of paratroopers still aboard after failing to locate the DZ. This was virtually a rerun of the US 51st Troop Carrier Wing's performance at the Primasole Bridge in Sicily in July 1943, as the commander of the British formation bluntly pointed out in a letter to the 52nd Wing and US 9th Troop Carrier Command. In addition, the 4th Parachute Brigade raised similar complaints about the US aircraft that dropped them for Exercise DOROTHY, also held in April 1944.[64] This suggests that none of the US Wings were especially competent, combat experience notwithstanding.

The subject appears, perhaps understandably, to have been a touchy one with the pilots, and became something of a hot potato after the late Stephen Ambrose somewhat crassly stated that all the D-Day pilots were 'afraid' without exception in his 1994 work on the invasion.[65] This, rightly or wrongly, was widely construed as an accusation of cowardice, and led to counter-accusations that Ambrose had demeaned and dishonoured brave veterans both living and deceased. Given that somewhere in the region of 1,724 C-47 pilots were involved in the US airborne lift, a blanket assertion of fear seems somewhat ill-advised to say the least. Had this been anywhere near the fact of the matter, the US airborne divisions would have been even more widely scattered. On the other hand, the drop pattern maps in the US official history, to say nothing of the numerous participant accounts, make it difficult to escape the conclusion that generally speaking, the US airborne soldiers were badly let down. This was equally applicable to their British counterparts, and all had a right to expect a better level of competence than was frequently evident over Normandy in the early hours of 6 June 1944.

Be that as it may, the scattering severely degraded the ability of the US airborne formations to carry out their assigned missions. The 501st Parachute Infantry, for example, failed to seal the eastern entrance into the Cotentin by destroying the bridge carrying the main Carentan to St Mère Église road over the River Douve, and the 505th Regiment was unable to secure the road hub at St Mère Église as assigned. However, the handicap was offset to a significant extent by a widespread and exemplary exhibition of what their British counterparts referred to as ABI, or Airborne Initiative. All over the Cotentin American paratroopers oriented themselves and began moving toward their objectives individually or in small groups, often without formal leadership, identifying friends with their specially issued metal clickers. One combat engineer attached to the 501st Regiment, for example, was part of a group tasked to destroy two small bridges over the River Douve near Carentan. After landing alone and in the river close to a German artillery position, he spent some time stealthily recovering his equipment, including sixty pounds of C-2 explosive, before setting off for his objective. On the way he linked up with seven men from his team and cut a variety of power cables before reaching the target bridges shortly before dawn.[66]

Inevitably, some of the roaming invaders ran into German troops, which sometimes resulted in the paratroopers being killed or captured. However, the sheer number of clashes confused the German defenders as to the scope and target of the US airborne landings, and interfered with their ability to formulate a response. Overall, the airborne assault came as a complete and unwelcome surprise, and the Germans did not invariably come out on top. One German NCO recalled seeing the unfortunate survivors of a German unit attacked by American paratroopers while carrying out night training with blank ammunition.[67] The shock effect was heightened by the aggressive activities of the airborne interlopers, who cut telephone lines and set up impromptu ambushes as they went. A party from the 508th Parachute Infantry led by Lieutenant Malcolm Brannen ambushed a German staff car near Picauville, for example. They killed the commander of *91 Luftlande Division*, *Generalmajor* Wilhelm Falley and his adjutant, who had been en route to a wargame exercise at *7 Armee* HQ in Rennes. Unsettled by Allied air activity, Falley had turned back for his HQ but ran into Brannen and his men within sight of his goal instead.[68]

This widespread determination in the face of adversity was responsible for the partially successful outcome of the most vital American airborne mission, that of securing the landward end of the four raised exit roads through the inundated area behind the UTAH landing area. The two northern exits were assigned to Colonel George Mosely's 502nd Parachute Infantry Regiment. Lieutenant-Colonel Robert G.

Cole, commanding the 502nd Regiment's 3rd Battalion, landed on the outskirts of St Mère Église, 5 miles away from his objective. After establishing his location he set out with six men, which grew to seventy or so en route, including several men from the 82nd Airborne. Cole's party fought a brief meeting engagement with a German marching column, discovered that the German artillery position near St Martin-de-Varreville had been evacuated, and secured Causeway Three without a fight at around 07:30. He then despatched part of his force north to assist two groups of the Regiment under Lieutenant-Colonels Patrick J. Cassidy and John H. Michaelis fighting to secure Causeway Four.

The two southern exits were assigned to the 506th Regiment. Despite strenuous efforts, a group led by Lieutenant-Colonel Robert Strayer did not reach Causeway Two at Houdienville before the sea landings began. Two groups moved on Causeway One at Pouppeville. Major-General Taylor, the 101st Division's commander, headed one which ended up containing a brigadier-general, one full and two lieutenant-colonels; Taylor joked that never had so few been led by so many.[69] The other consisted of fifty men led by Lieutenant-Colonel William L. Turner. Neither were totally successful; Pouppeville was not secured until around 11:00, several hours after the UTAH landing commenced. However, while they did not succeed in securing the two southern exits, the activities of the American paratroopers prevented the Germans from interfering with the egress of the sea landing force from the UTAH beach. The 101st Airborne's primary mission was thus achieved, if not quite in the manner envisaged.

While the American paratroopers were roaming the Cotentin Peninsula, their British counterparts were carrying out a number of special operations and receiving gliderborne reinforcements. The 6th Airborne's third lift, consisting of sixty-eight Horsas and four Hamilcars, began to lift off for DZ N from RAF Brize Norton, Harwell and Tarrant Rushton at 01:19. Four machines, including one of the Hamilcars, aborted over England. A further four ditched in the sea. One of these, flown by Staff-Sergeant Philip 'Tug' Wilson and Sergeant H. Harris, came down just off Worthing. Pilots and passengers took refuge atop their machine and were rescued by a RAF Air-Sea Rescue launch from nearby Shoreham; it was summoned by a RAF aircrewman in a nearby rest home who witnessed the ditching. Another Horsa came down just off Cabourg, and all aboard were captured when the wreck drifted ashore shortly afterward; in the meantime they were fired on several times by German shore positions. The other two Horsas simply disappeared.[70]

Not all the machines that reached the French coast landed where they were supposed to. Staff-Sergeant William Jones and Sergeant John Potts came down near Bolbec, east of Le Havre in the Pas de Calais. They were captured after a brief firefight with a German force expecting to round up a bomber crew, and a German newsreel film crew recorded the incident. The RAF tug apparently mistook the mouth of the west-flowing River Seine for the north-flowing Dives, a navigational error of 50 miles in a fifty-mile flight. One Horsa landed near Pont-L'Eveque, 20 miles east of the Dives, and another came down in the Dives itself near the bridge at Bures. One of the big Hamilcars came down in an orchard near St Vaast-en-Auge, 15 miles north east of the LZ, after a towrope failure. The Germans attacked the machine at first light, killing three passengers and mortally wounding one of the pilots.[71]

The vast majority, however, came down on or near LZ N, beginning at 03:20. One slightly prematurely released Horsa landed on a school playing field at Ranville. The remaining two Hamilcars alighted safely on the LZ, and made the welcome discovery that their wings were actually higher than the top of the *Rommelspargel* poles. One proved difficult to unload because of undercarriage damage; the Hamilcar was fitted with hydraulic landing struts that permitted the fuselage to be lowered. The glider pilots and gun crew – both Hamilcars were carrying a seventeen-pounder anti-tank gun with prime mover and crew – got around this by cutting off the machine's tail.[72] The crew of a Horsa carrying a small bulldozer experienced similar problems when the vehicle became jammed in the glider's side door. This was solved by yanking out the special props used to support the fuselage while unloading, which allowed the bulldozer to crash through the fuselage floor onto the ground. Fortunately, it survived in working order. The same glider also carried an unidentified para-trooper sergeant. Unable to parachute due to a shoulder injury, he had approached the glider pilots for a lift to France shortly before take off and disappeared into the Normandy night with a laconic comment that the landing had been 'a bit rough'.[73]

While all this was going on, the 3rd Parachute Brigade was busy carrying out its special tasks. Lieutenant-Colonel Pearson's 8th Parachute Battalion, reinforced by half the 3rd Parachute Squadron RE, was tasked to demolish three bridges over the River Dives at Bures and Troarn. The paratroopers were to occupy Troarn and cover the sappers, but only thirty men rallied at the battalion RV. By 03:30 this had grown to around 150, with no sign of the sappers from the 3rd Parachute Squadron apart from six men and a Jeep who had arrived by Horsa. Pearson waited another thirty minutes before moving off. In fact, the 3rd Parachute Squadron detachment were already en route after being misdropped on DZ N; two sappers were almost run down by a glider as they moved to recover one of their parachute contain-ers.[74] Undaunted, Major Tim Roseveare rallied his men, loaded the demolition stores onto special folding carts and set out for Troarn. On the way he commandeered an RAMC Jeep and trailer, cut a number of telephone wires in Hérouvillette, and ran into a large group from the 8th Battalion just outside the town.

Roseveare sent the paratroopers back to secure a road junction, despatched most of his sappers under Captain Tim Juckes to Bures, and took the Jeep, trailer and seven men into Troarn. After freeing the Jeep from a barbed wire roadblock, they stealthily penetrated into the outskirts before coming face to face with a German on a bicycle. The German was shot, and Roseveare raced the Jeep through Troarn under a hail of fire, with over a ton of explosives in the wildly bouncing trailer. In the process one of the sappers, travelling on the trailer with a Bren gun, was thrown clear and captured. The bridge was a mile east of Troarn. Roseveare's little band swiftly rigged their charges, blew the bridge and made their way back to 3rd Parachute Brigade HQ across country.[75] Pearson, meanwhile, was conducting his own

advance on Troarn. Leaving an ambush party with two PIATs to cover
the road to le Mesnil, he set up a firm base in the Bois de Bavent. The
ambush later destroyed six half-tracks from *21 Panzer Division*, apparently stymieing further German probes. Pearson also sent out a patrol
toward Troarn and despatched his six sappers and a platoon to attack
the two bridges at Bures, which had been already been demolished by
Captain Juckes.[76]

Two further bridges over the Dives, at la Bac de Varaville and
Robehomme, were the responsibility of the 1st Canadian Parachute
Battalion. Major Clayton Fuller was the first to reach the
Robehomme bridge, after landing in the Dives close by. He was
joined by Lieutenant Norman Toseland who had gathered a party of
men from his own unit, the 8th and 9th Parachute Battalions and
some sappers from the 3rd Parachute Squadron led by Sergeant Bill
Poole. Having lost their containers the sappers had no demolition
charges, but they managed to weaken the bridge with a thirty-pound
charge improvised from the blocks of plastic explosive carried by the
paratroopers to make Gammon bombs, sometime after 03:00. Another
party of sappers arrived with the proper kit and finished the job at
06:00. The second bridge was demolished at 08:30.[77]

The largest special operation was the elimination of the Merville
Battery by Lieutenant-Colonel Otway's 9th Parachute Battalion.
Otway was thrown out of his aircraft by flak, but was followed by the
rest of his stick. They landed near a large farmhouse housing a
German battalion HQ, 400 yards from DZ V. Otway hit the back wall
at first floor level, his batman crashed through a glass conservatory,
and two more men landed in the garden. One of the latter hurled a
brick for want of anything better at a German who investigated from
an upstairs window. All made good their escape as the Germans
turned out the guard. On the way to the DZ they assisted a radio
operator whose kit bag had become tangled in overhead power
cables, watched helplessly as two paratroopers were pulled under the
flood by the weight of their kit, and captured two elderly German
soldiers cycling nonchalantly down a lane. These at first refused to
believe Otway and his men were British; they were duly convinced,

disarmed and sent on their way, the paratroopers lacking the means to deal with POWs.

Otway arrived at DZ V at 01:30. By 02:35 only 110 had come in, mostly in ones or twos. This was a serious setback, for the 9th Battalion's carefully worked out and exhaustively rehearsed plan required the whole unit plus the attached sappers, special equipment and anti-tank guns. Only a single bundle of Bangalore torpedoes had been recovered, and all the battalion's organic heavy weapons were missing, apart from a single Vickers medium machine gun. Neither could Otway afford to tarry, for the Battery had to be eliminated no later than 05:30. At 02:45, as Otway passed the word to prepare to move out in five minutes, another group turned up, expanding the force to around 150. At 02:50 the severely depleted 9th Battalion set out, organised into the various groups worked out for the assault.

Major Smith and the Troubridge party had reached the battery after negotiating an extensive minefield, and penetrated into the badly cratered perimeter to ascertain if the battery were occupied. This was confirmed by a noisy general alarm provoked by the passage of a low flying glider combination, during which several machine guns and a 20mm gun opened fire. Satisfied, Smith withdrew to meet the main force, which arrived at 04:00. While three men under Captain Paul Greenway silently breached the barbed wire entanglement and marked four-foot wide lanes through the mines with white tape, the diversionary party moved around to the main gate. Parry reorganised the remainder into four groups, one for each of the Battery's case-mates. At 04:30, as they moved into their final positions for the attack, Otway's men came under fire from two groups of German machine guns located to the left and right of the Battery, which were engaged by the attacker's sole Vickers and the diversionary party.[78]

At that point the gliders scheduled to land atop the Battery arrived. The three Horsas had taken off from Brize Norton just after 02:15. One immediately developed a stability problem and was obliged to abort thirty minutes after take off. Despite being badly overloaded, it landed safely at RAF Odiham, where the alarmed pilots discovered that the towrope yoke had somehow looped over the wing and cut part way through it. Had the severely weakened wing given way, all would have been killed. The drogue parachute fitted to one of the other Horsas deployed in flight due to turbulence. The underpowered Albemarle tug almost stalled before the glider pilots managed to jettison the errant device.

Arriving near the battery but not seeing any identifying signals, this combination circled several times, with the tug's navigation lights illuminated to help the glider keep station. This courageous action attracted a good deal of flak, and the tug received several hits. On release, the Horsa was not able to decelerate sufficiently without the missing drogue parachute, and overshot the Battery by 200 yards. The third Horsa was hit by flak that wounded four passengers and set the glider on fire. Despite this, the pilot was heading for a landing within the Battery perimeter until he deployed the drogue parachute, which snagged on trees and brought the machine down in an orchard 50 yards short.[79] In the event this proved fortunate, for it placed the glider's passengers in a perfect ambush position to block the approach of German reinforcements from the nearby village of Gonneville-sur-Mer.

Otway launched the assault when the first glider overshot. Bangalore torpedoes marking the two marked lanes through the minefield were detonated and the assault groups rushed the Battery, urged on by Otway's exhortation to 'Get in, get in!' The Germans, alerted by the glider and the firefight with the flanking machine guns, responded immediately with small-arms and illumination flares. A number of men were killed and wounded in the initial charge, including the officers leading the way. Major Parry was hit in the thigh, and Captain Havelock Hudson was severely wounded in the stomach and lower back. Colonel Otway narrowly missed a similar fate; one bullet passed through the back of his Dennison smock and another pierced his water bottle.

The paratroopers penetrated rapidly into the battery position, overrunning trenches and closing rapidly on the four huge concrete casemates. Only four men of the group assigned to Casemate Four, on the left of the attack axis, survived to reach their objective. Finding the steel door secured, the paratroopers resorted to firing into apertures and dropping grenades into the air vents. The German gunners within made a break for it but most were shot down in the attempt. Two of the other casemates whose occupants had neglected to secure their doors were cleared with fragmentation and white phosphorous grenades. A handful of Germans were fortunate enough to have their surrender accepted on leaving the casemates, and the diversion party took a larger group near the Battery's main entrance. In all, between fourteen and twenty-three of the defenders were taken prisoner. Those who escaped claimed later that they had been overwhelmed by sheer weight of numbers and that the British had outnumbered them at least five to one. Otway would doubtless have wished this had been the case.[80] The battle lasted for twenty-five minutes and all the case-mates were taken by 05:00, but at a grievously heavy cost. At least fifty of Otway's paratroopers were dead and twenty-five wounded, some severely, a casualty ratio of almost exactly fifty per cent.[81]

With the casemates secured, the attackers made a rather unwel-come discovery. Instead of the 150mm artillery pieces the 9th Battalion had been briefed to expect, they contained First World War vintage 100mm field howitzers of Czech manufacture, complete with wooden spoked wheels. Lacking demolition charges, one was demol-ished by loading a shell into the breech and jamming another into the muzzle before firing the piece. Major Parry, still mobile despite his wound, supervised the spiking of another using Gammon bombs.[82] The destruction of the guns was less than thorough, however. The battery commander, who had been at his forward control post near Franceville Plage, returned to the Battery position after the 9th Battalion's withdrawal and got at least one of the howitzers back into working order.[83]

Having no radio the paratroopers were understandably reluctant to tarry. The cruiser HMS *Arethusa* was to bombard the battery unless a success signal was received by 05:30 at the latest. A carrier pigeon carried by Lieutenant Jimmy Loring was released with the success message, and Major Parry ordered yellow smoke candles lit atop one of the casemates, but there was no guarantee that *Arethusa* would be able to see the visual success signal. Unbeknown to the attackers, their

fears were misplaced because the cruiser had received additional
instructions not to fire unless it was certain the battery remained in
German hands.[84] The battery was under increasingly heavy German
mortar and artillery fire, however, called in by *Leutnant* Steiner from
the gun battery at Houlgate.[85] As this was making movement within
the battery perimeter extremely hazardous, Otway ordered a withdrawal. Three severely wounded airborne soldiers had to be left in
Casemate No. 4; they remained there, undisturbed by the Germans
who reoccupied the Battery in the evening of D-Day, until being
evacuated by No. 3 Commando in the afternoon of 7 June.[86] The
twenty-two wounded who could be moved were carried to a nearby
farm and left in the care of a German medical officer and orderlies
captured at the Battery.[87]

The able bodied and their POWs retired to a Calvary on the
Bréville road as planned, arriving at 05:30. Many required a pause for
psychological adjustment. Latecomers noted there were initially no
sentries in spite of the potential danger, with many men preferring to
rehash their recent experiences among themselves. Otway himself was
seen sitting for a time at the base of the Calvary with his head in his
hands, and did not respond to reports or enquiries.[88] The collective
mood passed as officers and NCOs gradually re-established control,
establishing a defensive perimeter and reorganising platoons and
sections around the missing. His force being too weak to carry out the
9th Battalion's subsidiary tasks, Otway thus moved directly to le Plein,
the Battalion's final objective.[89]

As they moved off at 06:00, another party left Varaville to meet
them, led by a recently arrived Brigadier Hill, fresh from picking his
way through the floods. Hill was accompanied by a number of men
from Brigade HQ, some Royal Navy Forward Observers, a small
party from 224 Parachute Field Ambulance and a mis-dropped group
from the 9th Battalion. Half an hour later both groups were caught in
a high level Allied bombing attack. Hill's party bore the brunt, with a
number of men being killed and wounded. Parachute Dog Glenn and
his handler, Private Emile Corteil, were among the dead. In the
confusion Hill's column became split. Half returned to Varaville after

dealing with the injured, Hill continued his quest for the 9th Battalion and Otway continued to le Plein, while the rest of the 6th Airborne braced itself for the German reaction to the south and the seaborne landings commenced across the Orne to the west.[90]

8

D-DAY
H-HOUR TO H PLUS 5 HOURS
30 MINUTES

(06:30 TO 12:00, TUESDAY 6 JUNE 1944)

The Allied airborne lift was complete by 03:45 on 6 June, and it achieved complete surprise. Among the reasons for this was inaccurate weather forecasting and faulty appreciation of how this would affect Allied invasion planning. German weather forecasts were based on reports from U-boats and weather flights over the western Atlantic, and one meteorologist claimed the data gathered was little better than observing the morning sky. This was an exaggeration, for German information was not significantly inferior in quality to that available to the Allies. The problem lay with its fragmentary and limited nature, which prevented the Germans tracking developments as closely and accurately as the Allies.[1] They thus missed the brief window of favourable weather that informed Eisenhower's decision to go ahead with the invasion on 6 June.

However, even had they detected that window, it is highly likely its significance would have been overlooked. German received wisdom held that a landing had to be launched on a high tide with a half moon at most, whereas the Allied plan incorporated a full moon and low tide.[2] This misconception was exacerbated by the usual poor-to-non existent German inter-service liaison, which also prevented a consensus on the optimum sea conditions. Whether the *Heer* and *Luftwaffe* had their own criteria is unclear, but the *Kriegsmarine* decided invasion would require a minimum of five consecutive days with visibility of no less than 3 miles, winds of 24 knots or less, and waves no more than 8 feet high.[3] Monday 5 June did not come close to this yardstick, and the prevailing conditions looked set to continue into Tuesday 6 June; weather reports received by *84 Korps* in St Lô thus stated rough seas would make any landing impossible.[4] In addition, German naval patrols in the western Channel were suspended on the night of 5-6 June, and the same logic presumably underlay the *Luftwaffe's* cessation of reconnaissance flights over the Channel and southern England after 1 June.[5] This effectively nullified what early warning mechanisms the Germans possessed.

The Germans did have very good intelligence on when the Allied blow would be launched, however. The British had developed a highly effective system for communicating with Resistance networks in occupied Europe using seemingly innocuous words and phrases inserted into open BBC broadcasts. In January 1944 the *Abwehr* obtained the signal that would be used to alert the Resistance when invasion was imminent. Consisting of the opening line from the 'Chanson d'Automne' by Paul Verlaine, the first half was a warning order to be broadcast on the first or fifteenth of the month. The second half confirmed the invasion would begin within forty-eight hours.[6] The immense task of monitoring BBC broadcasts to identify these signals fell to *Oberstleutnant* Hellmuth Meyer, intelligence officer at *15 Armee* HQ and his thirty-strong radio intercept section. The first half of the signal was picked up on the night of 1 June 1944 and German agents within the Resistance reported a further twenty-eight stand-by signals over the next two days. This coincided with the sudden imposition of Allied radio silence; the section's equipment was powerful enough to pick up routine radio transmissions from traffic control units in southern England. On the night of 4 June Meyer's section also intercepted a premature signal containing a press state-ment announcing the invasion.[7]

The second half of the Verlaine signal was intercepted on 5 June, just after 22:15.[8] Meyer immediately informed *15 Armee* and passed the information up to *Heeresgruppe B*, *Oberbefehlshaber West* and *OKW*. He did not, however, inform *7 Armee*, the formation responsible for the

Normandy coast west of Cabourg. That was the job of Rommel's *Heeresgruppe B*, which did not give the warning much credence, possibly due to a similar but fruitless alert on 1 June following the interception of the first half of the Verlaine signal. More likely, it was due to Rommel's stated opinion that invasion was unlikely before the end of June.[9] Rommel was so confident he left his HQ at La Roche-Guyon on the evening of 4 June to visit Hitler at Berchtesgaden.[10] Although his staff sought to conceal the fact, he departed earlier than strictly necessary to be with his wife for her birthday on 6 June.

Rommel was not the only high-ranking officer away from his post at this time. *Oberbefehlshaber West's* senior intelligence officer, *Oberst* Wilhelm Meyer-Detring, was on leave and Admiral Theodor Krancke, commanding *Marinegruppenkommando West*, left Paris for an inspection visit to Bordeaux.[11] In addition, *7 Armee* cancelled an alert planned for the night of 5 June, and instead summoned senior commanders to Rennes for a *kriegspiel* exercise on the morning of 6 June.[12] Prophetically, the scenario involved Allied airborne and sea landing in Normandy. The ramifications of removing senior commanders from their units concerned *7 Armee's* chief-of-staff, *Generalmajor* Max Pemsel. Privately convinced that any Allied attack would come at first light, Pemsel thus issued instructions that commanders were not to depart for Rennes before dawn on 6 June. Unfortunately some officers had jumped the gun. The commander of *709 Infanterie Division*, *Generalleutnant* Karl von Schlieben, was already in Rennes and *Generalmajor* Wilhelm Falley of the *91 Luftlande Division* left his HQ near Picauville at midnight.

On the other hand, *Generalleutnant* Wilhelm Richter, commanding *716 Infanterie Division* obeyed Pemsel's instruction, as did the commander of *84 Korps*, General Erich Marcks. The latter's staff had arranged a surprise midnight party to celebrate his birthday, which fell on 6 June. In addition, formations appear to have functioned perfectly well without their commanders. *709 Division*, for example, had alerted all its subordinate commands within an hour of the first American parachute landings in the Cotentin. Reports that something unusual was afoot were also prompt, although they were not always treated seriously. At 23:40 on 5 June a *Luftwaffe* radar station on Guernsey spotted a large, regularly spaced formation of aircraft shadowing bombers toward the Cotentin Peninsula. After double-checking *Oberst* Oelze called *84 Korps* and attempted to report to the chief of staff. He was fobbed off by the duty officer, who promised to relay the report and Oelze's considered opinion that invasion was imminent. A patronising staff officer called shortly afterward to wish Oelze a good night and advised him to look out for 'smaller ghosts' in the future.[13]

Within a couple of hours *84 Korps* had changed its tune. *716 Division* relayed word of British airborne landings east of the Orne at 02:11, and shortly afterward *709 Division* reported American parachute troops near St Marie-du-Mont, St Mère Église and astride the River Merderet. *84 Korps* issued a full alert and relayed the reports to *7 Armee*. The alert included *Oberst* Oelze, to whom it must have been a source of some satisfaction. *7 Armee* received the report at 02:15, and Pemsel immediately ordered the highest state of readiness and alerted *Generaloberst* Dollmann. He also telephoned his opposite number, *Generalmajor* Dr. Hans Speidel at *Heeresgruppe B*. Speidel received another call from *15 Armee* shortly afterwards. Von Salmuth had contacted *Generalmajor* Josef Reichert's *711 Infanterie Division*, at Cabourg on the boundary between *7 Armee* and *15 Armee*. He could clearly hear gunfire over the line as Reichert's HQ guard fought with stray British airborne troops.

Initially, *Heeresgruppe B* and *Oberbefehlshaber West* considered the airborne landings to be a diversionary effort. The Allies reinforced this by dropping hundreds of dummy paratroopers across northern France. Codenamed 'Ruperts', these were less elaborate than those featured in the film *The Longest Day*, being merely three-foot tall fabric outlines equipped with scaled-down parachutes and pyrotechnic gunfire simulators.[14] Ironically, the Allies had plagiarised the idea from the Germans, who employed similar devices in the Low Countries in May 1940.[15] Plagiarised or not, the idea had the desired effect. *84 Korps* was for a time misled into believing a large-scale airborne landing had taken place at the western base of the Cotentin Peninsula,[16] and *12 SS Panzer* stood to for a time after *711 Infanterie Division* reported parachute landings that turned out to be Ruperts.[17]

The unintended dispersion and aggressive behaviour of the real airborne troops reinforced German confusion. Misdropped paratroopers were probably the source of reports of major landings south of Carentan that drew *84 Korps* mobile reserve, three battalions from *352 Infanterie Division*, away from its position behind the OMAHA landing area.[18]

Nonetheless, *7 Armee* had correctly identified the centre of the two Allied airborne landings by 03:00. Pemsel was convinced this was the beginning of the real invasion, an opinion reinforced by reports of marine engine noise from *Kriegsmarine* sound direction stations near Cherbourg.[19] Within the hour the higher command levels had also begun having second thoughts; by 03:50 *Oberbefehlshaber West* was admitting that the scale of the airborne landings was overly large for a diversionary operation.[20] The reactions of *7 Armee* and its subordinate formations have been criticised by participants and more recent writers. One, for example, accuses *84 Korps* of sluggishness, *716 Division* of failing to provide centralised direction, and the German reaction generally of lacking momentum and being psychologically overawed.[21]

However, the evidence does not really support this verdict. *716 Division* swiftly identified the centre of the British airborne landing, despatched its mobile reserve to counter it, requested pre-arranged reinforcements from *21 Panzer Division* at 01:42, and ordered the Benouville bridges retaken less than an hour later, at 02:35. As a virtually immobile *bodenständige* formation, there was not realistically a lot more *716 Division* could do apart from defend its positions if attacked. Once appraised of the developing situation at 02:11, *84 Korps* and *7 Armee* reacted equally swiftly. The former requested and received control of *91 Luftlande Division* and drew up a scheme to reduce the Cotentin airhead with co-ordinated concentric attacks using *709* and *243 Infanterie Divisions*, *91 Luftlande Division*, *Fallschirmjäger Regiment 6* and *Panzer Ersatz Bataillon 100*. This effectively sealed off the US airborne incursion, and unwittingly laid the groundwork to do the same to the American sea landings at the UTAH beaches. *7 Armee* was also vociferous in persuading *Heeresgruppe B* of the magnitude of the threat, and rapid in requesting reinforcement. At 02:45 Pemsel asked that *12 SS Panzer Division* be placed on alert and prepare to recon-noitre the area east of the Orne, and at 04:30 requested and received permission to deploy *21 Panzer Division* in support of *716 Infanterie Division.*[22]

This was efficient work in the circumstances, and any tardiness was prompted by the need to clarify matters rather than psychological paralysis. Much of the contemporary criticism came from the *21 Panzer Division*, which was placed on stand-by for instant movement when its elements subordinated to *716 Division* were alerted at 01:40. *Oberst* Hermann von Oppeln-Bronikowski, commanding *Panzer Regiment 22*, was roused by *Generalleutnant* Feuchtinger personally and warned to stand by to clear the area between Caen and the coast. Oppeln-Bronikowski got his tanks on the road and briefed his commanders for a rapid advance to the coast.[23] He was then left kicking his heels for several hours awaiting further orders.[24] The commander of *Panzergrenadier Regiment 125*, Major Hans von Luck, underwent a similar process. Von Luck alerted his unit on receiving reports of parachute and glider landings, and was soon presented with irrefutable proof by his *II Bataillon*, which captured a British airborne officer near Troarn.[25] Von Luck was confident of his ability to destroy the British airborne force and retake the Benouville bridges, but no orders were forthcoming, and movement was strictly forbidden without specific authorisation.

Von Luck was later most vociferous in his criticism, accusing his superiors of condemning his unit to inactivity when rapid and deci-sive action was required. In this he was merely reflecting the standard German response to airborne landings, which was immediate and sustained attack once the location and objective of the landings was identified. The tactic was employed with salutary effect against the British 1st Airborne Division at Arnhem in September 1944. On that occasion, however, the landings took place in daylight, well away from possible ground reinforcement and their objective was immediately apparent. Things were not so clear cut on the night of 5–6 June, for while the area of the airborne landings was identified relatively quickly, their specific purpose was not. *21 Panzer Division* was *7 Armee's* sole mobile reserve, and the only armoured formation within immediate striking distance of the coast. Resisting premature commitment was thus both understandable and prudent. In addition, committing *21 Panzer* against Ranville effectively meant cutting it off from the bulk of *7 Armee's* coastal frontage, which lay west of the Orne. The decision was not therefore one to be taken lightly, and it is interesting to note that much of the criticism comes from those who would not have carried the can for any bad consequences.

Von Luck's recollections thus smack somewhat of hindsight, and he may also have been overestimating his ability vis-à-vis the British airborne troops. As they quickly demonstrated, the 6th Airborne Division's personnel were tough, highly motivated and aggressive. They were also thoroughly trained in taking on armoured vehicles with PIATs, Hawkins grenades and Gammon bombs; every man carried plastic explosive for fabricating the latter. This threat was not one to be taken lightly, especially at night; the destruction of six armoured half-tracks from *21 Panzer* by two PIAT teams from the 8th Parachute Battalion near Troarn in the early hours of 6 June illustrates the point. In addition, Major-General Gale's instructions to Brigadier Poett were uncompromising on the vital necessity of holding the Ranville area and Benouville bridges, and he was deadly serious when he ordered that the 'whole of this area must be held. Infantry positions will be fought to the last round and anti-tank guns to the muzzle'.[26] Had von Luck received permission to move on Ranville during the early hours of 6 June, he may therefore have received a rather stiffer reception than he anticipated.

While all this was going on, the Allied invasion fleet was approaching the Normandy coast. *Kriegsmarine* radar and listening posts picked up vessels 7 miles off the OMAHA landing area at 02:15, and large static contacts were identified by radar operators at Port-en-Bessin an hour later. At 03:40 German observers spotted a number of unidentified ships manoeuvring in the intermittent moonlight off the Orne estuary; visual observation further west was hampered by mist.[27] These reports and *7 Armee's* appreciation of the scale and significance of the airborne landings was relayed to Admiral Krancke at Bordeaux. At 03:50 he ordered the 5th and 9th Torpedo Boat Flotillas to sea from Le Havre and Cherbourg respectively, and summoned the 8th Destroyer Flotilla from Royan at the head of the Gironde estuary before leaving for *Marinegruppenkommando West* in Paris.[28]

Two hundred and fifty-five Allied minesweepers had begun clearing channels through the German minefields before midnight on 5 June, and completed their task between 02:00 and 03:00 the following morning.[29] The static contacts noted off Port-en-Bessin were the headquarters ship for Task Force O and the transports carrying the leading elements for the OMAHA landing area, which dropped anchor at 02:50. A similar grouping had dropped anchor off the UTAH beaches twenty minutes earlier.[30] The transports then began unloading the assault troops. Some had to climb down scrambling nets into their landing craft, a risky business in the heavy seas. One officer from the US 1st Infantry Division estimated that the landing craft were rising and falling thirty feet.[31] Being lowered aboard ready-loaded assault craft was only marginally safer, if at all. One boatload of Rangers was almost thrown into the sea when a wave struck the underside of their LCA.[32] Another carrying a battalion command group from the US 29th Division became stuck directly underneath the spurting effluent outlet from the transport's heads, and remained hanging there for the better part of half an hour.[33]

With the sea being whipped up by winds of between 16 and 20 knots, the troops were soaked by spray before they finished boarding. H-Hour for the US beaches was 06:30, which made this a miserable start to a passage that could conceivably last over four hours, depending on loading time and landing wave. Many landing craft thus spent a considerable period merely circling as the assault force was marshalled, their passengers standing in several inches of water and crushed together by their inflated life preservers and other equipment. The buffeting inflicted by the heavy seas caused widespread seasickness, obliging the use of greaseproof paper bags or, when those were used up, their helmets.

To the east the British and Canadian forces were going through much the same process, although the British selected loading areas 4 miles closer to the beaches. Aboard the Empire *Arquebus* heading for the GOLD landing area, stewards served breakfast to officers at 02:00 in dress uniform and white gloves.[34] Off the SWORD landing area men from the 1st Special Service Brigade aboard the SS *Astrid* were roused for breakfast at 03:30.[35] At around the same time, the nearby Empire *Cutlass*, carrying the assault companies of the 2nd East Yorks, began to launch its LCAs. Men on both ships witnessed the only *Kriegsmarine* action against the invasion fleet on 6 June. The commander of the 5th Torpedo Boat Flotilla, *Kapitänleutnant* Heinrich Hoffmann, left Le Havre with his three serviceable vessels after receiving Krancke's 03:50 order. Moving at 23 knots, Hoffmann's little flotilla approached a strange looking fog bank at around 04:30. This was in fact a smoke-screen laid to conceal the invasion fleet from shore observation, and on passing through it the German vessels found themselves surrounded by the flank element of the Eastern Task Force. In the immediate vicinity were the HQ ship HMS *Largs*, numerous destroy-ers, three cruisers, and two battleships.

Hoffmann's three boats promptly launched all of their eighteen torpedoes and zigzagged wildly back into the smokescreen, pursued by fifteen-inch shells from the battleship *Warspite*. Incredibly, all the German torpedoes save one failed to find a target. The exception struck the Norwegian destroyer *Svenner* amidships, and she broke in two and sank almost immediately.[36] One Commando aboard the SS *Astrid* described the *Svenner* folding up like a pocket-knife,[37] and another observer on the Empire *Cutlass* noted the automatic lights on the survivors life-jackets in the water; this was not considered a 'very heartening beginning' to the invasion.[38] Thirty of the *Svenner*'s crew were lost, although a further hundred were picked up by another destroyer. Hoffmann and his boats escaped unscathed, apart from a broken radio.

Shortly before 05:00 7 *Armee* HQ informed *Heeresgruppe B* that the sheer number of ships detected between the rivers Orne and Vire indicated a full-scale invasion. At around the same time *Generalfeldmarschall* von Runstedt was coming to the same conclu-sion at *Oberbefehlshaber West* in Paris. While still believing the main

Allied blow would come elsewhere, he nevertheless issued warning orders to *12 SS Panzer* and *Panzer Lehr Divisions*.[39] Dawn came at 05:15, although in places it took some time for the light to filter through the gloom and mist. The gathering light gave the Allied attackers their first, often uninspiring view of the misty French coast, and revealed the 6,000 vessel invasion fleet that had materialised on their doorstep to the Germans manning the beach defences. Two senior NCOs from *716 Infanterie Division* received their first glimpse of the hundreds of Allied vessels off the JUNO beaches while sharing a latrine near St Aubin-sur-Mer.[40] At the mouth of the River Vire the commander of *Infanterie Regiment 914's* heavy machine gun company saw the landing craft heading for UTAH across the estuary from a treetop observation post.[41]

The Eastern Task Force commenced its bombardment at 05:30, with what one eyewitness described as a single ripple of flashes running across the entire horizon. The heavy units concentrated on targets east of the Orne. The battleships *Warspite* and *Ramillies* targeted German shore batteries at Villerville and Benerville respectively, each broadside delivering in excess of three tons of explosives; this continued until the guns were so hot the rifling began to protrude from the gun muzzles.[42] The monitor *Roberts* hit the battery at Houlgate, which had been shelling the 9th Parachute Battalion at Merville. West of the Orne, each landing area was assigned a specific bombardment group made up of cruisers and destroyers. The former stood off and tackled the German shore batteries. HMS *Ajax*, joined later by HMS *Argonaut*, poured 179 shells into the Longue Battery from 6 miles out; two of four Type M272 casemates were knocked out and the battery temporarily silenced. HMS *Orion* shelled a battery covering the GOLD beaches, scoring twelve hits and putting it out of action. HMS *Frobisher*, HMS *Danae* and the Polish cruiser *Dragon* took on the gun batteries at Riva Bella and the Morris, Hillman and Daimler strongpoints inland from Ouistreham. The smaller vessels moved close inshore and shelled the German beach defences.

The Western Task Force, which was not scheduled to begin its bombardment until 05:50, began taking fire from German coastal guns from 05:05. Either or both the St Marcouf and Azeville Batteries opened fire on the US destroyers *Corry* and *Fitch* off the UTAH beaches. At 05:25 guns from two batteries at la Pernelle further north on the Cotentin fired on Allied minesweepers, and the battleship *Arkansas* was fired on by a battery near Port-en-Bessin at around 05:30.[43] Major Werner Pluskat, commanding *352 Infanterie Division's* artillery regiment, had been on alert at his observation bunker overlooking the approaches to the OMAHA beaches since 01:00. He had been observing the landing fleet since first light, and had the uncomfortable experience of watching the Allied warships traversing and elevating their guns in his direction in unison. Before the ships opened fire, however, he had to endure a final and sustained wave of bombing.[44]

The OMAHA bombing was carried out by 329 B-24 Liberator bombers from the US 8th Air Force, flying at 20,000 feet. To avoid accidentally hitting the landing fleet, bomb aimers were ordered to delay dropping for several seconds. As a result, the vast majority of the ordnance was scattered anywhere up to 3 miles inland, and the beach defences and minefields were left virtually unscathed.[45] It is unclear why the Liberators did not fly along the coast rather than across it, as the former tactic worked well against the UTAH defences.[46] *Leutnant* Jahnke at *Wiederstandnest* 5 watched a large formation of B-26 Marauder medium bombers approach from the sea and wheel to fly down the length of the beach and over his position at 500 feet. The attack wrecked some of his anti-tank guns, damaged several fighting bunkers, destroyed the ammunition shelter and filled in many of the open communications trenches and rifle pits.[47]

The bombing was followed by the Western Task Force's bombardment. Again the smaller vessels closed in to engage the German beach defences. Off OMAHA the US destroyer *Harding*, for example, began by shelling a German battery near Port-en-Bessin at a range of 4,800 yards at 05:37. Ten minutes later she closed to 3,000 yards and fired 100 five-inch shells into a group of bunkers in the Colleville exit from Fox

Green Beach, switching to radar gun-laying when smoke and dust obscured the target. At 06:10 a fortified house was engaged and smothered with another forty shells, and at 06:15 the Harding closed to 1,700 yards to deal with a German artillery piece located on the beach. Only at 06:20, with the first wave of landing craft just ten minutes out, did the Harding pull away.[48] Off UTAH the destroyers *Corry* and *Fitch* were engaging similar targets, until an aircraft detailed to stoke the protective smokescreen failed to materialise. The *Corry* was left exposed and the St Marcouf Battery's 210mm guns rapidly bracketed the vessel, which then struck one or possibly two German mines at 28 knots as it tried to escape. The crippled destroyer continued for 1,000 yards before coming to a stop, and the St Marcouf Battery promptly put nine shells into her, obliging the crew to abandon ship. The last man off stayed long enough to remove the ship's ensign from the stern and run it up the main mast; the mast and part of the superstructure remained above water when the wreck settled on the shallow bottom. Thirteen of her crew were killed and thirty-three injured.[49]

The heavier units took on better protected targets further inland. The US battleship *Nevada* and cruiser *Tuscaloosa* shelled the Azeville and St Marcouf Batteries until 06:20, when the former's fourteen-inch guns were turned against the concrete seawall backing the UTAH landing beaches. The USS *Texas*, assisted by the British cruiser *Glasgow*, spent twenty-five minutes hammering the Pointe du Hoc. At 06:14 the *Texas* shifted her fire to the Vierville exit from Dog Green Beach, next to where the *Arkansas* was pounding the les Moulins draw on the boundary between Dog Red and Easy Green beaches. Ammunition expenditure was prodigious. The *Nevada* expended 337 rounds of fourteen-inch ammunition, and 2,693 five-inch shells; the *Tuscaloosa* fired off 487 eight-inch shells and 115 rounds of five-inch ammunition.[50]

At 04:45 the two British miniature submarines *X20* and *X23* surfaced, no doubt to the great delight of all aboard. Two additional crewmen and additional equipment had been crammed into each vessel, and the postponement meant they had been off the Normandy coast since dawn on 4 June, submerged for twenty-one hours out of twenty-four to avoid detection. Their task was to act as navigation markers for the east and west boundaries of the British and Canadian landing sector, using radio and sonar emitters, and an 18-foot high telescopic mast mounting powerful flashing lights. Each also carried another light that was to be deployed by two men in an inflatable dinghy, to permit the invasion fleet to triangulate their position relative to the coast. Each submarine was also equipped with a huge yellow flag to avoid being run down by landing craft; providing a high-visibility target for the Germans was considered the lesser evil in this instance, even though the submarines would have to remain stationary for over two hours. The crew of X23 also planned to hoist a full-size Royal Navy battle ensign brought especially for the occasion.[51]

The first seaborne invaders to touch French soil went ashore, fifteen minutes before the X-Craft surfaced, at the Iles St Marcouf, two small, stony islands 3 miles off the Cotentin Peninsula. SHAEF decreed these had to be occupied because of their proximity to the UTAH beaches, and 132 men from the US 4th and 24th Cavalry Squadrons, commanded by Lieutenant-Colonel Edward C. Dunn, were to secure them in advance of the main landings. They found no Germans but unwelcome evidence of their presence in the shape of large numbers of anti-personnel mines. The cavalrymen lost two dead and seventeen wounded, some to S-mines and some to artillery fire when the Germans shelled the islands in the afternoon of 6 June, but Dunn was able to report his mission accomplished as planned.[52]

The invasion proper was supposed to begin at 06:25, when DD Sherman tanks were scheduled to go ashore at both the American landing areas. Two companies of the US 70th Tank Battalion, totalling thirty-two DD tanks, were assigned to lead the way onto the UTAH beaches; the Battalion's remaining company was to be landed by LCT. In the event, a mine sank one LCT carrying four DD tanks on the run in to the launch point, and the launch was delayed by the loss of three out of four control vessels to mines. The surviving DD tanks were launched at 3,000 rather than the planned 5,000 yards in an effort to make up for lost time.[53] However, they were overtaken by the LCVPs and LCTs carrying the first wave, and while all landed safely, they did so fifteen minutes after the infantry they were supposed to have been supporting.[54]

Things went even more awry at OMAHA, where two tank battalions were employed. The US 741st Tank Battalion was assigned to land ahead of the 16th Infantry Regiment on Easy Red and Fox Green Beaches, while the 743rd Tank Battalion was to support the adjacent 116th Infantry Regiment. The latter's frontage was spread across Dog Green, Dog White, Dog Red and Easy Green beaches. The sea was rougher off OMAHA, where the plan called for the DD tanks to be launched 6,000 yards offshore. The 741st missed a signal ordering the LCTs to carry the tanks all the way in, and twenty-nine DD tanks were launched at H Minus 50 Minutes. Twenty-seven sank in 30 metres of water, and only two made it safely to the beach, where they were joined by three more that had been unable to launch due to a ramp malfunction.[55] The 743rd Battalion's DD tanks only escaped a similar fate because the US Navy lieutenant in charge cancelled the launch and carried them all the way in on his own initiative.[56]

For over fifty years it was thought that the 741st Battalion's DD tanks had been swamped almost immediately after launch. However, a marine archaeological investigation in 2002 located and investigated nineteen of the unit's tanks on the sea bottom, and disproved this assumption in the process. The location of the wrecks showed that some had covered 3,000 yards before sinking, and their orientation also provided a highly plausible explanation for their loss. All were oriented on the church steeple at Colleville-sur-Mer, 1,500 yards inland from Fox Green Beach. The steeple was clearly visible from the sea, and was presumably a designated reference point for the DD tank commanders.

However, there was a strong current running east and roughly parallel to the coast, which the 741st Battalion's DD commanders do not appear to have been aware of. Attempting to remain oriented on the Colleville steeple meant rotating the tanks to the right relative to the coast, and thus exposing the sides of their flotation screens to the heavy seas rolling on to the beach. Because of their low freeboard and the fragility of the flotation screen, it was vital to keep the tank headed into the waves. One crewman recalled being called out of the vehicle to try and reinforce the side struts, which were buckling under the strain. The flotation screens could only stand so much and one by one the DD tanks were swamped, and their crews were left to swim for it. Despite claims that most of the DD crewmen drowned with their tanks,[57] losses were mercifully light. Eleven men were killed, five were listed as missing, and the remaining 119 were either picked up or made their own way on to the beach.[58]

Unexpected circumstances had a rather more fortunate outcome at UTAH, where the landing force was supposed to have gone ashore at Tare Green and Uncle Red beaches, fronting Causeways Three and Four. However, strong winds and offshore currents pushed the landing force south, a tendency that apparently went unnoticed because dust and smoke from the bombing and naval bombardment obscured reference points inland, and the lack of navigational clues was compounded by the loss of three control vessels to mines. Thus the landing force went ashore at 06:30 on Victor Green and Victor Red beaches, 2,000 yards south of its planned destination and straddling Causeway Two at la Grande Dune. The error side-stepped four beach-front resistance nests, a not inconsiderable boon given that the attackers were faced by 800 metres of open beach, and placed the landing force squarely in front of *Wiederstandnest 5*.

The initial wave of LCVPs, carrying two battalions from the 8th Infantry Regiment, was accompanied by thirty-three LCGs and LCT(R)s, which blanketed the dunes at the head of the beach with shells and five-inch rockets. *Leutnant* Jahnke, who had been observing the approaching armada, watched the landing craft beach and unload the assault wave, some on sandbars 200 yards or more from the surf line. The low-tide assault, he noted bitterly, nullified the beach obstacles erected with so much effort at a stroke. He fired two green flares to summon emergency artillery support and gave the order to fire when the attackers had closed to within 500 metres. However, the bombardment had left many of *Wiederstandnest 5's* garrison stunned, and had buried or damaged many of their weapons. The fire order thus prompted a spattering of rifle fire, supported by two machine guns, one mounted in an obsolete French tank turret, and an 80mm mortar. In desperation, Jahnke launched his Goliaths, remote-controlled armoured demolition charges containing 200 pounds of high explosive. The miniature tracked vehicles moved out of their shelters in the dunes but did not respond properly to their controllers; presumably the violent vibration from the bombardment disrupted their fragile electronics.[59]

Jahnke's call for artillery support went unanswered initially, although the resistance nest at les Dunes-de-Varreville, a mile to the north, opened long range fire with machine guns and anti-tank pieces at around 06:40. Consequently, many Americans thought their landing was totally unopposed. This was doubtless a welcome surprise, but the first US troops to reach the dunes made the less welcome discovery that they were not where they ought to have been. The first wave included the 4th Infantry Division's deputy commander, Brigadier-General Theodore Roosevelt Junior. The Division commander, Major-General Raymond O. Barton, was initially reluctant to permit Roosevelt to expose himself to such risk, partly because his deputy was overage and suffered from heart trouble, and also presumably because he was a close relative of the President. Roosevelt, however, persuaded Barton on the grounds that the presence of a general would be good for the troop's morale, and he thus sailed with the lead assault wave eschewing a helmet in favour of a knitted cap, and armed with a walking cane.

In the event, this proved to have been an extremely prescient arrangement. Roosevelt moved forward into the dunes, consulted with one of the lead company commanders and established their location. He then returned to the beach and conferred with Commodore James Arnold, the Navy Beach Control Officer, the commander of the 8th Infantry Regiment, Colonel Van Fleet, and two of the latter's battalion commanders; Van Fleet had come in with the fourth wave. To a background of engineers demolishing the beach obstacles and blasting gaps in the sea wall, the decision was taken to continue landing on the current beach, and to press inland immediately along

Causeways One and Two. Roosevelt then went on to fulfil his bargain about raising the troop's morale, walking up and down the beach, offering encouragement and directions with his cane and ignoring the increasingly heavy German artillery and mortar fire. His cool and sustained courage on the beach and later inland earned him the Medal of Honor, but he died of a heart attack on 12 July 1944, the very day he was given his own divisional command.[60]

While the Americans were reorganising, *Leutnant* Jahnke was trying to do the same. His last functioning anti-tank gun fired at the tanks of the 70th Tank Battalion's Company C as they waded ashore from their LCTs with the first wave. One US crewman recalled his tank taking four hits, which cracked but failed to penetrate the Sherman's armour, but permanently damaged his hearing.[61] This suggests the weapon was not an 88mm as Jahnke recalled, but the ex-French 47mm piece listed among *Wiederstandnest 5's* inventory, and which still guards the resistance nest today.[62] Whichever, the anti-tank gun then succumbed to damage inflicted in the bombardment, allowing Shermans to close up to the sea wall and shell the resistance nest's surviving positions with impunity. The machine gun mounted in the French tank turret was silenced, and Jahnke was wounded and half-buried in a rifle pit. He was pulled free and captured by the American infantrymen sweeping through the ruined position. Ironically, Jahnke was greeted amiably by two paratroopers from the 506th Parachute Infantry he had captured a few short hours before as he walked to a temporary POW cage.[63]

Once ashore, the US 8th Infantry Regiment despatched its battalions on their missions. The 3rd Battalion prepared to move on Causeway Two while a company from the 1st Battalion dealt with the resistance nest covering Causeway Three. The German survivors fled down the Causeway, unaware that a composite band of paratroopers led by Lieutenant-Colonel Robert G. Cole had seized the landward end at 07:30. They reached the far end at 09:30, and Cole's men killed over fifty without loss, before despatching a patrol to the beach to inform the 4th Division that Causeway Three was fully open.[64] The 8th Infantry's 2nd Battalion, supported by five Shermans, was assigned to advance down Causeway One toward Pouppeville. Three tanks and a number of infantry were lost to mines, but the survivors cleared some bunkers sited to cover the end of the Causeway, and captured a number of German troops guarding a culvert rigged for demolition. The charges were defused, and the cautious advance toward Pouppeville was resumed, where a close–quarter fight was already underway.[65]

Two separate groups of airborne soldiers had spent the hours of darkness making for Causeway One. The officer-heavy band led by Major-General Maxwell D. Taylor, swelled to around 150 by co-opting strays reached Pouppeville at 08:00. The village was held by seventy-odd men from *Infanterie Regiment 1058*, who were disinclined to give up without a fight. It took the Americans three hours of house-to-house fighting to clear the village, losing eighteen men in the process. The defenders lost twenty-five killed and wounded; forty more surrendered and six fled down Causeway One. Taylor immediately despatched a patrol under Lieutenant Eugene Brierre after them. They met the 2nd Battalion, 8th Infantry about half way, at exactly 11:10. The six German survivors of the Pouppeville surrendered.[66]

Causeway Four was assigned to the 22nd Infantry Regiment, the 3rd Battalion of which landed with the first wave at 06:30; the 1st and 2nd Battalions followed at 07:55. The Regiment seems to have become bogged down in clearing the four beach front resistance nests lying between the landing beach and the causeway, which was supposed to be open for the arrival of Colonel Russell P. Reeder's 12th Infantry Regiment at 10:30. At that time only Causeway Two was fully secure, but as it was jammed with vehicles and after conferring briefly with Roosevelt, Reeder opted to lead his entire Regiment in a straight line across the inundated area behind the beach to St Martin-de-Varreville. This rather surprising decision appears to have been based on an optimistic intelligence estimate that the flood was only ankle deep. Reeder may also have been trying to impress Roosevelt, having previously attempted to grandstand his command during training in the UK.[67] Be that as it may, the flood was frequently waist deep at best and over 6 feet at worst. In places it was thus necessary to despatch swimmers with ropes to haul the less capable across.[68] It took the 12th Infantry over four hours to cover 3 miles, and the exertion appears to have been needless; Roosevelt reached St Martin-de-Varreville via Causeway Two shortly after Reeder's men.[69]

Quite rightly, virtually every account of the UTAH landing stresses the light opposition, the consequent low level of casualties, and the speed and efficiency of the overall landing operation. In total, the 4th Division's three infantry regiments suffered between one hundred and eighty-seven and three hundred and fifteen casualties on 6 June, most of them to mines, and including personnel lost at sea.[70] This was a far lower figure than the 4th Division personnel killed during training in Britain prior to the invasion, including those lost in the E-Boat attack off Slapton Sands at the end of April 1944.[71] The unloading operation was undeniably impressive; 21,328 men, 1,742 assorted vehicles and 1,695 tons of supplies were delivered onto the UTAH beaches in the first eighteen hours after landing.[72]

What the accounts do not say, even though the evidence is abundantly clear, is that the 4th Division was extremely and inexplicably slow in moving inland. The 2nd Battalion, 8th Infantry took over four and a half hours to cover the 2 miles to where it linked up with Ewell's paratroopers on Causeway One. According to the officer heading the paratrooper patrol despatched along Causeway Three by Lieutenant-Colonel Cole, the 1st Battalion, 8th Infantry did not begin moving inland until 11:00 either.[73] Only the 12th Infantry Regiment seems to have acted with the haste the situation warranted, although little if any time was saved and the advance was conducted in a militarily unsound manner. Given the negligible level of resistance this was a pretty poor performance, even allowing for the confusion of landing in the wrong place, mines and the constricted egress from the beach. The root of the problem would appear to lie in the paucity and focus of the US training for the invasion discussed above. This appears to have left them extremely well prepared for cross loading from transports to assault craft and getting onto the beach, but rather less well prepared for what was supposed to come next, a tendency that was also apparent elsewhere.

The 4th Division only escaped the consequences of its tardiness at UTAH for two reasons. First was the quality and quantity of the immediate opposition. The bulk of this came from the thinly spread *709 Infanterie Division*, a virtually immobile *bodenständige* formation made up of average and/or medically sub-standard personnel with second-rate equipment. The second and more pertinent reason was the presence and actions of the airborne soldiers from the 82nd and 101st Airborne Divisions. The key proved to be the road hub of St Mère Église, which was secured by Lieutenant-Colonel Edward Krause's 3rd Battalion, 505th Parachute Infantry at 06:00.[74] Once the scale of the US airhead around the town was recognised, *7 Armee* focused its attention on its destruction and recapture of the town virtually to the exclusion of all else, which prevented *91 Luftlande Division* and *Fallschirmjäger Regiment 6* from addressing the more serious threat from the sea.[75]

The best German units in the Cotentin were thus distracted from the real threat, and the exemplary performance of the American paratroopers kept them that way. A combination of *bocage* and stubborn American resistance held *Infanterie Regiment 1057* west of the Merderet. Other German attacks, some supported by armour, against the south of St Mère Église were repulsed by Krause's 3rd Battalion. To the north, a forty-two strong platoon from the 2nd Battalion, 505th Parachute Infantry led by Lieutenant Turner Turnbull established a blocking position at Neuville-au-Plain, which was soon attacked by elements of *Infanterie Regiment 1058*. In the epic eight-hour battle that followed, the vastly outnumbered American paratroopers beat off numerous assaults, some supported by armoured vehicles, and the sixteen survivors only fell back to St Mère Église when they were all but encircled.[76] Neither were the activities of the American paratroopers restricted to the immediate area of St Mère Église. Attacks by the 501st Parachute Infantry trying to reach the road and rail crossings over the River Douve forced the *Fallschirmjäger Regiment 6* onto the defensive at St Côme-du-Mont. This effectively prevented them from moving on St Mère Église, or moving to assist the coastal defences.

Other American paratroopers were instrumental in limiting the amount of artillery fire the Germans were able to bring to bear on the beaches. Staff-Sergeant Harrison Summers of the 1st Battalion, 502nd

Parachute Infantry was despatched with fifteen men to deal with a large group of farm buildings serving as a German artillery barracks near St Martin-de-Varreville. Acting alone or with a single companion when most of his men proved reluctant to expose themselves, Summers methodically stormed one building after another. He finished the job in mid-afternoon shortly before elements of the US 4th Division began to arrive via Causeway Four; over sixty Germans were killed, most by Summers personally, and a further thirty-one surrendered.[77] To the south, Captain Richard Winters of Company E, 2nd Battalion, 506th Parachute Infantry was similarly detailed to eliminate a newly discovered battery of four German 105mm field guns that were shelling the UTAH landing beaches. Protected by around fifty men from the *Fallschirmjäger Regiment 6*, the battery was dug in at Brécourt Manor, north-east of St Marie-du-Mont. Winters gathered twelve men from Company E and carried out a hasty attack that carried them into the German trench system, from where they overran and spiked three guns in turn. A small reinforcing party of five led by another officer from the 2nd Battalion of the 506th destroyed the fourth gun. In the process twelve Germans surrendered, fifteen were killed and an unknown number wounded. American losses totalled four dead and two wounded.[78]

Without this kind of courage and professionalism on the part of the airborne soldiers they were supposed to be speeding to relieve, the 4th Division would have found itself facing much more competent and aggressive opposition, which need not have even necessarily physically attacked the invaders. The jammed Causeways, to say nothing of the 12th Infantry Regiment's impromptu wading exercise, were an artillery observer's dream. Had the airborne soldiers not over fulfilled their brief, it is extremely likely that events at UTAH would have turned out even worse than those unfolding a dozen miles to the east.

Whereas the Cotentin coast was low lying apart from the dunes immediately bordering the beach, sandy bluffs up to 170-feet high backed the OMAHA landing beaches, which ran for 4 miles between Vierville-sur-Mer in the west to Colleville-sur-Mer in the east. The bluffs were cleft by four re-entrants, or draws, leading inland. The western two, codenamed D1 and D3, were assigned to the 116th Infantry Regiment. The first ran inland to Vierville-sur-Mer, while the second was fronted by the seafront hamlet of les Moulins, with a track running inland to St Laurent-sur-Mer. The latter village lay roughly 1,000 yards behind the beach, almost equidistant between D3 and the next draw, E1. This was assigned to 16th Infantry Regiment, along with E3, which led to Colleville-sur-Mer.

The beaches were overlooked by thirteen resistance nests. Six were grouped into two strongpoints at the entrances to D1 and E3.[79] They were manned by *Infanterie Regiment 916* and *Infanterie Regiment 726* from *352 Infanterie Division* commanded by *Generalleutnant* Dietrich Kraiss. In one of its few lapses, Allied intelligence had this division located near St Lô. In fact, it had been given responsibility for a thirty-mile stretch of coast that included the OMAHA landing beaches on 15 March 1944.[80] As we have seen, *352 Division* was not a second-rate *bodenständige* formation, having been awarded the highest level of combat readiness by *OKW* in the spring of 1944.[81] Inaccurate bombing had left the defences virtually untouched, the rocket barrage from the LCT(R)s accompanying the landing wave was equally inaccurate,[82] and there was not sufficient time for the heavy naval units to take up the slack. Inescapable strategic and operational imperatives limited the length of the bombardment, and the Americans heading for the OMAHA beaches were about to pay the price for the technical shortcomings of aerial bombing.

Things began to go awry for the invaders before the Germans made their presence felt, however. The offshore current that swamped the 741st Tank Battalion's DD Shermans pushed most of the landing craft carrying the first wave of the OMAHA assault force east from their planned touch-down points. The 116th Regiment's Company G, for example, was driven 600 yards east from Dog White into Dog Red Beach, and became intermingled with Company F, and two of the 16th Infantry Regiment's companies were swept off the assigned beaches altogether. Eight LCTs carrying the 743rd Tank Battalion were supposed to touch down on Dog Green Beach at 06:30. Only two made it and several of their eight Shermans were lost to anti-tank guns as they tried to suppress the defences.[83] The infantry began to arrive at 06:31. The 116th Infantry's Company A lost two LCA's on the run in, one to four direct hits by mortar bombs 300 yards offshore.[84] The remaining four LCAs were the only craft in the first wave to reach the correct landing point. Unfortunately, Dog Green was almost exactly opposite the strongpoint guarding the entrance to draw D1, which remained unsuppressed by the best efforts of the USS Texas and her fourteen-inch guns.

German standing orders were to wait until the enemy was almost ashore before opening fire, and Company A was thus met with a storm of machine gun and mortar fire when the LCA ramps went down.[85] In a matter of moments ninety-one men were killed. Only twenty made it across the 350 yards of beach to the shelter of the sea wall, made up of wooden piles projecting 4 feet or so above the sand with breakwaters running toward the sea at 50-foot intervals. Some of the succeeding waves onto Dog Green also suffered heavily. The commander of Company B, which landed at 07:00, was killed 10 yards from his LCA, and every other man in the vessel was either killed or wounded. Company D, landing ten minutes later, lost thirty-nine killed and thirty-two wounded, including the company commander whose LCVP hit a mine 400 yards offshore.[86]

The LCAs carrying the 16th Infantry onto Fox Green Beach at the other end of OMAHA received a similar reception, and many of the hapless victims were not supposed to be there. The first ashore were an intermingled group made up of units slated for Easy Red and four loads from the 116th Infantry that should have landed at Easy Green, 2,000 yards to the west. The second wave onto OMAHA was made up of engineers tasked to clear lanes through the beach obstacles before they were covered by the rising tide. Some demolition teams were swept past their assigned objectives, and the rest were severely hampered by enemy fire. The 146th Engineer Combat Team, for example, was tasked to blow two 50-yard wide lanes on each of the 116th Infantry's four landing beaches. They succeeded in creating just two narrow corridors.[87]

This vision of untrammelled carnage with American infantrymen, bereft of close armoured support, being mown down as they emerged from their landing craft or struggled through the surf and shingle, has become the accepted view of events across the length of 'Bloody OMAHA'. Thus the troops have been referred to as 'visitors to Hell' where 'utter chaos reigned', and the beaches as a 'killing ground' with 'defences... simply too strong for the forces sent against them'.[88] This view has been firmly cemented in popular perception by the graphic depiction of events on Dog Green Beach in the film *Saving Private Ryan*. As a result, events at OMAHA are universally accepted as the uniquely awful low point of the D-Day landings. There can be no doubt that OMAHA was an extremely unhealthy place to be in the early morning of 6 June 1944, as dozens of eyewitness accounts eloquently, and frequently horrifyingly, testify. The question is whether the almost legendary reputation of OMAHA as an unmitigated bloodbath is accurate or justified.

Despite the fact that establishing accurate totals is problematic, casualty figures are frequently presented in support of this view.[89] The figures routinely cited for OMAHA are usually in the region of 2,000, between a third and twice those cited for the Anglo-Canadian beaches. However, bare casualty figures are at best a superficial method of judging the severity of any given engagement, not least because they rarely fully reflect the multiplicity of factors that influence outcomes. Merely comparing the losses at OMAHA and UTAH, for example, does not reflect the degree to which sheer luck minimised casualties on the latter. Casualties aside, examination of the evidence suggests that the popular perception of events at OMAHA is something of an oversimplification. More specifically, some of the underlying assumptions are not as clear-cut as they are often presented.

For example, the absence of the 741st Tank Battalion's DD Shermans is regularly cited as an important contributing factor in the casualties suffered by the 16th Infantry Regiment.[90] The problem with this is that the presence of the 743rd Tank Battalion's tanks on the 116th Regiment's beaches did little to suppress the fire that took such a toll of the infantry, even though they preceded the first wave of infantry as the DD tanks would have done. It is therefore difficult to see what difference the arrival of the DD tanks on schedule further east would have made, at least in the immediate term. The real problem with regard to armour at OMAHA was not the non-arrival of the 741st Tank Battalion's DD tanks, but that the landing frontage required significantly more tanks than were assigned to the landing overall. Including the specialised armour from the 79th Armoured Division, the initial British and Canadian landing waves deployed getting on for the equivalent of two tank battalions per beach, and frequently over much shorter landing frontages.

Received wisdom also cites the high combat status of *352 Infanterie Division* as an important contributing factor in the difficulties experienced by the Americans on OMAHA. This does not stand up to detailed scrutiny either. As we shall see, the performance of 352 Division was not significantly superior to that of the *bodenständige* formations that flanked it to the east, in either preventing the invaders getting off the beach or in holding the beachfront defences. Even the most obvious indicator, the higher number of casualties inflicted on the US assault force, has more to do with the Americans obligingly presenting themselves as targets in front of the highest concentration of machine guns than any particular expertise or tenacity on the part of the defenders.

In fact, overestimation of the strength and effectiveness of the German defences along the OMAHA landing beaches has been a key factor in the creation and maintenance of the popular perception of OMAHA as the scene of unrelenting slaughter. For proof one need look no further than the terms in which it is routinely described, which almost invariably suggest a fully developed defence system. One work, for example, refers to '…a deliberate defence years in the making', and another claims that a '…combination of man-made defences and natural obstacles had turned "Omaha" into a killing ground'.[91] Attractive as this explanation is, it is contradicted by two pieces of compelling evidence. First, the volume and accuracy of fire on OMAHA was not uniformly as intense as that encountered on Dog Green and Fox Green beaches, although eyewitness accounts from the latter two are almost invariably cited as evidence of the awfulness of the overall situation.

The 116th Infantry's Company G and most of Company F, for example, came ashore opposite exit D3 at les Moulins. Their landing was screened by smoke from burning vegetation on the bluffs, and both companies crossed the beach to the shelter of the seawall without difficulty and with few casualties. This area was something of a blind spot in the German defence. All four companies of the 116th Infantry's 3rd Battalion landed and crossed the beach there without losing a single man to enemy fire from 07:27; the only casualty was accidentally speared with a bayonet before disembarking.[92] Even where the German fire was heaviest and most accurate, some units crossed the beach with relatively few casualties. At Dog Green, over half of the 2nd Ranger Battalion's Company C made it across where the 116th Infantry's Company A had been destroyed. They were followed by the 116th Regiment's Company C, two more companies from the 2nd Ranger Battalion and the 5th Ranger Battalion in its entirety. None of these units suffered anywhere near the casualties inflicted on the first wave. The story was the same at the other end of OMAHA. At least eight boatloads from the 16th Infantry's first wave, along with four boatloads from the 116th Regiment's Company E crossed Fox Green virtually unscathed, followed by G Company from the second wave. The third wave, consisting of the 3rd Battalion 16th Infantry, also suffered few casualties in landing just east of the E3 exit leading to Colleville-sur-Mer.[93]

This suggests that the German defence was by no means as uniformly formidable as it is routinely portrayed, a contention reinforced by the way the Americans were able to move off the beach once they had reorganised themselves. The 116th Regiment's commander, Colonel Charles D. W. Canham, came ashore with his command group near the D3 exit at les Moulins at 07:30. He was accompanied by Brigadier-General Norman D. Cota, the 29th Division's deputy commander, who wanted to see conditions on the beach for himself. By this time the rising tide had narrowed the distance to the seawall to around 150 yards, and the command group found several hundred men sheltering in the 50-foot bays between the breakwaters jutting seaward from the seawall. Realising that the bays would be death traps once the Germans began dropping artillery and mortar fire into them, Cota and Canham split up and began moving along the seawall encouraging and cajoling the troops to move inland. One sergeant recalled Cota appearing next to where he and a group from the 5th Ranger Battalion were sheltering. Cota enquired who they were and on being told took the opportunity to remind them of their unit motto: 'Goddamit, if you're Rangers get up there and lead the way'.[94]

Cota personally led the way over the seawall and deployed a BAR gunner to give covering fire while a Bangalore torpedo was used to blow a hole in the concertina wire blocking further progress. When the first man through the gap was killed, Cota went through himself and led a growing stream of men across a flood meadow beyond the seawall and on up the face of the bluff. He reached the crest at some time between 08:30 and 09:00 and, after reorganising his motley band, led them west into Vierville-sur-Mer, where they met up with another group led by Canham. Canham then led a group east with the intention of clearing the D3 exit at les Moulins. Cota, accompanied by six men, cleared a position covering the draw and secured the D1 exit. He then organised engineers and a bulldozer to demolish a concrete wall blocking vehicular access through the draw, before moving back onto the beach to supervise the advance inland. Both Cota and Canham were awarded the Distinguished Service Cross for their actions.[95]

This was not an isolated incident, for the same process was taking place all along OMAHA. Companies G and K from the 3rd Battalion, 116th Infantry reached the crest of the bluffs to the east of the les Moulins D3 exit and began pushing inland toward St Laurent-sur-Mer. Further east, twenty-three men from the 2nd Battalion, 16th Infantry Regiment led by Second Lieutenant John M. Spalding attacked the resistance nest guarding the E1 exit from the rear and forced the garrison to surrender after a two hour battle. The 16th Infantry's 3rd Battalion also made its way up the bluffs to the east of the E3 draw and attacked another resistance nest located on the crest. With fire support from tanks and destroyers the nest was cleared by 09:00. The E3 exit proper was secured at 11:30 by the 1st Division's 18th Infantry Regiment, with assistance of an LCT and a LCI that rammed their way through the by now submerged obstacles and beached themselves to provide fire support at 10:30. Further fire support came from two destroyers that closed to under a thousand yards from the beach and plastered the German defences east of the les Moulins exit, covering engineers dealing with the minefields and other obstacles.[96]

Thus within four hours the Americans had overcome a badly disrupted landing, fought their way off the beach and secured or were well on the way to securing the four vehicle exits from the beaches, and were penetrating inland. This was laudable, especially in comparison with the tardy progress achieved over a similar timespan on the virtually uncontested UTAH landing beach. However, such progress would have been unlikely, if not impossible had the OMAHA defences been anywhere near as complete and impregnable as they are popularly portrayed. The crux of the problem was therefore that it took the American attackers an hour to start moving off the beach and, popular perceptions not withstanding, the above strongly suggests that this delay was not solely or even largely due to the German defence.

The two most common explanations for this initial inertia are that the carnage wrought by defensive fire on the attackers was magnified by their inexperience, and that it 'facilitated the onset of shock and paralysis'.[97] The former may be valid up to a point, but it has to be said that despite received wisdom, experience is not an infallible indicator of superior combat performance. The US 1st Division was deemed so experienced as not to require specialist assault training, but its performance was not markedly superior to that of the green 29th Division, whose troops proved equally capable when push came to shove on the bluffs above the landing beaches. The fact is that a combination of strong *esprit de corps* and intensive, realistic and properly configured training can provide a perfectly valid substitute for combat experience, as the performance of the equally green British 6th and US 101st Airborne Divisions clearly shows.

The shock and paralysis explanation appears to be more feasible, at least in the case of the survivors of initial waves. The commander of the 2nd Battalion 116th Infantry, Major Sidney Bingham, came across a party of 100 men near the les Moulins exit, many without weapons and seemingly unaware of their surroundings.[98] Another officer also referred to men staring into space and being physically incapable of holding weapons. A report from the 29th Division referred to men lying inert, seemingly in a daze, and a member of the 1st Division's 16th Infantry Regiment admitted to taking cover behind a beached landing craft and crying uncontrollably.[99] The visual evidence of the slaughter strewn across some of the beaches was certainly sufficient to trigger such responses, and not just among the assault waves. The rising tide had rimed the water's edge with scores of American dead, and one of Cota's staff officers estimated that every hundred square yards above the water line contained between thirty-five and fifty bodies.[100]

In addition, the impact of all this was exacerbated by unrealistic expectations of precisely what an opposed landing was likely to entail. Participant testimony shows the 1st and 2nd Battalion's of the 116th Infantry had been told to expect little if any resistance, and at least one company had been specifically ordered not to run across the beach.[101] This delusion was all the more damaging because it came straight from the top. US 1st Army commander Omar Bradley told the 116th Infantry that the naval and air bombardment would prepare their way so efficiently that they would be little more than spectators 'for the greatest show on earth'.[102] Brigadier-General Leonard T. Gerow, commanding the US 5th Corps, made the same point to his staff at a conference in February 1944, and repeated it publicly in a Corps address in the middle of May 1944.[103] On the other hand, Gerow can be partly excused because his address was attempting to counter damaging rumours that the invasion would entail very heavy casualties, and it should also be noted that such optimism was not universal at less exalted levels.

Colonel Canham, who played a key role in motivating the stalled attackers near the D1 beach exit, circulated a memo throughout the 116th Infantry Regiment warning of the dangers of underestimating German military prowess; this was read to the troops just before embarkation. Colonel Paul Goode, commanding the 175th Infantry, specifically warned his officers that the situation on the beach was likely not to conform to the plan. He emphasised the point by tossing the inches thick NEPTUNE operation order on the floor and stressing the crucial thing was going to be getting off the beach no matter what the conditions. General Cota was equally forthright, impressing on his staff that the invasion would be totally unlike past training exercises, presciently warning them that mislandings would be commonplace and that improvisation would be the key to success.[104] Quite how much of this was taken on board lower down the chain of command is open to question, however. The briefing given to the 29th Division's 115th Infantry Regiment, scheduled to land in the second wave onto OMAHA, specifically told the troops that they would merely have to hike inland to the D-Day Phase Line. There was thus much consternation on the run in to the beach when the Regiment was informed it would be landing in the middle of a battle.[105]

Unrealistic expectations thus doubtless contributed to the shock and paralysis, but whether to a degree sufficient to hold up the entire beachhead for over an hour is open to doubt. Where it did occur, the paralysis frequently appears to have been a short-lived and transitory occurrence rather than a permanently debilitating one. The soldier from the 16th Infantry cited above, for example, reported coming to his senses after a time and being able to function normally thereafter. Consequently, while the troops Cota and others found sheltering along the top of the OMAHA beaches may have been unwilling to stand up or move forward under their own volition, many were far from shocked, paralysed or quiescent. Eyewitness testimony shows many were firing their weapons at German positions they could see, including several .30 machine-guns, not the most unobtrusive or easily set up of weapons. Others were sorting out their kit and cleaning the sand from their weapons. In short, many if not most were willing to fight. They just needed someone to take the lead and tell them what to do.

This suggests leadership and small-unit cohesion, or more specifically a lack thereof, was the key factor in the initial hiatus, and this was not solely due to the loss of officers and NCOs on the beach. The US

1st and 29th Divisions' existing small-unit structure was reorganised for the landing, into specially configured assault platoons made up of rifle, BAR, wire cutting, flame-thrower and mortar teams; these teams were supposed to revert to their standard platoon and company organisations once the landing was complete.[106] The mandatory and blanket imposition of this removed and thus effectively destroyed whatever cohesion existed at the crucial squad and platoon levels. This was exacerbated yet further in some instances by the way the troops were assigned to their LCAs and LCVPs. The overriding principle was to fill the landing craft, which was often done by simply dividing the total number of men by the capacity of the landing craft. Although teams that made up the assault platoons were grouped together where possible, there was no binding allowance for the old or new tactical structures or the roles the individual passengers were supposed to perform on landing.

Given time, training could have offset this but as we have seen, that commodity was at a premium.[107] How assiduously training in the new organisation and specialisms was undertaken is also open to question, given that they were known to be a temporary arrangement and that the troops were being told to expect minimal resistance on the beaches. None of this is especially revelatory. One recent work on the subject devotes an entire chapter to an illuminating and well-referenced discussion of the matter, for example.[108] The problem is that it is tacked on as an epilogue, and thus still approaches the matter with the usual assumption that a particularly effective German defence was the catalyst for all that occurred on the OMAHA beaches.

However, the evidence points to an alternative and equally plausible interpretation. The plain if less than palatable fact is that overall, the American assault force was poorly prepared and insufficiently trained for the task it was assigned. The combination of time constraints and conflicting priorities left the US assault units tolerably well-drilled in trans-shipping from ship to landing craft, and debarking onto the beach in an orderly manner according to the plan. They were far less prepared to cope with what came thereafter, not least due to unfamiliarity with the practical workings of the special assault organisation, which reduced the basis for initiative that would otherwise have been present. This explains why the bulk of the troops on both landing areas ended up waiting passively for instructions. There had been no time for the intensive training and practice necessary to thoroughly inculcate all ranks in every aspect of their missions. Properly done, this would have dispensed with the need for tight formal leadership, an approach that proved highly successful in the airborne divisions. This in turn left the sea assault force highly vulnerable to any disruption of the plan, a rather dangerous state given the old military adage that no plan survives first contact with the enemy.

The clearest evidence to support this theory occurred not at OMAHA but at UTAH, where the 4th Infantry Division took several hours to initiate a hesitant advance with virtually no opposition. The two US landing areas have been invariably treated in isolation in the past, largely due to the disparity in resistance, but the particularist approach is both inaccurate and irrelevant in this instance. All of the American assault divisions underwent the same training, using the same facilities, practices and planning guidance, and under the same time constraints. Consequently, there is no reason to assume that the US 1st and 29th Division would have been any more competent than the 4th Division under the same precise circumstances. The true extent of American unpreparedness has thus been concealed by the inaccurate landing on UTAH, and the myth of a near impregnable German defence at OMAHA.

This is in no way intended as a criticism of the men who went ashore at OMAHA in the early morning of 6 June 1944, quite the contrary. It would be both unfair and unreasonable to hold the men at the sharp end responsible for the shape and extent of their training, over which they had a minimal influence at best. The same has to be said, at least to an extent, of those higher up the chain of command. General Huebner's 1st Infantry Division was given responsibility for the assault on OMAHA in its entirety. The problem was that neither Huebner nor his immediate superior, 5th Corps commander Gerow, were permitted more than minimal input to the assault plan. Everything, the attack frontage, the precise load out of the LCAs and LCVPs, the engineer obstacle clearing plan, the reorganisation into assault platoons, even the items of kit to be carried by individual soldiers within the latter, was passed down from on high.[109] The first waves from the 1st and 29th Divisions were thus facing not only the German defenders on OMAHA, but also handicaps imposed by their own side over and above those arising from the imperatives that guided the invasion overall. This renders the performance of the men placed on the spot all the more laudable.

Be that as it may, while the 1st and 29th Divisions were struggling ashore at OMAHA, the 2nd Ranger Battalion was fighting its own private battle at the Pointe du Hoc. The assault force, made up of Companies D, E and F led by Lieutenant-Colonel James E. Rudder, was carried in ten LCAs backed up with two DUKWs carrying hundred-foot extendable turntable ladders. Launched 12 miles offshore, the Rangers were scheduled to land at 06:30, but the British guide vessel led the flotilla toward another headland 4,000 metres to the east of their proper target. It took an additional thirty-five minutes to make up the distance, within small-arms range of the coast. In the process one troop-carrying LCA was swamped, although most of the Rangers aboard were rescued, as was another carrying ammunition, demolition charges and other equipment. A second supply vessel only avoided a similar fate by jettisoning most of its cargo.

The navigational error obliged the Rangers to land only on the east-facing beach below the cliffs. The seven surviving troop-carrying LCAs arrived along a 500-yard frontage between 07:00 and 07:05. At 07:10, having failed to receive the radio codeword 'Tilt' or detect any visual signals, the second turned away and headed for Dog Green Beach. By this time the Pointe du Hoc garrison was fully alert, and the Rangers could actually see many of them atop the cliff awaiting their approach. They were temporarily driven back by the destroyers HMS *Talybont* and USS *Satterlee*, which plastered the cliff-top and maintained a steady fire thereafter. This proved to be a mixed blessing, as the resulting debris rained down on the Rangers below; one large section of cliff narrowly missed Lieutenant-Colonel Rudder. The resultant build up did provide the Rangers with a useful platform from which to begin their climb, however.

The DUKWs mounting the turntable ladders had great difficulty negotiating the slippery shingle, and were prevented from closing up to the cliff by debris and craters from the pre-landing bombardment. One bogged at too acute an angle to deploy its ladder, but the other was raised with Sergeant William Stivison boldly manning the twin Lewis guns. However, once fully extended the ladder began oscillating at up to forty-five degrees, making accurate fire impossible, to say nothing of being extremely hazardous. One account describes Stivison arcing back and forth like a human metronome, and another eyewitness likened him to a circus performer.[110] The ladder was swiftly lowered again, doubtless to Stivison's relief. Much of the cliff climbing kit had been lost in the swamped supply LCA and not all of the remainder arrived in a usable condition. Many of the ropes had been thoroughly soaked in the approach or while being manhandled across the beach, and proved too heavy for the rockets to lift. The NCO charged with igniting the rocket-propelled grapnel ropes had to use an electrical igniter box with only one metre of cable, and was temporarily blinded by each launch.[111]

Many ropes that launched proved to be too slippery to climb, and the Germans atop the cliff severed several that grappled properly. One Ranger had two ropes cut from under him, and another found himself involuntarily ejected from the lightweight ladder he was climbing when his life preserver accidentally inflated. Some Rangers dispensed with ropes and ladders altogether and free-climbed up the cliff, cutting footholds with bayonets and fighting knives.[112] All the time the Germans were lobbing down hand-grenades and leaning over to fire on the Americans below, despite the best efforts of the *Talybont* and *Satterlee* and the Rangers on the beach. The climbing men also had to cope with large artillery shells suspended over the cliff by wires, which the defenders dropped onto the attackers.[113] Despite all this, the Ranger's intensive training and tenacity rapidly began to pay off. Among the first to make the clifftop was Private First Class Harry W. Roberts, who reached a shelf formed by a shell crater just below the edge of the cliff on his second attempt. He then used his body to secure a rope for the rest of his squad to join him, after which they went over the lip of the cliff and attacked a nearby bunker.[114]

By 07:30 the majority of Rudder's force had reached the cliff-top, at a cost of fifteen dead and fifty wounded. Rudder established a command post there fifteen minutes later, as his men fanned out to deal with their specific objectives within the battery position. They were aided by the results of the Allied air and sea bombardment, which had turned the battery position into a moonscape with craters up to 30 feet deep. However, the broken ground also severely hampered formal command and control, leaving individuals or small groups of Rangers to work things out for themselves. Occupied bunkers and defensive positions were cleared in a series of confused and vicious close-quarter fights. A bazooka rocket through the slit cleared the observation post at the tip of the promontory, and a machine gun position at the eastern end of the battery perimeter was despatched by the USS *Satterlee*. Ranger Lieutenant James W. Eikner controlled the destroyer's fire, using an ancient tripod-mounted signal lamp carried as a contingency measure in lieu of a radio.[115]

The Battery was secured at 08:15, and on reorganisation the Rangers discovered that the artillery casemates and emplacements were empty, and no guns were to be found within the perimeter. The Rangers then began patrolling inland. Sergeants Jack Kuhn and Leonard Lomell followed a heavily marked track, and came upon a camouflaged five-gun battery, complete with ammunition and ancillary equipment. Incredibly, there were no sentries, although the gunners were drawn up in a nearby field. Kuhn and Lomell detonated thermite grenades in the breech and traversing mechanism of two guns and smashed the sights of a third before leaving to collect more thermite grenades. On the way they were showered with debris when another patrol, led by Sergeant Fred Rupinski, destroyed a nearby artillery ammunition dump. Undaunted, Kuhn and Lomell gathered their fresh supply of thermite bombs, returned to the battery and demolished the remaining two artillery pieces before despatching a runner to inform Rudder that the guns had been located and destroyed. The time was about 09:00, and the Rangers had accomplished their mission against the odds and in the face of stiff resistance that had cost them around half their original number killed and wounded.

The survivors then turned their attention to preparing to defend their foothold in the battery position until relief arrived from OMAHA.[116]

The GOLD bombardment began at 05:45, and H-Hour was sixty minutes later than the US beaches because the landing vessels needed higher water to get over the Calvados Reef. In the event the British 50th (Northumbrian) Infantry Division began to go ashore on the Jig and King sectors five minutes early, at 07:25. DD Shermans from the 4th/7th Royal Dragoon Guards and the Sherwood Rangers Yeomanry were supposed to be launched 7,000 yards out, but the order was countermanded due to the rough sea. The LCTs thus carried their hybrid passengers much closer inshore and delivered them apparently at the individual whim of the LCT and tank unit commanders. Thus some of the Sherwood Rangers were launched 6-700 yards offshore, others 200 yards or closer, and one LCT with a damaged ramp carried its charges all the way onto the beach.

Lieutenant Stuart Hills, commanding a troop from C Squadron, was launched about 600 yards out and saw some of his comrade's tanks reach the beach as planned. Hills was not so lucky. His LCT ramp jammed, and two German shells hit the vessel while it was being freed, wounding two tankcrew caught standing atop their vehicles. The shells also damaged the underside of Hills' tank, which began to take water immediately on launching and sank after only 70 yards, thankfully with sufficient warning for the crew to bale out and take to their inflatable dinghy. Eight of the Sherwood Ranger's DD tanks foundered, and the 4th/7th Royal Dragoon Guards lost a further five. A passing LCG picked up Hills and his crew just as their dinghy was bracketed by German artillery, and they had the surreal experience of listening to the BBC reporting the activity in which they were involved. They finally made it ashore in their salvaged dinghy during the night of D Plus One, and rejoined their unit on 13 June.[117]

Some of the LCTs paid a high price for going in close. At least two were set ablaze by German fire and sank close inshore. Merely reaching the beach was no guarantee of safety either, for as at OMAHA the heavy bombers had delivered most of their ordnance harmlessly inland and fighter bomber strikes were ineffective, presumably due to the poor visibility. A Sherwood Rangers tank was hit while deflating its swimming screen, which caught fire and ignited spare fuel stowed on the vehicle; two of the crew were killed as they baled out.[118] Only one LCT carrying the Royal Marine Support Regiment made it ashore in the Jig sector, and all five Centaur close-support tanks were knocked out in quick succession.[119] Of one troop of Sherman Crabs from the Westminster Dragoons, only Trooper Joe Minogue's rear vehicle survived. The lead Crab stopped abruptly when its commander was killed, the second became bogged in a patch of clay while taking avoiding action, and an anti-tank gun knocked out the third and set it ablaze.[120]

All this interfered with the ability of the Funnies from 6 Assault Regiment RE to clear their lanes through the beach obstacles and minefields for the infantry assault wave, which began to land at 07:40. 231 Infantry Brigade was responsible for the Jig sector, and the 1st Hampshires were assigned to Jig Green, the most westerly of the GOLD beaches. The easterly current carried them part way onto the adjoining Jig Red Beach. B Company crossed the beach and overran the German resistance nest at les Roquettes, which was actually assigned to the neighbouring 1st Dorsets, before moving on to tackle another resistance inland at Asnelles-sur-Mer. A and C Companies, however, were pinned down on the beach by fire from the German resistance nest at le Hamel to the west.

Jig Green Beach straddled the boundary between *352* and *716 Infanterie Divisions*, and the le Hamel resistance nest was manned by personnel from the former's *Infanterie Regiment 726*. They relayed a running commentary on Allied activity, beginning with the appearance of the invasion fleet at 06:32, and reported enemy tanks moving inland toward Asnelles through the adjoining *716 Division* sector at 08:12. The assault was observed by the vanguard of a far more formidable foe. *Oberbefehlshaber West* had issued a warning order to *12 SS Panzer Division* at 04:00, and *SS Panzer Aufklärungs Abteilung 12* despatched five small patrols to clarify the situation. *Obersturmführer* Peter Hansemann's two Puma armoured cars were thus instructed to ascertain what was happening on the coast north of Bayeux.

Hansemann motored through Caen and Bayeux, alert for Allied
fighter bombers after daylight, and found a vantage point on the high
ground at Magny-en-Bessin, a mile south-west of the GOLD beaches.
This gave him a grandstand view of the fighting along the GOLD and
JUNO beaches and the invasion fleet stretching away towards the Orne
estuary in the east. After transmitting a report Hansemann continued
his patrol, returning east along the line of the coast.[121]

The 2nd Devons, and No. 47 (RM) Commando began landing on
Jig Green at 08:00, and were under fire before the ramps went down.
The Devons were quickly pinned down with the Hampshires, and the
Battalion's two command Jeeps were unloaded into several feet of
water, drowning both vehicles.[122] The Commandos lost two LCAs on
the run in, found its assembly area occupied by German troops, and
lost forty men clearing them out of it. The Hampshires were unable to
close on the le Hamel resistance nest, which was built around a stout
sea-front sanatorium building, without tank support; the tanks,
however, were unable to render assistance because of mines. The
impasse was broken by Trooper Minogue's Sherman Crab, which
cleared a lane for a Churchill AVRE, armed with a 290mm Petard
spigot mortar firing dustbin shaped round containing forty pounds of
explosive. Two rounds breached the sanatorium walls, allowing the
1st Hampshires to begin clearing the position while the AVRE shattered a now unsighted anti-tank gun bunker. The ensuing fight went
on until midday, when the surviving German defenders finally
surrendered.[123]

German resistance was equally stiff on the adjoining King sector.
Again the DD tanks, from the 4th/7th Royal Dragoon Guards, were
delivered close inshore or directly onto the beach, virtually alongside
the specialised armour. The King beaches were protected by a
number of machine gun positions, reinforced with at least two anti-
tank gun casemates. These knocked out the first Sherman Crab onto
the beach at 07:29, swiftly followed by two Churchill AVREs, and
several LCAs carrying the 5th East Yorks and 6th Green Howards
were sunk by mines attached to the beach obstacles.[124] Private Francis
Williams, a Bren gunner from the 6th Green Howards, landed in

chest-deep water that drowned several of his heavily laden comrades. After negotiating a burning Sherman Crab, Williams stormed a German machine-gun position, killing two and capturing six. Noticing one of the POWs wore an *Afrika Korps* cuff band, he identified himself as a Desert Rat in one of the less lethal Anglo-German encounters that morning, before moving off to rejoin his platoon.[125] The 6th Green Howards' first objective was a six-bunker resistance nest at Hable de Heurtot, covering King Green Beach. After reorganising at the seawall, the battalion attacked with support from a lone DD Sherman and set about clearing the bunkers and trenches. In the confusion an uncleared bunker was overlooked and opened fire on D Company's command group. CSM Stanley Hollis single-handedly attacked it with grenades and his Sten gun, killing two of the occupants and capturing the rest, before turning his attention to the occupants of a nearby trench. The battalion then moved on to its second objective, an artillery position at Mont Fleury, a mile and a half inland near Crépon.[126]

While all this was going on the 5th East Yorks were dealing with the German strongpoint built into the seafront town of la Rivière. Machine gun and mortar fire caused the East Yorks a number of casualties before they reached the seawall, where they were pinned for time by heavy fire. A lone DD tank succeeded in suppressing the defence sufficiently for two platoons to climb the wall and clear the machine-gun bunkers. At the same time another Sherman from the Westminster Dragoons knocked one of the anti-tank gun bunkers enfilading the beach with two rounds through the firing slit. The anti-tank guns were sited to provide mutual support, and a Churchill AVRE was then able to destroy another with a Petard round; the AVRE commander was awarded the MC. Another AVRE blew a gap in the seawall, which allowed other tanks to enter la Rivière and assist the East Yorks; the town was secured at around 09:00. The 7th Green Howards came ashore while the fight for la Rivière was underway, and bypassed the town to advance inland toward Vers-sur-Mer and Crépon, accompanied by tanks from the 4th/7th Royal Dragoon Guards. By the time the 50th Division's second echelon began landing at 11:00 therefore, the Division's lead elements were pushing well inland toward their D-Day boundary on the Caen-Bayeux road. The GOLD assault force had been allowed two hours to clear the beach defences. King Green and King Red beaches were cleared on or ahead of schedule. Most of the Jig sector was cleared with similar despatch, apart from the resistance nest in la Rivière, which took almost five hours to subdue.

The British 50th Division thus cleared a far more formidable set of defences in almost half the time as their counterparts on the adjacent OMAHA beaches. The above refutes the popular view that the GOLD landings were in some way easier, and there appear to be two reasons for the swifter and less costly progress. First was the sufficiency of armour, and especially the Sherman Crabs and Churchill AVREs belonging to the 79th Armoured Division. Conventionally armed tanks could provide a certain degree of supporting fire, but the latter vehicles packed sufficient punch to breach hardened fortifications, as demonstrated in the attack on the sanatorium strongpoint at le Hamel. They were equally effective against concrete obstacles, as demonstrated by the breaching of the seawall before la Rivière. This demolition capability would have been extremely useful on OMAHA. When Brigadier-General Cota found vehicular access up the Vierville Draw blocked by a concrete wall, he had to cast around for an engineer officer to demolish it, who in turn had to search out the necessary explosives, ancillary equipment and a bulldozer. An AVRE could doubtless have completed the job with one or two Petard rounds.

The second factor was the competence, aggression and speed of the 50th Division's infantry. Despite being delivered into chest deep water and coming under immediate mortar and machine-gun fire, the 6th Green Howards went straight after their primary objective. The account by Private Francis Williams MM cited above does not suggest he stumbled upon the German machine-gun position he wiped out single-handed. Rather, he appears to have known exactly where it was, which is extremely likely given that his battalion as a whole had exhaustively studied the layout of their objective. The upshot of this was that every man, and not just the senior NCOs and officers, had a full grasp of the plan and were thus capable and willing to act on their own initiative as and where necessary, even when delivered in the wrong location. Despite being delivered east of their planned landing place on Jig Red rather Jig Green Beach, B Company, 1st Hampshires attacked and overran the German resistance nest at les Roquettes assigned to a neighbouring unit.

That is not to suggest that this kind of performance was due to intrinsic British superiority, far from it. Most of the 1st Hampshires and the 2nd Dorsets were pinned down in the lee of the seawall near le Hamel, it will be recalled, as were the 5th East Yorks near la Rivière. The American infantrymen who landed at the OMAHA beaches acted in essentially the same way, it just took them longer to shake off the reaction to facing live enemy fire and get on with the job in hand. In part this was because there was not enough armour immediately available at OMAHA to shoot the infantry off the beach, in the way the British tanks of whatever type did on GOLD. It was also because the British infantry were operating in their accustomed sections, platoons and companies; any non-infantry tasks were left to either the specialised armour or attached detachments from specialist units. This allowed them to retain arguably their greatest strength, the cohesion generated by the tribal and familial nature of the British regimental system and infantry battalion structure. With the arguable exception of specially selected parachute and Ranger units, this was never an American strongpoint, but whatever cohesion and esprit the OMAHA assault units had was wiped out by the poorly thought-out and temporary reorganisation into specialist assault platoons. It is interesting to speculate on how things might have turned out had the OMAHA infantry commanders been left to organise their men as they saw fit, instead of being forced to conform to a poorly thought out scheme intended to temporarily transform line infantrymen into specialised assault troops hastily and on the cheap.

The JUNO landing area, a mile east of GOLD, was assigned to the 3rd Canadian Infantry Division. The landings were spread over five beaches with a combined frontage of 3.5 miles, straddling the small fishing port of Courseulles. Mike Green Beach stretched a mile west of Courseulles backed by sand dunes that screened the village of

Graye-sur-Mer. A strongpoint was built into the dunes and included the port and its immediate environs within its eastern perimeter. Mike Red straddled the port and extended onto the beach fronting Courseulles proper, which was located mainly to the east of the port. In all, the defences included at least one large calibre artillery casemate, anti-tank gun bunkers, over a dozen machine-gun positions, three mortar pits and a number of other fighting bunkers linked by trenches, and allegedly an anti-tank ditch behind the dunes to the west. According to one account, the Courseulles strongpoint was the strongest single German beach defence work on the invasion frontage.[127] The task of eliminating it was given to the 7th Canadian Infantry Brigade, supported by the cruisers Diadem and Belfast, eleven destroyers and a number of LCGs and LCT(R)s. H-Hour was set for 07:35, although this was extended to 07:47 because the rough seas delayed the forming up.

Nineteen DD Shermans from the 6th Canadian Armoured Regiment were launched 4,000 yards offshore instead of the planned 7,000 yards. Had they launched as planned it is highly likely the 6th Canadian Armoured would have suffered the same fate as the US 741st Tank Battalion off OMAHA. According to Sergeant Leo Gariepy, they were launched into a force seven wind, three categories above the normally accepted maximum, and his crew had to brace the flotation screen with whatever came to hand. Whether due to this or pure luck, Gariepy's tank was one of fourteen to land safely at 07:45, in front of the dunes west of the harbour. In this case the DD's alleged shock value appears to have paid off, as a number of the defenders abandoned their positions in panic. Gariepy machine-gunned a number of these unfortunates while deflating his flotation screen, and then moved off to tackle his primary objective, a large artillery casemate camouflaged as a beachfront house.

As the camouflaging structure was badly damaged and the casemate silent, Gariepy assumed it had been knocked out and halted close by to get his bearings and allow his crew to imbibe self-heating soup to stave off the after effects of sea-sickness. He was spectacularly advised of his error when the muzzle blast of the German gun lifted the thirty-ton Sherman up on its suspension. The Canadians responded by pumping several armour piercing rounds into the embrasure, followed by a number of high explosive shells into the rear door. Satisfied that the casemate was now out of action, Gariepy moved off into Courseulles to his designated rendezvous at the municipal grave-yard, driving through backyards to avoid any mines planted in the narrow streets. On the way he was side-tracked into spearheading an attack on a large group of Germans holed up in a park by the Regina Rifles, which netted thirty-two prisoners.[128]

Because of the rough sea, most of the DD tanks and specialised armour appear to have arrived on the Mike beaches after the assault-ing infantry. Mike Green was allocated to the Royal Winnipeg Rifles and a company from the Canadian Scottish Regiment. The H-Hour delay meant the tide had covered many of the beach obstacles, which obliged the landing craft to try and bull through; a third of the first wave LCAs were sunk or damaged. The surviving Winnipegs and Canadian Scottish landed at 07:49, accompanied by the latter's pipers playing 'Bonnie Dundee'. Once again the defences were largely untouched by the pre-landing bombardment, and the Canadians were greeted with artillery, mortar and machine gun fire. Understandably, the landing craft crews were thus eager to be off. The LCT carrying the Winnipeg's mortar platoon insisted they follow the tanks, despite warnings that the water was too deep. The lead Bren Gun Carrier promptly drowned, whereupon the Canadian sergeant in charge demanded to be carried onto the beach. He remained obdurate even when threatened with a court martial by the vessel's captain, which obliged the LCT to raise the ramp, circle and come in again. The remainder of the Winnipeg's mortar platoon landed dry-tracked.[129]

Fire from the unsubdued German defences caused the Canadian infantry a number of casualties as they struggled up the beach toward their tormentors in the dunes. Most of the Winnipegs made it to the seawall with moderate casualties, but B Company was particularly badly hit, being reduced to one officer and twenty-odd men.[130] Even harder hit were the sappers from the 6th Field Company, Royal Canadian Engineers, who suffered grievous losses attempting to clear lanes through the beach obstacles and mines ahead of the rapidly rising tide, unprotected from the German fire. Seventy-five per cent of the hundred-strong unit became casualties on 6 June, one of the highest casualty ratios anywhere along the invasion front.[131]

The situation eased somewhat as the tanks came ashore. Some sheltered the infantry as they moved up the beach, and provided fire support as they tackled the defences. Sergeant Harold Fielder's Churchill from the 26th Field Company RE carried a fascine to breach the anti-tank ditch behind the dunes fronting Graye-sur-Mer. The beach was littered with dead and wounded Canadians, and Fielder's tank had no option but to drive over several of the prone forms. The upset this caused Fielder and his crew was doubtless heightened by the discovery that the ditch they were supposed to fill did not actually exist. After discarding the fascine, Fielder then shot up a German bunker that was rash enough to fire on it, prompting five of the occupants to surrender, before returning to the beach to help clear the beach obstacles. This was done by dragging them aside with a towing hawser, and within a few hours Fielder had cleared the whole of his assigned beach above the water line.[132]

The Regina Rifles were assaulting Mike Red Beach, east of the harbour. Several men were drowned when their LCA unloaded them into deep water after grounding on a sandbar, and one sergeant had the unusual and alarming experience of seeing the vessel lifted bodily over him by the swell. He survived to deter a DD tank from shooting up a group of friendly infantry and directed the tank's fire against a German anti-tank gun instead.[133] The lead wave of Reginas also landed ahead of their supporting DD tanks, but cleared a number of harbour-side positions before penetrating into Courseulles. A number of machine-gun positions were built into or overlooking the sea wall supporting the Courseulles promenade. These were suppressed by the 6th Canadian Armoured Regiment's DD Shermans and then either cleared by the Reginas or demolished by AVRE Petard rounds. The latter also blew several gaps in the sea wall to allow other gun tanks off the beach and into Courseulles to support the advance through the town. The second wave of Reginas landed relatively uneventfully and with few casualties, although a number of its LCAs ran onto mined beach obstacles; only forty-nine men made it ashore from one company.[134]

The bulk of the JUNO landing frontage was the Nan Sector, which ran east from Courseulles for 3 miles. The sector was divided, reading west to east, into Nan Green, Nan White and Nan Red beaches. These fronted Bernières-sur-Mer and St Aubin-sur-Mer, a mile apart and within Nan White and Nan Red beaches respectively. The villages extended up to the seafront, numerous seafront dwellings had been constructed along the coast between them, and a substantial concrete seawall divided the beach from the dunes. The German garrison integrated many of the seafront properties into their defences, reinforcing cellars and blocking beach road exits with reinforced concrete walls. These augmented the specially constructed machine gun and anti-tank gun bunkers constructed as usual to enfilade the beach. At least one of these housed an 88mm gun. The Nan landings were assigned to the 8th Canadian Infantry Brigade, supported by DD Sherman tanks from the 10th Canadian Armoured Regiment and the usual array of specialised armour. The Queen's Own Rifles of Canada were assigned to Nan White Beach, fronting Bernières, and landed in two waves. H-Hour was originally scheduled for 07:50, but here too the landing was postponed because the supporting armour was behind schedule. Thus the first wave of the Queen's Own did not land until 08:15, and the second fifteen minutes later. The plan was for the first wave to secure the seawall and clear a path through the defences for the second wave, which was to occupy Bernières proper.

Things did not run as planned. Once again the infantry landed in advance of their supporting armour, and in the face of virtually untouched defences. The rocket barrage did manage to bring down a Spitfire that flew into the parabola of fire on the run in, however. Many of the Queen's Own went off the ramp into waist deep water or deeper, and one platoon was reduced from thirty-six to nine men in a matter of seconds. Another company fared even worse, landing directly in front of a German resistance nest.[135] Corporal Harold Brasier, moving to aid a wounded man in the surf, had the appalling experience of seeing the unfortunate man all but vaporised by a large calibre round that Brasier felt come over his shoulder. On reaching the seawall, one Canadian company commander attempted to tackle a bunker by firing his Sten through the firing embrasure. He was almost immediately rendered unconscious by a round that passed through his helmet and the back of his head, fired from a ventilation opening by one of the bunker's crew.[136] The second wave's problems began before they were delivered into the middle of a battle. Their LCAs were waved off to go round again after starting their run in, and when they did finally approach the beach almost half the landing craft were damaged or sunk by running onto mine-tipped beach obstacles.[137]

This time the arrival of the supporting armour did not immediately improve the situation. Captain Ian Hammerton's troop of Sherman Crabs landed safely on Nan White and succeeded in clearing a lane through the minefield up to the sea wall as planned. Things then went awry when a Churchill AVRE carrying a bridge section to cross the seawall was knocked out. When the seawall proved impervious to repeated hits from Petard rounds, other AVREs turned their attention to a concrete boat-launching ramp. A Belgian Gate obstacle was blasted off the ramp, but the lead AVRE slipped over the edge of the ramp trying to bulldoze the wreckage clear, and the next was disabled atop the wall by a mine while completing the debris clearance. Hammerton's tank attempted to pull the disabled AVRE back down the ramp with a towing hawser, but the incoming tide flooded the Sherman's engine compartment, obliging Hammerton and his crew to abandon their vehicle.[138] In the meantime many of the Queen's Own Rifles had gotten off the beach and penetrated into Bernières off their own bat, where they became bogged down in a protracted house-to-house fight that absorbed the follow-up battalion from the Régiment de la Chaudière.

The North Shore Regiment's initial reception on Nan Red Beach was less ferocious, although they came under fire from German positions in and around Langrune-sur-Mer on the left flank. The first wave of Canadians nonetheless made the seawall without serious mishap, cut through the wire topping it with wire cutters and Bangalore torpedoes and quickly penetrated into St Aubin-sur-Mer. There, however, the Germans had blocked the narrow streets with barbed wire and converted many of the buildings into strongpoints. The Canadians thus had to clear the village with little more than small arms once the assault engineer stores carried by some of the lead sections had been expended. Armoured support was needed, but as on the neighbouring Nan White, the tanks were unable to get over the seawall. Many were still stuck on the beach, some bogged in a wide bed of shingle when No. 48 (RM) Commando came ashore at 09:30.

No. 48 Commando was tasked to clear the German strongpoint in Langrune-sur-Mer before linking up with another Commando force moving west from the SWORD landing area. Lieutenant-Colonel James Moulton tried unsuccessfully to ascertain the situation as the LCIs carrying the Commandos started their run in at around 09:00. In an effort to screen their approach, he ordered his 2-inch mortars to drop smoke onto the beach; he was particularly concerned because the LCIs were wood and lacked the armour plating of the LCAs used by earlier waves. Relatively little fire was encountered on the run in, although some of that directed against the LCIs was uncomfortably accurate. Captain Dan Flunder spent the run in nonchalantly pacing the exposed bow superstructure of his LCI with his walking stick. He became aware of German fire when two men were hit and knocked overboard, and later discovered three bullet holes in the map case attached to his webbing.

The fire grew significantly heavier nearer the beach. Two LCIs were stranded a hundred yards or so offshore, one entangled ·with a submerged obstacle and the other after detonating a mine mounted on another obstacle. The heavy surf caused the LCIs that made the beach swing and pitch uncontrollably, a serious matter as the vessels used twin catwalks on either side of the bow rather than a ramp. Captain Flunder was catapulted off one of these gangways by an unexpectedly violent swell that went on to lift the vessel straight over his head, a process which tore off several items of his equipment and came very close to drowning him. A number of heavily laden Commandos were not so fortunate and drowned in the deep and turbulent water. The experience understandably left Flunder a little short tempered. After watching several buttoned-up tanks run over the wounded scattered across Nan Red, he attempted to direct another tank away from No. 48 Commando's padre, who had suffered a serious thigh wound. When the tank ignored his efforts, Flunder retaliated by blowing off the tank's drive sprocket and track with a Hawkins mine.[139]

The two stranded LCIs, each carrying a troop of Commandos apiece, attracted a growing volume of German fire but were too far out for their passengers to wade ashore. A passing LCA set up a shuttle to ferry one group ashore, and a LCT pulled alongside the other so the Commandos could cross-deck for the short passage to the beach, but not before a RM subaltern had drowned in a vain attempt to swim ashore with a line. The difficult landing extracted a heavy price from No. 48 Commando, which lost around half its strength and all its crew served weapons apart from a single 3-inch mortar. A Marine Thornton had made three hazardous trips across the beach on his own initiative to locate and retrieve the barrel, bipod and baseplate of the weapon. Despite being wounded by a mortar bomb, Moulton reorganised his depleted force and set out for Langrune-sur-Mer to deal with the strongpoint as ordered.[140]

The British 3rd Infantry Division went ashore on a single sector of the SWORD landing area, 3 miles east of the Canadians at JUNO. Three beaches were employed, Queen Green, Queen White and Queen Red, with a combined frontage of a mile and a quarter, bounded by Lion-sur-Mer and la Bréche. The story thus far has been one of plans frequently going awry, but here the carefully worked out scheme worked largely as advertised. Thirty-four DD Shermans from the 13th/18th Hussars were launched 4,000 rather than 5,000 yards offshore as a concession to the weather at around 06:15. Three sank en route, one after being rammed by the LCT which had launched it only minutes before; only the commander was rescued. Being run down by one of the mass of following landing vessels was a recurring fear among all the DD crews, understandably so given the extremely low silhouette and marginal seaworthiness of their craft.

The remaining thirty-one tanks made it ashore after about an hour wallowing through the heavy seas at a nominal five knots. Captain Robert Neave's tank touched down on Queen Red Beach on schedule at 07:20, five minutes before the designated H-Hour. Neave deflated and discarded his flotation screen before guiding his troop of four tanks gingerly through a maze of poles mounting large shells with contact fuses and into the dunes at the head of the beach. On the way he shot up a quiescent bunker which disgorged five prisoners, before pausing to confer with his other tank commanders, an act that almost cost him his life. As he remounted his tank a bullet passed just under his nose and passed between two fingers, just skinning the latter.[141] Lance-Corporal Patrick Hennessy's Sherman discarded its screen at the edge of the surf line and opened fire on its designated target, a row of houses at the head of the beach. A brief conference on whether to continue or wait for the Sherman Crabs to arrive in case of mines was settled when a large wave drowned the engine compartment.

Hennessy and his comrades literally stuck to their guns until the vehicle flooded, and then took to their inflatable dinghy with a dismounted .30 Browning. German fire then punctured the dinghy and wounded one man, leaving them to half swim, half wade ashore carrying their casualty. The final indignity came as Hennessy and his crew attempted to revive their spirits with cans of self heating soup, a beverage that crops up in a number of D-Day accounts. One RE Sergeant-Major received a nasty fright after a blow to the body left him covered in sticky red liquid. On reporting to an aid post he was highly embarrassed to discover that he was smothered in tomato soup; a self-heating can he was carrying had burst for some reason.[142] In the event, Hennessy and his crew were not to enjoy their soup. A passing and wrathful RE officer berated them for slacking and shooed them off the beach with the immortal words 'Get up Corporal! That's no way to win the Second Front'.[143] Some of the DD tanks faced with more than harsh language from 'friendly' quarters; one DD sergeant noted that the rocket barrage from the LCRs landed among the tanks on the beach and caused a number of casualties.

The pre-landing bombardment here was more effective than else-where, and many of the defenders were driven to take shelter; the arrival of the DD tanks came as an extra nasty surprise because the Germans assumed that Allied infantry would be first ashore. The specialised armour began to land at 07:25. The LCT carrying Major Tim Wheway's Sherman Crabs from the 22nd Dragoons ran ashore so hard it felt that the lead tank might be ejected prematurely through the closed ramp. The Crabs drove off the ramp into 3 feet of water and into a storm of fire from anti-tank pieces, machine guns and mortars which knocked out a number of them as they began flailing their way up the beach. One Crab took three armour-piercing hits in the turret that killed all but one of the crew, and another had one of its flail arms shot away.[144] A Royal Marine gunner aboard an LCF just off the beach saw another Crab take a large calibre hit that blew the turret clean off and left the burning hull rolling on for several yards. Being first ashore merely added to the hazardous nature of the Crab's job; by mid morning almost half of the twenty-six Crabs delivered onto the Queen beaches had been knocked out.[145]

The Crabs were followed by AVREs from 5 Assault Regiment RE, carrying fascines and bridging sections, which also suffered losses. One AVRE driver in a mixed LCT saw the two Crabs ahead of his vehicle burst into flames after being hit almost immediately on leaving the vessel. Avoiding a similar fate, the AVRE threaded its way through the booby-trapped beach obstacles to the head of the beach before a Teller mine blew off a bogey wheel and killed two crewmen. The driver estimated over half his unit never got off Queen Red Beach.[146] RE casualties were increased by the need for the assault sappers to leave the shelter of the AVREs to secure the bridging sections or to demolish obstacles, which exposed them to the German fire sweeping the beach. There were also less obvious dangers lying in wait for unwitting tank crews. One Sherman from the 44th Royal Tank Regiment drove off its LCT ramp and instead of wading through 6 feet of water fell straight into a 12-foot deep crater. The tank's water-proofing kept the sea at bay, but the top of the vehicle's air intake extensions were perilously close to the water's surface. The slightest movement risked flooding the tank and drowning the crew, so they were ordered to switch off and wait for the tide to drop, making their way ashore unaided after two interminable hours underwater.[147]

The specialist armour was closely followed by the assault infantry from the 8th Infantry Brigade. One LCA carried Major C.K. King, who spent the run in reciting the Agincourt speech from Shakespeare's *Henry V* through a megaphone.[148] Once again, the fierce surf created by the fast rising tide complicated disembarkation. Having suffered severely from seasickness on the run in, Lieutenant Edward Jones of the 1st South Lancs was almost crushed by the lurching LCA as he stepped off the ramp into 3 feet of water.[149] A private from the same unit, after noting the whiplash effect created by German shells dropping into the water through the hull of his LCA, was so relieved to touch dry land that he shot up the beach 'like a hare'. Another LCA passenger noted a similar effect created by the bombardment on shore silenced the quiet conversations aboard his vessel, to be replaced with the click-clack of weapons being cocked and put on safe.[150]

Two companies each from the 1st South Lancs and 2nd East Yorks led the way onto Queen Green and Queen Red beaches respectively at just after 07:30, with the rest of the two battalions coming in at 08:00. One of the South Lancs companies were tasked to clear the beach defences and mask the town of Lion-sur-Mer on the western boundary of Queen Green Beach. The other was to assist its neighbour in reducing the German strongpoint at la Brèche. The East Yorks were to deal with this strongpoint, codenamed Cod, along with two more strongpoints codenamed Sole and Daimler; the latter housed a battery of 155mm guns. This was a formidable array for a mere mile of sea front, and reflects the fact that the defences between Ouistreham and Courseulles were the most fully developed on the entire Normandy coast. The sector stretching inland from the Queen beaches was, in turn, the most fully developed in depth.

This explains the violent reaction that took such a toll on the invading armour, although this was not immediately apparent, at least on Queen Green Beach. Lieutenant Jones of the South Lancs, having recovered from his near crushing, reached the row of seafront houses that formed his primary objective without incident. The only minor hold up came from the barbed wire entanglement atop the seawall, which was cleared almost on cue by a passing AVRE. The reason for this easy passage became apparent when Jones' platoon began clearing the houses. The German defenders were still sheltering in the cellars from the bombardment, and Jones' platoon quickly despatch them to the rear, such as it was.[151] Things did not run so smoothly on Queen Red, where the assault wave ran into heavy machine-gun and mortar fire that killed or wounded 200 men in a matter of minutes.[152] One private likened the beach to a skittle alley.[153] Lieutenant H.T. Bone, who came ashore in the second wave, found the remnants of the first pinned down at the water's edge and rapidly joined them in scraping a hole in the sand for shelter.[154]

Despite this unpromising start, the first wave was making progress when the 8th Infantry Brigade's final unit, the 1st Suffolks, came ashore at 08:30. The Suffolks were tasked to regroup at la Brèche before moving inland to eliminate two fortified German positions. The first, codenamed Morris, contained a battery of 155mm guns and was located near Colleville-sur-Orne, a mile behind the beach. The second, with a pair of 105mm guns, lay a half-mile or so further south and was codenamed Hillman. Both were protected with mines, barbed wire and a full array of fighting bunkers and covered communication trenches. Most of the Suffolks' landed in chest deep water, but reached the beach largely without mishap, although one corporal from A Company dropped into much deeper water. He was obliged to abandon his weapons and equipment and swim ashore, where he re-equipped himself with a weapon and steel helmet from a dead soldier from the South Lancs before rejoining his platoon.[155] The first wave's slower than anticipated progress obliged the Suffolks to remain on the beach for a time, before regrouping and moving to an orchard where they remained until moving off to attack the Morris position in the late morning.[156]

The Suffolks were followed by a wave of Commandos. No. 41 (RM) Commando was tasked to eliminate a German defence posi-

tion and a château on the outskirts of Lion-sur-Mer, before moving
west to link up with No. 48 (RM) Commando from the JUNO
beaches. The Commando came ashore from LCIs at Queen Green
Beach but 200 yards farther west than expected, at 09:00. After
regrouping by the seawall, the Commando moved into Lion-sur-Mer.
The defensive position had been abandoned, but the garrison of the
chateau put up a spirited defence that caused the Commandos a
number of casualties including the unit CO. The château was then left
for the follow-up forces to deal with but the Commandos then
became bogged down in street fighting in Lion.[157]

A larger Commando contingent came ashore at the other end
of the SWORD landing area. The 1st Special Service Brigade,
commanded by Brigadier the Lord Lovat, consisted of Nos. 3, 4,
and 6 Commandos, 45 (RM) Commando and two troops of French
Commandos from No. 10 (Inter-Allied) Commando. No. 4
Commando and the French contingent were first ashore, at 08:20. At
that time the 2nd East Yorks were still pinned down and the
Commandos suffered forty casualties moving through them and off
the beach, overrunning a number of German bunkers and fighting
positions in the process. No. 4 Commando's mission was to eliminate
the artillery strongpoint at the mouth of the River Orne in
Ouistreham, while the French detachment dealt with the adjacent,
heavily fortified casino. A French civilian, presumably a member of
the Resistance, met the attackers in the outskirts of the town and
guided them through the streets to attack their objective from inland.
On the way they passed another Frenchman, dancing with joy in his
pyjamas and shouting 'C'est le jour! Le jour de la libération'.

The battery position was divided from Ouistreham by a concrete
anti-tank ditch, and reaching the start-line for the attack meant crossing an open area covered by a machine gun. While one troop
suppressed the gun, another improvised a plank bridge and pushed
over the ditch into the battery position. Using craters from the pre-
landing bombardment for cover, the Commandos methodically
cleared the strongpoint despite small-arms fire from nearby houses
and shelling from German artillery and Allied warships. The Naval

Forward Observer Officer attached to No. 4 Commando had been killed on the beach, his radio was rendered unserviceable and an Army artillery observer was unable to contact the ships to call off the fire. The latter subsequently confided to a Commando officer that he had just seen more action in half an hour than in all his previous service combined, including a stint at El Alamein. As at Merville and the Pointe du Hoc, the guns had once again been removed prior to the attack. Their mission complete, the Commandos fell back to recover their rucksacks, cached near the forming up point for the attack, and set off to rejoin the remainder of the 1st Special Service Brigade.[158]

No. 6 Commando accompanied by Lovat's forward brigade HQ landed in waist-deep water at 08:40. They were piped ashore by Piper Bill Millin, Lovat's personal piper, playing 'Blue Bonnets over the Border'. By this time the congestion on the beach had cleared as the East Yorks methodically eliminated the beach defences. The Commandos regrouped in the reinforced cellars of a number of demolished houses just off the beach and, on receiving confirmation that the Orne bridges were in airborne hands, they set out for Benouville. This involved filtering through the unsubdued German defences east and south of Ouistreham, followed by several hundred yards of marsh, bisected by dykes topped with barbed wire. The lead troop then had to put in a deliberate attack to clear a fortified German position in a copse surrounded by standing crops. Thus by late morning the Commandos were still some distance from the paratroopers and glider troops holding the Orne bridges.[159]

It is unclear how far east the sound of the pre-landing bombardment carried, but the airborne soldiers holding the bridges clearly heard the invasion begin. Major John Howard, who commanded the Ox and Bucks *coup de main* party that had seized the bridges, described the barrage as quite terrific and said that the smoke and dust was clearly visible to the north-west. It became even more noticeable after 07:00, when the bombardment shifted to targets around Caen. The next few hours must have been especially difficult for the airborne troops, who knew full well that their fate and indeed lives hung on the success or failure of the sea invasion. Howard's men were using the abandoned German positions on the east bank of the Orne Canal, and one enterprising group occupying the German anti-tank bunker by the bridge worked out how to operate the gun by trial and error. They then fired a number of rounds at a water tower and large château visible across the canal to the south-west in the belief it housed German snipers. They desisted when Howard noticed what they were up to and forcefully pointed out that the château reportedly housed a maternity hospital.[160]

Morale was lifted by a thoughtful Spitfire pilot who performed a victory roll over the bridges before jettisoning a container at around 08:00. It held copies of the British morning newspapers, all of which headlined with the invasion. The rank and file had other priorities, however, and there was some scuffling as the troops jostled to see 'Jane's' latest semi-naked cartoon adventures in the *Daily Mirror*.[161] A display of bravado by the 6th Airborne's senior commanders gave morale an additional boost an hour or so later, when Major-General Gale marched steadfastly down the road to the bridge from Ranville, unescorted except for Brigadiers Poett and Kindersley. Pointedly ignoring the occasional German rounds that were by then the norm in the bridge perimeter, Gale conferred briefly with Howard before moving on to find the commander of the 7th Battalion, Lieutenant-Colonel Pine-Coffin.

Shortly afterwards two German patrol craft approached the Orne Canal Bridge from Ouistreham, sparking one of the more unusual clashes on D-Day. Ignoring fire from the lead vessel's 20mm gun, the airborne soldiers waited until it was within PIAT range and then put a bomb straight into the wheelhouse and then opened fire from both sides of the canal. The vessel slewed round and ended up wedged across the canal; the crew fled to the stern and surrendered to the Ox and Bucks contingent, with the young captain ranting that the British invaders would be pushed back into the sea forthwith. The perception of German military superiority took a further dent at around 10:00, when a lone German fighter-bomber carried out a low-level bombing attack on the Orne Canal bridge. The bomb scored a direct hit on the tower housing the apparatus for raising the span but failed to explode, crashing instead to the road surface before rolling harmlessly into the canal.[162]

Such morale boosts were welcome, because German pressure on the 6th Airborne Division's widely spread perimeter was increasing. As a *bodenständige* formation, *716 Infanterie Division* had been assigned motorised units from *21 Panzer* as a mobile reserve, which were called in at 02:35. Thus a company-sized detachment from *II Bataillon, Panzergrenadier Regiment 192* with three assault guns, a number of anti-aircraft half-tracks and a mortar platoon arrived south of Benouville at 03:30.[163] This brought them up against the depleted 7th Parachute Battalion, holding the bridge perimeter west of the Orne Canal. B Company, occupying a wooded area between the Canal and the village of Le Port was kept under intermittent fire by elements of Infanterie Regiment 736, although this flagged markedly after a PIAT gunner removed the top of the village church tower. Subsequent investigation found a dozen German bodies in the rubble.[164]

The bulk of the 7th Parachute Battalion's strength was deployed facing south and south-west, the direction from which German attack was most expected. At around 07:00 C Company shot up the crews of a number of German light armoured vehicles that obligingly halted and dismounted for a conference in full view of their positions. These may have been the vanguard of the detachment *from Panzergrenadier Regiment 192*, who rapidly made their presence felt against the scattered platoons holding the southern fringe of Benouville village. The paratroopers beat off several infantry probes, but in the late morning close-range fire from the three assault guns obliged a withdrawal toward the centre of the village; one of the guns that pursued too closely was knocked out with a Gammon bomb. This kind of aggression appears to have caused the *panzergrenadiers* to overestimate the strength of their airborne opponents. One German senior NCO from the assault gun detachment, for example, claimed not only to have seen two British tanks near the road to the Orne bridges at this time, but also to have knocked one out; the other allegedly took up position in the British-held half of Benouville.[165] Lieutenant-Colonel Pine-Coffin and his men would doubtless have been delighted to know they had tank support, given that this occurred at least two hours before the Commandos from the 1st Special Service Brigade reached B Company's perimeter at le Port. Be that as it may, the perception of British strength was enough to keep the *panzergrenadiers* from pushing against the airborne perimeter as hard as they should have.

East of the Orne, the 3rd Parachute Brigade's dispersed battalions were largely shielded from German interference by the destruction of the Dives bridges. Lieutenant-Colonel Pearson's 8th Parachute Battalion withdrew from west of Troarn without incident and moved back to the Bois de Bavent. Having destroyed the bridges over the River Dives at Robehomme and la Bac de Varaville, the 1st Canadian Parachute Battalion spent most of D-Day morning fighting to secure the chateau in Varaville. The German garrison finally surrendered sometime after 10:00, and the Canadians occupied their positions and settled down to await relief by the 1st Special Service Brigade. To their west, the sorely depleted 9th Parachute arrived at le Plein at around 09:00, only to discover the village was occupied. A hasty attack overran and killed fifteen Germans near the village church, but the paratroopers were less successful in dealing with a large, walled property that housed the local German HQ; the attacking platoon were rebuffed and their commander was killed. Another dozen Germans were killed in an ill-fated counter-attack as the paratroopers were clearing the north end of the village. In all, the fight in le Plein reduced Lieutenant-Colonel Otway's little band to less than a hundred effectives, far too few to complete a mission intended for a full battalion. Otway therefore decided to withdraw to Amfreville and await relief from the 1st Special Service Brigade.[166]

The 5th Parachute Brigade's remaining two parachute battalions were deployed at les Bas de Ranville and Ranville proper. The 13th Parachute Battalion, manning the line facing east from Ranville had a relatively quiet morning time digging defensive positions and laying mines to protect them. One platoon endured persistent sniping that hit at least two men while laying their mines, using a wheelbarrow purloined from a nearby house. The four perpetrators were subsequently discovered in the house where the wheelbarrow came from, and surrendered after one paratrooper lobbed a grenade through a window.[167] The 12th Parachute Battalion occupied the western end of the perimeter, and was dug in around les Bas de Ranville with its right flank tied in to the bank of the Orne. In the late morning the 13th Battalion successfully rebuffed a probing attack by four German self-propelled guns from Hérouvillette; all four vehicles were knocked out by one of the Battalion's attached six-pounder guns. At around the same time a tank and infantry attack was made against the 12th Battalion after a sharp mortar bombardment. This attack was also rebuffed, with one tank knocked out and a number of Germans taken prisoner.

The most exposed position on the 13th Battalion's frontage was an outpost in a hedgerow 300 yards in front of the main position. It was commanded by Captain John Sim, and consisted of a rifle section reinforced with two extra Bren guns, a sniper, a six-pounder gun and a naval artillery observation team. To maintain their concealment Sim enforced strict fire discipline, with only his sniper being cleared to fire. The latter obliged by picking off a German investigating an abandoned container 400 yards distant. At around 10:00 a group of Germans were seen setting up an artillery piece of some kind. They were dispersed with a few salvos of naval gunfire called in by the observers. An hour or so later a fifty-strong group of German infantry was spotted moving parallel to, and then directly toward the outpost.

Because they wore camouflage smocks, the approaching Germans were at first thought to be either a British airborne patrol or rallying stragglers. The naval observers were unable to call in fire support because the guns were firing other missions, so Sim waited until the Germans began crossing a wire cattle fence 50 yards to his front before opening fire. The Germans went to ground in the long grass and called up two self-propelled guns. At this rather inopportune moment Sim discovered that his six-pounder had been damaged in landing and was unable to fire. Flare signals for emergency mortar support drew no response, and several airborne soldiers were killed and wounded as the guns methodically shelled their hedgerow. Sim's men responded by shooting a German infantryman who appeared in the hedge, and the commander of one of the self-propelled guns who was rash enough to leave his vehicle. This prompted a severe German mortar barrage, which was rendered all the more deadly by the bombs exploding in the tree branches with an airburst effect. By this time the outpost had been whittled down to Sim, his batman, the sniper and a sergeant, so Sim ordered a withdrawal down a ditch running back to the main perimeter. They were followed by the two self-propelled guns, which were then knocked out by a functioning six-pounder. The outpost was quickly retaken by a platoon from C Company, who discovered that the Germans had withdrawn. They also evacuated three badly wounded airborne survivors.[168] Thereafter there was a marked reduction in German activity along the 6th Airborne's perimeter on both sides of the Orne.

The German troops pushing against the Ranville perimeter also belonged to *21 Panzer Division*, specifically *Panzer Aufklärungs Abteilung 21* and *Panzergrenadier Regiment 125*. News of the airborne incursion had rapidly permeated the division's sub-units after the detachment from *Panzergrenadier Regiment 192* was alerted at 01:42. By the time the detachment was ordered to recover the Benouville bridges at 02:35, the rest of *21 Panzer* had been stood to, and most sub-units were ready to move shortly thereafter. *7 Armee* took operational control of the Division at 04:30, but orders to move against the British airhead were not forthcoming until around 06:00.

As we have seen, *21 Panzer's* subordinate commanders were champing at the bit to get at the British airhead around Ranville. The 06:00 orders were therefore received with no little enthusiasm, but they were nonetheless a serious error, which was compounded by the time it took for *21 Panzer* to actually begin moving against 6th Airborne's perimeter.

Even though the Division was ready to move, a combination of the constricted road net and the Allied air and sea bombardment seriously slowed deployment, especially in the region of Caen. *Obersturmführer* Hansemann of *12 SS Panzer's* reconnaissance battalion had to thread his way through streets crammed with vehicles from *Panzergrenadier Regiment 192* when he passed through Caen on his drive toward Bayeux.[169] Thus *21 Panzer Division* was not fully on the move toward Ranville until 09:00, and the the leading elements of the Division did not make begin to make deliberate contact with 6th Airborne's perimeter until an hour or so after that.

Thus by the time *21 Panzer* got around to launching its attack, the situation had undergone a drastic shift. By 08:12, *352 Division* was reporting that Allied tanks had broken through in *716 Division's* sector on its right flank, and twenty-five minutes later was reporting similar developments on its own frontage as Allied troops pushed past the strongpoint at le Hamel. At 08:21 *716 Division* relayed news of yet another breakout between la Brèche and Lion-sur-Mer. By the time similar news arrived from St Aubin and Bernières at 10:32, it was clear that the reduction of an airborne lodgement, no matter how awkwardly placed, had to be considered a secondary concern to the rapidly deteriorating situation on the coast.[170] The reasoning behind *7 Armee's* 06:00 decision is unclear, although the penalty is not. By casting caution aside and pandering to the aggressive instincts of its subordinate commanders, *7 Armee* nullified the ability of the sole German armoured force within immediate striking distance of the coast to interfere with the sea landings, by placing it on the wrong side of the River Orne.

The attack on the British airhead was cancelled at 10:30, and *21 Panzer* was ordered to shift its axis of advance west of the Orne and move on Lion-sur-Mer. The task was simplified at least to an extent by the fact that *Panzergrenadier Regiment 192* was approaching Caen, and could be transformed into the vanguard of the new advance. Reversing the remainder of the Division, and especially *Panzer Regiment 22*, was not so straightforward because they had to be directed back through the bottleneck at Caen, which was under heavy Allied artillery and air bombardment. The task was manageable, but was going to take several hours under the prevailing conditions, and time was a commodity the German defence could ill-afford.

Seizing the Benouville bridges and placing the 6th Airborne Division astride the River Orne thus succeeded beyond the invasion planner's most optimistic estimates. By attracting the immediate German reserve, 6th Airborne totally wrong-footed the German defence and bought the first wave of seaborne invaders several valuable hours, a prize for which the sacrifice of the airborne formation would have been a fair exchange. That they were not was purely a matter of coincidental timing. Had *21 Panzer* been turned loose in the early hours of 6 June, as advocated by von Luck et al, there is a good chance that the airborne soldiers could have given them serious pause, and possibly even held their own while it remained dark. The chances of them doing so decreased substantially after daylight, however. The ejection of Captain Sim's outpost from their hedgerow outpost illustrates in microcosm the probable result had *21 Panzer* been allowed to deliver the blow it planned against the Ranville perimeter.

Gale's men would doubtless have fought like tigers, but as their running mates in the 1st Airborne Division were to discover at Arnhem in September, the flimsiest armour plate was infinitely superior to a Denison smock. Even with their anti-tank guns, the lightly armed airborne soldiers would have been a relatively easy mark for a massed armoured attack in open country, and without effective means to strike back, bricks and mortar provided little protection against sustained, close-range fire from armoured vehicles. The Germans could have merely masked them off to be dealt with at leisure while they got down to the more serious business of striking over the Benouville bridges into the heart of the Allied landing area. All in all, therefore, the timing of *7 Armee's* attempt to correct its initial error in sending the *21 Panzer Division* after the British airhead was fortunate indeed for the 6th Airborne.

9

D-DAY
H PLUS 5 HOURS 30 MINUTES
TO H PLUS 18 HOURS

(12:00 TO 23:59, TUESDAY 6 JUNE 1944)

The first seaborne invaders to reach the British airborne soldiers at the Benouville bridges were not Commandos as planned, but members of the less glamorous but no less vital Royal Army Service Corps. Thirty-three trucks from 90 Company, RASC were to land in the early afternoon of D-Day carrying supplies for the 6th Airborne, and company commander Major James Cuthbertson landed at one of the SWORD beaches at 09:30 to carry out a personal reconnaissance of the route. Riding a motor cycle and accompanied by a despatch rider, he navigated serenely through enemy territory without seeing a soul, and arrived at the road junction leading to the Benouville bridges at 11:30. Fortunately the well-camouflaged paratroopers they stopped in front of held their fire, but they told Cuthbertson and his companion in no uncertain terms to seek cover as they were under enemy observation. The RASC men took the advice and settled down to wait for the arrival of the seaborne forces and liaison from 6th Airborne HQ in Ranville.[1]

They did not have a long wait. The 1st Special Service Brigade was scheduled to arrive at Benouville at midday. Some accounts claim the link up took place only a minute or two late, but airborne eyewitnesses clearly state the Commandos did not arrive until 13:30.[2] This was still no mean feat given the Commandos had fought their way across 7 miles of enemy held territory, and they made the link up in some style. Shortly after 13:00 the 7th Parachute Battalion at le Port heard the skirl of bagpipes, the recognition signal agreed by Lovat, Howard and Pine-Coffin back in England. Pine-Coffin's bugler responded as arranged, and Lord Lovat, wearing his green beret, a white roll-neck sweater and carrying a bulging Bergen rucksack, hove into view with Piper Millin, once again playing 'Blue Bonnets over the Border'. They were trailed by No. 6 Commando, a Churchill AVRE picked up on the way, No. 3 Commando and No. 45 (RM) Commando. The leading Commandos received an enthusiastic welcome, and not just from the airborne soldiers. Monsieur Gondrée, the owner of the café by the Orne Canal Bridge tried to present Lovat with a glass of champagne, but the Commando commander ignored the offer and pushed on over the bridge to meet Howard on the eastern bank. An enterprising private from the Ox and Bucks *coup de main* party gratefully appropriated the champagne.[3]

The Orne Canal Bridge was no place to tarry, being under intermittent German fire. A member of No. 6 Commando recalled rounds ricocheting off the steelwork as he ran across, although this did not prevent him from pausing to appropriate a .45 automatic from a dead airborne officer.[4] Once across, the Commandos fanned out to reinforce 6th Airborne's perimeter. No. 3 Commando was retained in the area of the Orne River Bridge on Gale's orders; Gale was concerned over the German pressure on the 12th Parachute Battalion's frontage, and wanted an emergency backstop. No. 6 Commando pushed north to link up with the 9th Parachute Battalion at Amfreville followed by No. 45 (RM) Commando. After pausing to dump the inflatable dinghies they had lugged all the way from the beach, the latter crossed the bridges in ones and twos as a concession to the increasingly heavy German fire and moved through No. 6 Commando to Franceville Plage, near the Merville Battery.

The Commandos were welcome, but 6th Airborne's position needed more substantial reinforcement, and the British armour was still fighting through the German coastal defences. A Company, 7th Parachute Battalion was still embroiled with *Panzergrenadier Regiment 192* in Benouville, which increased the pressure as the afternoon wore on. Major Nigel Taylor, commanding A Company, noted the preferred German tactic was to stand off and pound the British positions from armoured vehicles, to which the paratroopers had no effective reply. Taylor continued to command the embattled company despite a serious thigh wound, but was eventually obliged to hand over to the marginally less seriously wounded Captain James Webber. By the late afternoon A Company was cut off and down to twenty men, but the paratroopers stubbornly denied the Germans passage through the village. Relief finally arrived at 21:15, in the shape of the 2nd Battalion, The Royal Warwickshire Regiment from 185 Infantry Brigade. The Warwicks mounted an attack to allow A Company to regain British lines with their wounded, and the 7th Parachute Battalion formally handed to the Warwicks at 00:30 on 7 June.[5]

On the other side of the Orne Lieutenant-Colonel Pearson's 8th Parachute Battalion was regrouping at the south end of the Bois de Bavent ridge after its bridge-demolishing adventures. As he had heard nothing from Troarn, at midday Pearson despatched Captain Tim Juckes and a party from the 3rd Parachute Squadron RE to deal with it if necessary, escorted by Lieutenant Brown's platoon from B Company. Brown's paratroopers cleared two positions held by *Panzer Aufklärungs Abteilung 21* in Troarn, taking a number of prisoners at a cost of two wounded. Major Roseveare had blown the bridge a few hours earlier, so Juckes extended the damage before returning to the Bois de Bavent. In the meantime the 8th Battalion's strength had been augmented by fifty-five mis-dropped paratroopers, who fought their way through Hérouvillette to rally on green and white flares fired above the Bois de Bavent. This brought the 8th Battalion's strength up to approximately 250 all ranks, and permitted Pearson to set up standing and mobile patrols around his perimeter. B Company repulsed a probe by five German armoured vehicles at 17:40, and the patrols continued through the night.[6]

Similar moves were made against the 12th and 13th Parachute Battalions on Pearson's right at around the same time. Although *21 Panzer Division's* focus had shifted west of the Orne, it was also to maintain the pressure on the Ranville airhead. To this end

Kampfgruppe von Luck was formed, composed of two battalions from *Panzergrenadier Regiment 125*, a battalion from *Panzer Regiment 22*, *Sturmgeschütze Bataillon 200* and elements from the divisional reconnaissance and artillery units. Bringing these together took most of the afternoon; the assault gun battalion, for example, had already passed through the bottleneck at Caen heading west when it received word of its new assignment. Despite this, von Luck's men were able to make their presence felt again by the late afternoon, at the same time the rest of the Division made its main effort west of the Orne.

A company attack was made against the 13th Parachute Battalion at around 17:00, but was beaten off by the paratroopers. At around the same time a standing patrol in front of the 12th Parachute Battalion's C Company reported German activity near a feature dubbed the 'Ring Contour'. A platoon from B Company was later despatched to attack the feature, under cover of a barrage from the British 3rd Infantry Division's artillery, which was on call by the evening of 6 June. The platoon were driven back by heavy German fire, but the combination of artillery fire and infantry probe presumably stymied whatever *Kampfgruppe* von Luck was planning for the 12th Parachute Battalion's front for the time being.

On the Cotentin Peninsula at the other end of the invasion front, the US 4th Infantry Division spent the afternoon and evening of D-Day continuing its leisurely advance inland from UTAH beach. The 22nd and 12th Infantry Regiments were oriented northward, with the 3rd Battalion, 22nd Regiment pushing up the narrow strip between the beach and the inundated area immediately behind it. This involved clearing four German resistance nests, including the one at les Dunes de Varreville, which blocked the seaward end of Causeway Four. It then set up a night perimeter just short of Hamel de Cruttes, 3 miles north of its starting point. This placed it on line with the rest of the 22nd Regiment on the other side of the marshes, which had crossed Causeway Four in mid-afternoon to link up with the 1st Battalion, 502nd Parachute Infantry near St Martin-de-Varreville. The combined force then moved a mile north and set up a line running east from St Germain-de-Varreville, with the paratroopers on the left flank.

The line was extended further east by the 12th Infantry Regiment, which set up for the night near Beuzeville-au-Plain.

The 1st Battalion, 8th Infantry Regiment crossed the inundated area via Causeway Three. By nightfall it had advanced a mere 1.5 miles from the end of the causeway, and established a night perimeter just short of Turqueville. The 8th Infantry's other two battalions made somewhat better progress along a route 2 miles to the south. After linking up with the paratroopers near Pouppeville at the end of Causeway One, the 2nd Battalion advanced west to the village of les Forges on the St Mère Église-Carentan road, 4.5 miles from the Causeway exit. They were preceded by the 3rd Battalion, which had followed the same route after crossing Causeway Two, and had eliminated a German artillery position just outside St Marie-du-Mont on the way. The 3rd Battalion was oriented north, with an outpost from Company K set a mile north-west to cover the road leading to Chef-du-Pont.

Overall, this was a less than inspiring performance. The line established by the 12th and 22nd Infantry Regiments was 4 miles short of the 4th Division's D-Day Objective line. The official history admits that this was not due to German resistance and lays the blame on difficulties in crossing the inundated area behind the beach.[7] This does not really hold water, however, given the bulk of both regiments were across the marshes by the early afternoon, and moved only a mile or so thereafter. The 8th Infantry Regiment's advance did come to a halt in proximity to the enemy, with the 1st and 3rd Battalions running up against the western and southern edges of the German force that had been trying to break into St Mère Église from the south. However, the official history gives the distinct impression that the German presence was not detected until after the 8th Infantry had stopped, and that this permitted the Germans to consolidate on high ground to face the new American threat.[8] It is therefore difficult to escape the conclusion that the underlying problem was the marked lack of urgency the 4th Infantry Division had displayed from the outset. This would have been a less than ideal attitude at the best of times, but it was one that had no place in a formation that was supposed to be relieving an embattled airborne force, a task for which speed was the essence.

The 82nd Airborne Division had been tasked to seize St Mère Église, the causeways over the River Merderet at la Fière and Chef-du-Pont, and high ground west of the river. The original plan was badly disrupted by the scattered drop, although not as badly as it might have been. Only a handful of sticks from the 508th Parachute Infantry landed on DZ N, and the rest were scattered widely to the east and south. However, the bulk of the 507th Regiment was delivered in a fairly compact group just east of DZ T, albeit squarely in the inun-dated area flanking the Merderet, while the 505th Regiment enjoyed the most accurate delivery of any US airborne unit in the invasion. As we have seen, this was instrumental in permitting the 505th Regiment to seize St Mère Église and hold it through 6 June against German attack from the north and south.

The ring to the west of St Mère Église was held by a selection of mis-dropped elements from the 82nd Airborne's regiments. West of the Merderet, the commander of the 2nd Battalion, 507th Parachute Infantry, Lieutenant-Colonel Charles J. Timmes, was only able to spare ten men under Lieutenant Louis Levy to secure the 500-yard la Fière causeway and link up with the 505th Regiment supposedly holding the bridge. Levy incorporated another twenty men led by Lieutenant Joseph Kormylo en route, and the composite group reached Cauquigny, at the western end of the causeway at midday. Levy ordered his men to take a meal break before digging in around Cauquigny church, during which they were joined by thirty-nine men from the 508th Regiment. Unable to discern any friendly forces at the bridge, Levy settled down to await developments.

In fact, a minor battle had been underway across the river since an hour after first light. The east end of the bridge was held by thirty German troops at the hamlet of Manoir la Fière, who had coinciden-tally occupied the position for the first time at around 23:00 on the night of 5-6 June. The first Americans on the scene were Company A, 1st Battalion of the 505th Regiment led by Captain John J. Dolan. Dolan's company was stopped by German fire 500 yards short of

Manoir la Fière, but were subsequently joined by parties from the 507th and 508th Regiments seeking to cross the Merderet. These included 100 men from the 507th Regiment under Captain Ben Schwartzwalder, a large group led by the commander of the 508th Regiment, Lieutenant-Colonel Roy Lindquist and three hundred men led by Brigadier-General Gavin. After spending the morning probing and trying to outflank the Germans, Schwartzwalder and Dolan finally launched independent attacks on Manoir la Fière that cleared the village at around midday and netted twenty German prisoners.

Satisfied that the situation at la Fière was in hand, Gavin pushed south for the Chef-du-Pont Bridge with 200 men from the 507th Regiment. Behind him Schwartzwalder regrouped his band, reduced to around eighty, and launched a push over the la Fière bridge at 13:45. Schwartzwalder's point man, Private James L. Mattingly, single-handedly cleared two German slit trenches, killing one occupant and taking a further eleven prisoner; two emerged from a third, unseen, machine gun position that could have easily wiped out the Americans. Schwartzwalder had intended to push on to Amfreville, but after conferring with Lieutenant Levy decided to link up with Timmes and the main body of the 2nd Battalion of the 507th. Gavin's force, meanwhile, found the hamlet of Chef-du-Pont in German hands. A two-pronged attack drove the defenders out, but the survivors went to ground in slit trenches along the causeway, and others withdrew to similar shelter on the west side of the bridge.

The Germans were on the point of giving in, but that changed when two were deliberately shot in quick succession while trying to surrender. After two costly charges along the 100-yard long stretch of elevated road, the Americans finally succeeded in closing up to the bridge by crawling between the German slit trenches in the embankment. A stand-off then ensued, interspersed with occasional exchanges of fire and hand-grenades. By late afternoon the situation appeared to have settled down so the bulk of the American force was despatched back to la Fière bridge, where the situation had taken a turn for the worse. Thirty-four men were left, commanded by Captain Roy Creek.

Back at Cauquigny Lieutenant Levy was still worried about the size and isolation of his force. His concern deepened when Schwartzwalder's group moved on, taking all but ten of the newcomers from the 508th with them and his bazookas. Levy thus crossed the Merderet to discuss the matter with Lieutenant-Colonel Lindquist. Lindquist briefly inspected Levy's position and gave him another forty or fifty men as reinforcements. No sooner had the latter arrived than events took a series of turns for the worse. First came the unmistakable sound of tanks, followed by a German ambulance sweeping into Cauquigny. The ambulance paused, then raced back toward Amfreville. Within minutes artillery fire was falling around the church and along the riverbank, followed shortly thereafter by infantry from *Infanterie Regiment 1057*, supported by five ex-French Hotchkiss H39 tanks from *Panzer Ersatz Bataillon 100*.

This was part of a wider advance that had pinned Timmes' group from the 2nd Battalion, 507th Parachute Infantry against the marshland along the Merderet. Levy's position at the church was quickly overrun, although they disabled one or possibly two tanks with Gammon bombs; the reinforcements from the 508th Regiment decamped for la Fière in disorder. The Germans followed them onto the causeway, led by two more H39 tanks. Fortunately for the Americans, Dolan's Company A had been deployed to protect the bridge. Bazooka teams disabled one tank and set the other ablaze, a number of Germans were killed and the rest were driven off. They then settled down to pound the bridge and surrounding area with artillery.

Meanwhile, the situation was also deteriorating at Chef-du-Pont. Only minutes after most of the paratroopers withdrew to la Fière at 20:45, the Germans on the west bank wheeled out an artillery piece and opened direct fire at 600 yards' range. The American paratroopers had no answer to this, and within minutes fourteen had been killed or wounded. Even worse, another German force appeared on the east bank, moving to take Creek's force in the rear. It was at that point that salvation appeared literally from the heavens. A Waco CG4 glider, having overshot its assigned DZ by 3 miles, made a perfect landing in the centre of Creek's perimeter. The glider contained a 57mm anti-tank gun, which was swiftly unloaded and brought into action. The German artillery piece was knocked out with the second round, after which the gun was turned on the German infantry on the east bank, who broke and ran. Creek then received sufficient reinforcements to secure both ends of the bridge at dusk. The action cost the Americans thirteen dead and twice as many wounded; forty German bodies were counted along the causeway and around the bridge.[9]

It appears the possibility that the 4th Infantry Division might not move to aid their airborne comrades with sufficient urgency had occurred to someone in the US airborne hierarchy. Lieutenant-Colonel Edson D. Raff was given a special strike force, made up of a company from the 325th Glider Infantry Regiment, twenty Shermans from the 746th Tank Battalion and some glider gunners. He was ordered to force his way through to St Mère Église and link up with the 82nd Airborne Division as rapidly as possible. Raff came ashore in the late afternoon and appears to have arrived at the 8th Infantry Regiment's lines near the les Forges at around 18:00. On learning that the 8th Infantry's 3rd Battalion had no intention of attacking that night, Raff launched a series of probes that cost him a scout car and three Shermans by 20:00.[10]

Raff was not motivated solely by the desire to reach St Mère Église. He was also driven by the need to clear the two landing zones selected for a glider lift scheduled to begin at 21:00. LZ W was centred on les Forges, while LZ E lay to the south-east near Hiesville. The lift involved 172 Horsas and thirty-seven Waco CG4s, organised in three groups. Given the likely outcome of trying to land heavily laden gliders in the face of enemy fire, Raff was understandably concerned that the area be cleared of enemy troops before the gliders arrived. The first group wave of thirty-two Horsas, codenamed KEOKUK, were released at 21:53. Five landed on LZ E, and were shot up by the Germans; the remainder landed safely north-east of the LZ. The second group, codenamed ELMIRA, came in eleven minutes later on LZ W. Despite attempts to set up an alternative LZ, most of them landed accurately and became targets for the Germans, who also called down artillery fire. The third wave did not come in until sunset, at 23:05. Some of this group picked up the EUREKA beacon marking the alternative LZ, some landed on LZ W and others were scattered far and wide. Only eight landed without mishap, and the lift overall cost thirty-three dead and 124 wounded or injured.[11]

The American glider lift coincided with the largest German D-Day counter-attack in the Cotentin. *Fallschirmjäger Regiment 6* had been ordered to attack the American airhead in the early morning of 6 June, but took most of the day to concentrate near St Côme-du-Mont. The attack was launched at 19:30, and the advancing Germans overran a number of gliders, which they erroneously reported as being accompanied by a large parachute drop. German accounts also claim to have run into elements of the 8th Infantry Regiment, although by this time the 8th Regiment was firmly ensconced further north at les Forges. It is therefore more likely that the Germans were up against their opposite numbers from the US 501st and 506th Parachute Infantry Regiments; a composite group from both regiments held Hiesville and St Marie-du-Mont was firmly held by the 506th. In the event the attack was repulsed and one German battalion was cut off. *Fallschirmjäger Regiment 6* thus lost a third of its strength for no discernible return.[12]

To the east, the US 1st and 29th Divisions spent the afternoon pushing south off the OMAHA beaches. Many troops from the assault waves who succeeded in getting onto the bluffs pushed inland on their own initiative, fighting sharp actions with small parties of German troops as they went, and more formal attacks went in where forces of sufficient size were available. A force made up from the 1st and 2nd Battalions, 116th Infantry cleared Vierville-sur-Mer in the late morning. A detachment then moved south and set up a blocking position 1.5 miles to the south. The remainder, with the 5th Rangers and the elements of the 2nd Rangers who had landed at Dog Green Beach, began to advance west to relieve Rudder's force at the Pointe du Hoc. They were halted by German troops after only 800 yards, and set up a perimeter for the night. The remainder of the 116th Regiment tried several times to fight their way into St Laurent-sur-Mer, but without success.

Reinforcements for the assault wave began to land in the late morning. The 1st Division's 18th Infantry Regiment came ashore at 10:00, and finished clearing the German defences covering the E1 Draw leading to St Laurent-sur-Mer at around midday. The 29th Division's 115th Infantry Regiment was also ordered ashore ahead of schedule at 10:30. The 115th was intended to support the 116th Regiment, but the offshore current carried it east where it became entangled with the 18th Regiment on Easy Red Beach. After sorting out the confusion, the 115th Regiment moved up the E1 Draw. The Regiment's 2nd Battalion attacked St Laurent from the east, but with no more success than the 116th Infantry. The remainder of the 115th bypassed St Laurent and moved to its assembly area for the planned push to the D-Day Objective Line. The 18th Infantry meanwhile were assigned to reinforce the 16th Infantry, and to take over their missions where necessary. An attack by the 2nd Battalion, 16th Infantry on Colleville-sur-Mer drew a sharp German counter-attack that put the Americans on the defensive. The entire area between St Laurent and Colleville was the scene of confused fighting with isolated German elements until well after dark; the Americans ambushed many German troops trying to escape south from by-passed positions. A final wave of reinforcements, consisting of the 26th Infantry Regiment and seventeen tanks, came ashore in the early evening.

By nightfall the eastern flank was held by the 3rd Battalion, 16th Infantry in le Grand Homeau, a mile east of Colleville-sur-Mer. Eight US battalion perimeters of varying size stretched west to St Laurent-sur-Mer, on a line roughly 2,000 yards inland from the beach. There was a large gap between St Laurent and the mixed force of Rangers and 116th Infantry west of Vierville, but Ranger patrols criss-crossed the area and the German stragglers encountered showed little inclination to fight. A two-man Ranger outpost captured thirty-five to forty members of an *Ost Bataillon* complete with a cartload of wounded without firing a shot.[13] The Germans had attempted a number of piecemeal counter-attacks throughout the day, but they were unable to muster sufficient strength to make them count. By nightfall the

American foothold was narrower than the planners had envisaged, but there were more US troops ashore than the Germans could hope to drive back with the forces immediately to hand.[14] This was not apparent to many of the US troops, however, and the night was punctuated by bursts of fire as they cut loose on threats real and imagined. Brigadier-General Cota was convinced most of the fire came from his men firing at 'specters', although at one point his HQ guard were obliged to fire on a dog that attacked them; the men decided it must have been a German dog. In the area occupied by the 29th Division's formations, the night was also punctuated by the sound of explosions as men tried the technique of blowing instant slit trenches with blocks of plastic explosive; most found it dangerous and that it did not work as well as advertised.[15]

While the Americans were fighting their way inland from the OMAHA bluffs, their Canadian and British counterparts were penetrating much deeper south. The British 50th Division's follow-on formation at the GOLD landing area was the 56th Infantry Brigade, consisting of the 2nd Battalions of The South Wales Borderers, Gloucester and Essex Regiments. The Brigade was scheduled to land at 10:00, but due to the stubborn German resistance at le Hamel, the landing was postponed until the early afternoon and shifted east. The delay obliged the landing craft to circle for a considerable period, an uncomfortable experience for the troops in the heavy seas, while shifting the landing area involved crossing unused beach. The 2nd Essex Pioneer Platoon was therefore pushed forward to assist sappers clearing lanes through the German minefields. To the east, the 6th, 8th and 9th Battalions of the Durham Light Infantry from 151 Infantry Brigade came ashore on King Green Beach.

Both follow-up brigades pushed rapidly inland, through the assault battalions from 231 Infantry Brigade who were still engaged in clearing their assigned objectives inland. CSM Stanley Hollis, who had single-handedly stormed a German bunker on the beach, continued to act in a similar vein in the 6th Green Howards' fight to clear Crépon. Not content with taking on a German field gun with a PIAT, he also drew German fire to allow two of his men to regain friendly positions. In recognition of his courageous and selfless actions, CSM Hollis was awarded the Victoria Cross, the only such award made on D-Day.[16] 50th Division's D-Day objectives had been to reach the main Bayeux-Caen road, occupy Bayeux and link up with friendly troops on either flank. Nightfall found the invaders just over 2 miles short of the highway, a mile and a half short of Bayeux, and No. 47 (RM) Commando failed to reach Port-en-Bessin, forming a night perimeter to the south. However, a link up had been achieved with the Canadians on the left flank, reconnaissance patrols had penetrated into Bayeux, and a defensible line had been established almost 7 miles inland. This was a respectable degree of progress given the level of German resistance.

The 3rd Canadian Infantry Division's landing on the JUNO beaches followed a similar pattern. Having cleared the German defences in and behind the dunes west of Courseulles, the 7th Canadian Infantry Brigade pushed south and linked up with the 69th Infantry Brigade on the left of the GOLD landings. The 3rd Canadian Division's follow-up formation, the 9th Canadian Infantry Brigade, was supposed to land in the late morning opposite St Aubin-sur-Mer on Nan White Beach. In the event, the 9th Brigade and the follow-up elements of the 8th Canadian Brigade were diverted west to Nan Green Beach because of German resistance in St Aubin. The exit from Nan Green Beach led through Bernières-sur-Mer, however, which was unable to handle the increase in traffic. The snarl up, which effectively pinned the 8th Canadian Brigade on one of its phase lines, was reported to the divisional commander, Major-General R.F.L. Keller aboard the HQ ship *Hilary* at 12:15. Keller came ashore at 12:45, and within an hour or so the 9th Brigade was advancing south-east toward Caen.[17] Once again, the Canadian formations did not achieve their given objectives, which were to reach Caen and seize the Carpiquet airfield west of the town. However, by nightfall the Canadians had secured a lodgement 6 miles deep, with a spur projecting a further mile toward Caen, the deepest penetration of D-Day.

The most serious fighting on the afternoon of D-Day occurred inland from the SWORD landing beaches, where the Germans launched their heaviest counter-blow of the day. The 8th Infantry Brigade spent the time clearing German defences on and just inland from the beaches. The 1st Suffolks were tasked to eliminate two German strongpoints near Colleville-sur-Orne. The first objective, codenamed Morris, was reached at 13:00. Despite damage from the pre-landing bombardment, Morris was still firing its 155mm guns but the garrison surrendered as B Company prepared to breach the barbed wire defences. The Hillman position was assigned to A Company, supported by sappers from 246 Field Company RE. Approaching through standing crops, the sappers breached two belts of barbed wire and cleared a lane through the minefield. The attackers incurred casualties passing through the resulting gap and were then pinned down in craters and trenches just inside the inner perimeter.

The defences proved too strong for infantry alone, and the Suffolks pulled back to regroup. They attacked again at 20:00, with armoured support that cleared a wider path through the minefield. This permitted the Suffolks to clear the position, taking fifty prisoners and killing a number of the garrison who refused to surrender.[18] A further seventy men, including the commander of *Infanterie Regiment 736*, emerged from a deep bunker the next day.[19] The 8th Infantry Brigade's other two battalions were still engaged just behind the beaches. The 2nd East Yorks methodically eliminated the defences at la Brèche and Riva Bella, usually from the rear. A German artillery observer east of the Orne noted the extensive use of explosive charges and flame-throwers, possibly Churchill Crocodiles. German resistance ceased sometime around 16:00.[20] At the east end of the SWORD landing area, *III Bataillon, Infanterie Regiment 736* held out rather better against the attentions of the 1st South Lancs and No. 41 (RM). By late afternoon they were still stubbornly holding onto a number of positions in and around Lion-sur-Mer.

The British 3rd Infantry Division's plan called for its other two infantry brigades to push as quickly as possible to Caen, the main D-Day objective. Thus 185 Infantry Brigade was moving south even before the Suffolks had properly dealt with Hillman; the 1st Royal Norfolks suffered a number of casualties to fire from the strongpoint at 15:30.[21]

Two companies of the Norfolks then became embroiled at another strongpoint, codenamed Rover, which took over two hours to subdue. Despite the severity of the fighting, there were lighter moments too. A private from A Company marvelled at an elderly Frenchman calmly pushing a wheelbarrow of vegetables through a firefight and mortar barrage, and the commander of B Company watched with growing amusement as his second in command miscommunicated spectacularly with a group of agitated French civilians. As he was speaking Urdu, the mutual incomprehension was hardly surprising.[22] 185 Brigade was supposed to ride south on Shermans from the Staffordshire Yeomanry, but these were caught in jams at the SWORD so the 2nd Warwicks and 2nd King's Shropshire Light Infantry moved out on foot. As we have seen, part of the 2nd Warwicks were involved in relieving the 7th Parachute Battalion in Benouville. The rest continued south to Beuville and Biéville, 5 miles inland from the beaches. The former lay at the east end of the Périers Ridge, a stretch of high ground running west from Beuville that marked the half way point between Caen and the coast.

While all this was going on *21 Panzer Division* was preparing the counter-blow ordered by *7 Armee* at 10:30. Control of the Division had passed to *84 Korp*, and General Marcks moved from his HQ at St Lô to Lebisey, 2 miles north of Caen, to observe the attack west of the Orne. The portion of *21 Panzer* assigned to the attack was divided into *Kampfgruppe* Oppeln, made up of two battalions from *Panzer Regiment 22* and a battalion from *Panzergrenadier Regiment 192*, and *Kampfgruppe* Rauch consisting of the remaining two battalions from *Panzergrenadier Regiment 192*. Both were augmented with elements from divisional engineer and self-propelled artillery units. It took five and a half hours for the attackers to re-negotiate the growing traffic chaos in Caen.[23] Some of *22 Panzer Regiment's* tanks took a short cut over a bridge in the industrial Colombelles district in the north of the town. They were attacked by RAF Typhoons as they emerged from the western suburbs, which destroyed two *Panzer IV*s and damaged four more.[24]

The attack force finally concentrated at Lebisey sometime after 15:00. All the senior commanders were called to a conference with

Marcks on a hill above the village; one *Panzer* officer called it 'a proper general's hill' in reference to 19th Century military practice.[25] The attack was to be made in a single echelon. *Kampfgruppe* Oppeln was to head for the Périers Ridge, which was supposed to be held by elements of *Panzergrenadier Regiment 192*, and then onto the coast. *Kampfgruppe* Rauch was to hook to the west around the ridge and link up with the elements of *Infanterie Regiment 736* holding out in Lion-sur-Mer. Marcks made it clear that he expected *Oberst* von Oppeln-Bronikowski's ninety-odd *Panzer IV*s to play the crucial role. According to one source he finished the briefing by declaring 'Oppeln, if you don't succeed in driving the English into the sea, we've lost the war.'[26]

The attack was launched on both sides of the Orne at 16:20. *Kampfgruppe* von Luck's attack on the 6th Airborne was spearheaded by *Panzer Aufklärungs Abteilung 21*, supported by *Panzer IV*s and assault guns from *Panzer Regiment 22* and *Sturmgeschütze Battalion 200*. According to German sources, the attack proceeded well until the armour emerged into the open near Escoville, just south of Hérouvillette. There it came under concentrated attack from fighter-bombers and a devastating barrage from capital ships offshore. This broke the attack and obliged von Luck to withdraw and inform *21 Panzer Division* HQ that his attack had been stymied with no realistic prospect of success. This may have been the case, but such dramatic events do not seem to be reflected in British accounts. This is curious, given that the alleged scene of the action was in clear view from the British positions' airborne perimeter. The 13th Parachute Battalion merely recorded repulsing a company-size attack at around 17:00. The 12th Parachute Battalion did call in naval gunfire support, but at unspecified German activity near the Ring Contour to its front. Had this been in response to an onrushing horde of German armour, the 12th Battalion is rather unlikely to have despatched a platoon patrol to investigate as it did. This raises the suspicion that for *Kampfgruppe* von Luck, this was one of those frequent but underplayed occasions when the troops quietly declined to conform to that which their superiors proposed.

Be that as it may, the attack west of the Orne did not proceed as planned either. *Panzergrenadier Regiment 192* was no longer on the Périers Ridge, having been drawn into the fight at Benouville. It had been replaced in the afternoon by the 2nd Shropshire Light Infantry and a squadron of Shermans from the Staffordshire Yeomanry, supported by the 20th Anti-Tank Regiment RA. More of the Staffordshire's Shermans located around Beuville and Biéville on the left flank. The appearance of the first wave of forty Panzer IVs caused considerable alarm. Staffordshire tanks deployed back from the front line listened intently to the highly charged exchanges coming over the squadron and troop radio nets. Word of the German attack rapidly spread all the way back to the beach; the 1st Suffolks near Hillman were officially warned to expect a German armoured attack.[27]

Kampfgruppe Oppeln, however, was inadvertently moving into a killing ground. *I Bataillon, Panzer Regiment 22* on the left of *Kampfgruppe* Oppeln's frontage lost six or seven tanks in quick succession as it moved around Mathieu at the foot of the Périers Ridge. Return fire knocked out a British anti-tank gun, but the attempted ascent up the west end of the Ridge was repulsed with the loss of ten or more tanks. On the right, some tanks of *II Bataillon* spotted the Staffordshire's Shermans in Biéville and Beuville, and began to move to firing positions in the standing crops. The British fired first, knocking out five *Panzer IVs* with their initial volley of armour-piercing shot. Others *Panzers* attempted to manoeuvre into cover behind hedgerows and in small copses, but the British gunners in their elevated positions were able to pick them off, and the area below the Périers Ridge was soon littered with burning tanks and tall columns of oily black smoke.[28] *Kampfgruppe* Oppeln's push to the sea thus ended on the slopes of the Périers Ridge, just over 3 miles from where it had started. According to *21 Panzer Division's* commander the action cost his division 25 per cent of its tank strength.[29]

The British did not escape entirely unscathed. The Shropshire Light Infantry lost a relocating six-pounder and Universal Carrier, and a number of men were lost tackling a German anti-tank gun near the east end of the Ridge, the latter presumably one of those stationed there earlier with *Panzergrenadier Regiment 192*. The Staffordshire Yeomanry lost a number of tanks around Biéville; the burned-out hulks provided a graphic example of German anti-tank capabilities for passing units. They also prompted an early manifestation of the 'Tigerphobia' that was to grip Allied units later in the Normandy campaign, with one crewman from the 13th/18th Hussars remarking that they provided a sobering demonstration of what a Tiger could do to a Sherman.[30] The problem was that *21 Panzer Division* had no *Panzer VIs* in its order of battle. The nearest Tiger units were at that time located at Beauvais in Picardie and around Le Mans, over 100 miles to the east and south respectively.[31] Nonetheless, the action significantly boosted British morale, and went some way to exorcise the recurring nightmare of the much-vaunted *Panzers* again sweeping all before them into the sea.

With hindsight, it can be seen that *21 Panzer* committed a serious error in deploying all its tanks with *Kampfgruppe* Oppeln. The British 3rd Division's advance to Caen was angled to the south-east, and stubborn German resistance in Lion-sur-Mer therefore opened a gap on the right of the British SWORD incursion. *Kampfgruppe* Rauch was thus able to move unmolested around the Périers Ridge and drive north through Plumetot and Cresserons to all the way to Lion-sur-Mer. There it was enthusiastically received by the survivors of *Infanterie Regiment 736*. Had *Panzer Regiment 22* been more evenly divided between the three *Kampfgruppen*, this might have inflicted serious damage on the growing volume of traffic moving inland from the SWORD beaches. As it was, *Kampfgruppe* Rauch's half-tracks were too lightly armed and armoured for such an attack. Apparently unaware of what had befallen *Kampfgruppe* Oppeln, *Oberst* Rauch therefore elected to await armoured reinforcements.[32] His resolve, however, was severely jolted by the last major event of the day at the east end of the Allied landing front.

At 21:00 the first wave of the main British glider lift, consisting of 220 Horsas and thirty Hamilcars carrying the 6th Airlanding Brigade, arrived. The second wave came in at 21:30. 6th Airlanding Brigade HQ and the 1st Battalion the Royal Ulster Rifles landed on LZ N at Ranville.

The remainder of the 2nd Ox and Bucks, a company from the 12th Battalion the Devonshire Regiment, the 6th Airborne Armoured Reconnaissance Regiment and a number of Divisional units including 211th Airlanding Light Battery RA came down on LZ W. This was a new landing area on the west bank of the Orne, between Ouistreham and le Port. The landing was opposed by light flak that brought down at least one tug aircraft, and one of the Ox and Bucks' gliders broke up in mid-air while making its approach. Overall, casualties were remarkably light, however, even though the Germans quickly brought down mortar and small-arms fire that destroyed a Jeep and six-pounder on LZ N. There were also isolated German elements on the LZ W; one Horsa landed atop a German slit-trench, prompting its startled occupants to surrender to the British crew.

The 6th Airborne Reconnaissance Regiment lost one of its Tetrarch tanks over the Channel, which somehow became unshackled and broke through the nose of its Hamilcar, leaving both to fall hundreds of feet to the sea.[33] Bad landings and debris on the LZ depleted the armoured unit further still. Two Hamilcars collided on landing, and a Hamilcar travelling at over 90 miles per hour hit another Tetrarch. The seven and a half-ton tank was knocked upside down and came to rest underneath the Hamilcar; incredibly the crew escaped unscathed.[34] All the remaining tanks were then temporarily immobilised by parachute rigging lines entangled in their running gear. Some were so badly jammed that welding torches had to be used to free them.[35] Even so, the glider lift begat two historic events. The 6th Airborne Reconnaissance Regiment became the first British Army unit to fly tanks into action, and the 211th Airlanding Battery, which had its 75mm Pack Howitzers in action within thirty minutes of landing, was the first Royal Artillery unit to fly into action.[36]

Coming so soon after the trouncing of the German tank attack against the Périers Ridge, the sight of the British air armada serenely delivering its gliders and supply containers gave British morale a further lift. It had precisely the opposite effect on the German troops that witnessed it. This was especially the case with *Kampfgruppe* Rauch in its exposed position in Lion-sur-Mer, which was becoming increasingly vulnerable as British tanks closed on Cresserons and threatened the corridor to the coast. One company from *Panzergrenadier Regiment 192* fought its way into the German strongpoint at Douvres-la-Déliverande, a mile inland from Luc-sur-Mer. The remainder of *Kampfgruppe* Rauch fell back to Anguerny. Concerned that the British glider landing was a deliberate ploy to cut off *21 Panzer Division, 84 Korps* later pulled both western *Kampfgruppen* back to a line in front of Epron, just north of Caen.[37] This was close to where the afternoon attack had been launched just a few short hours before, and brought the first attempt to inflict a telling blow on the Allied invaders to an unsuccessful close.

It is worth noting two things at this point. First, in fighting *Kampfgruppe* Oppeln to a standstill, the lead elements of the British 3rd Infantry Division turned back the strongest and most dangerous threat to emerge anywhere along the Allied invasion front on 6 June. The half hearted attack by *Fallschirmjäger Regiment 6* toward the UTAH beaches was not in the same league in strength or possible consequence, and the moves against St Mère Église were probes rather than serious attacks. The same was true of the piecemeal local counterattacks made against the troops pushing inland from the OMAHA, GOLD and JUNO beaches. Second, this feat was achieved after the British formation had not only fought its way through a stubborn and heavily fortified beachfront defence, but through the most fully developed sector of the German defences in Normandy as well.

This is important because it contradicts a widespread misconception, popular in American circles, that is neatly encapsulated in the following quote: 'The British amphibious forces, encountering only light-to-moderate resistance, pushed inland with comparative ease.' The root of this appears to be US 1st Army commander Omar Bradley, who the same source quotes as saying 'In sum, the British and Canadian assault forces sat down. They had Caen in their grasp and let it slip away.'[38] These comments are breathtakingly inaccurate, for as we have seen there was nothing light or moderate about the resistance encountered on GOLD, JUNO or SWORD. It is also rather ironic, as the only unit that did any sitting down on D-Day was the US 4th Infantry

Division at UTAH, and also in view of Bradley's low expectations of his own troops. He apparently 'hoped' his men would have occupied Carentan by D Plus One, a mere 6 undefended miles inland from the UTAH beaches.[39] Given this, it is interesting and sobering to reflect on the likely outcome had two thirds of a *Panzer* division with getting on for 100 first-line tanks been directed against the UTAH or even OMAHA landing beaches.

It has to be acknowledged that Bradley's line was followed by the British official history. For some unfathomable reason, this characterised the British advance from the beaches as lacking urgency, presumably because the three assault divisions failed to fully achieve the unrealistic paper objectives they had been set.[40] This verdict, like Bradley's claim that the British let Caen slip out of their grasp, conveniently overlooks three crucial points. First, the advance from the GOLD and JUNO beaches was not a peacetime route march. As eyewitness accounts clearly show, it was a confused series of independent actions by platoons or companies, many of which do not appear in the official records. These fights erupted as the invaders ran unexpectedly into German resistance nests or units retiring from the broken beachfront defences, and overwhelmed them before pressing on for their assigned objectives.

Second, the advance inland from the SWORD beaches involved traversing the most heavily developed sector of the Normandy defences. This meant storming heavily fortified, carefully sited and stubbornly held defensive positions like the Hillman and Rover strongpoints. Given the strength of the German beach defences at SWORD and the density of those stretching inland behind them, the speed with which the lead elements of the British 3rd Division penetrated inland was laudable rather than tardy. Third and finally, the view that the 3rd Division in some way let Caen slip through its fingers conveniently overlooks a crucial fact. Even after the rebuff at the Périers Ridge, two thirds of *21 Panzer Division* with around seventy battleworthy tanks remained between the British invaders and Caen, reinforced in the late evening by the *panzergrenadiers* from *Kampfgruppe Rauch*. *21 Panzer Division* was thus perfectly capable and in the right place to mete out the same treatment to any rash British armoured advance on Caen. All in all, therefore, it would appear that any failings on the GOLD, JUNO and SWORD landing front lay with the planners and their unrealistic expectations, rather than the troops tasked to carry them out.

D-DAY PLUS 1
H PLUS 18 HOURS TO
H PLUS 30 HOURS

(00:00 TO 12:00, WEDNESDAY 7 JUNE 1944)

The failure of *21 Panzer Division* before Ranville and the Périers Ridge, and the enforced withdrawal west of the Orne to Epron left *7 Armee* bereft of an effective mobile reserve at the eastern end of the Allied landing frontage. However, relief was on the way. At midnight on 6 June *716 Infanterie Division* hosted a conference to work out a co-ordinated counter-blow against the Allied invaders at its tactical HQ west of Caen. Present was the commander of *716 Division*, *Generalleutnant* Wilhelm Richter, his opposite number from *21 Panzer Division* Edgar Feuchtinger and a liaison group from the *Panzer Lehr Division*. Last to arrive were a group from *12 SS Panzer Division*, led by the commander of *SS Panzergrenadier Regiment 25*, *Standartenführer* Kurt Meyer. Meyer confided to Richter that he had spent half of the eight-hour journey from Falaise sheltering in ditches from Allied fighter-bombers.[1]

The process which delivered the representatives of the two *Panzer* divisions to Richter's HQ began in the small hours of 6 June with *7 Armee* passing reports of Allied airborne landings to *Heeresgruppe* B at 02:15. These were passed up the chain to von Runstedt's *Oberbefehlshaber West* in Paris. At 02:30 the latter's chief of staff, *Generalleutnant* Gunther Blumentritt, ordered *12 SS Panzer Division* to reconnoitre east of Troarn on the River Dives. As we have seen, *12 SS Panzer* had been alerted following reports of parachute landings not long after midnight on the night of 5-6 June, and Meyer despatched patrols from *SS Panzergrenadier Regiment 25* toward Caen on his own initiative. It was Blumentritt's order that sent the five patrols from *SS Panzer Aufklärungs Abteilung 12* to ascertain the coastal situation west of the Orne.[2]

At 04:45 *Oberbefehlshaber West* requested operational control of *12 SS Panzer* and the *Panzer Lehr Divisions* from *OKW* and, assuming this would be forthcoming, issued orders to both formations. *Panzer Lehr* was instructed to prepare to move to a concentration area between Caen and Bayeux, and at 05:00 *12 SS Panzer* was placed under command of *Heeresgruppe* B, which handed it on to *84 Korps*. Forty-five minutes later *12 SS Panzer* was ordered to concentrate near Lisieux, 30 miles east of Caen. This obliged some rapid improvisation as the *SS* formation had no pre-planned scheme for a move to that location. A hurried reconnaissance showed the recommended concentration area was small and adjacent to obvious targets for Allied air attack, but orders were orders and the Division moved off at 10:00 with a battalion from *Panzergrenadier Regiment 25* in the lead.[3]

However, at 09:30 *Oberbefehlshaber West* discovered *OKW* was not going to authorise its assumption of control. *12 SS Panzer* was specifically not released from *OKW* control, and *Panzer Lehr* was only authorised to move 50 miles from Le Mans to Flers, midway to the coast. According to popular legend, this was because Hitler's staff were unwilling to awake the *Führer*, but this was not the case. Hitler had in fact given specific instructions that he was to be roused if anything of importance occurred after he had retired, and he was discussing the Normandy situation with his staff shortly after 08:00 on the morning of 6 June. The real reason for the delay was simply that Hitler and *OKW* were expecting the real Allied blow to fall on the Pas de Calais. This view shifted only slowly as reports revealed the magnitude of the Normandy landings, underlined by repeated requests from *84 Korps*, *7 Armee* and *Oberbefehlshaber West* for operational control of *12 SS Panzer* and *Panzer Lehr*.

OKW finally released the formations sometime between 14:30 and 15:00. *7 Armee* then ordered *Panzer Lehr* to proceed to Caen immediately, while *12 SS Panzer* was redirected to a concentration area south-west of Caen. *Generalleutnant* Fritz Bayerlein, commanding *Panzer Lehr*, was not happy with this turn of events, and neither was his opposite number from *12 SS Panzer*, *Brigadeführer* Fritz Witt. The latter formation had already arrived at Lisieux at 13:00, although it would have been easier to reach its new destination. Bayerlein asked to postpone his movement for the few hours until dusk, having experienced the capabilities of Allied tactical air power in North Africa. His request was denied, and *Panzer Lehr* began its march to Caen at 17:00. In all, the Division was moving 229 tanks and assault guns, 658 armoured half-tracks and over 1,000 assorted wheeled vehicles along three routes. As this mighty host moved off, the skies began to clear.[4]

Panzer Lehr's personnel carefully camouflaged their vehicles, but could do little to damp down the huge columns of dust that sprang up from the summer-dry French roads at any speed above a crawl. Thus alerted, Allied fighter-bombers were able to make almost constant attacks on the long columns of vehicles, and the march degenerated into a torturous stop-start process as individual vehicles hopped from cover to cover. Over thirty vehicles were destroyed on 6 June, and the harassment eased rather than ceased with the onset of darkness, as medium bombers continued to strafe the roads with the aid of flares. The rearmost and slowest elements of the division were the *Panzer IV* equipped battalions from *Panzer Lehr Regiment 130*. By the morning of 7 June one of these battalions had only covered a third of the distance to Caen, and was refuelling in a wood near Alençon when Allied fighter-bombers found them. *Panzer Lehr's* ordeal went on for a full forty-eight hours in some instances; *Panzergrenadier Regiment 901* did not reach the southern outskirts of Caen until 18:00 on 8 June. The march cost *Panzer Lehr* five tanks, eighty-four armoured half-tracks, ninety assorted wheeled vehicles and, arguably most seriously, fifty armoured fuel tankers.[5]

12 SS Panzer began moving from Lisieux at 17:40. The columns were spread out with intervals of a hundred metres or so between vehicles, which meant the average battalion column of 120 vehicles occupied 10 kilometres of road. They too were easily spotted by the

Allied fighter-bombers swarming over the German rear areas. At first
the occupants of tanks, trucks and half-tracks abandoned their vehicles
at the mere sight of a Typhoon, but they adapted rapidly and remained
aboard until an attack materialised. They also learned that while the
air attacks were extremely stressful, they were frequently less dangerous than the sound and fury suggested. Numerous attacks on *I
Bataillon, Panzergrenadier Regiment 25*, for example, destroyed or
damaged only six vehicles and an anti-tank gun, and killed four men
and wounded twelve more. The casualty toll for the entire Division on
6 June amounted to twenty-two dead and sixty-wounded.[6]

The heaviest cost for the German formations was thus reckoned in
time and fuel. For one three-hour period of the march at the height of
the air attacks, for example, *Panzergrenadier Regiment 25*'s average speed
was a mere 3 kilometres per hour.[7] Lead elements did not cross the
Orne south of Caen until 21:00, and reached the concentration area
near Evrecy at around 23:00. Other units continued to arrive
throughout the night and into 7 June, partly because of the air attacks
and partly because of wide variations in start points, which ranged
from 40 to 120 miles from Evrecy. On arrival all were in dire need of
fuel, as normal consumption was hugely inflated by the constant stopping and starting. The first forty-eight Panthers from *SS Panzer
Regiment 1* burned 8,000 gallons of fuel moving to Evrecy, and ran out
while still east of the Orne. Logistic units had managed to cache some
fuel in the concentration areas, but the Panthers were stranded for
some time.[8]

Meyer may have spent a good deal of the journey from Lisieux
sheltering in ditches, but neither the experience nor the less than
inspiring briefings at the 716th Divisions tactical HQ dampened his
ardour. The liaison team from the *Panzer Lehr* bluntly pointed out that
their formation would not be in a position to participate in any attack
on 7 June. Feuchtinger, having felt the power of the invaders, was of
the opinion that only a massed attack with a minimum of three divisions stood any prospect of success. While the conference was in
progress there was also an incident that underscored what they were
up against. Richter took a telephone call from the commander of

Infanterie Regiment 736 at the Hillman strongpoint. The unfortunate officer reported that he was cut off from his men, that the enemy were atop his bunker demanding his surrender, and asked for instructions. Richter told him to act on his own judgement and wished him well; the officer surrendered with some of his men the next day. None of this impressed Meyer, who contemptuously dismissed the capabilities of the Allied invaders with typical *Waffen* SS bravado: 'Little fish! We'll throw them back into the sea in the morning'. The conference decided that *12 SS* and *21 Panzer Divisions* would attack toward Douvres, into a gap identified between two of the Allied landing areas. The decision was confirmed shortly afterward by *12 SS Panzer's* commander, who ordered Meyer to ensure that the Allies did not gain control of Caen or the nearby airfield at Carpiquet, and to launch a co-ordinated attack with *21 Panzer* at 12:00 on 7 June.[9]

While *12 SS Panzer Division* was gathering in its far-flung elements, the first Allied troops into Normandy were busy maintaining their grip on the flanks of the landing area. On the north and east of the 6th Airborne's perimeter, the 3rd Parachute Brigade's three battalions spent the night and morning of 7 June in relative quiet. The 1st Canadian Parachute Battalion continued digging in and distributing a badly needed resupply of ammunition to make up for supplies lost in the drop, while the 9th Parachute Battalion assisted the Commandos in clearing the area around Amfreville. The 8th Parachute Battalion dominated the area around its firm if undermanned base at the south end of the Bois de Bavent Ridge with constant patrolling, a technique the 6th Airborne Division dubbed 'static offensive'. Pearson maintained a punishing schedule despite personal illness and adverse conditions. The extremely thick foliage in the wood was permanently wet, and full of voracious mosquitoes that ceaselessly tormented the tired paratroopers.

To the west, the arrival of the 6th Airlanding Brigade permitted Gale to reinforce and expand his southern perimeter. The 2nd Ox and Bucks moved across the Orne bridges from LZ W in the early hours of 7 June. At 04:30 the Battalion advanced on Hérouvillette, south-east of Ranville, and when the village proved to be undefended, prepared to move on Escoville a mile further on. This was also undefended, and by 11:00 the Ox and Bucks were digging in under German shell and mortar fire, having filled the gap between Pearson's isolated battalion and the main divisional perimeter. While the Ox and Bucks were moving on Escoville, the 1st Royal Ulster Rifles advanced south along the Orne to Longueval. When this proved to be empty of Germans the Battalion commander, Lieutenant-Colonel Jack Carson, opted to organise a hasty advance into the next village, St Honorine-la-Chardonnerette. This brought them up against elements of *Panzergrenadier Regiment 125* and *Sturmgeschütze Bataillon 200*. Despite confusion over the start time and heavy German artillery and mortar fire, two companies penetrated into St Honorine, but a strong German counter-attack drove them back in some disorder to Longueval. The attack cost the Rifles seven dead, ninety wounded and sixty-eight missing; twenty of the latter rejoined the Battalion over the next few days.[10]

Sixty miles to the west *Generalleutnant* Karl von Schlieben, commanding *709 Infanterie Division*, spent the night organising a renewed attack on St Mère Église. To the north, the *Infantry Regiment 1058* was reinforced with *7 Armee Sturm Abteilung*, a company of self-propelled guns and elements from three artillery battalions. After an artillery barrage, this force attacked down the Montebourg-St Mère Église road at dawn on 7 June. *Infanterie Regiment 1058* does not appear to have applied itself overly vigorously, but the *Sturm Abteilung* rapidly advanced to the outskirts of St Mère Église. This left them vulnerable to the US 4th Division's 12th Infantry Regiment, which spent the night of 6-7 June a mile north-east of St Mère Église, but the American unit appears to have been oblivious to its advantage and the Germans remained unmolested. Instead, the 12th Regiment spent the day moving just under 2 miles north. On its eastern flank the 22nd Infantry Regiment attacked the German gun batteries at Azeville and Crisbeq, and continued to advance against the German defences on the strip of solid ground between the beach and inundated area behind it.

East of St Mère Église, *Infanterie Regiment 1057* renewed the assault on the la Fière bridge at 08:00, again with the assistance of four ex-

French light tanks from *Panzer Ersatz Bataillon 100*. The German tanks and infantry advanced over the bridge against Company A, 1st Battalion, 505th Parachute Infantry. The lead tank was knocked out on the eastern causeway, but a close-range firefight then ensued, with German infantry using the knocked out tank and derelict vehicles pushed onto the causeway by the Americans for cover. The fight ceased when the Germans called for a truce to clear the wounded, and did not resume hostilities thereafter. This was fortuitous for the paratroopers, who had lost almost half their number killed or wounded; one platoon was reduced to fifteen men.[11]

By this time the 82nd Airborne's plight in and around St Mère Église was no secret. Major-General Ridgeway had despatched one of his staff officers with a small patrol to brief the commander of the 4th Division on the situation in the evening of 6 June. Having been awake for over forty-eight hours, the officer accepted a dose of Benzedrine before embarking on his mission,[12] and the patrol reached Major-General Barton's command post at Audouville-la-Hubert at around midnight. It brought the first official word on the situation beyond the 4th Division's shallow beachhead. Barton assured the exhausted paratroop staffer he would despatch assistance at first light, and passed word that contact had been made to VII Corps HQ, which was still aboard ship. This is usually presented in a manner that suggests the 4th Division would have moved faster had they been aware of airborne troop's predicament. Given what we have seen of the 4th Division's performance thus far however, this is a rather unlikely scenario and smacks more of an excuse than a serious explanation. Even if it were the case, it still demonstrates an inexcusable ignorance of the realities of airborne operations. In such circumstances it is a rather novel concept to operate on the assumption that all has gone well with friendly airborne landings, as the 4th Infantry Division appears to have done, and to move to their aid only if specifically requested to do so.

Be that as it may, the result was development that was finally to propel at least part of Barton's formation into acting with the urgency the situation warranted. The US VII Corps was commanded by Major-General Lawton J. Collins, a tough, no-nonsense officer who had commanded the US 25th Infantry Division on Guadalcanal and New Georgia in the South-West Pacific. Collins immediately went ashore to Barton's HQ to get the full situation report. He then ordered Barton, against the latter's will, to despatch a task force from his reserve tank battalion, the 746th Tank Battalion commanded by Lieutenant-Colonel C. G. Hupfer, to St Mère Église immediately. The 746th was located at Reuville, just under 2 miles east of St Mère Église, but it does not appear to have been ready for rapid action. Even though there were no German formations between Reuville and St Mère Église, the battalion's lead elements did not reach the town until the early afternoon.[13]

At around the time the German attack on the north of St Mère Église began, the US 8th Infantry Regiment and its attached companies from the 70th Tank Battalion roused themselves from their prematurely occupied night positions and tackled the German pocket blocking the southern approaches to St Mère Église. The 1st Battalion attacked toward Turqueville from the east while the 2nd and 3rd Battalions and Lieutenant-Colonel Raff's task force advanced north from les Forges. The 3rd Battalion was stymied by German troops atop the ridge running between Fauville to Ecoqueneauville, a mile south of St Mère Église. However, the 2nd Battalion advancing on the right outflanked the ridge, and the defenders surrendered readily after a stiff but short lived fight. Most were ex-Soviet POWs from *Ost Bataillon 795*. This suggests that a determined push the previous night might have broken through to the embattled 82nd Airborne. It is unclear how long clearing the ridge took, but the 8th Infantry took the rest of the morning to cover the last mile or so to St Mère Église.[14]

Shortly after the 8th Infantry began to move north from les Forges, GALVESTON arrived. This was the first of two glider lifts – the other was confusingly dubbed NEPTUNE – carrying the 325th Glider Infantry Regiment and an attached battalion from the 401st Glider Infantry. GALVESTON was divided into two echelons, the first of which was scheduled to begin landing on LZ E, south-east of les Forges, at 07:00. Made up of thirty-two Waco CG4s and eighteen Horsas, the first echelon actually arrived five minutes ahead of schedule, but the tug aircraft were all flying at three hundred feet or lower. This altitude only allowed the heavily laden machines a glide time of thirty seconds, and in combination with all but six tug aircraft releasing their tows prematurely, almost all came down in the marshy terrain between Causeways One and Two. The second echelon of fifty Waco CG4s fared slightly better. In all the landing killed seventeen men and injured eighty-five, many badly. The glider casualties, interestingly, in this case appear to refute routine American assertions that the Horsa was flimsy and unsafe. Ten Horsas and nine Waco CG4s were destroyed on landing, and seven and nine respectively were seriously damaged.

NEPTUNE came into LZ W around les Forges at 08:51, nine minutes early. Again, the lift was divided into two echelons, the first made up of thirty Horsas and twenty Waco CG4s. The second, trailing by eight minutes, consisted of fifty Waco CG4s. Again, the tugs did not do their job as well as they ought. Several gliders overshot the LZ to the west and came down among intact *Rommelspargel*, others came down on the northern end where German troops were still holding out, and several of those that came down on target collided with abandoned machines from earlier lifts. Sixteen Horsas and four Waco CG4s were destroyed, fifteen of their passengers were killed and fifty-nine injured. Despite this, 90 per cent of the 325th Glider infantry were assembled and ready to move by 10:15.[15] The 325th was supposed to become the 82nd Airborne's reserve regiment, but two battalions were immediately parcelled out, one to reinforce the units holding the east end of the la Fière causeway, and one to assist the paratroopers north of St Mère Église.[16]

While the 82nd Airborne was holding out around St Mère Église, elements of the 101st Airborne Division were doing the same on the River Douve. The 3rd Battalion, 506th Parachute Infantry Regiments were still holding the northern end of two bridges over the River Douve near le Port. A mile and a half to the west, elements of the 501st Parachute Infantry were holding the la Barquette locks, while the remainder of the Regiment occupied the villages of les Droueries and Basse Addeville to the north. As nothing had been heard from these units since the landings, Major-General Taylor despatched the 1st and 2nd Battalions of the 506th Parachute Infantry south-west toward St Côme-du-Mont to investigate. Company E from the 2nd Battalion led the way from night positions around Culoville at first light on 7 June, and quickly cleared Vierville. The advance then became a two-pronged affair, with the 1st Battalion continuing along the road to Beaumont while the 2nd Battalion struck off cross-country to the left toward Angoville-au-Plain. This brought both into contact with the Germans, and the advance was slowed until two platoons from the 746th Tank Battalion arrived.[17]

At the OMAHA landing area the commander of *352 Infanterie Division*, *Generalleutnant* Dietrich Kraiss, spent the night of 6-7 June in a desperate and fruitless attempt to erect an effective defence against the American incursions pressing inland. The Division's reserve formation, *Kampfgruppe* Meyer, had been split and sent against OMAHA and the British GOLD landings with little effect during the morning of 6 June. By the evening of D-Day Kraiss was forced to deploy his engineer battalion to St Laurent-sur-Mer as infantry, and to order up his replacement training battalion. An appeal to General Marcks at *84 Korps* for reinforcements elicited an admission that every available unit had already been committed, and an uncompromising order to hold in place until reinforcements could be drafted in from elsewhere.

Kraiss' counterpart from the US 29th Division, Major-General Charles Gerhardt, also received orders shortly before first light, from Major-General Gerow at US V Corps HQ. The 29th Division was to advance south-west and secure Isigny, 9 miles away at the junction of the Rivers Aure and Vire. Gerhardt was concerned over the state of his landed units, especially the 116th Infantry that had led the way ashore on D-Day, and by the presence of pockets of German resistance in the immediate area of the beaches. He therefore requested his 175th Infantry Regiment be released from Corps reserve to spearhead the advance. Gerow granted this request and moved the 175th Regiment up the disembarkation schedule to the late morning of 7 June. In the meantime the 115th Infantry made another attack against St Laurent. This met with more success than the previous evening, and the village was cleared by 09:00. They were accompanied by Brigadier-General

Cota, reprising his inspirational role of the previous day; at one point he personally led a squad against a German held house in an impromptu demonstration of house-clearing technique for a dumb-founded company commander. The 115th then turned its attention to organising a push south to cut the coast road near Vacqueville, in order to prevent German reinforcements reaching Vierville.

Most of the 116th Regiments were engaged in clearing German stragglers and isolated positions; several pockets of resistance were encountered in the supposedly clear D3 Exit at les Moulins. The 1st Battalion, however, was ordered to push with all possible speed to relieve the 2nd Ranger Battalion at the Pointe du Hoc. The 1st Battalion could only raise around 250 men, but they were augmented by elements of the 5th Ranger Battalion and elements of the 2nd Ranger Battalion that had been redirected to Dog Green Beach, and ten Sherman tanks. The Rangers had been rebuffed in a similar endeavour on the evening of D-Day, and spent the night on the extreme right of the American landing area in anticipation of another attempt. The relief force moved off at 08:00, and by 11:00 was at St Pierre-du-Mont, within a mile of the German battery position. There, however, things went awry and stubborn German resistance stopped the advance, which remained stalled for the rest of the day.[18]

Their presence does, however, appear to have distracted the German besiegers. Serious German efforts to eliminate Rudder's diminishing band appear to have begun in earnest in the early hours of 7 June, with three separate attacks coming in between 00:05 and 01:30. One overran a section of the perimeter held by the survivors of Company E, but the situation was resolved by their counterpart from Company F, although with less than fifty combat-effective Rangers remaining in total terms like company were relative at best. Another determined attack by *Infanterie Regiment 916* just before dawn pushed the Rangers back into a perimeter backing onto the cliffs, only 200 yards deep. Rudder's men held this perimeter through the day with the assistance of naval gunfire support summoned via their single working SCR-284 radio and Lieutenant Eikner's ancient signal lamp.[19]

On the other half of the OMAHA frontage, the US 1st Infantry Division was also engaged in expanding its lodgement with a six-battalion push south and east. Two battalions from the 16th Infantry, supported by the 1st Battalion, 26th Infantry Regiment advanced south-east with the aim of occupying high ground at St Cauvin and ultimately linking up with the British GOLD landings at Port-en-Bessin. The main effort was an attack to secure high ground south of the Bayeux-Isigny road by the 18th Infantry Regiment, supported on the right by the 3rd Battalion, 26th Infantry. The latter was to secure the village of Formigny, while the 1st and 3rd Battalions of the 18th Infantry advanced toward Engranville and Mandeville respectively. The 2nd Battalion, 18th Infantry angled south-east toward Mosles, actually on the main Bayeux-Isigny road. All the attacks appear to have begun in the late morning, and made good initial progress apart from the 3rd Battalion, 26th Infantry Battalion which, according to the US official history, '…was unable to get moving'. Their German opponents also noted this tardiness; *352 Infanterie Division* specifically contrasted the sluggishness of the battalion's set-piece attack with the individual initiative and aggression exhibited by American infantry-men in the fighting on the bluffs.[20]

The nearest British troops to the Americans on the morning of 7 June were No. 47 (RM) Commando, which had landed near le Hamel on D-Day. After a difficult landing that involved clearing German troops from the planned assembly area, the Commandos began their advance on Port-en-Bessin at 11:00. At around 17:30, following a 4-mile tactical advance through German occupied terri-tory they paused to rest and take stock. The result was not encourag-ing. Seventy-eight men were missing, and many Commandos had been obliged to acquire German weapons after losing their own in the landing or running short of ammunition. Most of the unit's radios were unserviceable after immersion in seawater, and all but one three-inch mortar had been lost. The surviving example lacked a sight, and most of the mortar ammunition and the Bangalore torpedoes the Commandos needed to breach the defences of the strongpoints guarding their objective were also missing.

Nonetheless, at 19:45 the Commando moved off again on the final leg of their journey. Their destination was Point 72, a hill just east of Escures, a mile and a half inland from Port-en-Bessin and 6 miles from their rest up point. The Commandos arrived there at around 22:30, dug in and spent a relatively quiet night apart from capturing two Germans who inadvertently wandered into their positions. The morning of 7 June was spent rejigging the assault plan and establishing communications with the units tasked to support the attack on the port. These included the cruiser HMS *Emerald* and an Army field artillery battery; close air support was to be provided by RAF Typhoons. The assault was scheduled to begin at 16:00.[21]

The process of dealing with pockets of German resistance and pushing inland to secure assigned objectives was repeated along the remainder of the invasion front on 7 June. Behind the GOLD beaches the British 50th Division's brigades pushed south for the main Caen-Bayeux road and south-west for Bayeux. The Germans had evacuated Bayeux on 6 June, and the 56th Infantry Brigade thus occupied it without a fight the following day. The advance in the SWORD sector was restricted to the British 3rd Infantry Division's follow up formation. The 8th Brigade needed time to reorganise after the daylong fight to clear the German beachfront defences at Riva Bella and Ouistreham, and 185 Infantry Brigade had become strung out between Benouville and the Périers Ridge. The advance was thus renewed by the 9th Infantry Brigade, which moved off in the morning for a concentration area near le Mesnil, at the western end of the Périers Ridge. From there it was scheduled to renew the attack toward Caen in the early afternoon.

Inland from the JUNO landing area, the 3rd Canadian Infantry Division also despatched its fresh follow up formation at Caen. On the right the 7th Canadian Infantry Brigade moved off at 06:00 for its D-Day phase line astride the Bayeux-Caen road. After three hours without encountering significant German opposition, the brigade was ordered to make a dash for its final objectives. By midday it was digging in around Putot-en-Bessin, Norrey-en-Bessin and Bretteville l'Orgueilleuse, astride the main road and rail line linking Caen and

Bayeux, 9 miles from the coast. The 8th Canadian Infantry Brigade was tasked to pinch out a bulge into the left flank of the Canadian lodgement centred on Douvres. This involved one battalion attacking two heavily defended radar stations near Douvres, while the rest of the brigade moved on the villages Anguerny and Colomby-sur-Thaon to the south. The latter task went more successfully than the former, and the Douvres radar stations were eventually left for follow up formations to deal with.

The attack toward Caen was thus left to the 9th Canadian Infantry Brigade, advancing south from the spur in the D-Day perimeter near Villons-les-Buissons. Its target was Carpiquet airfield, 4 miles west of Caen. The advance was spearheaded by Stuart light tanks from the 7th Canadian Reconnaissance Regiment and a company from the North Nova Scotia Highlanders; the remainder of the infantry battalion followed riding Shermans from the Canadian 27th Armoured Regiment. The force moved off at 07:45 and reached Buron by midday, an unopposed advance of 3 miles. A mile or so beyond Buron the force angled south-west toward Authie. On approaching Authie, the Shermans dropped off their passengers and deployed to shoot the vanguard company into the village. The reconnaissance tanks, meanwhile, continued to push south toward Franqueville, just short of the Bayeux-Caen road. This put the lead elements of the 9th Canadian Infantry Brigade within 2 miles of their objective at Carpiquet, and apparently with nothing to stop them.

11

D-DAY PLUS 1
H PLUS 30 HOURS TO
H PLUS 42 HOURS

(12:00 TO 23:59, WEDNESDAY 7 JUNE 1944)

On the east side of the River Orne, *Kampfgruppe* von Luck had spent the morning of 7 June exacting a heavy price from newly arrived 1st Royal Ulster Rifles in their attempt to penetrate into St Honorine-la-Chardonnerette. In the afternoon it was the turn of the 2nd Ox and Bucks, which by late morning was digging in around Hérouvillette and Escoville. This, however, brought them under direct German observation, and heavy artillery and mortar fire swiftly followed. This was in at least one instance augmented with direct fire; the battalion commander, Lieutenant-Colonel Michael Roberts, was prevented from setting up his command post in the Château d'Escoville by a German assault gun. More seriously, the Ox and Bucks were unable to bring up their anti-tank guns.

This proved to be a critical omission when the Germans attacked Escoville at 15:00. Once again German vehicles stood off and pounded the British positions while their infantry closed up for the assault. The Ox and Bucks had no real counter to this, and calls for assistance went unanswered because Battalion HQ was out of communications with the forward companies. They nonetheless fought stubbornly from house to house, but the position was untenable without anti-tank support and Lieutenant-Colonel Roberts ordered a withdrawal to Hérouvillette. This required a counter-attack to extricate two companies cut off in Escoville, after which the Ox and Bucks established a hasty defensive perimeter in Hérouvillette. The Germans, however, did not capitalise on their success and 6th Airborne's perimeter remained intact. The action cost the Ox and Bucks eighty-seven casualties, including Lieutenant-Colonel Roberts. Roberts had actually been injured in the 6 June glider landing, but insisted on carrying on until he could no longer stand.[1]

The German attack on Escoville appears to have been part of a general assault on the southern section of the 6th Airborne's perimeter. The equally violent reaction to the 1st Royal Ulster Rifles' incursion into St Honorine-la-Chardonnerette during the morning suggests that they had trespassed on a forming up area for the attack, which would explain the lack of follow-up to the disorderly British withdrawal to Longueval. Whether or not, at least seven tanks and an estimated 150 *Panzergrenadiers* fell on the 12th Parachute Battalion, overrunning part of the perimeter after the Battalion's sole anti-tank gun was knocked out. The incursion was contained thanks to the courageous actions of Private Hall, who braved heavy German fire to man the silent gun and quickly knocked out three of the attacking tanks. The 13th Parachute was assailed by a German force spearheaded by three assault guns, but this attack also faltered when all three vehicles were knocked out by the paratroopers.[2]

The two parachute battalions had been engaged virtually non-stop since the early hours of D-Day, and the 12th Battalion was doubtless delighted to be relieved by the final increment of the 6th Airlanding Brigade. The 12th Battalion, The Devonshire Regiment journeyed to Normandy by sea, and marched into the 6th Airborne Division's perimeter from the SWORD landing area, relieving the 12th Parachute Battalion in front of Ranville at some time between 17:00 and 18:15. The paratroopers were withdrawn to the relative quiet of the Chateau de Ranville, while the Devons dug in along the southern edge of the village. The Germans marked their arrival, knowingly or otherwise, with an air raid that killed three men and wounded a further sixteen.[3]

To the north of 6th Airborne Division's perimeter, the Commandos of the 1st Special Service Brigade were busy patrolling their new area of responsibility. In the early afternoon of 7 June No. 3

Commando, prompted by complaints about German shelling from the Merville Battery, despatched a strong fighting patrol to investigate. The patrol discovered the three badly wounded members of the 9th Parachute Battalion still ensconced in Casemate No. 4. The Commandos promised to evacuate the unfortunate paratroopers, but the appearance of two German self-propelled guns obliged them to withdraw, and the airborne wounded were once again left to their own devices.[4]

Brigadier Hill had set up 3rd Parachute Brigade near the le Mesnil crossroads, a mile north-east of Hérouvillette. The 1st Canadian Parachute Battalion was recalled there from Robehomme, while the 9th Parachute Battalion remained in Amfreville until relieved by the 1st Special Service Brigade at 21:30. As Lieutenant-Colonel Otway prepared to move, he received fresh orders to occupy the Château St Côme, located in a wooded area called the Bois de Mont a mile north of le Mesnil on the le Mesnil-Amfreville road. According to 3rd Parachute Brigade HQ, the Château was held by German troops, and Otway was ordered to seize and hold it at all costs.

Otway immediately despatched Major Eddie Charlton in a commandeered Renault car to reconnoitre the target. The rest of the 9th Battalion moved off at 23:30 accompanied by a heavily-loaded handcart and a horse-drawn brewer's dray; as a concession to stealth, the hooves were wrapped in strips of blanket. A fortuitous navigation error led the Battalion round rather than through Bréville, which unknown to Otway was occupied by German troops. At one point the column of paratroopers encountered two companies of German infantry marching openly in column. Probably fortunately for all concerned, Otway's lead scouts saw the Germans first, the horse handlers kept their charges quiet, and the Germans passed on their way. The 9th Battalion met Major Charlton near their objective at around 01:30 on 8 June, who reported the Chateau St Côme unoccupied. Otway decided to wait until daylight before moving on the Chateau, but did search a bungalow located in the woods next to the crossroads. It was occupied by the mayor of Bréville and his wife who, in one of those curious coincidences of war, turned out to be related to a man Otway knew from his time at the Royal Military Academy at Sandhurst.[5]

While the 9th Parachute Battalion was trekking through the darkness, Lieutenant-Colonel Pearson's 8th Parachute Battalion was busy dominating its area of responsibility a mile or so away at the south end of the Bois de Bavent. Pearson's aim was to create the illusion that his force was much larger than it in fact was, and to this end despatched a fighting patrol into Troarn to set up an ambush on the road leading north-east from the town. Pearson himself led a third patrol sparked by the arrival of a sergeant from the 9th Parachute Battalion at around 20:00. The Dakota carrying the sergeant's stick had crashed near Bassenville, a mile east of the Dives and a number of injured men were hidden in a large house near the village.

Pearson put together a sixty-four strong patrol equipped with two Jeeps, medical supplies and collapsible stretchers. Setting out after dark, the first stop was an abandoned glider near Bures to recover an inflatable dinghy. The original plan was to use the dinghy to cross the Dives, but one of the patrol punctured it with his fixed bayonet as he embarked; a furious Pearson kicked the miscreant into the river, and he received another withering rebuke from the RSM after being fished out. The patrol then picked its way across the wrecked Bures bridge and followed the railway track to Bassenville. Only three of the injured were mobile, so the remainder were dosed with morphine and loaded onto a farm cart. Part of the patrol had become separated on the approach, and Pearson ordered his party to sing 'Roll out the Barrel' as they passed back through Bassenville as a recognition sign. This saved them from a friendly ambush that mistook the noise of the cart's iron tyres on the cobbled road for an approaching German half-track. The wounded were carried over the Dives to the Jeeps, and Pearson and the rest of the patrol were back in the 8th Battalion's perimeter just before dawn.[6]

At the other end of the invasion frontage, the afternoon of 7 June finally saw relief for the embattled American airborne defenders of St Mère Église. In the early hours of the morning the commander of the US VII Corps, Major-General Lawton J. Collins, had ordered the unwilling commander of the US 4th Infantry Division to despatch part of his reserve tank battalion to St Mère Église immediately. It took another ten hours for the order to be carried out, although it is unclear whether this was due to tardiness in transmission or because Lieutenant-Colonel C.G. Hupfer's 746th Tank Battalion was not ready to move. Whichever, it was not until the early afternoon that a company of tanks moved into the suburbs of St Mère Église. Hupfer had been preceded by Brigadier-General Roosevelt Junior who, being a close friend of Ridgeway, reprised his earlier performance on the UTAH beach by taking a Jeep and pushing through to St Mère Église alone and unarmed apart from his walking cane. His arrival and nonchalant greeting – his first words to Ridgeway and his staff were 'Fellows, where's the picnic?' – was a tremendous morale boost for the tired paratroopers, and balanced the lack of immediate practical assistance from the 4th Division. It was this, in combination with his fearless behaviour at the UTAH beach that led to Roosevelt being awarded the Medal of Honour.[7]

A battalion from the US 8th Infantry Regiment, reinforced with two companies from the 70th Tank Battalion also arrived in St Mère Église in the early afternoon, along with Raff's task force from the 746th Tank Battalion and 325th Glider Infantry. The tanks linked up with the 2nd Battalion, 505th Parachute Infantry and launched a joint advance up the St Mère Église-Montebourg road to Neuville, where Lieutenant Turnbull's little band of paratroopers from the 2nd Battalion, 505th Parachute Infantry had fought their epic battle against *Infanterie Regiment 1058* on D-Day. Less than a mile out they ran into heavy German artillery fire and a number of assault guns, which prompted a long-range and inconclusive firefight. While this was going on Hupfer personally surveyed a trail east of the road, and led part of his force up it into Neuville. In the ensuing fight the Americans knocked out two assault guns, captured sixty assorted German troops and released sixteen American paratroopers being held in the town.

Thus by mid-afternoon there were around sixty American tanks in the region of St Mère Église. This, according to the US official history, was the '…first time in the early beachhead battles the Americans were confronting the Germans with something like massed armour in a relatively small sector.' This was perfectly true, but it is also worth noting some salient points the official history does not acknowledge. Much is made of the quality of the *Luftlande Division 91*, but the record clearly shows that the calibre of German opposition encountered north of St Mère Église did not really require massed armour. If that were the case, the *ad hoc* groupings of American paratroopers could not have held up *Infanterie Regiment 1058* as they did. All that was required was sufficient armour to provide fire support and counter the low-grade armour deployed by the Germans in the Cotentin, and this was available from at least the late afternoon of D-Day. The bulk of the 746th Tank Battalion, for example, was lying idle at Reuville, within 2 miles of St Mère Église in the early hours of 7 June. What was missing therefore was not massed armour but a little more application by those controlling the resources already available, which was not forthcoming until Major-General Collins arrived to galvanise Barton and the 4th Division staff into moving with the speed and aggression the situation warranted.

Be that as it may, the American attacks north of St Mère prompted a German collapse. *Infanterie Regiment 1058* was broken by the American thrust to Neuville and began a precipitate retreat that obliged a similar move by the intact *7 Armee Sturm Abteilung*. Personal intervention by *Generalleutnant* von Schlieben stemmed the retreat, and he established a hasty defence line a mile or so north of Neuville. The German failure convinced von Schlieben that he could do no more than contain the American incursion and prevent them from seizing Cherbourg. To this end he ordered a defence line established running from le Ham, on the Merderet 3 miles south-west of Montebourg, to Quinéville near the east Cotentin coast. German units garrisoning defence works along that coast were pulled back to man the new line, but the core of the defence was a *Kampfgruppe* under *Oberst* Helmuth Rohrbach, made up of *Infanterie Regiment 922* from *243 Infantry Division*, reinforced with a battalion from *Infanterie Regiment 919*.[8]

To the south of St Mère Église, the 101st Airborne was continuing its efforts to link up with its elements holding crossings and locks on the River Douve. The 1st and 2nd Battalions, 506th Parachute Infantry reached Vierville in the late morning. From there, the 1st Battalion pushed on through Beaumont toward St Côme-du-Mont, while the 2nd Battalion struck off across country toward Angoville-au-Plain with the idea of hooking south and then west to the Carentan - St Mère Église in order to come at St Côme-du-Mont from the south. Shortly thereafter the 1st Battalion ran into two of what it described as counter-attacks, but which may well have been probes from *Fallschirmjäger Regiment 6* in St Côme-du-Mont trying to locate their lost 1st Battalion. The latter unit had become cut off during the German attack toward St Marie-du-Mont on the afternoon of D-Day.

The 2nd Battalion of the 506th was also held up by German fire, but moved off again with support from two platoons of the 746th Tank Battalion and penetrated to within a mile of St Côme-du-Mont. Having rebuffed the German attacks, the 1st Battalion of the 506th Regiment continued south-west toward St Côme-du-Mont. In the process it linked up with the 2nd Battalion, 505th Parachute Infantry which had been attempting to push into the town from les Droueries. This attack made progress against stubborn resistance from *Fallschirmjäger Regiment 6*, but by nightfall it became apparent that it would not be able to link up with the 2nd Battalion, 506th Parachute Infantry. The latter therefore went firm in place while the 1st Battalion of the 506th withdrew to Beaumont. Both battalions spent the night reorganising in preparation for renewing the attack on the morning of 8 June.[9]

While all this was going on, the isolated American elements on the Douve were scoring their own victory. The failure of the German counter-attack toward St Marie-du-Mont in the evening of 6 June left *I Bataillon, Fallschirmjäger Regiment 6* cut off. Unable to move west, *I Bataillon* spent the night moving south toward the Douve in an effort to regain friendly territory. In the process it unwittingly manoeuvred between the 3rd Battalion, 506th Regiment holding the bridges near le Port and the 501st Parachute Infantry holding the la Barquette locks. In the mid-afternoon the 800-strong German battalion was spotted moving in the open. The American paratroopers opened fire on their counterparts caught cold in the open, killing many as they attempted to flee over the swampy ground. Realising their situation was hopeless, 250 *fallschirmjäger* surrendered to the 506th and the 501st took a further 350 prisoner. Only twenty-five evaded the American ambush and reached friendly lines at Carentan.[10]

On the other side of the Vire Estuary, *Generalleutnant* Kraiss, commanding *Infanterie Division 352*, could do little more than watch as the American invaders gathered strength and pushed slowly inland, destroying his formations piecemeal in the process. Appeals for reinforcement had merely underlined the fact that *84 Korps* had already comprehensively scraped the barrel. At midnight on 6 June General Marcks informed Kraiss that all available reserves had been committed and that his mission was now to hold out until *7 Armee* or *Heeresgruppe* B despatched reinforcements. The last of *84 Korps'* reserve reached Kraiss in the evening of 7 June. *Schnelle Brigade 30* was a bicycle-mounted formation located at Coutances, 35 miles inland from the OMAHA landing area. *352 Infanterie Division* received a single battalion; the other two were despatched to face the British incursion north of Bayeux.

The only bright spark for Kraiss in this gloomy situation was the capture of a complete set of US V Corps orders in the fighting around Vierville. The 29th Division's forward HQ was established near the mouth of the D1 Exit near Vierville, and Kraiss' men presumably happened upon a member of Major-General Gerhardt's staff. After marvelling at their scope and scale, Kraiss hurriedly despatched them up the chain of command, on the reasonable assumption that they would lead to a turnaround of the situation. One of *352 Division's* staff officers claimed that the orders were kept at *7 Armee* HQ for four days, which may or may not have been the case. Even had the orders been taken at face value, it is difficult to see how the knowledge could have been turned rapidly to German advantage, given the deteriorating situation along the entire invasion front.

In the early morning of 7 June USV Corps ordered Major-General Gerhardt to secure Isigny, 9 miles south-west of the OMAHA beaches at the junction of the Rivers Aure and Douve. The intent was to increase the security of the 29th Division's lodgement, which dovetailed neatly with subsequent instructions from 1st Army HQ in the afternoon. These came directly from Eisenhower, who had inspected the landing front by sea during the morning. The Supreme Commander instructed Bradley to organise a concerted drive to link the OMAHA and UTAH landing areas, beginning with the seizure of Isigny. At Gerhardt's request, V Corps had released the 175th Infantry Regiment from the Corps' reserve to spearhead the attack, and the Regiment had been bumped up the landing schedule to just before midday on 7 June.

As a reserve formation, the 175th Regiment had assumed its landing would be routine, a misconception of which it was rapidly disabused. Bumping the regiment up the timetable meant it arrived piecemeal, and while Gerhardt had planned for a landing on Dog Green Beach the Navy delivered them onto Easy Green instead, allegedly because the approaches to the former were not properly cleared of obstacles. Even then at least one landing craft hit a mined obstacle; one appalled observer noted the craft disintegrated rather than sank, and that the resulting debris rained down on other craft around it. Given that the D1 Exit from Dog Green was at that time jammed with troops and vehicles, however, it is in any case more likely that the Navy found it easier to slot the accelerated deployment of the 175th Infantry into the Easy Green landing schedule. Whatever the reason, when the first elements of the 175th Infantry waded ashore at 12:30 they were fired on by German stragglers holding out in the bluffs, and then had to make a mile and a half march west along the beach through the grisly detritus of the D-Day assault. Neither experience was good for the newcomer's morale, and one of Gerhardt's staff noted that many of them were 'spooked' by stepping over mangled bodies wearing the 29th Division patch. Gerhardt himself was annoyed with the Navy for both unilaterally shifting the 175th Regiment's landing place and for failing to deliver them in a single, coherent entity. These shortcomings stymied his plan to launch the 175th Infantry straight off the beach toward Isigny.

The last elements of the 175th landed at 16:30.[11] It thus took all afternoon and evening for the regiment to land, move to and struggle through the logjam at the D1 Exit and reach Gruchy, a crossroad hamlet a mile west of Vierville. Company F was side-tracked briefly by a female civilian who led them to a well-camouflaged German bunker hidden in a ravine. The bunker contained a number of German wounded, who were taken prisoner. To its credit, the 175th Infantry remained at Gruchy only long enough to reorganise and link up with supporting Shermans from the 747th Tank Battalion. The 1st Battalion then led a 2-mile column out of Gruchy after dark, following a track running south-west. The 2nd Battalion fought a brief skirmish with a party of Germans who blundered into the column at around midnight, and the Regiment halted for a three-hour rest at around 01:00 in the morning of 8 June.[12]

The 29th Division's other two infantry regiments spent the afternoon of 7 June clearing the area immediately behind the beach and preparing to resume the advance inland on 8 June. After finally clearing St Laurent-sur-Mer during the mid-morning, the 115th Infantry Regiment spent the rest of the day advancing 1.5 miles south-west to cut the road running south from Vierville to Formigny, where they set in for the night. The 2nd and 3rd Battalions, 116th Infantry Regiment spent the morning clearing tenacious pockets of German resistance from the supposedly secure les Moulins draw. That done, both battalions moved west along the sea line to the D1 Exit leading to Vierville, clearing more German stragglers from the bluffs in the process. After reorganising at Vierville they struck out for Louvières, 2 miles inland and one of the 116th Infantry's D-Day objectives. In the event, Louvières was not to be liberated on D Plus 1 either, as both Battalions were still short of the hamlet when darkness fell and the advance was called off until the morning of 8 June.

The depleted 1st Battalion, 116th Infantry spent 7 June trying unsuccessfully to reach Lieutenant-Colonel Rudder's embattled Rangers at the Pointe du Hoc, with the rest of the Provisional Ranger Group. After initially making good progress, the relief force spent the afternoon trying to force its way through stubborn resistance from

Infanterie Regiment 914 in St Pierre-du-Mont, a mile short of the
Pointe du Hoc position. In the early afternoon a Major Street
succeeded in getting rations, ammunition and a reinforcing platoon
from the 5th Ranger Battalion into the Pointe du Hoc perimeter
from the sea. The landward relief force made two attacks against
German units in the vicinity of St Pierre-du-Mont; when these were
rebuffed it was suggested Rudder's men try and break out to meet
them at around 17:00. The German ring proved too strong, however,
and the relief force dug in for a troubled night thanks to German
infiltrators.[13]

On the right of the US 1st Infantry Division's frontage, *Infanterie
Regiment 916* kept the newly arrived 3rd Battalion, 26th Infantry out
of Formigny, but the other two battalions in the attack forged ahead.
With support from five Shermans from the 741st Tank Battalion, the
1st Battalion, 18th Infantry Regiment advanced 2 miles to
Engranville, and drove a company-sized force of Germans off the high
ground overlooking the village in a fight that lasted most of the afternoon. The 3rd Battalion of the 18th Infantry made even better
progress and reached Mandeville, 3 miles from the start line and a mile
south of the Bayeux-Isigny road. The 1st Division's attack east, to link
up with the British GOLD lodgement, made similar progress. The 2nd
Battalion, 18th Infantry pressed south-east to Mosles on the main
Bayeux-Isigny road, and the 3rd Battalion, 16th Infantry pushed east 2
miles to Huppain, less than a mile from Port-en-Bessin. The task of
linking up with the British was entrusted to the 26th Infantry
Regiment, the 1st Battalion of which advanced to a line running
between Mosles and Huppain. It was followed by the 2nd Battalion
after it was released from 1st Division reserve at 17:45.

In conjunction with moves west by the British 231 and 56th
Infantry Brigades from the GOLD beaches, the American advance had
the effect of squeezing the remnants of *Infanterie Regiment 726* and
Schnelle Brigade 30 into a narrow corridor between the OMAHA and
GOLD lodgements. At 16:00, after a two-hour bombardment, No. 47
(RM) Commando began to close off the head of the corridor. The
axis for the assault was the road from Escures to Port-en-Bessin,

supported by the sightless three-inch mortar and the destroyer HMS *Emerald*. One troop was delayed on the start line after taking a number of casualties from what turned out to be a German sniping school located in Fosse Soucy, half a mile south-west. The remainder of the Commando quickly overran three resistance nests guarding the approaches to the port, and pressed on to clear the harbour and two flanking features. Two German Flak ships interfered with clearing the harbour, and a German counter-attack from the western feature had to be beaten off, but Port-en Bessin was secured as darkness fell, at around 22:00.[14]

As on D-Day, the heaviest fighting on 7 June took place on the approaches to Caen. Brigadier D.G. Cunningham's 9th Canadian Infantry Brigade, supported by the 7th Canadian Reconnaissance Regiment and 27th Canadian Armoured Regiment (The Sherbrooke Fusiliers), had pushed south from Villons-les-Buissons toward Carpiquet airfield, 4 miles west of Caen, at 07:45. The advance was led by Stuart reconnaissance tanks and C Company, The North Nova Scotia Highlanders, followed by the remainder of the North Nova Scotia Highlanders riding on the Sherbrooke's Shermans. At 11:50 the advance guard entered Buron, 3 miles from the start point. By 13:00 the main body of the North Nova Scotia Highlanders was deploying to advance on foot to Authie, while the reconnaissance elements pushed toward Franqueville, just short of the Bayeux-Caen road. By this point the Canadian force was fully extended without a covering foot on the ground, and had moved beyond the range of its supporting artillery. While this was going on, the British 9th Infantry Brigade, supported by the 27th Armoured Brigade were preparing to renew the advance on Caen. The attack was spearheaded by the 2nd Royal Ulster Rifles and 1st East Riding Yeomanry, which moved off toward Cambes at around 14:00.

Following the midnight conference at *716 Infanterie Division* HQ, *12 SS Panzer Division* had been ordered to attack with *21 Panzer Division* at 12:00 on 7 June. The objective was the coast near Langrune-sur-Mer, along the axis formed by the Caen-Luc-sur-Mer railway. *21 Panzer Division* contributed three companies from *Panzer*

Regiment 22 and two battalions from *Panzergrenadier Regiment 192*, which were to renew the attack toward Blainville and Biéville, just west of the Orne Canal. The commander of *SS Panzergrenadier Regiment 25*, *Standartenführer* Kurt Meyer, had ordered a reconnaissance north-west of Carpiquet at 01:00, which reported no enemy presence closer than Villons-les-Buissons. Meyer therefore set up his HQ in the grounds of the ruined Ardenne Abbey 2 miles north-west of Caen, with the commanders of the *SS Panzer Regiment 12* and *III Bataillon, SS Panzer Artillerie Regiment 12*. The Abbey's twin towers, which gave a panoramic view of the ground to the north-west, were quickly colonised by artillery observation teams.

Meyer deployed his units along a line running from Franqueville in the south to St Contest. At the northern end of the line, the 1st Battalion, *SS Panzergrenadier Regiment 25* and *SS Panzer Pionier Kompanie 16* were deployed around Epron and la Folie. *II Bataillon, SS Panzergrenadier Regiment 25* was deployed across the front of the Ardenne Abbey. *III Bataillon* was still en route from Lisieux, and was scheduled to reach the start line sometime in the mid afternoon.[15] Partly because of this the attack start time was put back from midday to 16:00; *III Bataillon* was to join the left flank of the attack, straddling the Caen-Bayeux road. At 10:00 the *Panzer IVs* from *II Bataillon, SS Panzer Regiment 12* arrived to take its place on the start line; *I Bataillon's* Panthers were still immobilised by lack of fuel east of Caen. Meyer distributed the tank companies among his *SS Panzergrenadier* battalions.

The Canadian advance came under observation from the *12 SS* from midday, when their lead elements moved from Buron toward Authie; Meyer watched personally from one of the Ardenne Abbey's towers. As they pushed south the Canadians thus unknowingly exposed the whole of their left flank to *II Bataillon, SS Panzergrenadier Regiment 25*, and cadre from *1 SS Panzer Division* had taught their young charges well. Their camouflage and fire discipline was superb and the *SS Panzergrenadiers* and *Panzer* crewmen sat immobile as a succession of tempting targets moved oblivious across their front for around two hours. Meyer waited until the Canadian reconnaissance elements moved south from Franqueville and then ordered the attack.

The spearhead company of the North Nova Scotia Highlanders was quickly overrun by *SS Panzer Kompanie 6* and elements of the newly arrived *III Bataillon, SS Panzergrenadier Regiment 25*, and another Canadian company was overcome as it attempted to withdraw onto high ground north of Authie. The SS then pressed into Buron, which was cleared by late afternoon. *II Bataillon, SS Panzergrenadier Regiment 25* joined the assault at 15:00, attacking flanking elements of the Sherbrooke Fusiliers near St Contest. Several *Panzer IV*s were lost and the unit's commander was decapitated by a Canadian shell. The Canadian survivors withdrew to Villons-les-Buissons, held by the 9th Canadian Brigade's other two infantry battalions. While this fight was going on, the right wing of *12 SS Panzer Division's* attack jumped off at 16:15, heading for Anguerny, 6 miles to the north. The SS made just under half this distance before running into the 2nd Royal Ulster Rifles and East Riding Yeomanry near Cambes. The first five *Panzer IVs* were knocked out, along with three Shermans, allegedly at close range with *Panzerfausts*.[16] The resulting fight cost the Rifles over thirty casualties and they were obliged to withdraw to their start point at le Mesnil under cover of naval gunfire.

All this gave the SS pause, although Meyer blamed the check on *21 Panzer Division*, which he claimed had left *12 SS Panzer's* right flank vulnerable by not joining the attack as arranged. Feuchtinger, on the other hand, claimed that Meyer's men did not reach the agreed start line because of Allied naval gunfire. The truth probably lay somewhere in the middle. Meyer had a well-founded reputation for impetuosity, and Feuchtinger can perhaps be forgiven for being somewhat more circumspect after the rough handling his formation had suffered the previous day. Whichever, 7 June had been a costly day for both sides, measured in both casualties and frustrated objectives. *12 SS Panzer Division's* six-hour baptism of fire cost the North Nova Scotia Highlanders eighty-four dead and 158 wounded. The Sherbrooke Fusiliers lost twenty-eight Sherman tanks knocked out and a further eight damaged, along with twenty-six dead and thirty-four wounded. The fighting cost *12 SS Panzer* approximately seventy-three dead and

227 wounded. Nine *Panzer IVs* were destroyed and a number of others damaged, although the Canadians claimed thirty-one *Panzers* including eleven Tigers, another early example of Allied Tigerphobia. In fact the nearest Tiger unit, *schwere SS Panzer Abteilung 101* did not begin to move from Beauvais until 7 June, and were still 180 miles from the front on the evening of 8 June.[17]

By midnight on 7 June, *12 SS Panzer* was holding a curving front stretching from Franqueville to Cambes, while *21 Panzer* held the sector between Cambes and the Orne. Meyer had not come close to sweeping the little fish into the sea, but there was still room for satisfaction. The *Hitlerjugend* had made a superlative combat debut, fighting the main Allied effort on D Plus One to a standstill and rebuffing the attackers to their start line, and this while the main body of the *Division* and *Panzer Lehr* were still closing up to the battlefield. From their perspective Meyer and his men were thus justified in viewing the little fish as having postponed rather than avoided their assigned fate.

D-DAY PLUS 2
H PLUS 42 HOURS TO
H PLUS 66 HOURS

(00:00 TO 23:59, THURSDAY 8 JUNE 1944)

The heaviest fighting on 8 June took place once again west and north-west of Caen. When *12 SS Panzer* and *Panzer Lehr Divisions* were released to *7 Armee* in the afternoon of 6 June, OKW decreed that they should be commanded by *I SS Panzer Korps* HQ, commanded by *Oberstgruppenführer* Sepp Dietrich. It was Dietrich who implemented the instructions from *7 Armee* for *21 Panzer*, *12 SS Panzer* and *Panzer Lehr Divisions* to launch a co-ordinated drive to the coast. In the early hours of 8 June Dietrich reiterated this course of action, timed to commence at 10:00, although he was aware that the main burden would fall on *12 SS Panzer Division*. *21 Panzer Division* was hamstrung by its commitment either side of the River Orne, and *Panzer Lehr* was still making its painful way to the battlefield from Le Mans; its lead elements only reached Tilly-sur-Seulles, 10 miles west of Caen after dark on 7 June. Dietrich therefore instructed *Panzer Lehr* to fall in on *12 SS Panzer's* left as and when its units reached the battle area.

Panzergrenadier Regiment 25 was willing and capable of resuming the attack, but the fighting on 7 June had left it spread along a curving frontage running from Franqueville, north of the Caen-Bayeux railway line, to *21 Panzer's* line near Cambes. *SS Panzer Aufklärungs Abteilung 12* screened the left flank, with patrols on high ground near Audrieu, 10 miles west of Caen, although it would be capable of doing little more than provide warning of enemy approach. Of particular concern was the area encompassing Norrey–en–Bessin, Putot–en–Bessin and Bretteville l'Orgueilleuse, 4 miles west of Caen. This straddled the Caen–Bayeux road and rail line, and was held by the 7th Canadian Infantry Brigade. Dietrich therefore ordered *Panzergrenadier Regiment 26*, commanded by *Standartenführer* Wilhelm Mohnke, to protect Meyer's left flank, although it was still closing up to the front; *I Bataillon, Panzergrenadier Regiment 26* was scheduled to arrive in the late afternoon of 7 June.

Mohnke decided to launch a night attack on the 7th Canadian Infantry Brigade from the south. *I Bataillon, SS Panzergrenadier Regiment 26* reached the jump off point near Cheux in the early hours of 8 June, and was directed to attack Norrey–en–Bessin, held as a forward outpost by D Company, The Regina Rifle Regiment. The rest of the Reginas were dug in at Bretteville l'Orgueilleuse, astride the Caen–Bayeux road, while the Royal Winnipeg Rifle Regiment held Putot–en–Bessin to the west. Brigadier Harry Foster established 7th Brigade HQ to the north with the 1st Canadian Scottish at Secqueville–en–Bessin. Mohnke's *II Bataillon*, which was still en route to the assembly area, was to attack Norrey–en–Bessin, and *Standartenführer* Erich Olboeter's *III Bataillon* was ordered to seize the village of Brouay, west of Putot from a separate assembly area near Cristot, 2 miles south of his objective.

Sturmbannführer Bernhard Krause's *I Bataillon* launched its attack against Norrey–en–Bessin at 03:00. The resultant battle went on for eight hours and ended in failure. The Regina Rifles put up fierce resistance, fighting from house to house, and their on–call artillery support proved the deciding factor, obliging Krause to break off the attack at 11:00 after losing five dead and twenty wounded. *II Bataillon*, commanded by *Sturmbannführer* Bernhard Siebken, arrived too late to co–ordinate its attack with *I Bataillon* and went straight into the attack from the line of march at 06:30. This involved crossing the Caen–Bayeux railway embankment and a wide stretch of open ground fronting Putot. The Royal Winnipeg Rifles had deployed three rifle companies to cover this approach, and *II Bataillon* came under fire as soon as it crested the embankment.

The resulting fight was brutal. The Winnipegs inflicted a number of casualties on the SS as they crossed the open ground, but the *panzergrenadiers* pushed into the village, sparking a bitter house-to-house fight. By 13:30 the surviving Canadians were encircled and had to break out, with the aid of an artillery smokescreen, to rejoin Battalion HQ and D Company to the east. In all, the fight cost the Winnipegs 105 dead and 151 wounded; a third of the battalion's total strength. In the late afternoon 7th Brigade organised a counter-attack using the 1st Canadian Scottish, supported by a squadron of tanks from the 6th Canadian Armoured Regiment. The attack went in at 20:30 under a barrage from two field artillery regiments. Within an hour Siebken's men had been driven out and were organising a defensive line along the railway they had crossed fifteen hours earlier. Retaking Putot cost the Canadians another forty-five dead and eighty wounded; *II Bataillon* lost nineteen dead and eighty-nine wounded or missing.[1]

III Bataillon, SS Panzergrenadier Regiment 26 left its armoured half-tracks at Fontenay-le-Pesnel in the early hours of 8 June and moved to Cristot on foot. The plan was to move two companies, supported by six fire-support half-tracks through Brouay. Allied shellfire got the advance off to an unpromising start by wounding both company commanders during *Sturmbannführer* Olboeter's orders group, but the attack force nonetheless moved off for Brouay at around 08:00. The lead *SS* company were surprised to find *I Panzergrenadier Bataillon* of the *Panzer Lehr Division's Infanterie Regiment 902* in the woods south-west of the village. The second *SS* company was even more surprised when they passed through the area at midday. In the interim, elements of the British 61st Reconnaissance Regiment had stumbled on the *Panzer Lehr* elements and called down naval gunfire support and field artillery. This all but destroyed the *Panzer Lehr* unit; an *SS* eyewitness reported a devastated landscape with corpses and parts thereof decorating the shattered trees, littered with smashed half-tracks and other equipment.[2] It was an early demonstration of Allied firepower, with which the Germans were to become intimately acquainted over the following weeks and months.

The Canadians had also intended to return to the offensive on 8 June. Following a Divisional conference at 11:00, the 7th Canadian Infantry Brigade was to hold in place, while Brigadier R.J. Cunningham's 9th Canadian Infantry Brigade, having recovered overnight from the bruising encounter with *SS Panzergrenadier Regiment 25* on 7 June, was ordered to retake Buron. By the time Keller issued his orders, however, 7th Brigade was already embroiled with Siebken's *II Bataillon* at Putot, and the Germans were shifting their focus. Rommel, having returned post-haste from Germany, made the rounds of his various subordinate HQs on the afternoon of 8 June, receiving the latest situation reports and issuing instructions. This was to be his last opportunity to exercise direct control over the *panzer* formations, for on 7 June von Runstedt had decided to centralise them under a branch of his own staff, *Panzergruppe West* commanded by General Leo Freiherr Geyr von Schweppenburg. Von Schweppenburg was delayed and did not take over until the night of 9–10 June.

Rommel cancelled *Panzer Lehr's* collaboration with *12 SS Panzer*, and Bayerlein was ordered to concentrate at Tilly-sur-Seulles for an attack up the Tilly-Bayeux road on the morning of 9 June, with the objective of retaking Bayeux. *12 SS Panzer Division* appears to have been ordered to continue to press north toward Langrune-sur-Mer, but the events of the day required some tidying up of the situation before a concerted Divisional attack could be made. The Caen-Bayeux railway line was chosen as the start line for the renewed effort, but this meant eradicating the Canadian foothold at Norrey-en-Bessin, and clearing the rest of the 7th Canadian Infantry Brigade from its positions on or overlooking the railway line around Bretteville l'Orgueilleuse. The Germans also thought, mistakenly, that the Canadians had occupied the nearby village of Rots.

In line with Rommel's intentions the commander of *12 SS Panzer*, *Brigadeführer* Fritz Witt, ordered Mohnke's *SS Panzergrenadier Regiment 26* take Norrey-en-Bessin. Meyer was ordered to seize Bretteville and Rots, for which he was given the Panther-equipped *I Bataillon, SS Panzer Regiment 12*, which had finally secured sufficient fuel to reach the battle area, and a battery of 105mm self propelled guns.

Meyer married the Panthers up with *SS Aufklärungs Kompanie 15*, which were to accompany the Panthers as infantry. The attack was scheduled for 22:00, partly to avoid unwelcome attention from Allied fighter-bombers, and partly because it was thought a dusk attack would catch the Canadians by surprise. In the event, the Regina Rifles repulsed *SS Panzergrenadier Regiment 26* once again. Why the attack failed is unclear, for at least one Panther penetrated into Norrey from the north looking for Mohnke's men, but was driven off. Presumably the failure was due to poor co-operation that left the *panzergrenadiers* lacking the firepower to suppress the Canadian defenders.

Meyer's attack did not go as planned. *SS Panzer Regiment 12's* Panthers spearheaded the assault, carrying the recce troops on their decks. Finding Rots empty of Canadians the Panthers, carrying the recce troops on their decks, pressed swiftly on into Bretteville using the shock tactics that had worked well in Russia. Unfortunately, they were less effective against the Regina Rifles. Without sufficient infantry to neutralise the anti-tank guns and deal with the Canadian infantry, the Panthers could do little more than circle the Regina's positions, for venturing alone into the narrow village streets could be lethally hazardous. According to Canadian reports five Panthers were knocked out in the vicinity of the Regina's HQ, and one PIAT gunner scored what may be the sole recorded example of sniping with that weapon, scoring a direct hit on an *SS* officer dismounting from his *Kubelwagen*. Recognising the impossibility of securing Bretteville with the forces to hand, Meyer ordered a withdrawal to Rots. The ferocity of the fight is again clear from the casualty roll. *SS Panzergrenadier Regiment 26* lost twelve dead and forty-nine wounded, while Meyer's *ad hoc* force suffered thirty-one killed and sixty other casualties and lost six Panthers. In all, since being committed to battle in the afternoon of 6 June, *12 SS Panzer Division* had suffered 186 killed and over 500 wounded, injured and missing.[3]

To the east of the River Orne, *Kampfgruppe* von Luck made another attack on the 13th Parachute Battalion on the morning of 8 June. This was once again rebuffed with the loss of six armoured vehicles; according to one source this prompted an armoured follow-up force to abandon the attack.[4] On the paratroopers' right, the 12th Devons were spared a direct attack but in the late morning came under a sustained mortar barrage that went on for most of the day. This may have been intended to prevent them interfering with the attack on the 13th Battalion. It is unclear whether the Germans also mortared the 1st Royal Ulster Rifles, ensconced in Longueval to the Devon's front, but they did receive the unwanted attentions of 'friendly' field artillery. When radio appeals failed Captain Robin Rigby swam the Orne River and Canal, got the commander of a British infantry battalion on the west bank to call off the guns and then repeated the double swim back to his platoon.[5]

In the afternoon a German patrol managed to infiltrate the Ulster Rifles' positions, but was spotted as it prepared to attack Battalion HQ. The Battalion Defence and Intelligence Section, assisted by clerks and the unit Adjutant and RSM, brought the would-be attackers under fire, and B Company shot them up as they retreated. This was followed by a lone tank, reportedly a *Panzer IV*, shelling Battalion HQ from the high ground to the north-east of Longueval. An appeal to 6th Airlanding Brigade HQ prompted a foray by two borrowed M10 Wolverine tank destroyers accompanied by two Jeeps carrying Bren teams, led by Brigadier Kindersley in person. Two German tanks were spotted and withdrew with no noticeable damage after being engaged by the M10s; whether this was due to Brigadier Kindersley, who was keen to try his hand at gunlaying, is unclear.[6]

Thus far, German activity had been directed against the southern portion of the 6th Airborne Division's perimeter, but the focus began to shift to the northern sector on 8 June. The 8th Parachute Battalion was acting in a virtually independent capacity at the southern end of the Bois de Bavent ridge, and the reinforcing Commandos were acting in a similar capacity to the north-west. This left the 3rd Parachute Brigade with two understrength battalions to hold a frontage of over 3 miles, most of which was broken and wooded country. Brigadier Hill could therefore do little more than set up isolated outposts at key points to act as a tripwire to warn of enemy approach, and hope that a combination of aggressive patrolling and the destruction of the Dives bridges would keep the Germans at bay.

It was this policy that brought the 9th Parachute Battalion to the Château St Côme, a mile north of le Mesnil, in the early hours of 8 June. The paratroopers dug in around a house set in the Bois du Mont, 250 yards west of the Château. As became apparent once it grew light, the position provided an unbroken view over the 6th Airborne Division's perimeter, and was a perfect launch point for an attack against the Orne bridges and beyond into the flank of the SWORD lodgement. It also went at least some way to closing the mile-wide gap between the 3rd Parachute Brigade and No. 6 Commando in Amfreville. This was especially important, as the Germans had occupied Bréville, in the low ground between the northern end of the Bois de Bavent ridge and the Amfreville plateau.

A patrol under Lieutenant Dennis Slade checked the Château, which contained a hastily vacated German HQ that had already been looted of rations and a motorcycle combination by B Company's CSM. Otway did not occupy it because his existing position in the woods was superior and he lacked the men to occupy both, and because it was a good target for German artillery. Even then, the 9th Battalion's depleted state precluded a formal defence, so standing patrols were established with orders to remain hidden and to fire only if the enemy came within 20 yards of their location; Bren gunners were to restrict their fire to single shots to conceal their presence. Small patrols were also run in the immediate vicinity of the Battalion perimeter, and in the late morning one of these clashed with a platoon of Germans near the Château.[7]

The 3rd Parachute Brigade HQ and 1st Canadian Parachute Battalion at the le Mesnil crossroads had a more eventful morning. A *Nebelwerfer* barrage began at 05:30, followed by an infantry attack from elements of *346 Infanterie Division*, supported by self-propelled guns and at least one *Panzer IV*. This was a mobile formation belonging to *15 Armee*, quartered near Le Havre; the attacking elements had presumably crossed the Dives via Cabourg before closing unseen on the British airborne perimeter. Their arrival showed that the destruction of the Dives bridges had become a complication rather than a complete block to German movement into the area between the Orne and Dives north of Ranville.

One German thrust penetrated into the Brigade HQ area and came close to the crossroads before being repulsed.[8] Another group assembled in column on the road leading into le Mesnil from Varaville was caught by the Canadian paratrooper's mortars. A *Panzer IV* supported by a number of infantry penetrated between B and C Companies, inflicting numerous casualties until the tank was driven off by PIAT fire; B Company then launched a bayonet charge that drove the Germans out of the perimeter. At one point the situation grew so critical that Brigadier Hill requested assistance from the 9th Battalion. Otway personally led a party from his HQ and C Companies accompanied by a fire group carrying two MG 42s. They arrived as the Germans were being pushed out of the Brigade perimeter, and all but wiped out a ten-strong German machine gun group before becoming side tracked into the adjacent woods.[9] By 09:00 the perimeter cleared of intruders and the 9th Battalion group returned to the Bois du Mont.

However, some Germans regrouped in a farmhouse only 200 yards from the crossroads, and the Canadians were ordered to eject them. An outlying German detachment was overrun, but the farm contained several armoured vehicles and more infantry than expected. The Germans then launched a counter-attack of their own that obliged the Canadians to carry out a fighting withdrawal. In the process they caught a number of the pursuing Germans in the open and inflicted at least fifty casualties. The action cost the 1st Canadian Parachute Battalion eight dead and thirteen wounded, but the Germans abandoned the farmhouse shortly thereafter.[10] The cost to the attackers was graphically noted by Airborne medics sent out from the Brigade Main Dressing Station to assist the German wounded. One field, probably where the retreating Canadians had turned the tables on their pursuers, was littered with dozens of German dead clearly caught by machine-gun fire. The medics were only able to find around a dozen wounded to assist across the whole brigade perimeter.[11]

German probing attacks against the 3rd Parachute Brigade's perimeter continued through the afternoon and night, and they also began to feel out the 9th Battalion's position in the Bois du Mont. At around midday a platoon-size unit approached the north-western sector of the 9th Battalion's perimeter. The paratroopers allowed them to get within 50 yards before opening fire; one sergeant noted they were so close he could see the dust puffing from the Germans' uniforms as they were hit. This was the first of several stealthy attempts to infiltrate into the paratroopers' positions through the woods. One group closed to within 6 feet or so of a B Company position before being spotted, and several were captured after being hit by a well-placed hand grenade.

The probing ceased in the early afternoon as the Germans prepared their attack. This came in at 16:30, against the driveway leading up to the Château St Côme. It was driven off with the assistance of a Vickers medium machine-gun team commanded by Sergeant Sammy McGeever, which ran forward from the Château and set up their gun in the open for a clear shot at the attackers. One man held the rear leg of the tripod steady and watched the belt feed while another climbed into a nearby tree to direct fire. The attack was repulsed, and the Germans fell back on nuisance tactics, firing randomly into the British perimeter, calling out in English and occasionally closing to throw grenades. The idea appeared to be to keep the tired paratroopers on edge and provoke them into firing and exposing their location; one German wag took to shouting 'Stand Down!' in response to the paratroopers' 'Stand To' alert calls. There were no more attacks, however, and the 9th Battalion passed a relatively peaceful, if less than quiet, night in the Bois du Mont.[12]

While the British and Canadian paratroopers were fighting their defensive battle at le Mesnil, their American counterparts from the 1st and 2nd Battalions, 506th Parachute Infantry Regiment were renewing their attack on St Côme-du-Mont at the base of the Cotentin Peninsula. During the night the 506th Regiment's axis of attack was reinforced with the 3rd Battalion, 501st Parachute Infantry, the 1st Battalion, 401st Glider Infantry Regiment,[13] and the detachment from the 746th Tank Battalion was reinforced with eight light tanks. The Germans also did some reinforcing, moving two companies from *III Bataillon, Fallschirmjäger Regiment 6* to stiffen the battalion from *Infanterie Regiment 1058* facing the Americans south-east of St Côme-du-Mont. The American attack began at 05:00 with a heavy artillery barrage on the town. The 3rd battalion, 501st Parachute Infantry hooked south and west to cut the road to Carentan, while the battalion from the 401st Glider Infantry moved south to secure and destroy the bridge carrying it over the River Douve.

The Americans made extensive use of their supporting artillery, although this could be a mixed blessing in the vision-restricting *bocage*. A salvo of eight-inch shells from the USS Quincy comprehensively demolished a farmhouse assigned to one of the 501st Parachute Infantry's units, to the unanimous approval of the paratroopers; their opinion changed somewhat when the next salvo landed among them, killing five and wounding another eight. Nonetheless, within a couple of hours a combination of artillery and close-quarter fighting among the dense hedgerows began to tell, and *Regiment 1058* began to melt away. When the Americans began to overrun positions held by the reinforcements from *Fallschirmjäger Regiment 6*, Major von der Heydte cut his losses and pulled them and the survivors of *Regiment 1058* back to St Côme-du-Mont.

By 08:00 the 3rd Battalion 501st Parachute Infantry had cut the Carentan-St Mère Église road, isolating the elements of *Fallschirmjäger Regiment 6* holding out in St Côme-du-Mont. The Americans then had to hold against a series of counter-attacks from *III Bataillon, Fallschirmjäger Regiment 6* in Carentan trying to re-open the escape route for their comrades in St Côme. Learning from their experience the previous day, the two battalions from the 506th Regiment had attacked St Côme-du-Mont behind a heavy rolling barrage from naval and field guns thickened with smoke. The field artillery battalion supporting the attack fired 2,500 rounds of 105mm ammunition in the first hour and a half of the attack. This got the 506th Infantry into the approaches to the town but the *fallschirmjäger* put up stubborn resistance that obliged the Americans to dig them out hedge by hedge and house by house.[14]

By the afternoon, fatigue was becoming a serious drag on the combat effectiveness of the American paratroopers. One officer noted that his ability to talk coherently had virtually disappeared, and that his men were equally incapable of absorbing his orders.[15] This probably explains why the elements of *Fallschirmjäger Regiment 6* north of the River Douve were able to escape. The two companies that withdrew into St Côme when the *Regiment 1058* battalion collapsed retired into the inundated area to the west and swam the Douve to safety. *II Bataillon, Fallschirmjäger Regiment 6*, which had been holding back the US airborne advance north-east of St Côme-du-Mont, broke contact, crossed the swamp to the Carentan-Cherbourg railway line and also crossed the Douve, reaching Carentan virtually intact. Major von der Heydte was thus able to deploy the unit as a complete entity east of Carentan on the night of 8 June when he heard that American troops from the OMAHA beaches had seized Isigny.

With German opposition banished from St Côme-du-Mont, the 101st Airborne moved up to the Douve and relieved the elements of the 501st and 506th Parachute Infantry holding the crossings at la Barquette and le Port. Attention then turned to the seizure of Carentan, and the Division deployed along the Douve in accordance with a pre-arranged scheme. The 502nd Regiment covered the right flank, south-west of Côme-du-Mont and blocking the gap in the marshes created by the railway line from Carentan. The 506th Regiment was deployed astride the Carentan-St Mère Église road, the 327th Glider Infantry on the left along the Douve to le Port, and the 501st Regiment was placed in reserve. The scheme envisaged an attack over the Douve at la Barquette and le Port toward Brevands on the high ground 3 miles north-east of Carentan. This would place the Americans in place to attack Carentan from the flank, and to link up with US forces from the OMAHA beaches. In the event a patrol by the 2nd Battalion, 506th Parachute Infantry on 9 June discovered that the causeway on the main Carentan-St Mère Église road was passable. The 502nd Regiment was detailed to cross and establish a blocking position south-west of Carentan, while the rest of the plan remained essentially unchanged. The attack was scheduled for the night of 9-10 June.

The advance north of St Mère Église was renewed at 08:00. The 505th Parachute Infantry, reinforced by the 2nd Battalion, 325th Glider Infantry Regiment and the 8th Infantry were on the left of the St Mère Église to Montebourg road, and the 12th and 22nd Infantry Regiments were on the right. The objective was to occupy a ridge of high ground running east from Montebourg to Quinéville, but in the evening reconnaissance patrols 'revealed what seemed to be a prepared defence',[16] with machine gun positions dug into the tributary banks and artillery pre-registered on lines of approach. With the onset of darkness the American units stopped and dug in for the night. In doing so, they handed the Germans a breathing space and helped prepare a rod for their own back, for on the evening of 8 June the German defence line was a far from solid barrier. The outpost line that stopped the American advance consisted of hurriedly constructed positions manned largely by the remains of *Infanterie Regiment 1058* and garrison units drawn from the abandoned coastal defences commanded by *Oberst* Helmuth Rohrbach. Rohrbach made good use of his unexpected time bonus; it took the US 8th Infantry Regiment two days to eliminate the outpost line and close up to the main German position.

By then it had become a properly-constructed defence line occupied by *7 Armee Sturm Abteilung* and units drawn from *91 Luftlande Division* and *243* and *709 Infanterie Divisions*, organised into three autonomous *Kampfgruppen*. These were supported by a strong concentration of artillery made up from four artillery battalions, ex-Soviet and French medium field pieces from positions covering the eastern beaches, and larger guns removed from coastal batteries near Quinéville. Given that they had been in almost continuous combat for around seventy-two hours, the 505th Parachute Infantry can perhaps be forgiven its reluctance to press forward on the night of 8-9 June. The line infantry units had less excuse. Had they pressed forward they would certainly have unhinged the still forming German defence and probably avoided the subsequent costly fighting to clear the Cotentin Peninsula, which went on for another two weeks, followed by another week to reduce and secure Cherbourg.[17]

The situation to the west of St Mère Église remained uncertain. Company A, 1st Battalion, 505th Parachute Infantry was still holding precariously at la Fière, while the Chef-du-Pont bridge was held by the 508th Parachute Infantry, which had relieved Captain Creek's little band with their heaven-sent 57mm anti-tank gun during the night of 7-8 June. To the west of the Merderet, the 2nd Battalion, 507th Parachute Infantry and an assortment of misdropped paratroopers were pinned against the marshland bordering the river just north of the la Fière crossing. To their south, elements of Lieutenant-Colonel John B. Shanley's 3rd Battalion, 508th Parachute Infantry Regiment were holding a piece of high ground dubbed Hill 30. This had been the 508th Regiment's rally point for the D-Day drop, and was located roughly midway between the two crossings but separated from them by the marshes. Securing the Merderet crossings had been one of the 82nd Airborne's D-Day tasks and Ridgeway was reluctant to leave the job unfinished. He and Gavin therefore came up with a two-part plan to complete the mission before the Division was relieved by seaborne reinforcements.

Colonel Roy Lindquist's 508th Parachute Infantry was ordered to advance over the Chef-du-Pont bridge and link up with Shanley's force on Hill 30. As Creek's party had only cleared the eastern causeway and the bridge, Lindquist ordered Shanley to clear the three-mile road linking the causeway to Pont l'Abbé. Shanley in turn despatched a twenty-three-strong patrol commanded by Lieutenants Lloyd L. Pollette and Woodrow W. Millsap, who not only cleared the road but fought their way up the causeway and over the Chef-du-Pont bridge to report their progress to Lindquist in person. However, the Germans responded by bringing down heavy artillery fire on the western causeway, and Lindquist cancelled the advance west as a result. What Millsap, Pollette and their surviving men made of this can be well imagined, but the result was to leave Shanley's battalion isolated and in line to receive any German retribution.[18]

The second part of the plan was aimed at the la Fière crossing. A submerged ford over the Merderet north of the la Fière crossing had been pointed out to the Americans by French civilians, and Major

Edward Sanford's 1st Battalion, 325th Glider Infantry Regiment crossed to the west bank at 23:00 on 8 June. Sanford linked up with the group accreted around the 2nd Battalion, 507th Parachute Infantry backed up against the marshes in an area dubbed 'Timmes' Orchard'. The combined force then marched south to attack Cauquigny, which controlled the exit from la Fière causeway. They were accompanied by Lieutenant Louis Levy, whose valiant little band had been overrun in the village by German tanks on the afternoon of D-Day.

One company was left as a blocking force to prevent German rein-forcements from Amfreville interfering, one moved against the nearby village of le Motey, and the third moved against Cauquigny. At around 03:30 on the morning of 9 June the latter ran into a German artillery position on the outskirts of the village. A two-hour firefight ensued, but the paratroopers were unable to break through the hurriedly roused gunners. The 325th Regiment then withdrew to Timmes' Orchard, arriving after daylight. Thus the 82nd Airborne's second attempt to secure the Merderet crossings failed, and *Infanterie Regiment 1057* remained in control on the west bank of the river.[19]

At the OMAHA landing area, 8 June marked the point where the 29th Division finally started to make progress on the western end of the lodgement. The 115th Infantry Regiment spent the night of 7-8 June near St Laurent-sur-Mer, after clearing the village and its environs. In the morning Major-General Gerhardt ordered Colonel Eugene Slappey to advance south and cross the River Aure valley, which ran parallel with, and 5 miles behind, the western half of the OMAHA landing area. As the valley was inundated it was unclear if this was feasible, but as Gerhardt pointed out to his staff, it was the 115th Infantry's job to find out. The Regiment duly moved off toward Longueville, 4.5 miles inland on the Bayeux-Isigny road.

This carried it into the *bocage*, with all the navigation and commu-nication problems that entailed. At one point during the morning Brigadier-General Cota, leading from the front as usual, went forward by Jeep to the 115th Regiment's reported position to see the situation for himself. On arrival at the designated spot, they were nowhere to be seen, but a timely outbreak of small-arms fire guided him to the Regiment's 2nd Battalion; all 800 men had been sitting unseen within 200 yards. German resistance was sporadic, and the 2nd Battalion and Regimental HQ arrived in Longueville at around noon. There was no resistance, but the amount of abandoned German kit and weaponry indicated a recent and hasty withdrawal.

This was indeed the case. As we have seen, the *352 Infanterie Division* had received its final reinforcement from *84 Korps* on 7 June, in the shape of a bicycle battalion from *Schnelle Brigade 30*. On 8 June *Generalleutnant* Kraiss was informed that no reinforcements would be forthcoming for at least two days. Acting on his own initiative, Kraiss then ordered the surviving elements of his Division to hold their positions until nightfall and then retire under cover of darkness; the garrison of Longueval appears to have jumped the gun. As the Aure valley was considered impassable, the withdrawal would effectively split Kraiss' formation in two. Thus the remains of *Schnelle Brigade 30*, *Infanterie Regiment 916* and *Infanterie Regiment 726* were to pull back to a line running south-east from the head of the Aure valley. *Infanterie Regiment 914*, *Ost Bataillon 439* and elements of *Artillerie Regiment 352* were to withdraw west through Isigny, in the narrow gap between the end of the Aure valley and the River Vire, blowing the Aure bridge after crossing. The sole exception to the withdrawal order was the garrison of Grandcamp-les-Bains, 2.5 miles west of the Pointe du Hoc. The port was to be held at all costs.[20]

In line with Gerhardt's orders, Slappey despatched a platoon from the 2nd Battalion's Company E, led by Lieutenant Kermit Miller to ascertain if the Aure Valley was traversable. Miller's little band set out at 17:30, and emerged on the south side of the swamp shortly before midnight near the village of Colombières. Three less than alert German sentries were captured on the outskirts of the village, but the rest of the garrison were made of sterner stuff and the American's had to storm the house they occupied, killing several and taking a number of prisoners at a cost of three wounded. The patrol set off back across the swamp after first light and after a journey complicated by carrying their wounded and prisoners reported that the Aure valley was indeed traversable. Lieutenant

Miller was awarded the Distinguished Service Cross for his efforts.[21]

The 2nd and 3rd Battalions, 116th Infantry Regiment spent the night of 7–8 June near the hamlet of Louvières, a mile or so inland from Vierville-sur-Mer. In the morning both units moved west to link up with the 1st Battalion, which was stalled at St Pierre-du-Mont. The 1st of the 116th had spent 7 June in company with the 5th Ranger Battalion trying to reach the embattled remnants of the 2nd Ranger Battalion holding out in the Pointe du Hoc battery. By 8 June Rudder's force had less than fifty effectives remaining, many of whom were wounded. In the event, the renewed advance did not elicit anything like the degree of resistance experienced hitherto; possibly the elements of *Infanterie Regiment 914* had also made an early start in complying with Kraiss' withdrawal order. Whether or not, the 1st Battalion, 116th Infantry and accompanying tanks pushed easily into the battery position, which had been turned into a moonscape of craters by preparatory bombing and the pre-landing bombardment. At the very last moment several of the besieged Rangers were killed by fire from the incoming American infantry and their accompanying Shermans. According to one source, the unfortunate Rangers were using German weapons, and the relief force fired on their distinctive sound. Whatever the reason, it was a sad note on which to conclude such an epic feat of arms. The battery position was cleared by midday, in the process of which a number of badly wounded Rangers were discovered. These unfortunates were gathered in and despatched to the 29th Division rear for treatment. The surviving Rangers and the rest of the relief force then reorganised and prepared to move on Grandcamp-les-Bains.

Grandcamp was occupied by *III Bataillon, Infanterie Regiment 914* and *Artillerie Regiment 1716*, and the approaches were restricted by marshes along the coast road and a bridge 600 yards east of the port. The Rangers leading the advance reached the bridge in the early afternoon, and called down naval gunfire when German fire prevented them from crossing. The 1st Battalion, 116th Infantry skirted south of the marshland and pushed west to outflank Grandcamp, while the 3rd Battalion and some of their supporting

Shermans rushed the bridge, losing one tank to a mine in the process. This brought the 2nd and 3rd Battalions up against prepared German positions linked together by trenches. In the fight that followed Sergeant Frank Peregory of the 3rd Battalion's Company K carried out a one-man attack into a German strongpoint that knocked out two machine-gun positions, killed several of the defenders and took several more prisoner. Peregory was awarded the Medal of Honour for this action, although he was killed six days later before learning of his award. Grandcamp was cleared by mid-afternoon, while the 1st Battalion followed the coast road toward Isigny, dealing with a number of German delaying positions in the process. With the area between Grandcamp and Isigny cleared, the 116th Infantry was officially designated the 29th Division reserve and allowed a well deserved rest in Grandcamp.[22]

The formation that did most to disrupt the German withdrawal to the west was the 175th Infantry Regiment, albeit in a somewhat halting manner. After a drawn-out landing in the afternoon of 7 June that involved hiking through the material and human detritus on Easy Green, Dog Red, Dog White and Dog Green beaches, the regiment reorganised near the village of Gruchy. At around 23:00 it moved off following a track running south-west, fighting a brief skirmish with a party of German troops in the darkness before halting at 01:00 in the morning of 8 June to allow the men to catch a little rest. The regiment roused itself at 04:00, two hours before first light, and resumed the move south-west with the 1st Battalion in the lead. At sometime after 06:00 the lead scouts came to the main Bayeux-Isigny road, turned west and ran into a German blocking force in a group of farm buildings outside the village of la Cambe. The German force knocked out the lead Sherman and inflicted a number of casualties before working the difficult trick of breaking contact after the Americans had begun to deploy, but before their attack was launched.

The 1st Battalion paused in la Cambe while the remainder of the Regiment closed up. At that point the Regimental column was strafed repeatedly by RAF Typhoons as it approached the village. Six Americans were killed and a further eighteen were wounded. The incident appears to have shaken the confidence of the 175th Regiment's commander, Colonel Paul Goode. Instead of pressing on to Isigny as instructed, Goode decided to hold until his artillery unit caught up, and set up his Regimental HQ in the village just after 09:00. A sweep of the area around the village netted a number of prisoners, which were handed over to the HQ for interrogation. A number were Mongolian ex-Soviet POWS from *Ost Bataillon 439*, whose appearance aroused considerable surprise among their captors and may have given rise to the enduring legend of Imperial Japanese Army troops being captured in Normandy.[23]

In mid afternoon Major-General Gerhardt paid a flying visit to Goode's HQ and reiterated his instruction. Unconvinced that Goode was going to comply with sufficient despatch, Gerhardt sent the indomitable Brigadier-Cota to 'light a fire' under Goode. Cota worked out a plan with Goode that involved the 175th Regiment's 3rd Battalion and supporting tanks from the 747th Tank Battalion leading the renewed advance down the main Bayeux-Isigny road. When Gerhardt returned to la Cambe at 19:00, however, the 175th was still immobile. In a terse, largely one-way conversation that lasted only a few minutes, Goode's excuses were brushed aside and he was left in absolutely no doubt he was to move on Isigny immediately. Even then, the advance did not begin until shortly before dark, although this proved fortuitous. The Germans had set up another delaying position with an anti-gun a mile up the road at Arthenay, but darkness permitted the Americans to knock out the gun before it could do any damage, and the supporting German infantry pulled when tracer rounds set the buildings they were occupying ablaze. As the advance resumed, most of the 2nd Battalion struck off to deal with a German radar station near Cardonville, just north of the Bayeux-Isigny road.

By midnight the rest of the 175th were within 2 miles of Isigny where one of the lead Shermans lost a track, allegedly to a mine. This brought the advance to a halt in sight of their objective, which was burning after an Allied bombing raid. They were still there when Gerhardt arrived sometime after 01:00 on the morning of 9 June. The

29th Division's commander was as forthright as before and, brushing aside Goode's protests that the road ahead was mined, ordered him to '[get] those damn tanks going and follow them into Isigny'. Gerhardt's boldness paid off, for there were no mines, no German defence in Isigny and the bridge over the River Aure was intact. Predictably, Cota was one of the first Americans over the bridge, accompanied by the commander of the 3rd Battalion and men from Company K. By daylight a few German stragglers in the town had been driven off, Isigny was in American hands and those elements of *Infanterie Regiment 914, Ost Bataillon 439* and *Artillerie Regiment 352* that had not already withdrawn through the town were cut off.[24]

At the other end of the OMAHA lodgement the US 1st Division was pushing south and east to link up with the GOLD landing area. The 16th Infantry Regiment remained in place at Hupain, just west of Port-en-Bessin on the boundary line between the OMAHA and GOLD landing areas. To the south the 1st Battalion, 18th Infantry rectified the failure of the 26th Infantry's 3rd Battalion by clearing Formigny. This pinched out a possible salient and brought the right flank of the 18th Infantry more in line with the 115th Infantry on the north edge of the Aure valley. The 3rd Battalion, 18th Infantry remained ensconced in the centre of the Regimental frontage at Mandeville, which unbeknown to the Americans brought them up against the *352 Division's* new line of resistance. A probe by the 18th Regiment's 2nd Battalion south from Mosles also ran into the new German line.

The 26th Infantry Regiment had been tasked to effect the link up with the British 50th Infantry Division. The 1st Battalion had moved up to Huppain toward the end of 7 June, but ran into obstinate resistance in Etreham, where elements of *Infanterie Regiment 726* refused to relinquish a bridge over the River Aure. The 2nd Battalion bypassed the fight in Etreham, moved south-east and occupied a crossroads on the Bayeux-Isigny road, midway between Mosles and Tour-en-Bessin. To the east, the British 56th Infantry Brigade had seized the village of Sully on the high ground overlooking the road and the River Drôme, a north-flowing tributary of the Aure. A British attempt to seize a nearby bridge over the Drôme was less successful, however, and determined German counter-attacks obliged the British to withdraw back across the river. There was a good reason for German sensitivity. It will be recalled that *Generalleutnant* Kraiss had ordered his *352 Infanterie Division* to withdraw after dark on 8 June to a line running south-east from the head of the Aure valley. Counter-attacks against the GOLD landing area on 6 and 7 June had left all or part of a number of units in what the Americans referred to as the Drôme Corridor, squeezed between the American and British forces. These included *II Bataillon, Infanterie Regiment 915, Fuesilier Regiment 352, Schnelle Brigade 30, II Bataillon, Infanterie Regiment 916, Infanterie Regiment 726* and *III Bataillon, Artillerie Regiment 1352*; the latter unit had destroyed its guns and was fighting as infantry. Should the American and British forces effect a link up along the Bayeux-Isigny road, these units would be cut off.

This explains why the Germans reacted so sharply in Etreham and Sully, and the ferocity of the resistance encountered by the 3rd Battalion, 26th Infantry Regiment. This unit had been held near Formigny until the afternoon of 8 June, after which it moved straight down the Bayeux-Isigny road to the crossroad position held by the 2nd Battalion. After regrouping, the newcomers attacked through the 2nd Battalion's positions toward Tour-en-Bessin at 18:00. The attack penetrated through Tour-en-Bessin, but ran into extremely stiff German resistance when it reached the hamlet of St Anne at around midnight. The reason for the resistance was simple. The American arrival at St Anne narrowed the exit from the Drôme Corridor to less than a mile, and the withdrawal ordered by Kraiss was in full swing. Confused fighting went on in and around St Anne through the night, but by daylight on 9 June the bulk of the German force had succeeded in extricating itself from the Allied trap.

This was a noteworthy achievement, and not merely because it rescued a good number of German troops to fight another day. It was also the first retirement from the coastal defences to be sanctioned by both division and corps level HQs. Kraiss had ordered his division to withdraw on his own authority, in direct contravention of his orders from *84 Korps* in the early hours of 7 June. On that occasion General Marcks had informed Kraiss that he was to hold to the last man and the last bullet. By 8 June, however, Marcks had either changed his view or was less sanguine about ordering men to fight to the death in person. At around 15:00 Kraiss had made radio contact with the isolated commander of *Infanterie Regiment 726*, and passed on his order to put up resistance until dark and then withdraw south to the new defence line. Shortly afterwards Marcks arrived at Kraiss' HQ, and the latter asked him to approve the withdrawal order. Marcks reportedly paused for a long time before finally giving his assent. It was the first retirement to be authorised by a German corps level command or above in the Normandy campaign. It was not to be the last.

13

D-DAY PLUS 3
H PLUS 72 HOURS

(06:00, FRIDAY 9 JUNE 1944) SITUATION REPORT

By dawn on 9 June, the Allies had established a pretty secure lodgement on the Normandy coast. On the Cotentin Peninsula the US 4th Infantry Division had extended the Allied perimeter 5 miles north of St Mère Église, which itself lay 5 miles inland from the UTAH beaches. They were up against a hastily drawn and thinly spread defensive line defended by elements from three German divisions (*91 Luftlande*, *243* and *709 Infanterie*), reinforced by artillery units drawn from abandoned seafront defences. To the south, the 101st Airborne Division had cleared the area between St Mère Église and the River Douve, and was preparing to cross the river to take Carentan and start the link up with the OMAHA landing force. Carentan was held by what remained of *Fallschirmjäger Regiment 6*, which was at that time holding the ring south of the Cotentin alone. Concerns over additional Allied landings in Brittany delayed the despatch of *77 Infanterie* and *17 SS Panzergrenadier Division* to assist, and the latter did not arrive until after the 101st Airborne secured Carentan on 12 June.[1] The 82nd Airborne were still holding, albeit somewhat tenuously, the crossings over the River Merderet at la Fière and Chef-du-Pont west of St Mère Église, and maintaining two pockets on the west bank of the Merderet against solid resistance from *Infanterie Regiment 1057* and *Panzer Ersatz Bataillon 100*.

To the east, the US 29th Infantry Division had relieved the 2nd Rangers at the Pointe du Hoc and taken the fortified port of

Grandcamp-les-Bains. In addition, it had cleared the 5 miles between the right half of the OMAHA beaches and the inundated Aure Valley, penetrated across the latter and, more importantly, seized the town of Isigny blocking the narrow strip between the mouth of the valley and the River Vire. On the left, the US 1st Infantry had penetrated a similar distance inland and had closed up to *352 Infanterie Division's* hastily drawn up fall back line east of the head of the Aure Valley. Elements of the Division had also closed the gap with the British units from the adjoining GOLD landing area on the Bayeux-Isigny road, squeezing out a large German pocket trapped along the River Drôme in the process.

Behind the GOLD landing area, the British 50th Infantry Division had cleared the area up to the boundary with the US V Corps, occupied Bayeux and was probing south St Léger on the Caen-Bayeux road, toward Tilly-sur-Seulles and Brouay, 10 miles inland from the beaches. This was carrying them toward the still forming *Panzer Lehr Division*, which had been ordered by Rommel to attack independently toward Bayeux on the morning of 9 June. The 3rd Canadian Infantry Division had penetrated a similar distance to Putot-en-Bessin and Norrey-en-Bessin, south of the Caen-Bayeux railway line, and the British 3rd Infantry Division was facing elements of *21 Panzer* and *12 SS Panzer Divisions* a couple of miles north of Caen. To the east of the Orne the 6th Airborne Division was holding fast as planned, against the remainder of *21 Panzer Division* and elements of *346 Infanterie Division* from the north-east.

It should be noted that with the exception of the British 3rd Infantry Division which was supposed to have been in Caen, these Allied positions were virtually on the D-Day Objective Lines assigned to the various units. The British 3rd Infantry has been much castigated for its alleged failure, but the reality is that it was by no means alone. None of the D-Day assault formations achieved their D-Day objectives, and most took between forty-eight and seventy-two hours to do so. This suggests that any fault lay not with the men at the sharp end, but with the planners for setting D-Day objectives that were simply too ambitious. Although the American formations, and in particular the 4th Infantry Divisions did not move as swiftly as they could and should have in some instances, none of the assault formations appear to have been overly reluctant to close with the enemy. It is therefore difficult to see what other reason there can have been for failure across the board.

The planners also appear to have expected too much of the assault formations, and as a result neglected to push others forward fast enough to relieve them. The American parachute company commander cited above who was too weary to speak coherently was by no means alone by 8 June, and a definite slackening in the tempo of Allied activity can be detected in the push inland by D-Day Plus Two. Nonetheless, the assault divisions carried the burden virtually alone for the first seventy-two hours of the invasion, even though formations were available to relieve them. The US 90th Infantry Division, for example, began to come ashore at UTAH on 6 June, but was not ordered to the front until three days later.[2] The US 2nd Infantry Division began to come ashore at OMAHA in the evening of 7 June, but did not move up to the line in the US 1st Infantry sector until midday on 9 June.[3] The British 51st Highland Division came ashore at SWORD at the same time and while elements supported the 6th Airborne and 3rd Canadian Infantry Divisions, it was not deployed in its entirety until 10 June.[4] Similarly, the British 4th Armoured Brigade came ashore at the same place and over the same time period.[5] It is interesting to speculate on how events might have turned out had these and other formations been pushed forward in their entirety more rapidly, rather than after waiting in the wings for days. The presence of a fresh armoured formation to push through the British 3rd Infantry Division after *21 Panzer Division* on the night of 6–7 June might have reached Caen after all, and might have changed the whole course of the subsequent campaign.

Events in the first seventy-two hours of the invasion also set the pattern for virtually the next three months. In the wider sense, the attraction of the most powerful German units to the British end of the beachhead continued for the next three months. Rivers of ink have been spilt arguing whether this was a deliberate policy, as claimed by

Montgomery, or merely an excuse to cover failed breakout attempts like Operation EPSOM and GOODWOOD. The truth probably lies somewhere in the middle, but the point here is that the attraction was extremely fortuitous for the Americans, for the poor performance of the 4th Infantry Division was not an isolated tendency.

When the 82nd Airborne's attack over the Merderet failed on 9 June, the US 90th Infantry Division was pushed forward to relieve the exhausted paratroopers and lead the drive west to cut the Cotentin Peninsula. The formation, which Bradley later acknowledged as being one of the worst in the European Theatre of Operations, performed abysmally. VII Corps' commander Collins promptly relieved the division commander and those of the 90th Infantry's infantry regiments, and prevailed on Bradley to not only keep the 82nd Airborne in the line, but to spearhead the drive west. Ridgeway and Gavin concurred with the decision but probably for different reasons; Gavin was the consummate military professional, whereas Ridgeway was generally rather more concerned with the pursuit of greatness. Whichever, the feelings of their exhausted paratroopers, who had been going virtually non-stop for four days at this point, can be well imagined.[6] The salient point here is that the American performance for the first month in the Cotentin and southward was not especially impressive in the face of generally inferior German opposition. Up to at least the beginning of July there were seven panzer divisions facing the British and Canadians, as opposed to a single panzer and panzergrenadier division facing the Americans to the west. Had the Germans been able to re-deploy some or all of the formations near Caen, the story of the Normandy campaign might well have turned out very differently.

Be all that as it may, by the early morning of 9 June the initial assault on the Normandy beaches had come to a close, and the formations involved had done their job, if not as promptly as the OVERLORD planners had envisaged. It was now time for the follow-up formations to step forward and continue what they had begun.

MAPS

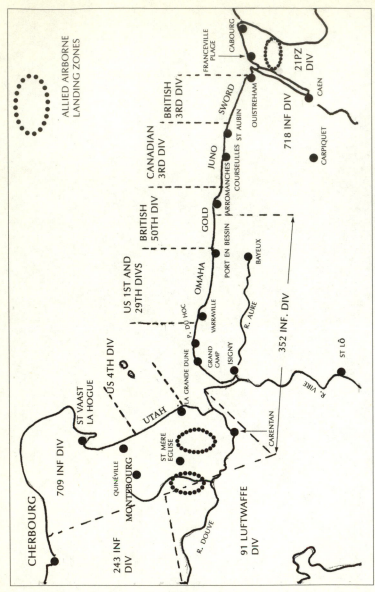

Normandy: the beaches and German dispositions.

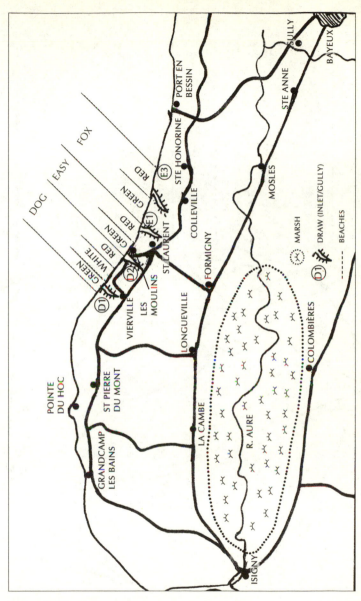

OMAHA landing area.

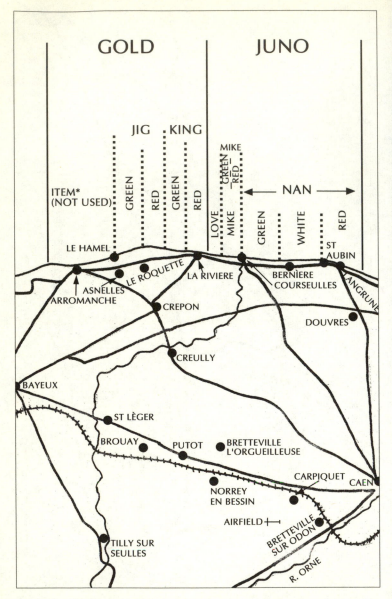

The GOLD and JUNO landing areas. *The area of the beach codenamed ITEM was ultimately not used as a landing site.

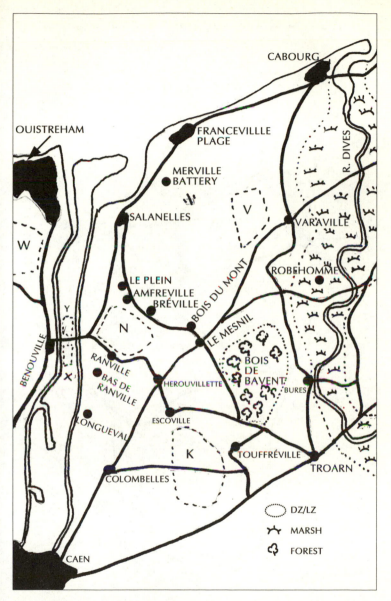

The Eastern flank and British landing zones.

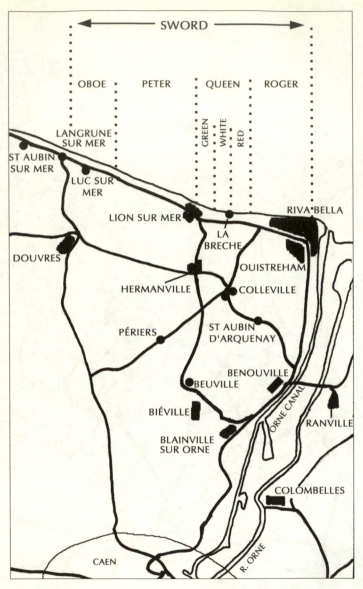

The SWORD landing area.

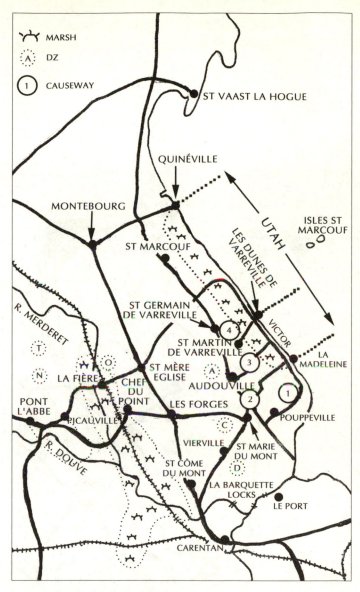

UTAH and the US airborne landing zones.

NOTES

CHAPTER ONE

1   *Militärgeschichtliches Forschungsamt* (Research Institute for Military History), (Eds), *Germany and the Second World War, Volume II*, pp. 254, 275-276; and Cajus Bekker, *The Luftwaffe War Diaries*, pp. 58-59, 97-139.

2   Operation DYNAMO ended on 4 June 1940. The precise figure of evacuees will probably never be known; figures cited in Nicholas Harmon, *Dunkirk: The Necessary Myth*, Appendix I, p. 250.

3   For example, Major L.F. Ellis, *The War in France and Flanders*, pp. 244-246, 305.

4   Figures from Ellis, pp. 326-327.

5   PRO *CAB 120/414*, minute from PM to Ismay, dated 3 June 1940.

6   PRO *CAB 120/414*, minute from PM to Ismay, dated 5 June 1940.

7   Charles Messenger, *The Commandos*, pp. 26-28.

8   PRO *WO 32/4723*, doc. 1B, dated 9 June 1940.

9   PRO *WO 193/27* minute from War Office MO1 to War Office SD1, dated 10 June 1940.

10   Messenger, p. 32.

11   ibid., p. 36.

12   ibid., pp. 33-35.

13   PRO *WO 32/4723*, note from WO DRO to WO AG 17, dated 2 October 1940.

14   PRO *WO 32/4723*, signal from WO AG 17 to HoFor, dated 4 October 1940; signal from Southern Command to WO AG 17, nd c. 3 October 1940; message from WO AG 17 to Southern Command, dated 5 October 1940; and teleprint from HoFor to WO AG 17, nd, c. 5 October 1940.

15   PRO *WO 32/4723*, letter from WO DRO to GOCs Northern and Southern Commands, dated 9 June 1940.

16   PRO *WO 32/4723*, letter from GOC Northern Command to WO, dated 28 July 1940; and PRO *CAB 120/262*, conference minutes 'Minutes of the War Cabinet Chiefs of Staff Committee, 6 August 1940', dated 6 August 1940.

17   PRO *WO 32/4723*, memo from WO DRO to All Home Commands, dated 26 June 1940.

18   PRO *WO 32/4723*, memo from WO DMO&P to Commander Special Service Brigade, dated 15 April 1941; and series of letters from Ministry of Food to WO, dated from 1-5 April 1941.

19   See for example Field Marshal Viscount Slim, *Defeat Into Victory*, pp. 546-549; and John Terraine, *Right of the Line*, pp. 642, 669.

20   PRO *WO 3/4723*, memo from WO DMO&P, dated 13 June 1940; see also for example PRO *WO 193/384*, signal from WO DMO&P dated 20 June 1940.

21   M.R.D. Foot, *SOE in France*, pp. 2-6.

22   For a brief account see Messenger, pp. 19-25.

23   PRO *WO 32/4723*, memo from WO DMO&P to WO DRO, dated 12 June 1940.

24   PRO *AIR 2/7239*, note 'Development of Parachute Troops', from AM Department of Plans to various AM departments, dated 08/06/1940; and *AIR 2/7338*, extract from Chiefs of Staff Meeting to PM, dated 06 August 1940.

25   PRO *AIR 32/2*, paper from Major John Rock RE, n.d., c. July/August 1940.

26   PRO *AIR 32/2*, 'Airborne Brigade Group', n.d., c. August 1940; and doc. 14, paper 'Airborne Troops – Policy For', from War Office SD4 to Director Military Co-operation, Air Ministry, dated 10 January 1941.

27   Interview with Admiral Lord Louis Mountbatten, 'The World at War', Thames Television/IWM; also cited in Carlo D'Este, *Decision in Normandy*, p. 21.

28   PRO *CAB 69/1*, minutes of Defence Committee meeting, dated 19 June 1940; and

PRO *CAB 120/262*, letter from PM to Ismay, dated 22 June 1940.

29 PRO *PREM 3/103/1*, minute from PM to Eden, dated 25 August 1940; also cited in Messenger, p. 39.

30 Lieutenant-Colonel T.B.H. Otway DSO, *Airborne Forces*, pp. 65-70; for a more detailed account see George Millar, *The Bruneval Raid*.

31 James D. Ladd, *Commandos and Rangers of World War II*, pp. 40-52; for a more detailed account see C.E. Lucas Phillips, *The Greatest Raid of All*.

32 Ladd, p. 33.

33 ibid., pp. 21-38.

34 Gordon A. Harrison, *Cross-Channel Attack*, pp. 7-8.

35 PRO *WO 205/901*, directive from Chiefs of Staff to C-in-C Home Forces and Director Combined operations, April 1942.

36 Julian Thompson, *Ready For Anything*, p. 40.

37 ibid., p. 40.

38 Otway, p. 62.

39 Figures from Robin Neillands, *By Sea and Land*, pp. 49 & 52.

40 Figures from ibid., p. 73.

41 Gordon L. Rottman, *US Army Rangers & LRRP Units 1942-87*, p. 5.

42 Ladd, p. 85.

43 Brian Loring Villa, *Unauthorised Action: Mountbatten and the Dieppe Raid*.

44 Ladd, p. 85 and Appendix 4, p. 245.

45 Ladd, p. 82.

46 Harrison, p. 9; foregoing details from ibid., pp. 1-2, 9.

47 For ROUNDUP, see ibid., pp. 7-8.

48 ibid., pp. 2-4, and Chart 1, p. 3.

49 ibid., pp. 16-17.

50 ibid., p. 19.

51 Figures from ibid., pp. 46-47.

52 D'Este, p. 34.

53 Harrison, p. 49.

54 ibid., pp. 57-59.

55 ibid., footnotes 73 & 75, pp. 105-106.

56 D'Este, pp. 43-44.

57 ibid., p. 58.

58 For a detailed account, see Jozef Garlinski, *Intercept: The Enigma War*.

59 Ladd, pp. 57-67, 173-177.

60 Harrison, pp. 194-196.

61 Alfred Price, 'The Air Battle' in *D-Day: Operation Overlord*, p. 130; and Max Hastings, *Das Reich*, p. 56.

62 Hastings, *Das Reich*, p. 88.

63 Figures from Harrison, pp. 204, 230.

64 Edwin P. Hoyt, *The Invasion Before*

Normandy, pp. 74, 80.

65 Figure cited in Stephen Badsey, 'Preparations for Overlord' in *D-Day: Operation Overlord*, p. 39.

66 Hoyt, pp. 153-161.

67 Ryan, *The Longest Day*, pp. 46-48.

68 F.O. Miksche, *Paratroops*, diagrams 10 and 15, pp. 64, 98.

69 Hoyt, pp. 57-59.

CHAPTER TWO

1 George Forty, *Fortress Europe*, pp. 51-53, 146-147.

2 *Oberkommando der Wehrmacht*: Armed forces High Command.

3 *Westwall*: the fixed defensive line built on the western German border in the 1930s, as a rough equivalent to the Maginot Line. Also known as the Siegfried Line.

4 Forty, p. 11.

5 For Directive No. 40 in full, see Forty, pp. 15-17.

6 *Heer*: German Army; *Kriegsmarine*: German Navy after Hitler's ascent to power in 1933.

7 Forty, pp. 6-9.

8 Anthony Saunders, *Hitler's Atlantic Wall*, p. 23.

9 ibid., p. 5.

10 ibid., p. 80.

11 The officer was General Hans Speidel, chief of staff to *Generalfeldmarschall* Erwin Rommel during the latter's stint as commander of *Heeresgruppe* B; ibid., p. 6.

12 Figures from Forty, p. 50.

13 Figures from Saunders, p. 22.

14 Hitler's 'Fortification Order for the Channel Islands' is translated in full in Forty, p. 22.

15 For details of Führer Directive No. 51 see Forty, pp. 22-24.

16 Figures from Detlef Vogel, 'The German Defences' in *D-Day: Operation Overlord*, p. 47.

17 For a full list see Saunders, Appendix A, 'Atlantic Wall Structures', pp. 191-199.

18 PAK: abbreviation of German PanzerAbwehrKanone, or anti-tank gun.

19 For details and scale diagrams of all the structures mentioned, see Forty, pp. 51-58.

20 See for example Ken Tout, *The Bloody Battle for Tilly*.

21 Paul Carell, *Invasion!*, pp. 41-42.

22 Figure from Vogel, 'The German Defences' in *D-Day: Operation Overlord*, p. 47.

23 Teller mine: German anti-tank mine containing 4.5 kg of explosive.

24 For details and illustrations of these beach

obstacles, see *D-Day: Operation Overlord*, pp. 48–49; and Forty, pp. 84–85.

25 See upper plate of Trouville casino in Saunders, p. 20.

26 Figure cited in Vogel, 'The German Defences' in *D-Day: Operation Overlord*, p. 47.

27 Flak: anti-aircraft guns, abbreviation of *FlugzeugAbwehrKanone*; light flak is usually classified as single or multiple barrelled 20mm and 37mm pieces.

28 For details and diagrams of these defence works see Saunders, pp. 26–30.

29 Saunders, p. 145; for a diagram of the Merville Battery, see Peter Harclerode, '*Go To It!*', p. 70.

30 Figure from Robert J. Kershaw, *D-Day: Piercing the Atlantic Wall*, p. 28.

31 For a diagram of *Wiederstandnest* 5, see Saunders, p. 28.

32 ibid., pp. 155–158.

33 *Luftwaffe* Field divisions were ground combat units raised to prevent the *Heer* siphoning off *Luftwaffe*; for a brief account of their formation and combat record, see Kevin Conley Ruffner, *Luftwaffe Field Divisions 1941–45*, especially pp. 19–33.

34 Harrison, op. cit., pp. 237–238.

35 ibid., p. 260.

36 Joseph Balkoski, *Beyond the Beachhead*, pp. 67–71; for locations of *352 Division's* units, see Map 4, p. 74.

37 *Panzer*: tank or armoured; literally an abbreviation of PanzerKampfWagen or armoured fighting vehicle.

38 Kershaw, p. 28.

39 Martin Windrow, *The Panzer Divisions*, p. 11.

40 *Waffen SS*: military arm of the Nazi paramilitary political organisation.

41 Michael Reynolds, *Steel Inferno*, p. 18.

42 ibid., p. 20.

43 Figures from Kershaw, p. 29.

44 Harrison, p. 234.

45 Kershaw, pp. 29–32.

46 Windrow, p. 12.

CHAPTER THREE
1 Figures from Harrison, op. cit., pp. 64–66.

2 Figures from Ambrose, *D-Day, June 6, 1944*, pp.257–258.

3 David Massam, *British Maritime Strategy and Amphibious Capability*, PhD Thesis, Oxford University, 1995, pp. 124–135.

4 PRO *CAB 120/414*, minute from PM to

Ismay, dated 5 June 1940.

5 Harrison, pp. 196–197; and Adrian R. Lewis, *Omaha Beach: A Flawed Victory*, p. 213.

6 Harrison, p. 197.

7 Lewis, *Omaha Beach*, p. 219.

8 For a breakdown of ship assignments, see *D-Day: Operation Overlord*, map 'Allied Bombardment Ships and their D-Day Targets, p. 68.

9 Quote from Lewis, *Omaha Beach*, p. 2.

10 ibid., p. 55.

11 Meirion and Susie Harries, *Soldiers of the Sun*, pp. 373–374.

12 Harrison, p. 194.

13 Robin Neillands and Roderick Norman, *D-Day, 1944: Voices from Normandy*, p. 53.

14 Blair, op. cit., p. 184; and Devlin, op. cit., pp. 224–237.

15 Quoted from Lewis, *Omaha Beach*, p. 80.

16 For details of the Churchill and Sherman derivatives, see Peter Chamberlain and Chris Ellis, *British and American Tanks of World War II*, pp. 69–76, 130–137; for a vivid memoir of a Crocodile commander see Andrew Wilson, *Flame Thrower*.

17 For details of DD tanks see Chamberlain and Ellis, pp. 61–63, 132–133.

18 Figure from Neillands and de Norman, p. 40.

19 For details of the C-47 see Owen Thetford, *Aircraft of the Royal Air Force Since 1918*, pp. 227–228; US figures cited in Blair, pp. 218, 226; British figures cited in Otway, op. cit., p. 166.

20 James Sims, *Arnhem Spearhead*, pp. 16–19.

21 For details of the Stirling, see Thetford, pp. 459–462; and Otway, Appendix B, pp. 399–400; D-Day figures cited in ibid., p. 166.

22 For details see Thetford, pp. 296–301; and Otway, Appendix B, p. 399.

23 S.L.A. Marshall, *Night Drop*, p. 96.

24 Otway, Appendix A, p. 392.

25 For details of the Horsa and Hamilcar, see Thetford, pp. 620–622; and Otway, Appendix A, pp. 391–395.

26 For details of the D-Day glider loadouts, see Shannon and Wright, op. cit., Appendix Three, pp. 195–196.

CHAPTER FOUR
1 See Otway, op. cit., pp. 60–61, 93–94.

2 PRO *AIR 2/7338*, doc. 55'B', 'Minutes of Meeting, Air Ministry 11 December 1940,

dated 11/12/1940, especially closing
comments from DCAS Arthur Harris.

3   PRO *AIR 32/3*, doc. 10B, letter from AM to
70 Group, dated 25/07/1941.

4   PRO *AIR 2/7574*, doc. 3C, 'Minutes of Air
Ministry Conference to Discuss the
Provision of Flying Personnel for Airborne
Forces', dated 22/08/1941.

5   Otway, pp. 42, 55–56.

6   Edward Storey, '1st Canadian Parachute
Battalion, 1942–45 (1)',
in *Military Illustrated Past and Present*, No. 48,
May 1992, pp. 11–17.

7   See for example Terraine, op. cit.,
p. 642.

8   PRO *WO 32/9778*, doc. 24B, paper
'Formation of Further Parachute
Battalions', n.d., c. 07/07/1941.

9   Thompson, op. cit., p. 26.

10 PRO *WO 32/9778*, doc. 24A, covering letter
from Rock CLE to WO SD4, dated
07/07/1941; and doc. 24B, paper 'Formation
of Further Parachute Battalions', n.d.,
c.07/07/1941.

11 For a full list of the 6th Airborne Division's
parachute battalions and their forebears, see
Peter Harclerode, *Go To It!*, p. 19; and
Otway,
pp. 90, 140.

12 Otway, p. 59.

13 Harclerode, p. 27.

14 Storey, p. 14.

15 Thompson, p. 98.

16 Otway, p. 169.

17 General Richard Gale, *Call To Arms*, p. 136.

18 Otway, pp. 172–173.

19 Thompson, p. 102.

20 ibid., pp. 78, 82–3.

21 ibid., pp. 103–104.

22 Shannon and Wright, *One Night In June*, p. 18.

23 Ambrose cites twenty sappers, Harclerode
refers to thirty; Stephen E. Ambrose, *Pegasus
Bridge*, Appendix, p. 186; and Harclerode,
p. 11.

24 Bangalore torpedo: metal tubes filled with
explosive, capable of being linked together
and detonated by a variable time fuse, used
for breaching barbed wire obstacles.
Allegedly invented by Indian Army Sappers
and Miners at Bangalore.

25 Ambrose, pp. 50–55. The dates in this
account do not tally with the primary
documentation. Ambrose claims the initial
three day exercise ended on 18 April 1944,
and that D Company took two weeks leave
before returning for Exercise MUSH. The

unit War Diary, however, clearly states that
MUSH ran from 21 to 23 April. Either the
initial exercise was held earlier, although
there is no mention of it in the unit war
diary, or Ambrose confused his dates. This is
the more likely explanation, as this is not an
isolated error in Ambrose's work. His
account of operations in the region of
Eindhoven by Easy Company, 2nd Battalion
506th Parachute Infantry on 19 September
1944, is similarly at odds with the War Diary
of British armoured unit involved and with
the US official history; see PRO
WO171/589, 1st Airlanding Brigade War
Diary, Summary for April 1944; Ambrose,
Band of Brothers, pp. 128–130; War Diary of
the 15/19 King's Royal Hussars, entry for 19
September 1944; and Leonard Rapport and
Arthur Northwood, *Rendezvous With
Destiny*, pp. 320–321.

26 Ambrose, *Pegasus Bridge*, pp. 65–66.

27 ibid., p. 66.

28 Thunderflash: British pyrotechnic device
used to simulate hand grenades for training.
Essentially an oversized cardboard firework
with a friction fuse, but containing sufficient
explosive to cause considerable injury; the
standard safety demonstration used to
involve blowing a steel helmet thirty feet in
the air.

29 Ambrose, *Pegasus Bridge*, pp. 61–63, 68–72.

30 Brigadier George Chatterton DSO OBE,
The Wings of Pegasus, pp. 127–128.

31 Lawrence Wright, *The Wooden Sword*, pp. 7,
20–21.

32 Ambrose, *Pegasus Bridge*, pp. 56, 72–73.

33 Chatterton, p. 128.

34 Figure cited in Ambrose, *Pegasus Bridge*, p.
56.

35 Thompson, p. 106.

36 Rapport and Northwood, pp. 23–24.

37 Clay Blair, *Ridgeway's Paratroopers*,
p. 17.

38 For a detailed account of the Test Platoon
phase, see Gerard M. Devlin, *Paratrooper!*, pp.
47–75.

39 ibid., pp. 80–82.

40 ibid., p. 32.

41 Blair, p. 20.

42 Devlin, p. 128; and Rapport and
Northwood, p. 3.

43 Blair, pp. 39–44.

44 ibid., p. 52.

45 ibid., pp. 50–52.

46 ibid., p. 71.

47 Devlin, pp. 213–214 and endnote 5, p. 680.

48 ibid., pp. 221, 224–229.

49 Blair, pp. 92–94; and Devlin, pp. 229-230.
50 Devlin, p. 240.
51 All figures from Blair, pp. 100-102.
52 ibid., pp. 236-237; and Devlin, pp. 97-99; the ridge is spelled Biazzo and Biazza in different accounts.
53 Devlin, pp. 246-248.
54 Blair, pp. 106-107.
55 ibid., pp. 150-153.
56 Rapport and Northwood, pp. 13-21.
57 The programme is reproduced in part in Rapport and Northwood, pp. 26-27.
58 ibid., p. 28.
59 Blair, p. 205.
60 The 82nd Airborne consisted of the 504th, 505th, 507th and 508th Parachute Infantry Regiments, the 325th Glider Infantry Regiment, the 376th and 456th Parachute Field Artillery Battalions and the 319th and 320th Glider Field Artillery Battalions. The 101st Airborne was made up of the 501st, 502nd and 506th Parachute Infantry Regiment, the 327th Glider infantry Regiment, the 377th and 463rd Parachute Field Artillery Battalions and the 312th and 907th Glider Field Artillery Battalions. Glider Infantry Regiments originally had two battalions; in March 1944 the 401st Glider Infantry Regiment was split up and divided between the 325th and 327th Glider Infantry Regiments to bring them up to three battalions; see Rapport and Northwood, p. 87n; for a breakdown of organisation including all divisional units for both divisions, see Gordon Rottman, US Army Airborne 1940-90, Table 'World War II Airborne Divisions, 1942-45', p. 8.
6   Harrison, Cross Channel Attack, pp. 184-185; and Blair, pp. 178-190. Harrison gives the impression that Marshall did not unveil his plan until February 1944, but Blair cites other primary sources to reinforce the autumn 1943 start date; Blair, p. 543n.
62 Rapport and Northwood, pp. 51-52, 57; Devlin, p. 326; and Blair, p. 183.
63 Blair, p. 184.
64 ibid., p. 188.
65 Harrison, p. 186; and Blair, pp. 207-209.
66 Devlin, pp. 176-188.
67 Otway, p. 36; and Chatterton, pp 21-24.
68 Quoted from 'Army Air Forces Historical Study No.1: Development and Procurement of Gliders in the Army Air Forces 1941-1944' (Washington, DC: AAF Historical Office, 1946), p. 20; cited in Devlin, p. 73.
69 Devlin, pp. 118-120; and Rapport and Northwood, pp. 19-20.
70 For a brief account see Rottman, US Army Rangers and LRRP Units, pp. 5-10; see also Ladd, op. cit., Chaps. 7, 8 and 9.
71 Rottman, US Army Rangers, pp. 10-13; and Ladd, Appendix 7, pp. 265-267.
72 Ladd, pp. 188-189 and Appendix 3, p. 241; and Ryan, op. cit., p. 236.

CHAPTER FIVE
1   PRO WO 32/4723, doc. 14A, copy of letter from WO DRO to All Home Commands, dated 17/06/1940, and doc. 11A, typed addendum dated 17/06/1940.
2   Peter Chamberlain and Chris Ellis, British and American Tanks of World War II, pp. 41-42.
3   Figures cited in Philip Katcher, The US 1st Infantry Division, 1939-45, p. 14.
4   Harrison, op. cit., Map XII, 'Omaha Beach Assault (Infantry)', between pp. 104-105.
5   ibid., p. 192.
6   ibid., Map XI, 'V Corps D-Day Objectives', between pp. 104-105.
7   The 115th Infantry Regiment traced its origins back to the Colonial 1st Maryland Regiment, and units of that name served on both sides in the American Civil War; the 116th Infantry was originally the 2nd Virginia Regiment, raised in 1760, which served in the Confederate Stonewall Brigade in the War Between the States; and the 175th Infantry traced its origins back to the 'Dandy 5th' Maryland Infantry Regiment, which fought the British at the Battle of Long Island on 27 August 1776; see Balkoski, Beyond the Beachhead, pp. 24-25.
8   ibid., pp. 36-52; and Harrison, p. 162.
9   Harrison, Map XI, 'V Corps D-Day Objectives', between pp. 104-105; and Balkoski, p. 168.
10 ibid., p. 302; and Map VIII, 'The Airborne Assault', between pp. 104-105.
11 Figures from Eric Morris, Circles of Hell, p. 148.
12 Harrison, Map XIII, 'The Second British Army on D Day', between pp. 104-105.
13 PRO WO 219/1942, MARTIAN 95, 10 May 1944; MARTIAN Reports contained information gathered from sources besides ULTRA, and were issued by SHAEF's Theatre Intelligence Section; cited in D'Este, p. 125.
14 PRO DEFE 3/155, Message KV 3892 dated 15 May 1944, Decrypt of signal from German 7th Army HQ, dated 5 May 1944; cited in D'Este, p. 124.
15 PRO WO 219/1919, SHAEF Weekly Intelligence Summaries Nos. 8 & 9, dated 13

May and 20 May 1944 respectively; cited in
D'Este, p. 122.

16 PRO *WO 285/3*, The Dempsey Papers,
Second Army Planning Intelligence
Summary No. 23, dated 22 May 1944; cited
in D'Este, p. 123.

17 This information appeared in the 3rd
Infantry Division Final Operation Order,
Divisional Intelligence Summary, dated 14
May 1944; quoted in Norman Scarfe, *Assault
Division*, p. 66; cited in D'Este, p. 124.

18 PRO *WO 179/2839*, 2nd Canadian
Armoured Brigade War Diary, Operation
Order No. 1, dated 23 May 1944 ; and *WO
171/613*, 8th Armoured Brigade War Diary,
Brigade Intelligence Summary dated 25
May 1944.

19 Robert J. Kershaw, *D-Day: Piercing the
Atlantic Wall*, p. 28; and D'Este, p. 125.

20 D'Este, pp. 125-127.

21 The officer concerned was Major Brian
Urquhart, Senior Intelligence Officer at
British 1st Airborne Corps HQ; see for
example A. D. Harvey, *Arnhem*, p. 34; and
PRO *WO 171/393*, 1 Airborne Division War
Diary.

CHAPTER SIX

1   Ambrose, *D-Day, June 6 1944*, p. 48.
2   John Ellis, *The Sharp End*, p. 12.
3   Ambrose, *D-Day, June 6 1944*, pp. 48-51.
4   ibid., p. 50.
5   Thompson, op. cit., pp. 96, 103.
6   John Foley, *Mailed Fist*, pp. 26-30.
7   David French, *Raising Churchill's Army*, pp.
205-206.
8   Cited in Timothy Harrison Place, *Tactical
Doctrine and Training in the Infantry and
Armoured Arms of the British Army, 1940-1944*
(Ph.D. Thesis, University of Leeds, 1997), pp.
269-278.
9   For example, Montgomery was involved in
shelving the personal observations of an
officer attached to the 36th Infantry Brigade
in Sicily which claimed that in any average
rifle platoon, around a quarter could be
expected to run away in action, and that the
remainder were drawn on by around six
individuals. He also had a June 1944 report
by a senior officer in the 7th Armoured
Division that compared British tanks
unfavourably to their German counterparts
toned down before circulation; see Harrison
Place, pp. 29-31.
10 French, p. 210.
11 Hastings, OVERLORD, p. 57.

12 Jon E. Lewis (Ed), *Eye-Witness D-Day*,
extract from unpublished memoir by Major
F.D. Goode, The Gloucestershire Regiment,
p. 37.
13 Hastings, OVERLORD, pp. 311, 371.
14 ibid., p. 57.
15 ibid., p. 63.
16 Balkoski, *Beyond The Beachhead*, pp. 41-64.
17 According to Lewis, there were eight US
invasion training centres in the UK.
However, no locations except Woolacombe
and Slapton Sands are cited in his work or in
any of the other works consulted. It is possible that the two locations hosted multiple
specialised training facilities; Lewis, *Omaha
Beach*, p. 108.
18 Hoyt, *The Invasion Before Normandy*, p. 37.
19 Balkoski, p. 52; and Harrison, *Cross Channel
Attack*, p. 162.
20 Hoyt, pp. 81-83.
21 figures from Hoyt, p. 160; for a detailed
account of the attack on the TIGER convoy
and its immediate aftermath, see ibid., pp.
99-119.
22 Harrison, pp. 162-164.
23 Russell Miller, *Nothing Less Than Victory*,
interview with Private Dennis Brown, 5th
East Yorks, pp. 101-106.
24 Figures and raid cited in Harrison, pp. 269-
270.
25 Lewis, extracts from unpublished narratives
by P.H.B. Pritchard, No. 6 Commando, and
T. Tateson, The Green Howards, pp. 28-29.
26 Miller, extract from unpublished memoir by
then Sergeant John R. Slaughter, 1st Bn.
116th Infantry Regiment, p. 117.
27 Foley, pp. 30, 35-36.
28 Ellis, p. 60.
29 Mike Chappell, *British Infantry Equipments
1908-80*, pp. 21-23 and Plate 'E', between pp.
24-25.
30 Donald R. Burgett, *Currahee!*, pp. 77-79.
31 Rapport and Northwood, op. cit., extract
from the diary of Specialist 5th Class
George E. Koskimaki, pp. 77-79.
32 Lewis, extract from unpublished memoir by
Major F.D. Goode, The Gloucestershire
Regiment, and interview with Donald S.
Vaughan, 5th Assault Regiment, 79th
Armoured Division, pp. 34-35, 37.
33 Lewis, extract from interview with Trooper
Peter Davies, 1st East Riding Yeomanry, pp.
33-34.
34 Miller, extract from account by PFC
William E. Jones, 8th Infantry Regiment,
US 4th Infantry Division, pp. 118-119.
35 Ryan, op. cit., pp. 42-44.

36   Harrison, p. 272.
37   Ambrose, *D-Day, June 6 1944*, pp. 184-186.
38   Miller, extracts from interviews with
     Edward C. Boccafogli, 508th Parachute
     Infantry Regiment and Major E.H. Steele-
     Baume, 2 i/c, 7th Parachute Battalion, p.
     150.
39   Harrison, p. 274. See also Miller, extract
     from a television interview with Group-
     Captain James Stagg, pp. 155-158.
40   Ambrose, *D-Day June 6, 1944*, pp. 188-189.

CHAPTER SEVEN

1   Rapport and Northwood, op. cit., p. 79.
2   Miller, op. cit., interviews with Edward C.
     Boccafogli, 508th Parachute Infantry
     Regiment, p. 150.
3   Ambrose, *Pegasus Bridge*, pp. 78-79.
4   ibid., p. 79; and Burgett, op. cit, p. 74.
5   Barber, *The Day the Devils Dropped In*, inter-
     view with Private Ron Gregory, p. 41.
6   Shannon and Wright, *One Night In June*, p.
     36.
7   Lewis, op. cit., p. 64.
8   Burgett, pp. 76-77.
9   The officer was Lieutenant Wallace Strobel.
     His conversation with Eisenhower was
     photographed and has become one of the
     most frequently reproduced images of the
     immediate pre-invasion period; see
     Ambrose, *D-Day June 6, 1944*, p.193.
10   John Keegan, *Six Armies in Normandy*, pp.
     84-85.
11   For details of the kit bags see Otway, op. cit.,
     Appendix E, pp. 410-411.
12   Ambrose, *Band of Brothers*, pp. 64-65.
13   The Hawkins No. 75 Grenade was an
     explosive charge in a metal container
     resembling a flat polish tin, complete with
     screw top.
14   Ambrose, *D-Day June 6, 1944*, p. 194.
15   Miller, extract from letter by Sergeant Jack
     Harries, A Company, 9th Parachute
     Battalion, pp. 179-180.
16   Warner, *The D-Day Landings*, account by
     the Reverend Lieutenant-Colonel A. R.
     Clark MC, p. 36.
17   Barber, extract from interview with Major
     Allen Parry, 9th Parachute Battalion, p. 41.
18   Otway, Appendix F, Annexure II: Navigation
     and Employment of Pathfinder Units, pp.
     421-424.
19   Ambrose, *D-Day June 6, 1944*, p. 196.
20   Miller, account by Corporal J. Frank
     Brumbaugh, 508th Parachute Infantry
     Regiment, pp. 196-197.
21   Ambrose, *Pegasus Bridge*, p. 80.

22   Miller, extract from unpublished memoir by
     Sergeant Len Drake, 22nd Independent
     Parachute Company, pp. 187-189.
23   The official history cites sixteen Albemarles,
     but a more recent account refers to four-
     teen; see Otway, p. 176; and Barber, p. 44.
24   Otway, pp. 176-177.
25   Details from Shannon and Wright,
     Appendix Three, 'Individual Glider Loads
     (Where Known)', p. 195.
26   Ambrose, *Pegasus Bridge*, pp. 90-92; and
     Carell, op. cit., p. 38.
27   Shannon and Wright, p. 49.
28   For a detailed account, see ibid.,
     pp. 43-50; and Ambrose, *Pegasus Bridge*, pp.
     82-99.
29   Otway, *Airborne Forces*, p. 177.
30   Miller, extract from unpublished memoir by
     Sergeant Len Drake, 22nd Independent
     Parachute Company, pp. 187-189.
31   Shannon and Wright, p. 52.
32   Harclerode, *'Go To It!'*, p. 71.
33   Barber, p. 48.
34   ibid., p. 32.
35   Otway, p. 179.
36   Barber, pp. 50-51.
37   Warner, interview with Flight-Lieutenant
     P.M. Bristow, RAF
     No. 575 Squadron, pp. 27-30.
38   Barber, pp. 51-53, 62-63.
39   Kershaw, op. cit., p. 80.
40   Shannon and Wright, pp. 54-68 and
     Appendix One 'Comments on Tonga
     Gliders', pp. 186-191.
41   Kershaw, pp. 80-82; and Ambrose, *Pegasus
     Bridge*, p. 110.
42   Ambrose, *Pegasus Bridge*, p. 110.
43   PIAT: Projector, Infantry, Anti-Tank, a
     spring and recoil operated bomb thrower
     with hollow charge ammunition.
44   Ambrose, *Pegasus Bridge*, pp. 105-106.
45   ibid., pp. 115-117.
46   Kershaw, p. 83.
47   Ambrose, *D-Day June 6, 1944*, p. 201.
48   Keegan, account by Sergeant Louis E. Traux,
     1st Battalion, 506th Parachute Infantry
     Regiment, pp. 84-85.
49   Ambrose, *Band of Brothers*, p. 68.
50   Burgett, pp. 86-87.
51   Blair, op. cit., pp. 219.
52   Harrison, op. cit., Map IX, '101st Airborne
     Division Drop Patterns,
     6 June 1944', between pp. 104-105.
53   Blair, p. 222.
54   Harrison refers to Hoffman hearing unusual
     aircraft noise from 01:30, and seeing the
     paratroopers coming down 02:00, whereas

Carell cites an approximate time of 00:40.
Given that the paratroopers appear to have
been from the 101st, and 101st began
jumping at 00:45, Carell's time appears the
most likely; see Harrison, p. 278; and Carell,
p. 36.

55   Carell, pp. 43-45, 49-51.

56   Blair, p. 227.

57   Miller, account by Sergeant William T.
Dunfee, 3rd Battalion, 505th Parachute
Infantry Regiment, pp. 201-202.

58   ibid., account by Harold Canyon, 2nd
Battalion, 508th Parachute Infantry
Regiment, pp. 193-194.

59   ibid., account by Sergeant Dan Furlong,
508th Parachute Infantry Regiment, pp.
193-194.

60   Ryan, op. cit., pp. 130-133; and Neillands
and de Normann, *D-Day, 1944: Voices from
Normandy*, p. 115.

61   Harrison, Map X, '82nd Airborne Division
Drop Pattern, 6 June 1944', between pp.
104-105.

62   Blair, pp. 234-235.

63   ibid., p. 236.

64   PRO *WO 171/592*, 1st Parachute Brigade
War Diary, Summary for April 1944; and
PRO *WO 171/594*, 4th Parachute Brigade
War Diary, Summary for April 1944.

65   'The pilots were afraid.'; Ambrose, *D-Day
June 6, 1944*, p. 198.

66   Neillands and de Normann, account by
John D. Kutz, p. 103.

67   Neillands and de Normann, account by
Sergeant Rainer Hartmetz, p. 101.

68   Carell, pp. 57-58; and Devlin, *Paratrooper!*, pp.
388-389.

69   Blair, p. 238.

70   Shannon and Wright, pp. 93-100.

71   ibid., pp. 122-123.

72   ibid., p. 121.

73   ibid., p. 104.

74   Miller, extract from unpublished memoir by
Sapper Benny Jordan,
3rd Parachute Squadron RE, pp. 205-206.

75   ibid., interviews with Major Tim 'Rosie'
Roseveare and Lance-Sergeant Bill Irving,
3rd Parachute Squadron RE, pp. 207-211.

76   Harclerode, p. 71; and Thompson, op. cit.,
pp. 124-127.

77   Harclerode, pp. 72-73

78   Barber, pp. 54-78.

79   Shannon and Wright, pp. 83-92.

80   Kershaw, p. 84.

81   Figures from Barber, p. 99.

82   For a highly detailed account of the attack
with numerous participant accounts, see

ibid., pp. 77-91.

83   Saunders, op. cit., p. 145; and Barber,
Appendix 5, 'Controversial Issues
Surrounding the Merville Battery', Point 5,
pp. 212-213.

84   Barber, pp. 91-92.

85   Saunders, p. 146; and Carell, p. 57.

86   Barber, p. 92, 123, 129.

87   ibid., p. 97.

88   ibid., p. 95.

89   ibid., p. 99.

90   ibid., pp. 100-101.

CHAPTER EIGHT

1   Harrison, *Cross Channel Attack*,
p. 276.

2   Kershaw, *D-Day: Piercing the Atlantic Wall*, p.
52.

3   Harrison, p. 276.

4   Kershaw, p. 52.

5   Harrison, p. 275.

6   The line ran: '*Les sanglots longs des violons de
l'automne/ Blessent mon coeur d'une langeur
monotone*' [The long sobs of the violins of
autumn/ Wound my heart with a monoto-
nous languor]; Ryan, *The Longest Day*, p. 33.

7   ibid., pp. 30-34.

8   German clocks were set to Central
European Time (CET), which was one hour
behind the Allies, who used British Double
Summer Time (BDST). The present author
has endeavoured to use BDST throughout,
although some sources are unclear as to
which time is being referred to.

9   Ryan, pp. 20-21.

10   Harrison, p. 275.

11   Ryan, p. 81.

12   *Kriegspiel*: a map-based war game widely
used as a training aid by the German Army
from the 19th century.

13   Kershaw, p. 63.

14   Otway, p. 177; for a picture of a Rupert, see
D-Day: Operation Overlord, p. 39.

15   Bekker, op. cit., p. 128.

16   Ryan, p. 147.

17   Kershaw, p. 89.

18   ibid., p. 88.

19   Ryan, p. 148; and Harrison, p. 278.

20   Kershaw, p. 89.

21   ibid., pp. 82, 88-89.

22   ibid., pp. 89-90.

23   Miller, *Nothing Less Than Victory*, extract
from interview with *Hauptmann* Curt
Fromm, No. 6 Company, 100 Panzer
Brigade,
22 Panzer Division, pp. 237-238.
As 22 Panzer Division was destroyed near

Stalingrad in late 1942, it is more likely the interviewee was a member of 21 *Panzer Division's Panzer Regiment 22.*

24 Ryan, pp. 151-152; and Lewis, *Eye-Witness D-Day*, extract from interview with *Gefreiter* Werner Kortenhaus, 22nd Panzer Regiment, 21st Panzer Division, p. 92.

25 Kershaw, p. 80; and Miller, extract from interview with *Oberleutnant* Helmut Liebeskind, Adjutant, 125 Panzergrenadier Regiment, 21st Panzer Division, pp. 235-236.

27 Otway, Appendix K, 'The Normandy Operations: Commander 6 Airborne Division's Planning Instructions, Part 2: For Commander 5 Parachute Brigade', pp. 430-432.

27 Kershaw, p. 92.

28 Harrison, p. 301; and Ryan, p. 150.

29 Figure from Ambrose, *D-Day: June 6 1944*, p. 254.

30 Harrison, p. 301.

31 Kershaw, p. 95.

32 Ryan, pp. 192-193.

33 Ambrose, *D-Day: June 6 1944*, p. 260.

34 ibid., p. 260.

35 Donald Gilchrist, *Don't Cry For Me*, pp. 46-47.

36 Ryan, pp. 150-151, 195-196; and Kershaw, pp. 98-99.

37 Lewis, interview with Ken Wright, 1st Special Service Brigade, p. 93.

38 Warner, account by Reverend P.C. Webber, formerly Lieutenant P. Webber, 2nd Battalion the Middlesex Regiment, p. 186.

39 Ryan, pp. 183-184.

40 Kershaw, p. 92.

41 Miller, account from Hauptmann Ernst During, Commander Machine Gun Company, 914 Regiment, 352nd Infantry Division, pp. 240-242.

42 Kershaw, p. 99.

43 ibid., p. 96.

44 Miller, account by Major Werner Pluskat, 352 Artillery Regiment, 352nd Infantry Division, pp. 243-245.

45 Harrison, pp. 300-301.

46 Ambrose, *D-Day, June 6 1944*, pp. 241-246.

47 Carell, op. cit., pp. 58-62.

48 Ambrose, *D-Day, June 6 1944*, pp. 264-265.

49 ibid., pp. 266-267; and Ryan, pp. 233-236.

50 Figures from Kershaw, p. 99.

51 Ryan, pp. 42-45, 182-183.

52 ibid., p. 159; and Harrison, p. 304.

53 Ambrose, *D-Day, June 6 1944*, p. 276.

54 Harrison, p. 304; and Neillands and de Normann, p. 125.

55 Harrison, p. 309; and Neillands and de Normann, p. 141.

56 Balkoski, p. 129.

57 Neillands and de Normann, p. 141.

58 See television documentary series *Journeys to the Bottom of the Sea: D-Day: The Untold Story*, BBC/ Discovery Channel Co-production, broadcast on British BBC2 television, 30 May 2002.

59 Carell, pp. 65-67.

60 Ambrose, pp. 276-279; and Ryan, pp. 231-233, 286.

61 Neillands and de Normann, p. 126.

62 For Jahnke's reference to an 88mm, see Carell, p. 66; according to a detailed diagram of *Wiederstandnest* 5, the only anti-tank guns deployed there were three 50mm and one ex-French 47mm pieces; see Saunders, *Hitler's Atlantic Wall*, p. 28.

63 Carell, p. 71.

64 Ambrose, *D-Day, June 6 1944*, p. 297.

65 ibid., pp. 283-284.

66 ibid., p. 300; and Harrison, p. 283.

67 Neillands and de Normann, p. 129.

68 Ambrose, *D-Day, June 6 1944*, p. 287.

69 ibid., pp. 286-287.

70 The differing casualty figures are cited in Ambrose, *D-Day, June 6 1944*, p. 292; and Kershaw, p. 105.

71 Ambrose, *D-Day, June 6 1944*, p. 292.

72 Figures from Kershaw, p. 106.

73 Ambrose, *D-Day, June 6 1944*, account by Captain L. Johnson, p. 297.

74 Harrison, pp. 289-290.

75 ibid., pp. 293-294.

76 For a detailed account, see S.L.A. Marshall, *Night Drop*, pp. 31-39.

77 For a detailed account, see ibid., pp. 216-212.

78 For a detailed account of this action, see Ambrose, *Band of Brothers*, pp. 77-84; and Miller, extract from interview with Private Don Malarkey, Company E, 2nd Battalion 506th Parachute Infantry Regiment, pp. 433-435.

79 Harrison, Map XI, 'V Corps D-Day Objectives', between pp. 104-105.

80 Balkoski, p. 71.

81 ibid., p. 67.

82 Lewis, *Omaha Beach*, pp. 16-17.

83 Harrison, p. 315.

84   ibid., p. 313; and Ryan, pp. 208–209.
85   Carell, p. 84.
86   Figures from Neillands and de Normann, p. 147; for a detailed account see Balkoski, pp. 125–130.
87   Balkoski, p. 129.
88   First two quotes from Ambrose, *D-Day: June 6 1944*, pp. 320, 346, latter two from Neillands and de Normann, pp. 140, 142.
89   The most up to date figures for D-Day casualties the author has seen were posted by Mr Richard Anderson of the Deputy Institute as a review of a work in progress on the TankNet Military Forums internet discussion forum on 29 October 2002. Some difficulties were encountered in contacting
     Mr Anderson, which resulted in the information being obtained too late for incorporation inthe main text.
     Mr Anderson's research suggests a combined total of between 2,515 and 3,380 British and Canadian casualties on the JUNO, GOLD and SWORD landing areas, and a combined total of between 2,616 and 3,114 on the OMAHA and UTAH landing areas. The figures were obtained from the following sources: PRO WO 205/405, *British Casualties During the First Month of Operation Overlord*, nd.; *The Victory Campaign*, Appendix B, Canadian Army Casualties – Normandy – 6 June 1944m p. 650; ibid. Appendix C, Approximate Casualties of the Allied Armies by Sectors, Normandy 6 1944, p. 651–652; 'A' SITREP Reports, 21 Army Group Files; USV Corps History.
     I am indebted to Mr Anderson for providing this information and for his kind permission to cite it.
90   See for example Neillands and de Normann, p. 141.
91   Lewis, *Omaha Beach*, p, 2; and Neillands and de Normann, p. 140.
92   Balkoski, pp. 125–132.
93   Harrison, p. 318.
94   Lewis, extract from account by Sergeant Mike Rehm, US 5th Ranger Regiment, p. 105.
95   Balkoski, pp. 135–139; and Harrison, p. 324.
96   Harrison, pp. 324–325.
97   See for example Lewis, *Omaha Beach*, p. 299.
98   Balkoski, p. 132.
99   Lewis, pp. 298–299.
100 Balkoski, p. 138.
101 Miller, account from Sergeant John R. Slaughter, Company D, 1st Battalion, 116th Infantry Regiment, pp. 250–253; and Balkoski, comment from Private August Bruno, Company G, 2nd battalion, 116th Infantry Regiment, p. 127.
102 Balkoski, p. 63.
103 The address is reproduced in full in Lewis, pp. 297–298, and n. 12 & 13, p. 352.
104 Balkoski, pp. 63–64.
105 Lewis, p. 296.
106 Harrison, p. 192.
107 ibid., pp. 162–164.
108 Lewis, *Omaha Beach*, 'Epilogue: The Question of American Military Skill', pp. 291–307.
109 ibid., pp. 258–259.
110 Ambrose, *D-Day, June 6 1944*, p. 407; and Kershaw, p. 121.
111 Ladd, op. cit., p. 191.
112 Ryan, p. 237.
113 Ladd, p. 189.
114 ibid., p. 189.
115 Kershaw, p. 121; and Ambrose, *D-Day, June 6 1944*, pp. 413–414.
116 Ambrose, *D-Day, June 6 1944*, pp. 415–416.
117 Stuart Hills, *By Tank Into Normandy*, pp. 75–79, 84–91.
118 ibid., p. 79.
119 Neillands and de Normann, p. 161.
120 Miller, interview with Private Joe Minogue, 7th Armoured Division, pp. 344–347.
121 Kershaw, pp. 164–168.
122 Miller, extract from account by Sergeant W.E. Wills, 2nd Battalion, The Devonshire Regiment, pp. 348–351.
123 Neillands and de Normann, pp. 164–165.
124 Kershaw, p. 149; and Neillands and de Normann, p. 167.
125 Miller, account by Private Francis Williams MM, 6th Battalion, The Green Howards, pp. 343–344.
126 Neillands and de Normann, p. 167.
127 ibid., p. 188.
128 Miller, account by Sergeant Leo Gariepy, B Squadron, 6th Armoured Regiment, Canadian Armoured Corps, pp. 323–326.
129 Ambrose, *D-Day: June 6, 1944*, p. 539.
130 ibid., p. 539.
131 Neillands and de Normann, p. 189.
132 Miller, interview with Sergeant Harold Fielder, 26 Field Company, Royal Engineers, pp. 322–323.
133 Ambrose, *D-Day: June 6, 1944*, pp. 538–539.

134 Neillands and de Normann,
    pp. 188-189.
135 ibid., pp. 196-197.
136 Kershaw, p. 141.
137 Neillands and de Normann,
    pp. 186, 194-195.
138 Kershaw, pp. 143-144.
139 Neillands and de Normann, p. 200.
140 Ladd, p. 187.
141 Miller, extract from interview with Captain
    Robert Neave, B Squadron, 13th/18th
    Hussars, pp. 308-310.
142 ibid., extract from interview with Sergeant-
    Major H.E. Harrison, Royal Engineers, pp.
    318-319.
143 ibid., extract from interview with Lance-
    Corporal Patrick Hennessy, 13th/18th
    Hussars, pp. 315-316.
144 Warner, extract from the diary of Major
    Tim Wheway MC, C Squadron, 22nd
    Dragoons,
    pp. 147-151.
145 Kershaw, p. 132.
146 Neillands and de Normann,
    pp. 209-210.
147 Miller, extract from account held at D-Day
    Museum, pp. 314-315.
148 Ryan, p. 241.
149 Neillands and de Normann, p. 210.
150 Kershaw, p. 133.
151 Neillands and de Normann,
    pp. 210-211.
152 Figure from Kershaw, p. 138.
153 Lewis, comment attributed to anonymous
    private from the East Yorkshire Regiment, p.
    120.
154 ibid., account by Lieutenant H.T. Bone, 2nd
    Battalion the East Yorkshire Regiment, pp.
    119-120.
155 Neillands and de Normann, account by
    Corporal Rayson, 9 Platoon, A Company,
    1st Battalion the Suffolk Regiment, p. 212.
156 Warner, extract from a letter by former
    Private R. Harris, B Company, 1st Battalion
    the Suffolk Regiment, pp. 183-184.
157 Ladd, pp. 186-187; and Neillands,
    By Sea and Land, pp. 135-140.
158 Ladd, pp. 184-185; and Gilchrist,
    pp. 57-59.
159 Warner, account by Trooper P.H.B.
    Pritchard, No. 6 Commando,
    pp. 227-230; and Ladd, pp. 185-186.
160 Ambrose, Pegasus Bridge, pp. 129-131.
161 ibid., p. 132.
162 Ambrose, Pegasus Bridge, pp. 133-135.
163 Carell, p. 104.
164 Thompson, p. 121.

165 Carell, pp. 104-105.
166 Harclerode, p. 71; and Barber,
    pp. 107-111.
167 Thompson, p. 122.
168 ibid., account by Captain John Sim, pp. 121-
    122.
169 Kershaw, p. 164.
170 Timings from Kershaw, pp. 165-167.

CHAPTER NINE
1   Neillands and de Normann, D-Day 1944,
    account by Major James Cuthbertson, pp.
    216-217.
2   ibid., p. 217; and Ryan, op. cit.,
    p. 293.
3   Ambrose, Pegasus Bridge, p. 144.
4   Warner, The D-Day Landings, account by
    Trooper P.H.B. Pritchard, pp. 227-230.
5   Thompson, op. cit., pp. 119-120;
    and Harclerode, op. cit., pp. 64-65.
6   Thompson, pp. 126-127.
7   Harrison, op. cit., p. 329.
8   Ibid., pp. 328-329.
9   Ibid., pp. 291-293; Blair, op. cit.,
    pp. 246-250; and Marshall, Night Drop, pp.
    51-83.
10 Harrison, p. 329; and Devlin, Paratrooper!, pp.
    373-374, 406-407.
11 For a detailed account, see Blair,
    pp. 254-255.
12 Kershaw, op. cit., pp. 180-183.
13 Miller, extract from interview with PFC
    Carl Weast, 5th Ranger Battalion, pp. 429-
    431.
14 Harrison, pp. 325-330; and Kershaw, pp. 159-
    163.
15 Balkoski, op. cit., p. 146.
16 Neillands and de Normann,
    pp. 168-169.
17 ibid., p. 201.
18 Lincoln, Thank God and the Infantry, p. 21.
19 Warner, extract from a letter by former
    Private R. Harris,
    B Company, 1st Battalion the Suffolk
    Regiment, pp. 185-186; and Neillands and
    de Normann, accounts by Private Eric
    Rowland and Corporal Rayson, A
    Company, 1st Battalion the Suffolk
    Regiment and Sapper Richard Ellis, 246
    Field Company RE, pp. 221-223.
20 Kershaw, p. 173.
21 Lincoln, p. 21.
22 Neillands and de Normann, p. 225.
23 Miller, extract from account by Oberleutnant
    Herr, Panzer Regiment 22, pp. 395-397.
24 Kershaw, pp. 174-175.
25 Carell, Invasion!, p. 107.

26 Ibid., p. 107.
27 Warner, extract from a letter by Private R. Harris, B Company, 1st Battalion the Suffolk Regiment, p. 185.
28 Kershaw, pp. 175-176; and Miller, extract from account by *Oberleutnant* Herr, *Panzer Regiment 22*, pp. 397-399.
29 Miller, extract from interview with *Generalleutnant* Edgar Feuchtinger, commander 21st Panzer Division, p. 395.
30 Kershaw, comment by Lance-Corporal Patrick Hennessy, 13th/18th Hussars, p. 178.
31 *Schwere SS Panzer Abteilung 101*, equipped with Tiger Is was located at Beauvais; *schwere Panzer Abteilung 503*, equipped with a mix of Tiger I and Tiger II tanks was attached to *Panzer Lehr* near Le Mans. The latter unit was in the process of moving to Poland when the invasion began and it took five days to get them back; see Reynolds, *Steel Inferno*, p. 70; and Carell, p. 111.
32 Kershaw, pp. 176, 178.
33 ibid., p. 184.
34 ibid., p. 185.
35 Neillands and de Normann, p. 88.
36 Otway, op. cit., pp. 177, 181-182; and Harclerode, pp. 75-76.
37 Kershaw, pp. 180, 185.
38 Blair, p. 242; for the Bradley quote, see n. 8, p. 548.
39 Ibid., p. 240.
40 L.F. Ellis, *Victory in the West*, Volume One, pp. 212-213; cited in Blair, p. 548.

CHAPTER TEN
1 Reynolds, *Steel Inferno*, pp. 59-60.
2 ibid., pp. 53-54.
3 ibid., p. 54.
4 Kershaw, *D-Day: Piercing the Atlantic Wall*, p. 192.
5 ibid., pp. 196-199; and Carell, *Invasion!*, pp. 111-117.
6 Kershaw, p. 194.
7 ibid., p. 196.
8 Reynolds, p. 55.
9 ibid., pp. 60-61; and Kershaw, pp. 199-201.
10 Harclerode, *'Go To It!'*, pp. 78, 85.
11 Harrison, *Cross Channel Attack*, pp. 342, 345-346.
12 Blair, *Ridgeway's Paratroopers*, p. 257.
13 Harrison, p. 344.
14 ibid., p. 342.
15 Devlin, *Silent Wings*, pp. 197-199.
16 Harrison, p. 345.
17 Ambrose, *Band of Brothers*, p. 89; and Harrison, p. 347.
18 Balkoski, op. cit., pp. 150-151, 155-159.
19 Ladd, op. cit., pp. 192-193; and Harrison, pp. 340-341.
20 Harrison, p. 337.
21 Neillands, *By Sea and Land*, pp. 158-163.

CHAPTER ELEVEN
1 Harclerode, op. cit., p. 78.
2 ibid., p. 85.
3 ibid., pp. 78-79; and Otway, op. cit., p. 184.
4 Barber, op. cit., p. 129.
5 ibid., pp. 134-135.
6 Thompson, op. cit., pp. 127-128.
7 Blair, op. cit., pp. 259-260.
8 Harrison, op. cit., pp. 344-345, 386-387.
9 ibid., pp. 347-348.
10 ibid., p. 347.
11 ibid., p. 337.
12 Balkoski, op. cit., pp. 152-154, 168.
13 ibid., pp. 157-159; and Ladd, op. cit., p. 193.
14 Neillands, *By Sea and Land*, pp. 163-166.
15 Reynolds cites a time of 15:00 from Meyer's personal account, at which time the attack on the advancing Canadians was also launched. However, he also states that the Canadians requested armoured assistance at 14:30, after the engagement began. It is therefore unclear whether the 3rd Battalion arrived ahead of schedule, or whether one side or the other were in error in their records; see Reynolds, op. cit., pp. 66-67.
16 *Panzerfaust*: literally 'armoured fist', a hand-held, single-shot disposable rocket launcher.
17 For a detailed account of the engagement, see Reynolds, pp. 63-71, 80; and Kershaw, op. cit., pp. 205-208.

CHAPTER TWELVE
1 Reynolds, op. cit., p. 76.
2 ibid., pp. 73-75.
3 ibid., pp. 75-80.
4 Thompson, op. cit., p. 133.
5 Harclerode, op. cit., p. 79.
6 ibid., Harclerode, op. cit., pp. 78-79.
7 Barber, pp. 136-142.
8 For a detailed account of this part of the action, see ibid., pp. 142-143.
9 ibid., pp. 144-145.
10 Harclerode, pp. 82-83.
11 Barber, p. 145.
12 ibid., pp. 146-149.
13 The 1st Battalion, 401st Glider Infantry was

attached to the 327th Glider Infantry Regiment. US Glider Infantry Regiments had only two integral infantry battalions at that time, and an extra battalion was routinely attached to them.

14   Harrison, op. cit., p. 356; and Kershaw, op. cit., pp. 219–222.
15   Kershaw, p. 222.
16   Harrison, p. 386.
17   ibid., pp. 386–387, 441.
18   Blair, op. cit., pp. 267–268.
19   ibid., pp. 268–269; and Marshall, op. cit., pp. 129–137.
20   Harrison, p. 353.
21   Balkoski, op. cit., p. 167.

22   ibid., pp. 163–164.
23   ibid., pp. 168–170.
24   ibid., pp. 170–173.

CHAPTER THIRTEEN
1   Harrison, op. cit., p. 349.
2   ibid., p. 401.
3   ibid., p. 366.
4   Patrick Delaforce, *Monty's Highlanders: 51st Highland Division in World War Two*, p. 126.
5   id., *Monty's Marauders,* pp. 73–74.
6   Blair, op. cit., pp. 280–283.

GLOSSARY

AA	Anti-aircraft
Abteilung (Ger.)	battalion
Airlanded	British term for units landed by powered aircraft
Airlanding	British term for glider units
AT	anti-tank
Aufklärungs (Ger.)	reconnaissance, literally 'enlightenment'
AVRE	Armoured Vehicle Royal Engineers
Bodenständige (Ger.)	static formation, literally 'firmly based'
C-47	militarised version of the Douglas DC-3 airliner, standard US military transport aircraft during the Second World War.
CIGS	Chief of the Imperial General Staff
COPP	Combined Operations Pilotage Party
COSSAC	Chief of Staff to the Supreme Allied Commander
DD	Duplex Drive
Despatcher	aircraft crewman charged with supervising parachute or supply drops; jumpmaster in US parlance
DZ	Drop Zone, for parachute landings
Fallschirmjäger (Ger.)	paratrooper, literally 'parachute hunter'
Festung (Ger.)	fortress
Flak (Ger.)	anti-aircraft fire; abbreviation of German *Flugzeugabwehrkanone*
Führerprinzip (Ger.)	leader's prerogative, literally 'leader principle'
Hamilcar	Large British glider, capable of lifting a maximum load of 7.8 tons. Possible loads were a single Tetrarch light tank, or two Universal carriers, or a 17-pounder AT gun with prime mover.
Heeresgruppe (Ger.)	Army Group
Horsa	Standard British troop-carrying glider. Capable of carrying 29 passengers plus two pilots, or a variety of heavy equipment including the jeep with or without trailer and various artillery pieces
Heer (Ger.)	German army
Jumpmaster	see Despatcher
Kampfgruppe (Ger.)	Battlegroup
Kriegsmarine (Ger.)	German Navy
LCA	Landing Craft Assault
LCF	Landing Craft Flak
LCG	Landing Craft Gun
LCM	Landing Craft, Mechanised
LCN	Landing Craft Navigation
LCR	Landing Craft Rocket
LCT	Landing Craft Tank
LCVP	Landing Craft Vehicle Personnel
LSD	Landing Ship Dock
LSI	Landing Ship, Infantry
LST	Landing Ship, Tank
Luftlande (Ger.)	Airlanding

Luftwaffe (Ger.)	German air force from 1933
LZ	Landing Zone, for gliders or powered aircraft
Oberbefehlshaber West (Ger.)	Commander-in-Chief West
Oberkommando der Wehrmacht,	
OKW (Ger.)	Armed Forces High Command
Panzer (Ger.)	tank or armoured
Panzerjäger (Ger.)	literally 'tankhunter', usually applied to self-propelled anti-tank vehicles & units
PIAT	Projector, Infantry, Anti-Tank. British spring and recoil operated hand-held bomb thrower, with hollow charge projectile.
RA	Royal Artillery
RAF	Royal Air Force
RASC	Royal Army Service Corps
RE	Royal Engineers
Rommelspargel (Ger.)	Rommel Asparagus
RTR	Royal Tank Regiment
Serial	group of transport aircraft or glider tugs within a larger formation. Usually all the aircraft carrying a specified unit or team for a task
SHAEF	Supreme Headquarters Allied Expeditionary Force
SOE	Special Operations Executive
Stick	group of parachutists scheduled to exit the aircraft during one run over the DZ; usually the whole complement except on restricted DZs requiring two or more runs
Sturmgeschütz (Ger.)	assault gun
Stützpunkt (Ger.)	strongpoint
USAAF	United States Army Air Force
Waco CG4	Standard US glider, capable of carrying 15 passengers. Called the Hadrian in British parlance
Waffen SS	military arm of the Nazi para-military political organisation
Widerstandnest (Ger.)	Resistance Nest

BIBLIOGRAPHY

UNPUBLISHED SOURCES

Public Record Office Files.
AIR 2/7239 1940-1942 Airborne Forces: Organisation.
AIR 2/7338 1940-1941 Airborne Forces: Provision of Aircraft – Policy.
AIR 2/7574 1941 Parachute Troops: Training.
AIR 32/2 Provision of an Airborne Force.
CAB 69/1 Minutes of Defence Committee Meetings.
WO 32/4723 Badges for Paratroops.
WO 32/9778 1940-1943 Airborne Forces: Policy.
WO 171/393, 1 Airborne Division War Diary.
WO 171/589 1st Airlanding Brigade War Diary.
WO 171/592 1st Parachute Brigade War Diary.
WO 171/594 4th Parachute Brigade War Diary.
WO 171/613 8th Armoured Brigade War Diary.
WO 179/2839 2nd Canadian Armoured Brigade War Diary.
WO 193/27 1940 June-1941 January Formation of Parachute and Glider Units.
WO 193/384 Combined Operations 2: Independent Companies 20 June-December 1940.
WO 219/1919, SHAEF Weekly Intelligence Summaries.
WO 219/1942, MARTIAN 95.
WO 285/3, The Dempsey Papers.

PUBLISHED SOURCES

Ambrose, Stephen E., *D-Day, June 6, 1944* (London: Pocket Books, 2002).
Id., *Pegasus Bridge* (London: Pocket Books, 1994).
Id., *Band of Brothers* (New York: Touchstone Books, 1992).
Balkoski, Joseph, *Beyond the Beachhead* (Mechanicsburg PA: Stackpole Books, 1999).
Barber, Neil, *The Day the Devils Dropped In: The 9th Parachute Battalion in Normandy – D-Day to D+6* (London: Pen and Sword, 2002).
Bekker, Cajus, *The Luftwaffe War Diaries* (New York: MacDonald 1966).
Blair, Clay, *Ridgeway's Paratroopers: The American Airborne in World War II* (New York: The Dial Press, 1985).
Burgett, Donald R., *Currahee! A Screaming Eagle at Normandy* (New York: Dell Books, 2000).
Carell, Paul, INVASION! *They're Coming! The German Account of the D-Day Landings and the 80 Days Battle for France* (Atglen, PA: Schiffer Publishing, 1995).
Chamberlain, Peter and Chris Ellis, *British and American Tanks of World War II: The Complete Illustrated History of British, American and Commonwealth Tanks, 1939-1945* (New York: Arco Publishing, 1981).
Chappell, Mike *British Infantry Equipments 1908-80* (London: Osprey Publishing, 1980).
Chatterton, Brigadier George, DSO OBE, *The Wings of Pegasus: The Story of the Glider Pilot Regiment* (Nashville: The Battery Press, 1982).
Delaforce, Patrick *Monty's Highlanders: 51st Highland Division in World War Two* (London: Chancellor Press, 2000).
Id., *Monty's Marauders* (London: Chancellor Press, 2000).
D'Este, Carlo, *Decision in Normandy: The Unwritten Story of Montgomery and the Allied Campaign* (London: Collins, 1983).
Devlin, Gerard M. *Paratrooper! The Saga of US Army and Marine Parachute and Glider Combat Troops During World War II* (New York: St Martins Press, 1979).

Id., *Silent Wings: The Story of the Glider Pilots of World War II* (London: W.H. Allen, 1985).

Ellis, Major L. F., CVO, CBE, DSO, MC *The War in France and Flanders 1939-1940* (London: HMSO, 1953).

Id., *Victory in the West*, Volume I (London: HMSO, 1962).

Ellis, John, *The Sharp End: The Fighting Man in World War II* (London: Pimlico, 1993).

Foley, John, *Mailed Fist* (London: Granada, 1982).

Forty, George, *Fortress Europe: Hitler's Atlantic Wall*, (Surrey: Ian Allan, 2002).

Foot, M.R.D., SOE *in France: An Account of the Work of the British Special Operations Executive in France, 1940-1944* (London: HMSO, 1966).

French, David, *Raising Churchill's Army: The British Army and the War Against Germany 1919-1945* (Oxford: OUP, 2000).

Gale, General Sir Richard, *Call To Arms: An Autobiography* (London: Hutchinson, 1968).

Gilchrist, Donald *Don't Cry For Me: The Commandos, D-Day and After* (London: Robert Hale, 1982).

Hall, Tony (Ed), *D-Day Operation Overlord: From Its Planning to the Liberation of Paris* (London: BCA, 1993).

Harclerode, Peter, *'Go To It!' The Illustrated History of the 6th Airborne Division* (London: Caxton Editions, 1990).

Harrison, Gordon A., *United States Army in World War II, The European Theatre of Operations: Cross-Channel Attack* (Old Saybrook CT: Konecky & Konecky, 1950).

Harmon, Nicholas, *Dunkirk: The Necessary Myth* (London: Hodder & Stoughton, 1980).

Harvey, A.D. *Arnhem* (London: Cassell, 2001).

Hastings, Max, *Das Reich: The March of the 2nd SS Panzer Division Through France, June 1944* (London: Pan, 1983).

Id., *Overlord: D-Day and the Battle for Normandy 1944* (London, Pan, 1985).

Hills, Stuart MC, *By Tank Into Normandy: A Memoir of the Campaign in North-West Europe from D-Day to VE Day* (London: Cassell, 2002).

Hoyt, Edwin P., *The Invasion Before Normandy: The Secret Battle of Slapton Sands* (New York: Military Heritage Press, 1985).

Katcher, Philip *The US 1st Infantry Division, 1939-45* (London: Osprey, 1978).

Keegan, John *Six Armies in Normandy* (London: Pan, 1982).

Kershaw, Robert J., *D-Day: Piercing the Atlantic Wall* (Surrey: Ian Allan, 1993).

Ladd, James D., *Commandos and Rangers of World War II* (London: BCA, 1978).

Lewis, Adrian R. *Omaha Beach: A Flawed Victory* (London: University of North Carolina Press, 2001).

Lewis, Jon E. (Ed), *Eye-Witness D-Day: The Story of the Battle By Those Who Were There* (London: Robinson, 1994).

Lincoln, John *Thank God and the Infantry: From D-Day to VE-Day with the 1st Battalion the Royal Norfolk Regiment* (Stroud: Sutton Publishing, 1999).

Lucas Phillips, C.E., *The Greatest Raid of All: St. Nazaire 1942* (London: Heinemann, 1958).

Miller, Russell, *Nothing Less Than Victory: An Oral History of D-Day* (London: Penguin, 1994).

Morris, Eric *Circles of Hell: The War in Italy 1943-1945* (London: Hutchinson, 1993).

Harries, Meirion and Susie, *Soldiers of the Sun: The Rise and Fall of the Imperial Japanese Army 1868-1945* (London: Heinemann, 1991).

Marshall, S.L.A. *Night Drop: The American Airborne Invasion of Normandy* (London: Macmillan, 1962).

Messenger, Charles, *The Commandos 1940-1946* (London: Kimber, 1985).

Milit

ärgeschichtliches Forschungsamt, Freiburg (Eds) (Research Institute for Military History), *Germany and the Second World War, Volume II: Germany's Initial Conquests in Europe* (Oxford: Clarendon Press, 1991).

Millar, George, *The Bruneval Raid: Flashpoint of the Radar War* (London: Bodley Head, 1974).

Miksche, F.O., *Paratroops: The History, Organisation and Tactical Use of Airborne Formations* (London: Faber & Faber, 1943).

Neillands, Robin, *By Sea and Land: The Story of the Royal Marines Commandos* (London: Fontana, 1988).

Id. and Roderick Norman, *D-Day, 1944: Voices from Normandy* (London: Weidenfeld & Nicolson, 1993).

Otway, Lieutenant-Colonel T.B.H., DSO, *The Second World War 1939-1945 Army: Airborne Forces* (London: War Office, 1950: facsimile IWM, 1990).

Pöppel, Martin, *Heaven & Hell: The War Diary of a German Paratrooper* (Staplehurst: Spellmount Publishing, 2000).

Rapport, Leonard and Arthur Northwood, *Rendezvous With Destiny: A History of the 101st Airborne Division* (Fort Campbell, Kentucky: 101st Airborne Division Association, 1948).

Reynolds, Michael, *Steel Inferno: I SS Panzer Corps in Normandy* (Staplehurst: Spellmount, 1997).

Rottman, Gordon L., *US Army Rangers & LRRP Units 1942-87* (London: Osprey, 1987).

Id., *US Army Airborne 1940-90* (London: Osprey, 1990).

Ruffner, Kevin Conley, *Luftwaffe Field Divisions 1941-45* (London: Osprey, 1990).

Ryan, Cornelius, *The Longest Day* (London: Wordsworth Editions, 1999).

Saunders, Anthony, *Hitler's Atlantic Wall* (Stroud: Sutton Publishing, 2001).

Scarfe, Norman, *Assault Division* (London: Collins, 1952).

Shannon, Kevin and Stephen Wright, *One Night In June* (Shrewsbury: Airlife Publishing, 1994).

Sims, James *Arnhem Spearhead: A Private Soldier's Story* (London: IWM, 1978).

Slim, Field Marshal Viscount, DSO, MC *Defeat Into Victory* (London: Pan, 1999).

Terraine, John, *Right of the Line: The Royal Air Force in the European War 1939-1945* (London: Sceptre, 1988).

Thetford, Owen, *Aircraft of the Royal Air Force Since 1918* (London: Putnam, 1979).

Thompson, Julian, *Ready For Anything: The Parachute Regiment at War, 1940-1982* (London: Weidenfeld & Nicolson, 1989).

Tout, Ken, *The Bloody Battle for Tilly: Normandy 1944* (Stroud: Sutton Publishing, 2000).

Warner, Philip, *The D-Day Landings* (London: Mandarin, 1990).

Wilson, Andrew, MC, *Flame Thrower* (London: Corgi, 1973).

Windrow, Martin, *The Panzer Divisions* (Revised Edition), (London: Osprey, 1982).

Wright, Lawrence, *The Wooden Sword: The Untold Story of the Gliders in World War II* (London: Elek, 1967).

INDEX

INDEX

If you are interested in purchasing other books published by Tempus,
or in case you have difficulty finding any Tempus books in your local bookshop,
you can also place orders directly through our website

www.tempus-publishing.com

or from

BOOKPOST, Freepost, PO Box 29, Douglas, Isle of Man IM99 1BQ
Tel 01624 836000   email bookshop@enterprise.net